THE MODERN CULTURE OF REGINALD FARRER
LANDSCAPE, LITERATURE AND BUDDHISM

LEGENDA

LEGENDA is the Modern Humanities Research Association's book imprint for new research in the Humanities. Founded in 1995 by Malcolm Bowie and others within the University of Oxford, Legenda has always been a collaborative publishing enterprise, directly governed by scholars. The Modern Humanities Research Association (MHRA) joined this collaboration in 1998, became half-owner in 2004, in partnership with Maney Publishing and then Routledge, and has since 2016 been sole owner. Titles range from medieval texts to contemporary cinema and form a widely comparative view of the modern humanities, including works on Arabic, Catalan, English, French, German, Greek, Italian, Portuguese, Russian, Spanish, and Yiddish literature. Editorial boards and committees of more than 60 leading academic specialists work in collaboration with bodies such as the Society for French Studies, the British Comparative Literature Association and the Association of Hispanists of Great Britain & Ireland.

The MHRA encourages and promotes advanced study and research in the field of the modern humanities, especially modern European languages and literature, including English, and also cinema. It aims to break down the barriers between scholars working in different disciplines and to maintain the unity of humanistic scholarship. The Association fulfils this purpose through the publication of journals, bibliographies, monographs, critical editions, and the MHRA Style Guide, and by making grants in support of research. Membership is open to all who work in the Humanities, whether independent or in a University post, and the participation of younger colleagues entering the field is especially welcomed.

STUDIES IN COMPARATIVE LITERATURE

Studies in Comparative Literature are produced in close collaboration with the British Comparative Literature Association, and range widely across comparative and theoretical topics in literary and translation studies, accommodating research at the interface between different artistic media and between the humanities and the sciences.

The Modern Culture of Reginald Farrer

Landscape, Literature and Buddhism

Michael Charlesworth

LEGENDA

Studies in Comparative Literature 36
Modern Humanities Research Association
2018

Published by Legenda
an imprint of the Modern Humanities Research Association
Salisbury House, Station Road, Cambridge CB1 2LA

ISBN 978-1-78188-694-6

First published 2018

Copy-Editor: Birgit Mikus

CONTENTS

I. M.

my aunt
Thora Elizabeth Barker, *née* Charlesworth
d. 21/6/2012

my uncle
James Wemyss Barker
1925–2010
late 14th Army, Burma Campaign 1944–45
and member of the Alpine Garden Society

ACKNOWLEDGEMENTS

A surprisingly large number of people have helped me during the process of writing this book, and I would like to thank the following. Henry Noltie, a curator at the Royal Botanic Garden Edinburgh, for generously saving me from many errors; Leonie Paterson, Adele Smith and staff at the Library and Archives of the Royal Botanic Garden Edinburgh; Lucy Waitt and Liz Taylor at the Lindley Library of the Royal Horticultural Society.

Annie Farrer helped; and I heard her speak at a Study Day for Reginald Farrer organized by the Yorkshire Gardens Trust at which Patrick Eyres ensured I had a place. Patrick also kindly read a chapter of the manuscript and made a crucial suggestion. Donald S. Lopez Jr., Jishnu Shankar, Oliver Freiburger and Patrick Olivelle helped me to understand specific concepts in Buddhist thought, which is not my field, as any remaining errors will show. The last three names on this list reveal how I have benefitted from working at a university that has a vigorous South Asia Center. Thanks must go to Simon Edsor and staff at the Fine Art Society, London, for spontaneously-offered assistance; and to Nigel Price, for the guided tour of Crarae. The late Puff Miller-Thomas provided the introduction to Crarae. Thanks to Antony and Margaret for a small but important bit of help in your garden.

Janice Leoshko offered crucial help without which this book could not have been written, and enthusiastic encouragement. By coincidence, her uncle, serving in the US Air Force during the Second World War, flew 'the Hump,' to supply the Chinese Nationalist allies from airfields in Assam, and therefore flew over Reginald Farrer's grave. Janice also happens to be my partner, and her gentle spirit informs the best pages of this study.

The Royal Asiatic Society of Sri Lanka offered me an early forum for trying out some ideas about Farrer's account of his time in Sri Lanka. This episode of his life was further illuminated by my visits to museum libraries and I thank staff of the libraries of the National Museum, Colombo, Sri Lanka, and the Museum of Fine Arts, Boston; as well as the Sri Lanka National Archives.

Osmund Bopearachi, for such a stylish introduction to Sri Lanka! For a charming evening in Colombo with Dr Leoshko and me, Tamara Loos; and for letting me see a draft of a chapter of her book about Prince Prisdang in Sri Lanka, with a photograph of the Prince in company of a skull and bones. Dr Loos also helped me to improve my narrative.

Research performed in three continents needs practical support, and I was fortunate to obtain this from John Rogers and the American Institute for Sri Lankan Studies; the Houston Foundation; the Kimbell Foundation of Fort Worth, Texas;

and from two units of the University of Texas at Austin: the South Asia Center and the College of Fine Arts; particular thanks are due to Jack Risley, Kamran Ali, Dean Douglas Dempster and Professor Jeffrey Chipps Smith. Publication of colour photographs is assisted by a University of Texas at Austin Subvention Grant awarded by the Office of the President.

Finally I should say that the best academic decision I ever made was to ask Stephen Bann to be my doctoral advisor. He has always set me an example of the highest standard in scholarship, and shown by his work and through his friendship how humanity and humour can quietly inform what historians do. The standard that he sets has always been too high for me to reach, but he has always greatly encouraged my efforts to do so; as again with this book.

M.C., Austin, Texas, December 2017

LIST OF ILLUSTRATIONS

❖

A RATHER PERSONAL PREFACE

I was in the library at UCLA, walking fast through the book-stacks, heading for the section on garden history. The spine of a small pale book caught my eye as I hustled past. *The Silent Traveller in the Yorkshire Dales.* I was young, in a hurry. My family comes from Yorkshire. I thought I knew the county. I was far from home, a little homesick. I had never heard of this book. I stopped and took it off the shelf.

It had been written by a Chinaman, some time in the 1930s. He had illustrated it with reproductions of his own paintings. They made Yorkshire look *exactly* like China. This was delightful, and fascinating. I remembered I was in a hurry, and put the book back.

Years later, after arriving in Austin, Texas, and being provided with a personal computer by the Dean of the college, I remembered the book, used the search engine Alta Vista, found the book, and bought a copy. Poor Chiang Yee! A Chinese exile in 1930s Britain, vastly homesick, a lover of landscape, he had visited the regions of famous scenery in Britain (North Wales, the Lake District, etc.) asking himself always, 'Does it remind me of home?' And answering, 'Yes — but no, not really' (I paraphrase) and thus being disappointed. Until he was taken to one place that did it. 'This takes me there,' he said. Took him back to China. It was a garden made by a man of whom, although I am a garden historian, I had never heard: Reginald Farrer.

Years later, after a long-standing friend of mine had acquired new hips, we decided to celebrate with a walk up one of the Yorkshire mountains. I suggested Ingleborough, because we could also look at the garden at the foot of it that had so pleased Chiang Yee. We found an interesting bridge, little paths, bamboos, dead leaves, rhododendrons, invasive sycamores. Then we puffed our way to the top of the mountain in a cold east wind.

The following year and another summer trip to England. My friend Patrick had put my name down to participate in a Study Day about Reginald Farrer, to be staged in his old home, Ingleborough Hall, by the sterling personalities of the Yorkshire Gardens Trust. The day before the Day, I was in a distant part of Yorkshire, visiting my aunt and uncle. The latter was making a desperate effort to stave off kidney dialysis by taking a complicated regime of tablets. I had seen him the previous year. On this occasion he greeted me at the door with an unusual conversational gambit: 'Since I last saw you, I've taken six and a half thousand pills!' We laughed. I went in, and over a cup of tea told them: 'I'm on my way to a Study Day on some bloke called Reginald Farrer.' My uncle nearly had apoplexy. 'Some bloke!?' he exclaimed. 'Some bloke!!?' he repeated. 'Only the father of the

Alpine Garden Society!!! Only the greatest rock gardener we've ever had in this country!!!!" And he stumped off to his library to retrieve a book to show me. He was, of course, a member of the Alpine Garden Society.

So that is how I found Reginald Farrer: through a Chinese exile, a good Dean, an old friend, and an uncle I had known and loved all my life. Or, to put it another way, the tale shows the value, incalculable, immense, of being in a proper library, where accidental finds can be made, as in old attics, or adit-mines; and not having to rely on electronic 'searches' where you need to know in advance what you are looking for in order to find it. My experience shows the value of friends and relations and conversation. The value of clubs of like-minded people, meeting in places off the beaten track; and, yes, the value of the internet and the computer — only as a means of getting to somewhere else, though, rather than as a place to linger.

And then the enquiry, and the work, began...

The courses of the world have divorced our modern civilized life from rough primary emotion.

Reginald Farrer, *The House of Shadows,* 1906.

I myself have been spending the last 10 weeks having my inside salubriously removed and repaired and put back.

Farrer, about his sixth operation, January 1919.

The camp suggests an Abbey of Theleme, with me in the midst, seated at my tent-door, with a paint-brush in one hand, and an open umbrella in the other, attempting to portray a primula [...] through a dense fog of midges and of stinging blue smoke designed, quite vainly to keep them off.

Farrer, letter from his camp in Burma, 1919.

In the powdered gold of early sunset I rode leisurely into the Halls of Heaven.

Farrer (1880–1920), *The Rainbow Bridge,* 1921.

.

INTRODUCTION

This book examines the relationship, or connection, between two powerful cultural forces: British modernism of the early twentieth century, and Buddhist thought. It addresses this large question by focussing on the work and life of the relatively unknown Reginald Farrer (1880–1920): rock gardener, father of the Alpine Garden Society, plant collector, travel-writer, novelist, wartime propagandist, writer on plants and garden design, poet, Buddhist, and amateur water-colour painter.

Farrer was active in many fields. Nevertheless, one idea that permeates his activities is the question of how the individual responds to the circumstances in which it finds itself. It is a question that is comprehensive, open to both scientific and artistic approaches, psychological, philosophical, experiential, existential. The 'circumstances' particularly considered by Farrer were less sociological or political than physical and inter-individual, leading up to the threshold of the metaphysical: a threshold that he never hesitated to cross. This question of indi- vidual and circumstance is not expressed here as a determinism, a question of how the environment acts upon an individual. Farrer would have had no patience with such a limit. It also stops short of being a completely ecological view, which would include insights into how a class of individuals act upon their environment or circumstances. He investigated the question through botany, gardening, plant- collecting and writing novels. Farrer was partly a scientist (at least, he was an expert botanist), and even more, as the great plant-collector Frank Kingdon Ward wrote, he was 'an artist, not merely looking at things from a new angle, but creating a new idea.'[1]

Physically handicapped, he had an urgent existential reason why the question of how individuals respond to their circumstances should be the most important intellectual orientation of his life. It was fundamental for Farrer not to do things the way that other people did them. We perceive this tendency in his flower paintings, his approach to gardens, and in his verbal expressions, both private in letters and in his published travel accounts and plant-writing. In pursuing his own course, Farrer probably felt that he could not *be* ordinary, given his handicaps and the strangeness of his early life, and that to try to be so would be both futile and impeding. Instead he had to make his own individual perceptions, sensibility, impressions, and thoughts, informative, useful, provoking, and delightful for other people: an audience or readership. The road he chose was not that of determinism, but of individuation: of leading a more fulfilled life by cultivating the individual that he was and wanted to be.

A factor no doubt contributing to this was his sexual preference. Other writers have argued that Farrer was homoerotic in his feelings. This study will present evidence that corroborates this view, as well as new evidence that shows him to have been, intermittently at least, homosexual in his actions. Farrer was fifteen years old at the time of Oscar Wilde's trial and imprisonment, and he died forty-seven years before sexual relations between consenting adult men in private were made legal in England and Wales. His sexuality was therefore transgressive of legal norms and social expectations. His peculiarly close and intimate way of writing about plants, suffused with remarkably strong sensuality, can be seen as a sublimation of sexual feelings defined in his lifetime as criminal. Faced with imprisonment or other punishment for the exercise of their sexuality, gay men, to fulfil their natures, by definition were obliged to subvert or transgress the law that surrounded them as well as resist the forceful social pressures encompassing them. The fate of Sir Hector Macdonald shows the frustrations, the equivocation, the repression, agonies and sometime unsuppressed violence by which gay lives were encompassed.[2]

Given the era in which he lived, and the fact that Farrer experienced modernity — defined as the psychological, and even social, response to experience of radical modernisation — this study examines the extent to which he and the modernisation he brought about in his chosen fields can be related to *modernism*. After reading the discussion presented here, the reader might decide that Farrer is very modern now, very much our contemporary. This might be because of his suitability as a subject for disability history, and queer theory; but it may as strongly be attributable to his openness to, even embrace of, contingency: — unplanned, unwanted, unexpected events — in the process of individuation. There are many ways of being modern.

On 25th December, 2015, *The New York Times* printed on its front page an article about the unseasonable warmth being experienced in New York City. Mentioned in the article, with its delicate pink flowers illustrated in a colour photograph, was a viburnum, blooming unusually early in Central Park. Its sweet scent was extolled. The botanical name for the plant was not mentioned in the article; it is *Viburnum farreri*, often referred to as *V. fragrans*, seed of which Reginald Farrer had collected in the wild in China in 1914, and sent back to Britain to spread as a garden plant in the West. The plant is perhaps the most successful of all Farrer's introductions (Figure 1). The newspaper article did not mention Farrer's name. This incident exemplifies the way in which the products of modernisation are all around us, whether we realize it or not. The effects and changes brought about by historical figures affect our lives, to be appreciated or regretted, even as the people who caused them are forgotten. In particular the article testifies to both the achievement and the obscurity of Farrer; the modernisation of life through exotic plant introductions; and the way in which modernisation in the West depended on borrowings from other geographical regions. These dynamics are underlying themes of this book; but they are not the only themes. In fact, readers deeply enthusiastic about the history of plant introductions and plant-collecting may judge that I should have spent more time discussing Farrer's plants and his achievements as nurseryman and collector.

This book presents the first full-length study of the works of Reginald Farrer in their previously unsuspected diversity, and it is exploratory rather than definitive.

Fig. I.1. *Viburnum farreri*. Photo: author.

There are few guides, and none that are comprehensive. Farrer has never been made the subject of a proper full-length biography. While the present study is not that, its first three chapters provide an extended biographical sketch of his life, which builds on, revises, and I hope will supersede, the slight existing accounts.[3] Farrer's varied creations span a range of literary, garden-related, visual and theatrical activities; but very little of this output — beyond his seeds, herbarium sheets, and seminal essay on Jane Austen — has been thoroughly investigated or scrutinized. As a result, Farrer is a largely unsung hero of twentieth century culture.

A book dedicated to the study of the achievements of such a figure needs to pay due attention to the adjective 'unsung'. While he is almost completely unknown on a popular level, in fact Farrer, and some of his achievements, are remembered by four groups of people limited in numbers but not insignificant: members of the Alpine Garden Society, which his example was instrumental in forming; historians of twentieth-century British gardening; and scholarly rock-gardeners (enthusiasts for the cultivation of garden plants in an artificial geological setting), who tend to revere Farrer as a great innovator. To these we should add scholars of critical views of Jane Austen's work. One point I need to make immediately, therefore, is that my research has not included reading the archives of all the gardens asserted to be designed by him or under his influence in order to find out who did what when. I have taken his gardening interests as one element (though a very important one) in a more holistic approach to his work and achievements. Given his large output of varied types of literary works, much of this book will pursue a literary enquiry, although I will not examine Farrer's 1917 essay on Jane Austen, as the essay has already been carefully discussed by literary historians, and at the moment I have nothing to add to those discussions. And it is important to note here that, in the attention that has been paid to him, Farrer's interest in Buddhism has been entirely shunned.

In determining the structure of the book I have started from the assumption that most readers will need to be introduced to Farrer and his activities before being able to assess his literary and artistic contributions and my discussions of them. So the first three chapters are more introductory than this brief Introduction. Chapters 1 and 3 provide a chronological biographical sketch, while Chapter 2 interposes into this an analysis of his account of visiting Sri Lanka for two months in 1908: his book *In Old Ceylon*. I have arranged it this way because his book contributes greatly to our biographical understanding of him, but also to introduce more incisive scrutiny of his writing at an early stage of the present study. My purpose here is less biographical than it is to consider Farrer's cultural interventions and contributions, and his aesthetics, so treatment of his other books, paintings, and gardens are laid out in chapters subsequent to the biographical sketch. If the book is about Farrer's works, the reader may ask, why bother with biographical chapters? The answer is that they tell us much information about his time in Sri Lanka, the nature of the war years, and his expedition to Burma, which is not available from published sources. Readers who are exclusively interested in his works, however, can be directed to read Chapter 2 and start again at Chapter 4.

After the first three chapters, the book is arranged thematically, although in accordance with a rough chronological sequence. Farrer is best remembered in relation to plants: as a writer about them, collector, and gardener; the activities that up until now have tended to define him. Chapter 4 therefore examines elements of his thinking about plants and gardens. The influence of Japan on him was powerful, given his nine months' stay in Japan in 1902–03, and so Chapter 5 discusses his first published book, an account of this visit. Chapter 6 studies four of his novels (published 1906–1912), while Chapter 7 takes as its subject his account of the first year of his great expedition to far northwest China and north-eastern Tibet, the 2-volume *On the Eaves of the World*. The first year of the expedition, when the events were lived, was 1914, and the book was written largely in the winter of 1915–1916 in China, and published in October 1917. Chapter 8 considers his paintings of Asian plants and landscapes from both this expedition and his fatal Burmese expedition of 1919–1920. Chapter 9 studies the book of propaganda that Farrer produced during the war years while employed at the Department (later Ministry) of Information. He gathered material for the book in the autumn of 1917, wrote the text immediately, and it was published at the end of 1918. Chapter 10 has as its subject his account of the second year of the China-Tibet expedition (1915), written in 1918 and eventually published posthumously as *The Rainbow Bridge* at the end of 1921. Taken together, his three published volumes describing the expedition were hailed by a review in the *Times Literary Supplement* in 1921 as another work of literary art: 'a classic of travel'.

The reader will gather from this account that the chapters here abide by the temporal sequence according to which the works under discussion were written, rather than the dates described by Farrer's narratives. There is an obvious emphasis in this, acknowledging Farrer's writing as primary and his biography as subordinated to that. An Afterword and an Appendix conclude the work by discussing his verse drama on a directly Buddhist theme, *Vasanta the Beautiful*, and the changes he made to his family's landscape garden at Ingleborough Hall, Clapham, Yorkshire.

I have arranged the book in this way because in a relatively short life, and one that I shall show ended unexpectedly, Farrer was prodigious in his production of books, articles, thoughts in letters to friends, new plants, gardening innovations, paintings and photographs. There is more clarity in a thematic organisation of these materials than in a purely chronological one. A sequence of ideas can be followed, including Appendix and Afterword, with particularly intense examples drawn from the major themes announced at the very beginning of this study: Buddhist thought, landscape, and the effect of gardens. I make no apology for quoting extensively Farrer's own words. Were he better known, it might be less necessary. By means of fairly extensive quotation, readers will have at least some material to help them judge the artistry and the poetics of Farrer's writings.

Among recent secondary sources, I make multiple references to Nicola Shulman's book about Farrer. In the chapters that follow the reader might think that I deal a little severely with what is, after all, a slight (ca 30,000 words, 115 pages) and journalistic essay. But Shulman's book is condensed, pithy, elegantly written, widely available and has been influential.[4] In the virtual vacuum that is Reginald Farrer Studies, Shulman's work has had its effect, so its errors must be corrected and its tendentious arguments contested, while its strengths are acknowledged.

Among academics, even with the great expansion of cultural studies of the last generation, there has been no interest in Farrer's Buddhism, and only a handful of scholars have written about any aspect of his activities. The cultural geographers Setsu Tachibana, Stephen Daniels, and Charles Watkins include a discussion of the garden Farrer made at his family's home, Ingleborough Hall, in an article about 'Japanese' gardens in Edwardian Britain.[5] While Farrer made part of the garden under the influence of Japanese gardens and aesthetics, as my Chapter 4 will show, and planted his waterfalls with bamboo, while training Wisteria down a cliff in emulation of sights he had seen in Matsushima, Japan,[6] this was not a serious attempt to conjure up the appearance of Japanese terrain. A few years later however, in an equally important development, he did try to evoke the look of Chinese countryside in other parts of the garden, which will be discussed in the Afterword.

So far as other notice has been taken of Farrer by academics: in a rather strange approach, the anthropologist Erik Mueggler convicted Farrer of being unable to assimilate to local life during his expedition to Burma (1919–1920).[7] He terms this an inability to 'see'. Unfortunately for the effectiveness of Mueggler's rather conventional argument, both the photograph and the written account upon which his argument substantially hangs, came not from Farrer but from his travelling companion, E. H. M. Cox. Farrer is therefore convicted of imperialist failings that were in this case committed by a different person. Possibly Farrer had imperialist failings of his own, but as my book will show, he made great efforts to discard the worst elements of his formation in Britain and to embrace Eastern civilisations. In any case, the purpose of my work is not to focus on imperialist failings as central. Before rushing to convict him of imperialism we first need to understand better who he was and what he actually did. Mueggler shows much more sympathy in this way with the plant collector Joseph Rock in his fine study *The Paper Road*.[8]

Farrer's account of visiting the battlefields of the First World War has been used briefly by several scholars to evoke the appearance and feeling of those battlefields, which leaves all the other very illuminating qualities of his account of them hitherto undiscussed.[9] During the war, Farrer found time to write one of the seminal essays on the work of Jane Austen, and scholars of the history of critical insights into Jane Austen's novels also remember his work with respect. For Brian Southam, Farrer's essay, distinguished by the existence of an 'acute critical edge' within Farrer's admiration for Austen, 'holds an important place in the historiography of criticism'.[10] Recently Jeff Mather has had the interesting idea that Farrer's reading of Jane Austen's work on his plant-collecting expeditions in remote Asia 'mediates the reality' of travel and therefore of travel-writing.[11] The precise workings of this mediation remain to be elucidated. Finally, Jill Didur brings her background in an English Department to bear on the subject of Farrer's plant collecting. Writing in the conviction that 'narratives about botanical exploration and rock and alpine gardening can be a resource for countercolonial thought in the environmental humanities', she argues that Farrer 'saw the need for plant hunters and gardeners to enter into relations of interdependence not only with the plants they collected, but also with the people, landscapes, and ecological conditions from which they had been extracted.'[12] She thus directly contradicts Mueggler. In my work the underlying dynamics providing the energy for Farrer's sympathetic view of other cultures, and the plants of their geographical regions, will be examined for the first time.

This quick survey of recent academic studies at least indicates that it is not only Farrer's travel writing that is of interest to scholars, if firmly in second place to his involvement with plants. In order to come to terms with the wide range of his activity, a variety of critical approaches is needed. I employ biographical insights; literary criticism, including some semiotics; rhetorical analysis; psycho-geography; an element of queer theory; some history of religion; art history; and garden history, in my exploration of his activities and the aesthetics of his chosen fields.

The word 'culture' in my title has a multiple application. It refers to Farrer's culture of plants (perhaps his greatest contribution, horticulture). It also refers to self-culture through education and self-education that emerges strongly in his writings. That Farrer was self-taught as an expert botanist is very surprising. 'Culture' also refers to the culture that formed him and that surrounded him during his years of formation and maturity: primarily, that is, Britain in the years 1880–1920, in all its political and artistic feverishness. Finally the word 'culture' refers to the other cultures through which Farrer wandered, especially those of Asia — Japan, Korea, China, Tibet, Ceylon (Sri Lanka) and Burma. These wanderings occupied five of the last eighteen years of his life. I shall show that he absorbed a great deal from the cultures of these places, and from them he learned. His interest in Asian cultures was also informed, on a deep internal level, by Buddhism, which Farrer encountered in Japan and Sri Lanka (then Ceylon). He also mixed with Buddhist enthusiasts in London. The Farrer family into which Reginald was born had a strong history of involvement with Evangelical Christianity, even a brush, through a marriage or two, with Calvinism. Yet Farrer became a Buddhist in Sri Lanka in 1908. Not the least value of his copious writings is that they show a western Buddhist attempting to live his Buddhism — in the unpropitious circumstances of upper-class expectations of a stifling conformism to Christianity, and the even worse circumstances of the Great War into which Britain was led by other kinds of upper-class expectations. My book about his life and work is thus not justified simply by being the first full-length study of the life and work of a virtually unknown character; that would leave open a contrary response that he was a historical anomaly whom some might say would have been better left undisturbed. Rather, Farrer is interesting for exemplifying, indeed incarnating, the question of the extent to which western culture in the early twentieth century engaged with Buddhist thought. His life and example elucidates the interconnection with peculiar intensity.

Our understanding of the representation of Asia in Britain, and Asian influence on British arts and modernism thus receives a contribution from the present study. The development of a modern sensibility by means of borrowing from geographically remote cultures is a central theme. The conversion into practical concrete effects of a liking for, and loyalty towards, such remote cultures, for example in garden design, or the writing of novels, or water-colour painting, is an essential part of the inquiry conducted here: in a sense its most important and original element. These Asian countries also provided some of the landscapes in which Farrer lived and which he represented vividly in paint, photographs, gardens, and words.

Farrer's preference in landscape was for mountains. He loved mountains. Writing in 1913 about the pleasures of the European Dolomites, he breaks off to consider the reasons why people love mountains. He discounts beauty, since mountains tend to be ugly.

> Perhaps a generation or two ago their Byronic savagery might have had its hold, but nowadays nobody is Byronic any more. [...] Is it that they are lonely? Is it that they are austere, defensive, defiant, independent? Of course, that is the pathetic fallacy (or enslaving modern fashion); but if one led them to breed those feelings in oneself, then some of their hold would be accounted for.

A dynamic of reciprocity is clear: they have a hold on us. We invest them with human properties. They can create those properties in us. Our relationship with the natural world is intersubjective; it has agency in us, whether we understand why (or whether we want it to) or not. Farrer's questioning has only just begun:

> [The Alps have] the impressiveness of size, which to everyone but a confirmed megalomaniac is no impressiveness at all. We are a flock of sheep, and now that mountains are in fashion, we pretend an indiscriminate worship. This is nonsense.

Entirely characteristic of Farrer's thinking is the way a deeply sceptical temperament helps him to discount the false and search further for something he can consider bedrock truth.

> No, it is in loneliness and lack of motive and the solemn splendour of their air that the secret charm of the mountains consists. I know well that they are often rude and angry and ugly; I puzzle again and again to analyze what it is I really find in them. And my conclusion always is that anyhow I would (usually, and for my best moments) rather be alone on the ugliest mountain [...] than in the finest palace ever made by man. The deepest reason (for pure light and air and solitude are only contributories) in reality is, I am sure, that on the mountains one is less than ever distracted from one's peace. [...] In fact, by long roads of personal inquiry, I come back at last to the knowledge of the Lord Buddha (and the great saints before and after) that in the high places of the world the being is better able to look itself undisturbed in the face, and learn the truth and the true proportions of things.[13]

Buddhist ideas give Farrer confirmation of his own feelings and rational direction to thoughts that might otherwise be difficult to bring to convincing conclusion (that otherwise might seem irreducibly individual or eccentric); while mountains themselves help to get everything into perspective. If we go back to the beginning of this quotation, we see one factor from the pathetic fallacy ('loneliness'), another from basic empirical observation of the natural environment (the 'splendour of their air') combined with a much more enigmatic utterance (their 'lack of motive'). What could this last have meant? Does it mean that mountains are unmotivated? In the seventeenth century, Thomas Burnet published an influential work that saw mountains as the ruins of the first world that the Old Testament God created and then had to destroy when God needed to drown almost the whole human race in Noah's flood.[14] This was a view of mountains that saw them as thoroughly motivated. The English deists argued for a motivation in the opposite direction: a benevolent deity created mountains to regulate the circulation of air and rainfall.[15] Thus rather than being ruins they are useful and beneficial. Does Farrer mean that in an age of geological science, God and the creating deity have faded from the picture, and so mountains emerge as an area unaffected by the Old Testament or Deism? It is quite possible. Equally possible is the idea that in the mountains one is set free from most of the quotidian concerns of the world of humans: alienation caused by politics, law, sexuality, economics (expenses vs. earning, wealth/poverty, search for the things we want to buy, cost-effectiveness, value for money, can I afford this?). The world implied by views of cities, towns, mines, quarries, and farms. Mountains are free from human motivation. Perhaps he means that we are not motivated to like mountains in the ways we are to like countryside imbued with the promise of hospitality, cosiness, productivity, comfort, and religious establishment. Farrer has found a phrase that sends readers' thoughts in a wide range of directions.

Chief among Farrer's internalized landscapes was that of Ingleborough, the Pennine Mountain on the lower slopes of which his ancestral home was located. It constitutes a comparative memory when he assesses remote Asian country-sides, and it features in romantic descriptions in his novels. Location of his greatest loyalties because it was the place of his early passionate discoveries of plants and of himself, yielding self-knowledge as well as early knowledge of the natural world, which provided him with an indication of a route through life. Ingleborough was the place where his curiosity unfolded fully, and a place which amply rewarded that curiosity. His curiosity centred around alpine plants, and it is Farrer's commitment to searching for, collecting, and distributing such plants, which can be understood as the smallest individual units of landscape, contributing to the composition of larger wholes, that justifies the inclusion of 'landscape' as a theme of the book and its inclusion in my title. Readers should be warned, though, that the grand picture of landscape is not often figured here; rather the concept revolves around the small constituent units of it — the plants.

A critical inquiry, then, into the works that Farrer left behind is this book, and a reflection on his processes, weighted by biographical insights. Farrer's lifetime saw a rapid process of modernisation in Britain, Europe and the USA, exemplified by a series of inventions. To select a few: the phonograph, telephone, steam turbine, motor-car, aeroplane, tanks on the battlefield, and concentration camps. Farrer's lifetime saw the Scramble for Africa, and the nations ploughing into the First World War, which changed the world comprehensively. Farrer himself benefitted from or came into contact with some of these developments. Whether as a response to this modernisation, or not, and the feeling of modernity it brought about (the psychological and social experience of de-stabilizing modernisation), literature and the other forms of art registered a new phase of radical modernism. Here is not the place to decide when and where modernism began: whether around 1908, or in the 1860s with Manet and others in Paris, or earlier in nineteenth-century or even eighteenth-century Britain, or with sixteenth-century religious changes.[16] I will say, though, that rather than staking everything on formal breaks and formal experimentation in the arts in the first two decades of the twentieth century, it is more interesting, as David Peters Corbett and others have argued, to examine the continuities between the 1880s and 90s and 1920.[17] Corbett's article is particularly about the interesting figure of Laurence Binyon, among whose many achievements is included the publication in 1908 of *Painting in the Far East: an Introduction to the History of Pictorial Art in Asia, Especially China and Japan*, a contribution to a scholarly and artistic interest within Britain in Chinese and Japanese culture. Imagism in poetry, partially indebted to far Eastern example, began the same year with the work of F.S. Flint and others.[18] Farrer was at least in sympathy with these interests before the opening of the Japan-British Exhibition of 1910. At the beginning of his book *In a Yorkshire Garden* (1909) he writes: 'The Japanese cherish their gift of condensing a whole aspect of nature and emotion into one tiny phrase: listen: Furu-dera ya; | Kane-mono iwazu | Sakura chiru. For here is crystallized loneliness of spirit: "Ancient temple; voiceless bells; falling cherry-petals." What could be more delicately and more completely pictorial?'[19] Farrer's interest in far Eastern culture and its possibilities for British culture was much stronger by virtue of the nine months he had spent in Japan.

The present study thus contributes to a newly emerging area of scholarly activity in the intercultural questions involved with Western artists' interest in the East, and particularly with Buddhism, in the early twentieth century. R. R. Arrowsmith's *Modernism and the Museum: Asian, African and Pacific Art and the London Avant-Garde* focusses on the effect of the cultures he specifies on the work and thought of Joseph Epstein, Eric Gill and Ezra Pound, all visitors to Binyon's area of the British Museum — the Print Collection. Arrowsmith's interest is not in the impact of Eastern religious beliefs, however, so much as the general visual appearance of Eastern works and the ways they reflect varied cultural dynamics that may or may not have been fully understood by the Western artists. Like other scholarship in this field, the focus is on how Eastern motifs and iconography are taken up by Western literary and visual artists. With the exception of studies of the work of Ezra Pound and Lafcadio Hearne, the specific question of the effect of Eastern *religion* (either deeply understood or shared by Western figures) on literary and visual art in the West during Farrer's lifetime has scarcely been successfully pursued at all. Janice Leoshko's article, 'What is in *Kim*? Rudyard Kipling and Tibetan Buddhist Traditions', about the profound understanding of Buddhism in Rudyard Kipling's novel *Kim* was pioneering.[20] Jacquelynn Baas's *Smile of the Buddha: Eastern Philosophy and Western Art from Monet to Today* (University of California Press, 2005) presents case studies on Monet, van Gogh, Gauguin, Redon, Kandinsky before proceeding to later artists. I have made a contribution so modest as to be hardly worth mentioning in my chapter about the work of Paul Gauguin in *Landscape and Vision in Nineteenth-Century Britain and France*.[21] I have to say that anyone embarking on an enquiry such as this has a great debt of gratitude to clarifications achieved by scholars of Buddhist studies and history of religions: especially, in the present instance (and as will become apparent in subsequent pages), to Donald S. Lopez, Guy Welbon, and Lambert Schmithausen. The latter's study on the sentience of plants in early Buddhism has proved invaluable to my researches: all the more so since Farrer left no trace of personal statements about the effect of his embrace of Buddhism on his views about plants in the form of letters or diaries in the archives, and I have had to work out his views by studying clues scattered in his published books on gardens and garden design.

There are published works by Farrer that are not mentioned in this study. Little attention is given to his books about plant collecting in the Cottian Alps, the Alpes Maritimes, and the Dolomites; his verse drama *The Dowager of Jerusalem* (1908) will not be examined at all. He was a very prolific writer. A study such as this cannot encompass everything, so I have omitted works that are less pertinent to my theme. Lacunae in our knowledge of his works and their whereabouts also remain and have affected the scope of this study. His last novel may still exist somewhere in manuscript, but is lost. While most of his flower-paintings are accounted for, the bulk of his landscape paintings wait to be re-discovered.

Notes to the Introduction

1. Anonymous obituary notice, *The Gardeners' Chronicle* 1769 (Sat. Nov. 20, 1920), p. 247. Close stylistic and conceptual continuities with Kingdon Ward's signed obituary in the *Geographical Journal* lead me to conclude that both were written by Kingdon Ward.

2. Sir Hector Macdonald's vexed life and unfortunate end are described in the *Oxford Dictionary of National Biography*. His case is also examined in Robert Aldrich, *Cultural Encounters and Homoeroticism in Sri Lanka: Sex and Serendipity* (London: Routledge, 2014). Farrer also visited Sri Lanka, and it is this coincidence that makes me choose Macdonald's case from among several possibilities.

3. *Oxford Dictionary of National Biography* and Nicola Shulman's *A Rage for Rock Gardening*, (see note 4) together with their derivatives.

4. Nicola Shulman, *A Rage for Rock Gardening: The story of Reginald Farrer Gardener, Writer and Plant Collector* (London: Short Books, 2002; 1st U.S. Edition, Boston, Mass.: Godine, 2004). Shulman's account has had a bad effect, for example, on Robert Aldrich, who imports into his two pages on Farrer in Ceylon several mistakes from Shulman; Aldrich, *Cultural Encounters and Homoeroticism in Sri Lanka*, pp. 41–42. Despite putting Farrer in this book, Aldrich decides that Farrer was 'seemingly blameless' in Ceylon in 1908. It is rather strange that a book about homoeroticism uses the language of blame and guilt. More serious perhaps is that in his page and a half describing Farrer's life, Aldrich makes ten errors of fact. Not all are derived from Nicola Shulman's book; Aldrich adds others of his own. Examples: Farrer did not travel to Japan in 1904, but in 1902; his fiction was not, as we shall see, 'poorly received by critics and readers'; he did not think that all Ceylonese 'merchants were dishonest'; or find Ceylonese 'rest-houses uncomfortable'; in China and Tibet he certainly wasn't 'doing research for a 2-vol encyclopedia of alpine plants'.

5. Tachibana, Setsu, S. Daniels, C. Watkins, 'Japanese Gardens in Edwardian Britain: Landscape and Transculturation', *Journal of Historical Geography* 30, 2 (2004), 364–95.

6. Reginald Farrer, *In a Yorkshire Garden* (London: Arnold, 1909), pp. 273–74, 303.

7. Erik Mueggler, 'The Eyes of Others: Race, "Gaping", and Companionship in the Scientific Exploration of Southwest China', in *Explorers and Scientists in China's Borderlands 1880–1950*, ed. by D. M. Glover et al. (Seattle: University of Washington Press, 2011), pp. 26–56.

8. Erik Mueggler, *The Paper Road: Archive and Experience in the Botanical Exploration of West China and Tibet* (Berkeley: University of California Press, 2011).

9. Paul Fussell, *The Great War and Modern Memory* (Oxford: Oxford University Press, 1975) quotes Farrer's work, pp. 237–38, 301, 327; Stephen Kern, *The Culture of Time and Space 1880–1918* (New Haven: Harvard University Press, 1983 & 2003), p. 301; see also Paul Gough, 'The Living, the Dead, and the Imagery of Emptiness and Re-appearance on the Battlefields of the Western Front', in *Deathscapes:New Spaces for Death, Dying, and Bereavement* (Farnham: Ashgate, 2010), pp. 263–81.

10. See Brian Southam, *Jane Austen: The Critical Heritage Vol. 2 1870–1940* (London: Routledge, 1987), esp. pp. 90–93. Quotations from pp. 85, 92. See also Claudia L. Johnson, *Jane Austen's Cults and Cultures* (Chicago: University of Chicago Press, 2012), pp. 98–100, 105–10.

11. Jeff Mather, 'Camping in China with the Divine Jane: The Travel Writing of Reginald Farrer', *Journeys* 10, 2 (2009), 45–64. Unfortunately Mather's article starts with a series of errors: Charles Lyte was not Farrer's travelling companion (p. 48); Farrer did not lack 'professional seriousness' (p. 48); and Farrer's *The English Rock Garden* (1919) was not the book that 'truly launched Farrer's career as a gardening writer' (p. 49): the launch had happened twelve years earlier. Mather is insightful, though, in discerning the influence on Farrer's writing style of Joseph Conrad, and in noticing that, of Jane Austen's characters, the only ones Farrer compares himself to are female (pp. 50, 53–54).

12. Jill Didur, '"The Perverse Little People of the Hills": Unearthing Ecology and Transculturation in Reginald Farrer's Alpine Plant Hunting', in *Global Ecologies and the Environmental Humanities: Postcolonial Approaches*, ed. by E. DeLoughry, J. Didur, A Carrigan (London: Routledge, 2015), pp. 51–72, quotations from pp. 51, 54. The volume explains that 'environmental humanities' is

conceived as an effort by scholars in the Humanities to 'develop strategies for negotiating this multidimensional environmental crisis' that we are experiencing (p. xiii).

13. Quotations from Farrer, *The Dolomites: King Laurin's Garden* (London: Black, 1913), pp. 70–72.

14. Thomas Burnet, *The Sacred Theory of the Earth* (London, 1684). There had been a Latin edition in 1681.

15. See particularly John Ray, *The Wisdom of God Manifested in the Works of the Creation* (London, 1691).

16. These are all possibilities offered in Stephen Bann, *Ways Around Modernism* (London: Routledge, 2007).

17. David Peters Corbett, 'Crossing the Boundary: British Art across Victorianism and Modernism', in *A Companion to British Art 1600 to the Present*, ed. by Dana Arnold and David Peters Corbett (Chichester: Wiley-Blackwell, 2013), pp. 131–55. This interest in continuity is the central argument of Bann's book too, which covers a longer temporal span.

18. See J. B. Harmer, *Victory in Limbo: imagism, 1908–1917* (London: Secker & Warburg, 1975).

19. Reginald Farrer, *In a Yorkshire Garden*, pp. 2–3.

20. J. Leoshko, 'What is in *Kim*? Rudyard Kipling and Tibetan Buddhist Traditions', *South Asia Research*, 21, 1 (2001), 51–75.

21. Michael Charlesworth, *Landscape and Vision in Nineteenth-Century Britain and France* (Aldershot: Ashgate, 2008), pp. 138–53. In the literary field, the (somewhat speculative) articles contributed by Peter Caracciolo to the journal of the Joseph Conrad Society should probably be mentioned: 'Buddhist Teaching Stories and their Influence on Conrad, Wells, and Kipling: the Reception of the Jataka and Allied Genres in Victorian Culture', *The Conradian*, 11, 1 (May 1986), 24–34; 'Buddhist Typologies in "Heart of Darkness" and "Victory" and their Contribution to the Modernism of Jacob Epstein, Wyndham Lewis and T. S. Eliot', *The Conradian*, 14, 1/2 (December 1989), 67–91.

CHAPTER 1

A Distant Bell:
Biography 1880–1908

Born into a stratum of British society that he came to reject, even hate, Reginald
Farrer started life with a cleft palate and a hare-lip. While Farrer was very young,
the medical profession attempted various times to seal up these lacks, these absences,
in ways torturous for the small boy. An operation when very young indeed
would have been almost inevitable, as the contents of the mouth can exit through
the nose when nursing, among other difficulties. 'Standard procedures', we are
told, 'involved hot tongs, sulphuric acid, and metal bridles'.[1] He probably needed a
further corrective operation after his permanent teeth came through.[2] In due course
he was able to grow a thick black moustache to conceal the scars of his upper lip.
Photographs show his lips pulled round slightly to the left, presumably as a result
of the handicap. His front teeth were, of necessity, artificial. As a boy, until he
reached about the age of fifteen, we are told that only his mother could properly
understand what he was trying to say, and despite the operations on his soft palate,
his voice throughout his life remained high-pitched, whistling, squawky. He was
also very small in stature (standing around 5' high in his prime) with extremely
narrow shoulders surmounted by a normal-sized head, which added to the oddity
of his appearance.

Unlucky, Farrer was in other ways very lucky. His parents decided, given his
difficulties, not to send him to boarding school, where he would certainly have been
heavily teased and bullied. He was educated first at home by a succession of tutors
and then in the household of a clergyman expert in tutoring.[3] He was educated
well: his published writings are full of apposite allusions to a range of literary and
historical references. The boy who could rarely make himself understood became
a most eloquent man, lecturing to various sorts of audience from election crowds
to villagers and the Royal Geographical Society, writing hundreds of articles, and
publishing nineteen books in seventeen years.

He was also lucky in that his family owned 11,000 acres of land: not the best-
quality farmland, but including most of the mountain of Ingleborough, at the foot
of which stood their country house, Ingleborough Hall in the village of Clapham.
It was on the slopes of this Pennine landmark that the young Farrer played and
explored and made his first botanical discovery, a new locality for *Arenaria gothica*
(now known as *Arenaria norvegica* subsp. *anglica*, a subspecies endemic to the Craven

limestone). He wrote a letter about this which was published in the *Journal of Botany*.[4] His first published work, therefore, at the perhaps impressionable age of 14, came out of his love for flowering plants growing above the treeline in one of the rockier and more infertile parts of the earth. Such plants are known as alpines. His mother had encouraged an interest in plants and flowers from a very early age, gardening being also one of her pastimes. A few years later, Farrer discovered, also on Ingleborough, a nondescript hybrid saxifrage that was eventually named after him.[5]

Farrer went as an undergraduate to Balliol College, Oxford, in 1898. While there he helped the Bursar of St. John's College make a rock garden. He made friends among his peers in the privileged class: particularly with Harold Brewer Hartley, who became an experimental chemist, Aubrey Herbert, the son of the Earl of Carnarvon, Alfred Gathorne Hardy, the son of Lord Cranbrook, and Raymond Asquith, the son of the Liberal politician, party leader and eventual Prime Minister. Farrer's letters after he got to Oxford indicate an impatience with the parochialism of home. In one letter of 1900 to his mother he parodies back to her her own sermonising style of homily: 'Dear Lady', he writes,

> Sorry to hear of your perturbation of spirit — if only you *determine not* to give *way* and fight the good fight *humbly* and *teachably*, you will find that *strength* will *come* and you will be no more *perturbed* — also a little port is an excellent thing.

This letter also indicates, on a different level, that Farrer was used to being indulged by his parents. First-born, handicapped, disfigured when very young, he nevertheless grew up with confidence in himself, and their indulgence will have been a contributing factor in that. On another occasion he gives advice about a practical matter: 'Dear Lady, The Library carpet will *not* fit in the Smoking Room, as is obvious to the naked eye.' Perhaps his purchase of a Kelmscott Press *Maud* was a departure from the family's normal dour attitude to possessions.[6] Perhaps it betokened an interest in the values of the arts and crafts movement, or even a respect for William Morris's socialism. Farrer graduated (1902) with a degree in Literae Humaniores — a 3rd class degree: 'to his and our own disappointment', writes his father.[7]

As a sort of post-graduation jaunt, Farrer went to Japan in 1902. His experience there is described in his first published book, *The Garden of Asia: Impressions from Japan* (1904), which I will discuss in Chapter 5. Here I shall simply note a few facts from unpublished materials. Farrer left from Genoa on October 10, and thereafter, in his own words, 'Yokohama Nov. 20 (?) 1902. Lived at 12 Hirokicho, Akasaka, Tokyo till July 15 1903 (March to April 15 in China and Korea). Home Aug 10 1903 (date of month not sworn to)'.[8] He was in Japan and China with Aubrey Herbert, who was taking up a post attached to the British Embassy in Tokyo; Herbert's brother Mervyn; and other friends, Gerard and Eric Collier, sons of Lord Monkswell. Gertrude Bell travelled in China with them, her informal photograph of the Empress finding its way into Farrer's album; and Lady Carnarvon also joined them for the trip to China. Farrer was deeply impressed by the sheer gloominess of Korea (and published an article about it in 1903 in the journal *The Nineteenth*

Century): 'Death, in this strange country, is in fuller evidence than life. It is, indeed, a land sacred and set apart for the dead. The living have here no place [...] this enormous graveyard that is Korea.'[9] He also noted in passing the savagery of Japanese methods of diplomacy.[10] The stay in Japan taught Farrer a great deal about designing with plants, and about Buddhism, and I shall discuss these topics in a later chapter. Returning home to Ingleborough Hall after a long time in the Far East did not make the young man of 23 feel like a hero or an adventurer:

> All the claws of the old life closed on me — the East dropped away from me so suddenly that it was almost tragic: at a blow it faded, and the house and the place were just as they had always been — till I felt in an hour I had never been away at all.[11]

The suggestions of physical pain ('claws' and 'a blow') together with the curious use of 'the old life' are enough to intimate the depth of emotional distress Farrer felt from his family's indifference ('My people are less interested than anybody'[12]). We might also note the implication that the implied 'new life' is, by contrast, to be lived in 'the East'.

In some respects the atmosphere at home while Reginald was growing up was not happy. His mother was very religiose, and in the early nineteenth century Farrer ancestors had espoused a Calvinist Evangelicalism.[13] Farrer's cousin Osbert Sitwell describes a Protestant gloom pervading Reginald's parents' household, where

> you could have possessions so long as you did not enjoy them, and where every Sunday dragged after it a weary, weekly train of charitable village functions, jumble sale or jamboree, and the more purely domestic orgies of missionary meeting and simple family prayer.[14]

Farrer's father was a Liberal barrister who stood unsuccessfully for Parliament, and a relative of Lord Farrer of Godalming, founder of the Victorian Board of Trade and one of the three indispensible men of the nineteenth century civil service. Public service and the Church therefore tended to dominate the atmosphere. Once he became an adult, parental indulgence, while not disappearing altogether, was curtailed. Reginald complained about not being treated with enough generosity.[15] In 1904 he was given an income of £100 p.a. from the Ingleborough estates. Given the costs and habits of the time, this was little more than pocket-money. In itself it did not enable independence, though by 1909 at least it was made up to £400 p.a. out of the parents' own incomes. In 1910, as a result of the resettlement of the estate to try to avoid taxes, his allowance went up to £500 p.a. paid entirely from estate income.[16] This was about what a gentleman-bachelor could live on unostentatiously in the countryside.[17]

By 1902 Farrer had started the Craven Nursery, a small business in Clapham which raised and sold plants, especially alpines, and was still functioning in 1921.[18] Apart from this, and an unsuccessful attempt to win the parliamentary seat of Ashford (Kent) in 1910, he seems to have resisted attempts by his parents to induce him to gain a conventionally respectable and professional way of making a living. In a letter home as late as 1915 he wrote,

> You haven't realised yet that the Craven Nursery is to be a large, serious and moving concern [...] why do you seem to think that in order not to be dilettante one must neglect the opportunity of making strenuous money out of what one already knows and likes, and spend weary hours gathering doubtful and meagre profit out of what one neither knows nor likes. This is a silly waste of time and trouble. We will say no more about it.[19]

That a man aged 35 was forced to remonstrate like this with his own parents suggests considerable difficulties in the relationships with them. As he was the elder son, the next in line to inherit the whole estate, he was unable to break entirely free from being beholden to his parents. His reference to not being 'dilettante' is sufficient to indicate the character of the mother and father's remonstrances. To Aubrey Herbert he complained of the Baudelairean phenomenon, horror of home: 'We really get on exceedingly ill, but we pretend that this is not so [...] Home life has all the disadvantages of solitude, and none of its delights.'[20] Other letters from before 1915 indicate how the atmosphere of home was felt by Farrer: 'Bill and I took out the motor the other day alone, and broke it in a by-lane, and walked home *miles,* and were hours late for dinner, and found everybody weeping, stuttering, and voiceless with rage.'[21] In a letter of 1907 he grumbles mightily about the family, and adds the final insult they have caused him: 'add to all that they are getting up a play of mine in a neighbouring little bloody metropolis [the small town of Settle], in which I have to act a burglar disguised as a widow, in black silk and a saffron wig.' The (typewritten) letter asks Herbert to write:

> for it is only by the letters of friends that I can feed the illusion that I still live. At present, as I say, I have all the drawbacks of death, with none of its countervailing calm . .--- And the damned blasted typewriter has come back from town after its rest-cure, in an even more atrocious temper than my own.[22]

To do some justice to the parents' concerns, I should clarify that generations of Farrers, including Reginald's own father, had been involved in the Law, as solicitors, even acting for Government (or in his father's case as a barrister). His paternal grandfather Matthew had been a clergyman. Profits from legal fees had bought the Ingleborough estate at the end of the eighteenth century, and they, together with some East India money and profits from directorships of banks, had enabled parcels of lands to be added to it as they had become available throughout the next century.[23] A recent writer on the Ingleborough estate, though somewhat contradictory in her presentation of evidence, is clear enough when she writes that, throughout the second half of the nineteenth century, income from rents failed to keep up with expenses of the estate. So the solicitors' and clergyman's livings had supplemented rents to contribute in a necessary way to the style of life that approximated, or affected, that of owners of more profitable lands.[24] His parents must have wondered what Reginald was going to contribute in that regard, and whether he would ever be in a position to add more land. They probably thought (though this point is more speculative) that, as he showed no inclination, and less aptitude, for the Law, and yet had become eloquent, he would have made a good vicar. Osbert Sitwell reports his grandmother as fantasizing a 'career of Low Church devotion' for Reginald.[25]

Correspondence about the garden that Farrer was creating at the ancestral home could be even more acrimonious than that about the Nursery. At the age of 30 (in 1910) Farrer had to write as follows to his mother. The background to this letter, which I shall quote at length, is that over the years Farrer had not only created two rock gardens at Ingleborough Hall, but had also appropriated a large cliff of bare limestone that looms over the eastern side of the lake in the garden (the lake itself being artificial, the work of Farrer ancestors in the 1830s). Here Farrer had successfully sown alpines. Yet his parents had decided to make paths through, and plant other plants in, his areas (the 'cave' in the letter refers to Ingleborough Cave, which had developed into a visitors' attraction):

> Don't be annoyed if I say you really must try to drop 'scaring'. For the ten or twelve parties who are annually shown my Cliff, you have four or five hundred who are allowed up to see the cave: so do leave off the attempt to make a grievance out of that! As to 'adding to expenses', how ridiculously ill comes this from you, when it is exactly this addition to upkeep-expenses that *you* are committing and *I* am asking you to refrain from! And your allusions to the Nursery have nothing to do with this point, but are merely designed to 'score'. With regard to my father, do let us for once be frank; you paint him as a stern-willed tyrant whenever it suits your argument: but both you and I know that he does, or refrains more or less exactly as you tell him! So that, if, instead of encouraging him to plant good plants in hopeless places, or horrible weeds in good ones, you advised him to rely on the advice of me, one of the best authorities in the Kingdom, he would agree at once, without any further feeling! So do make an effort. You say *he* never objected to his father's work: well, do I ever say what I feel about the rest of the garden, even, or any other subject? Yes, sometimes: because the way in which one is absolutely ignored, is sometimes beyond one's bearing: but as seldom *as possible*. Yet even *he* would have protested if his father had insisted in making bad chalk drawings all over his photographs! And that is exactly what you, and he, are doing. You are spoiling my work: making it hideous and ridiculous. He has all the rest of the garden and all the estate to play with, without a word from me: in decency and chivalry I require, and demand, that you, and he, leave to my sole control the one little tiny strip which belongs to me absolutely because it comes into the subject on which I am a final authority. If you stopped to think you would be only too thankful to have me there: *do* leave off being so jealous and grudging in your recognition; and, for Goodness sake leave off pretending that it's my *father's* uncontrollable wish to ruin my pet work by sticking weeds all over the ground which I am gradually (having the knowledge) going to make the miracle of England. Hang it, you and he have everything else; you needn't grudge me just half an acre or so, uninterfered with by zeal and ignorance!! My position between you isn't always easy already: I'm sure you and he don't want to make it more difficult still. You see, I speak to *you*. I know whatever paths *he* might have made, he would never have planted, but for you: it is to you, then, I turn, to have this wasteful trial stopped. Leave me my valley, rocks and cliff: go and stick Polygonums, etc. elsewhere. You have 14,000 acres: leave me two!![26]

Many years of frustration no doubt lie behind this letter. By the time of this protest against his parents' planting over his own garden spaces, and their invasive path-making, Farrer had published three books and several scholarly articles on gardening and garden plants, and repeatedly won prizes for design with plants. His claim to be 'one of the best authorities in the Kingdom' about alpines, rock-gardening, and thus gardening generally, was justified. Yet there his parents are, blithely going their own narrow way over his work, which he intends to make 'the miracle of England'. In that extraordinary ambition, straightforwardly expressed, and couched in language of the immeasurable ('miracle'), we sense the powerful purpose, the extent, the naivety and dramatic character of Farrer's motivation: the confidence with which he contemplates the possibility of accomplishing something extraordinary and memorable within the annals of national achievements.

Sitwell states that Farrer took to referring to his family as 'the Watsons',[27] assuming this to have been a reference to Dr. Watson in Conan Doyle's Sherlock Holmes stories, an idea endorsed by Nicola Shulman.[28] It seems to me much more likely to have been a reference to a work by Farrer's favourite novelist, Jane Austen. Her fragment of an undeveloped novel, *The Watsons*, describes a family that never has enough money to live up to the members' social pretensions. They are middle-class, but lack the money to live comfortably in the higher social stratum to which they think they belong. Unlike other of Austen's fictional families, who live with 'some style and elegance' despite financial difficulties, the Watsons 'were waited on by Nanny, and had to worry themselves about domestic matters like "the great wash".[29] The heroine, Emma, having grown up elsewhere, returns home to find 'an unequal society, and family discord'.[30] In an extraordinary scene, Emma's sister Margaret, her brother, and her sister-in-law all complain and nag snidely and half-covertly at each other. The sister-in-law lies to her child, Margaret lies to Emma and the brother 'irritated and grieved' her.[31] Emma has returned to 'the immediate endurance of hard-hearted prosperity, low-minded conceit, and wrong-headed folly' where she is 'surrounded by inferior minds with little chance of domestic comfort, and as little hope of future support.'[32] All of this seems to fit Farrer's mature appraisal of his own family better than does the example of the unimaginative, subservient, patient and yet sometimes enthusiastic Dr. Watson.

Several years passed before Farrer could return to the East. He worked at the Craven Nursery, which won prizes at Royal Horticultural Society shows, and, like his father, took an interest in Liberal Party politics. The party won a very large majority in the General Election of 1906, and set about a programme of social legislation. Farrer also wrote: *The Garden of Asia* appeared in 1904, his first novel in 1906 and a book about rock gardens the following year. Travel outside Britain was confined to Italy or France. Then in January 1908 he and Aubrey Herbert embarked on the Royal Mail Ship *Ophir*: Farrer was bound for Ceylon, and Herbert for Australia. Farrer arrived in Ceylon at 6am on the 3rd of February, after 'half a gale' in the Red Sea.[33] Two days later something very unusual and truly epoch-making happened: Farrer made vows not to kill, to steal, to lie, to commit adultery, or to touch alcohol; he knelt with his forehead on the floor in front of two aged men, one Sinhalese and one Siamese, and took refuge in the Buddha, the Dharma (Buddhist doctrine or teaching), and the Sangha (the Buddhist community). That is to say, he became a Buddhist.

Thus in the year of his grand climacteric, Farrer reoriented his life. As he confided in a letter to Herbert, he was only able to achieve this new state by winning a victory over himself. The two elderly men were monks: Prince Prisdang of Siam, a priest of the Dipaduttaramaya Temple at Kotahena (part of Colombo) whom Farrer calls 'His Highness' the 'Prince-Priest'; and the more senior 'Primate', Sumangăla, 'a tiny, decrepit old man of eighty-two, with one of the grandest heads I've ever seen'.[34] They conducted the ceremony. The day is surely worth dwelling on, given its supreme importance in Farrer's life. To begin, he called at the Kotahena Temple to take His Highness to Sri Sumangăla's college where the ceremony was to take place. Farrer was kept waiting an hour, rather un-Buddhistically writing: 'I fuming the while with thought of the dominant race being compelled to wait.' The previous day, in conversation with Farrer, the Prince-Priest ('small and frail and impressive, with keen face and eyes,' says Farrer) had had a Bishop Heber-like moment, confiding that he was 'miserable' in Ceylon, where, in ten years 'he has not found one true or honest soul.'[35] It is worth dwelling on possible reasons for this pessimism. Anne Blackburn's book, *Locations of Buddhism: Colonialism and Modernity in Sri Lanka* analyzes in detail the politics of Buddhism in the island over the period 1870–1910. She discusses the status of the Prince-Priest, more properly known as Jinavaravamsa.[36] Tamara Loos's invaluable work about the life of Prince Prisdang in the context of Thai history, *Bones Around My Neck: The Life and Exile of a Prince Provocateur,* elaborates and explains events very fully from Jinavaravamsa's point of view.[37] He was a grandson of a King of Siam, and cousin of another. He had been educated in England and had represented his country as a diplomat in Europe before becoming a monk in Ceylon in 1896. His first major task had been to help arrange a visit to Ceylon by the King of Siam in 1897. The King, a Buddhist himself, monarch of an independent nation (not taken into one of the European empires) wished to see the Tooth-Relic in its temple-shrine in Kandy. This was a very holy and amazing relic, a tooth of the Buddha (Gautama) himself. When the great moment came and the relic was unveiled to him, the King wished to handle the tooth. The tooth's guardians would not allow the King to touch it, fearing that he might steal it, or make off with it by replacing it with a false substitute. The King departed in a huff, sent back the gifts that the temple had presented to him, and demanded the return of the gifts that he had given the temple. This was a disaster, and was written up in both Sinhalese and English-language newspapers as a diplomatic fiasco. The Prince-Priest must have felt, with respect to his standing in the divided world of Buddhist monasticism in Ceylon, that the rug had been pulled out from under him. Some Sinhalese Buddhists welcomed closer ties with Siam, especially given that in their homeland there was no authoritative Buddhist temporal ruler who could help to regulate Buddhist affairs and arbitrate disagreement between monks; others were strongly opposed.

Now, on 5th February 1908, while the Prince-Priest finished his nap, 'fuming' Farrer: 'had to lap tepid lemonade and discuss the end of the world (through an interpreter) with an ardent Cinhalese monk.'[38] At last they set off, and arrived at Sumangăla's college (Vidyodaya Pirivena), where 'crowds of yellow robed monks escorted us to a hideous European room'. Here Farrer took his vows. The personages involved then repaired to 'a stifling little chapel' where Farrer disapproved inwardly of the tastelessness of the decoration:

> It's astounding, after the gorgeous dignity of the Japanese Buddhism (at which the Cinhalese sniff awfully) to note the dreadful tawdry tastelessness almost Roman Catholic in its gimcrackry squalor, which prevails [...] However the complete lack of dignity was an effectual safeguard against any religious emotionalism in me — a weakness of mine, and one I specially dread.

Things were not propitious, therefore. Squalor, tastelessness, lack of dignity, 'a mob of monks' to witness this Englishman's spiritual step. Farrer continues,

> Having kindled candles on the altars, I knelt and adored the Buddhas: — one bends one's head three times to the earth, where one's forehead rests for an awful apoplectic moment, during which one's chief prevailing thought is of the uncomfortable and humiliating protrusion of one's bottom.

After this, Farrer was guided through the 'Litany of reception' (pronounced by Sumangăla in the Pali language) and his responses by the Prince-Priest. So far so good. Then comes a crisis. Herbert and Farrer had evidently been discussing race on board ship, and when he had to bow down and put his forehead on the floor in obeisance to Jinavaravamsa and Sumangăla, Farrer writes,

> The ceremony concluded by my prostrate adoration of Sri Sumangăla and H.H. Now here comes a funny thing. So far, unimpressed, emotionally, I therefore coldly realised that I was doing the right inevitable thing, but at this point your 'little yellow people' surged up in my gorge and I found myself influenced emotionally by all that damned 'dominant race' rubbish — which, however true and valuable politically, is such utter balls in the higher sphere of ethics. It was quite a second before I realised that, in morals, there can never be any dominance but goodness and wisdom — quite a second before I could honestly stick out my bottom and plump down my head on the floor before two ancient men, probably of fifty times my pedigree, and certainly of a hundred hundred times my wisdom, knowledge and virtue.

So the whole morning, and the ceremony, had offended many of Farrer's sensibilities, but he had had the sense not to lose his head and abandon his purpose. The sense of adventure; of doing something because of its very strangeness and difficulty, is clear in this part of the letter. Farrer achieved a victory over lingering racial prejudice — a victory over his formation, his upbringing and the cultural forces of Victorian and Edwardian Britain he had lived amongst and that tried to determine his response — a victory of free will. He was left with a sense of the positive attraction of Buddhism and the way it answered a need in him, as he explained in another letter to Herbert a few weeks later:

> The really religious mind is absolutely bound to take refuge in the world of ideas, and rigidly to avoid sight or contact of any professional religions — most especially those who pretend to his own faith. For religion lives in the heart: any attempt to give it form in ordinance or liturgy or priesthood, immediately brings the holy thing into grip of the everyday world, and in that vulgarizing

material grasp the holy thing evaporates at once, leaving only a delusive shell behind.[39]

Independence, individuation, the reluctance to join a community regulated by a priesthood, are dominant here; Farrer clearly believes that Buddhism makes possible the realisation of these modern demands of his. The letter continues,

> By the way, logic does play a part in my religion, if only in so far that I imperatively demand of my religion that at least it should not be violently abhorrent from logic, like theological Christianity. Gautama's system touches me in the bull's eye because it fully satisfies my sense of religious mystery, my love of ethics and ideals, and above all craving for a reasonable — not a *proved* but a reasonable and coherent view of the scheme of things.

The letter is quite clear about the appeal of Buddhism to Farrer's imagination, his reason, and his idealism. He goes on immediately,

> — a view in which evolution and development and eternity have their due place, and where no single notion, out of the Indian jungle five and twenty centuries ago, conflicts at any point with the views of accurate science today.

We might sense something slightly wrong here. The last phrase, 'the views of accurate science today' strikes the wrong note. In deploying a cliché, it reveals itself as a phrase not of Farrer's making. He is rehearsing someone else's position. And he may have been a good botanist, but apart from that, how is he to judge, of the whole of 'science,' what is 'accurate' or not? Donald S. Lopez has looked at the crafting of a 'modern' Buddhism, trimmed down and made fit for Western societies of the twentieth century, and he reminds us that 'an attraction of Buddhism to European intellectuals during the Victorian period was that it presented an ethical system that did not require God, yet somehow seemed consistent with Darwinism.'[40] Lopez quotes 'the leading British scholar of Buddhism of the day, Thomas W. Rhys Davids,' in a lecture of 1881: 'the more thorough-going the Evolutionist, [...] the greater will be his appreciation of the strangeness of the fact that a theory so far consistent with what he holds to be true should have been possible at all in so remote a past.'[41] Lopez clarifies that it is the Buddhist doctrine of *karma* that is the subject. T. H. Huxley, the eventual defender of Darwin, wrote in 1894 that, 'like the doctrine of evolution itself, that of transmigration has its roots in the world of reality; and it may claim such support as the great argument from analogy is capable of supplying.'[42] Lopez also cites an essay of 1905 in *The Fortnightly Review*: 'The religion of the Buddha is not in conflict with modern science; he anticipated many of its most important conclusions; its primary principle of evolution is one with his central tenet.'[43]

Clearly, during his lifetime there was a certain amount of debate and discussion of the idea, on which Farrer relies in his letter, that Buddhism is a religion compatible with modern science. Rhys Davids establishes this statement of the congruence between Evolution and Buddhism, within the discourse of Buddhism; it is then restated and confirmed by other writers.[44] Farrer, of course, was interested in the practice at least as much as the discourse, and equally clearly, if he was able to take his step into the Buddhist congregation the second day after disembarkation, he had prepared for it while he was still in Britain. *The Times of Ceylon* printed an article about him, together with a short interview, to mark his arrival, under the heading 'A European Convert to Buddhism'. The article tells us that 'Mr. Farrer is an active member of the council of the Boddhasasana of Rangoon, a branch of which has been formed in London under the Presidency of Professor Rhys Davids'. The interview elaborates:

> He [Farrer] had studied a good deal of Buddhist literature for many years, and had always been sympathetic to Eastern religions. He came to the Island with his mind quite settled on the subject. His initiation [...] was quite impossible at home, there being no priests of that religion in England to perform the rites [...] there were many others who were willing to be initiated into Buddhism but the absence of means [...] prevented them from carrying their wishes into effect. Ananda Maitriya of Rangoon, who will pass through Colombo, in a short while, [on his way to London] is expected to help these enthusiasts [...] A few months ago a branch of the International Buddhist Association was established in London with Prof. Rhys Davids as President. Mr. Farrer is a member of the council of this Association.

Asked if he intends to become a priest, Farrer demurs that he is not learned enough.[45] The article claims for Farrer a certain level of immersion in the society of the other Buddhist sympathisers, and in available Buddhist literature; it also clarifies some of the company he was keeping. Rhys Davids' translation activities via the Pali Text Society (and earlier his years of residence in Ceylon) had made him a pre-eminent authority of the moment, and the Buddhist Society of Great Britain had been founded in November 1907. Ananda Maitriya's original name was Allan Bennett. A former member of the Hermetic Order of the Golden Dawn, he was an associate of Aleister Crowley, who had paid for Bennett to travel to Ceylon in 1900. Bennett became a Buddhist monk there the following year, before going on to Burma, where he started the Buddhasasana Samagama, an International Buddhist Society, in 1903.[46]

   It is difficult to be exact about when Farrer might first have become attracted to Buddhism, if that interest pre-dates his experiences in Japan and China. In 1899 as a student he had written home about his coming winter holiday in Clapham, 'I hope to get plenty of shooting.'[47] At this date he was not, we can therefore judge, an exponent of Buddhism, with its emphasis on compassion for other sentient beings, and its injunction against taking any life. A later letter from Japan to his father in 1903 re-states Farrer's enthusiasm for shooting.[48] In his account of Japan he cites Rudyard Kipling's novel, *Kim*, which appeared in book form in 1901, and Farrer's photograph album from Japan labels one of his photographs of a statue of the Buddha in Shiba Park as: 'the best friend of all the world', a phrase used of the character Kim in that novel (figure 1.1).[49] The later letter of 28 February 1908 to Herbert confides that: 'I do not mind a label: in fact, I like it. I am very certain indeed of where I want to go. I want to go away from the everlasting recurrence of desire and disappointment — I want to get off the Wheel.' The reference here is to the *Bhavachakra,* (the 'Wheel of Life', figure 1.2), paintings of which became

FIG. 1.1. Reginald Farrer's photograph of a statue of the
Buddha in Shiba Park, Tokyo, 1902/3.

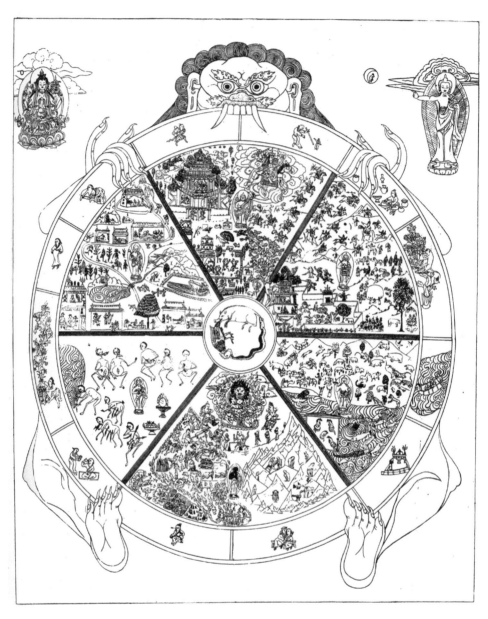

FIG. 1.2. The Tibetan Buddhist 'Wheel of Life' (from L. A. Waddell,
The Buddhism of Tibet, or Lamaism, 1895).

a central diagram of Tibetan Buddhist teaching, familiarly known (particularly by the characters in *Kim*) as 'the Wheel'. Farrer's use of this term might indicate a greater familiarity with *Kim* (and with Waddell's book from which the diagram comes) than with typical Buddhist terms for the same visual device. Such greater familiarity might have been Farrer's or Herbert's; but in any case Kipling's *Kim* seems to have exerted an influence over Farrer: indeed, a spiritual or philosophical one. Along the felloes of the wheel the *Bhavachakra* lays out the concept of the cycle of dependent origination, which is an analysis of the processes that keep us here in the world enduring many deaths and rebirths. The hub of the wheel, around which the whole thing pivots, features the cockerel of desire, the snake of anger and the pig of ignorance. The Lama in *Kim* expresses a desire to 'get off the Wheel'. To make such an escape from the suffering of endless rebirths one needs to overcome desire, anger and ignorance to become awakened.[50]

Farrer expresses optimism that he will, at some stage, 'get off the Wheel'; it's just a question of when. In this optimism, as in his conviction that Buddhism embraces evolution, and is 'reasonable,' Farrer gets quite close to certain aspects of Sir Edwin Arnold's view of Buddhism. Arnold, a keen promoter of Buddhism in all sorts of ways, had in 1879 written the highly influential poem, *The Light of Asia*, celebrating the Buddha. In a somewhat tendentious lecture published in 1891, he said,

> when Darwin shows us life passing onward and upward through a series of constantly improving forms towards the Better and the Best, each individual starting in new existence with the records of bygone good and evil stamped deeply and ineffaceably from the old ones, what is this again but the Buddhist doctrine of Dharma and of Karma?[51]

What, indeed, we might think, when put like that. But Arnold attributes an optimism to both Darwin and Buddhism that is not necessarily present in either system. He also attributes to Darwinism a belief that 'each individual [starts] in new existence', as if having been sent round again; as if it is the existence which is new, not the individual. Arnold also erroneously attributes to Darwin a moralism ('Better and Best [...] good and evil'). However, my purpose is not to take issue with Arnold so much as to indicate one of the possible sources for Farrer's own optimism about the relationship between Buddhism and science.

A final point made in the crucially important earlier letter to Herbert (5 February) concerns what Farrer, in embracing Buddhism, felt himself to be getting away from. He congratulates himself on: 'saying goodbye to the hideous Hebraica-Byzantine Gods of Christian theology, patched up with contradictions, alternatively vindictive, impotent and ineffectual, in all their Homo-ousic, Homoiousic subtleties.' This amounts to a rather splendid dismissal of the religion of his family. In a letter to his father dated July 15, 1903 from Hotel Badminton, Vancouver, during his return from Japan, he writes that 'a small work on the subject that I am bringing home shows to my complete satisfaction at least that both John and Jesus were clearly disciples following the better way of Gautama', that is, the Buddha.[52] So Christianity did not answer Farrer's spiritual needs, his impulse to belief, while Buddhism did.

The letter of 5 February to Aubrey Herbert describing the ceremony, and showing in splendid detail Farrer's most inward, personal responses, contains, on lines
3–6 of the first page, the revealing assertion: 'now, secure in the belief that you
will never receive this, I write out at random the flippant impressions of an overwrought mind.' I understand from this that what survives in the archive is therefore
a 'copy' of a letter that was never sent. So the letter was for Farrer alone. Not even
his closest friend was told all his secrets. A further point needs to be made about
this document, now revealed as a record, and perhaps a revelation, of the self to
the self. Farrer reminds himself (and inadvertently reveals to us) that he is prone
to: 'religious emotionalism [...] — a weakness of mine, and one I specially dread.'
It is worth considering this personality trait. It probably arose from his experience
in the Church of England as a boy, under the encouragement and perhaps example
of his mother. Yet, on another level, what is involved in psychological terms?
Religious emotionalism is an effacing or submerging of the self in the greater
whole: in the deity (presumably); and/or the community of the like-minded. By
contrast, Reginald Farrer's entire life was engaged in a process of individuation: an
attempt to become an individual, which involved the choosing and making of the
individual that he wanted to be. He tried to rise above all the forces of determinism
which acted upon him: physical handicaps, early isolation, inability to make himself
understood, early experience of considerable physical pain, family social life with
'The Watsons', smallness and strangeness of his appearance (unattractiveness). In this
process the earlier religious experiences under the aegis of his mother and father
had no doubt played their useful part; now, however, their usefulness was long
past and therefore the tendency had to be dreaded. Farrer's demand was modern:
that his spiritual beliefs, in so far as embodied in and satisfied by a religion, should
be rational; capable of accommodating evolution, while making no demands on
displays of emotion. In the end, if Farrer's approach to Buddhism retained strong
Protestant outlines from his earlier religious experience (not least obvious in his
condemnation of Roman Catholic 'gimcrackry squalor'), they were undemanding
outlines, not requiring an emotional confession of one's personal relationship
with God.

We can also perhaps regard Farrer's step into Buddhism as enlightened and modern
in that it entailed a conquest of racism. Farrer loathed the British plantation-owners
and overseers (the 'planters') he encountered in Ceylon, accusing them of racism,
among other faults. He relished stories that put British racial arrogance in its place.
In his account of 5 February he includes an anecdote that he has heard:

> the story of a planter who, with his friends, was in a 1st Class Railway Carriage.
> He was leaning out to keep it for himself, when, to his horror, up comes an
> old yellow Buddhist monk, and tries to get in. Planter, in vulgarest coolie
> Cinhalese, tells him he has made a mistake and can go to Hell. 3rd Class.
> To which monk, in perfect English, blandly replies 'It is probably far more
> unpleasant for me to travel with you, than it is for you to travel with me:
> however I have paid for a first Class Ticket, and I mean to use it. Kindly get
> out of the way!' — Utter Collapse of planter.

The monk was, of course, Jinavaravamsa, Prince Prisdang. Farrer also relays the story, heard in Colombo, that Bishop Heber's well-known disgust with the inhabitants of Ceylon, expressed in his mission hymn, 'where every prospect pleases | and only man is vile' was caused by a fit of pique after being cheated buying gems. 'Buying green glass for emeralds', he 'damned all the Cinhalese collectively for the crime of one'.[53]

In one other element of relations with authorities in Ceylon, Farrer was lucky. His letter of introduction, after his acceptance into the Buddhist 'congregation', from 'P.C. Jinavaramsa Thero' to 'the Venerable Nakaya' includes the statement that Farrer 'brings messages from H H Princess Louise'.[54] Queen Victoria's artistic daughter, the sculptress Princess Louise, had become Duchess of Argyll in 1900 on the death of her father-in-law. Farrer's mother's sister Grace had married into the Campbell clan to become Lady Campbell of Succoth, and lived at Crarae, a few miles down Loch Fyne from the Campbell/Argyll seat at Inverary.[55] It was presumably this connection that enabled Farrer to meet, and have a boisterous time with, another Princess Louise: Queen Victoria's grand-daughter, Princess Louise Augusta of Schleswig-Holstein. In a letter to Herbert, Farrer had written: 'Here I am talking all day long against Princess Louise Augusta. She shouts, and I shout too, and occasionally remember to poke in a "ma'am", and altogether it is great fun.'[56] The letter is addressed from 'Lunefield', a house in Lancashire belonging to Alice, Countess of Bective, a friend of Farrer's mentioned in his Will, so the introduction to Princess Louise Augusta might simply have come through her. At any rate, this Princess had visited Ceylon in the winter of 1903–1904, and again in 1906.[57] In a letter of 4 February 1908 to his mother he reports, 'I had tea with H.H. [Princess Louise Augusta] before leaving town, and her introductions will open, I fancy, most doors.'[58]

If this connection benefitted Farrer, another family connection caused him embarrassment. His mother had written to an Anson cousin in Ceylon (Reginald's father bore the middle name 'Anson' after his grandfather's evidently advantageous marriage to an Anson in the mid-19th century) asking if he would take Reginald as a paying guest.[59] Farrer writes back to his mother alleging that 'such a proposal is an insult in the East' and that Anson has warned him off.[60] No doubt Farrer would have devised any excuse to avoid being within the oversight of the family. Arthur Anson, the cousin, was a planter: after reporting Anson's negative response, Farrer writes,

> Praise be, say I: for I found out at once what H.H. told me, ^and I guessed,^ that, for my purposes it is absolutely essential to keep clear of the whole planter element. The planters form a close intolerant caste, hardened into a cast-iron crust of Englishry, hating the country, bored with its history, only bent on making every Club & settlement, as far as possible, an exact replica of Ealing or Wimbledon. Add to which that they (as a class) booze and keep black women to an extent that would not interest me![61]

That Farrer was warned by Queen Victoria's grand-daughter against the intransigent cultural and racial intolerance of the economic exploiters of the island provides an interesting footnote on the political history of royalty and the varied

FIG. 1.3. Reginald Farrer's photograph of the geishas, Tokyo, (1903).
Lady Little Willow Tree sits second from the right.

approaches of various royal family members to their roles and places in society. Farrer doesn't bother to keep the family connection (Anson) outside the target area of his condemnations.

The question of how sincere was Farrer's commitment to the Way of Buddhism can only reasonably be gauged by consideration of its effects on his writings and gardening activities, which I will undertake in later chapters. Certain immediate evidence makes us dubious about his commitment to some of the vows of abstinence that he had made. Already in the document of 5th February (the earlier 'letter to Herbert') he writes parenthetically after reporting his vow not to lie: '(oh har!)'. This incoherent exclamation seems to indicate that he himself is sceptical about his intention in the vow, or about his ability to refrain from lying! He certainly drank alcohol after the date of his vows. Over three weeks later in the later letter to

Herbert (February 28) from the Residency in Anuradhapura, in the northern plain of the island, he reports that he had found:

> a very nice woman interested in Theosophy: a most delicious dove, whom even you would admit to be exquisite, an absolutely 'obvious' person, and just the subtle sparkler, tinged with intellectual emotionalism, to whom my genius and eccentricities most appeal. Houses on fire are not in it: she has a husband, but has very sensibly left him behind. So Kandy was all right.[62]

Yet two days earlier he had written to Mervyn Herbert at the British Embassy in Rome, that 'solitary travel' is 'an ideal bliss'.[63] Farrer's account of this incident doesn't imply sexual activity, or even that he would abandon his vow against adultery if given the chance. It raises a question, though, about Farrer's sexuality. The evidence, at least for this stage in Farrer's life, is unclear.[64] Basil Morgan, in the *Oxford Dictionary of Biography* entry on Farrer (2002) states that he 'had an affair with a geisha girl' in Japan.[65] The geisha in question went by the professional name of 'Korin (Lady Little Willow Tree)', but whether she was male or female (biologically) has not yet been established (figure 1.3).

So Farrer may have had genuine conflicts about his vows and purposes (for example, wishing to overcome 'desire and disappointment' and yet falling at the first hurdle). This does not necessarily mean that his embrace of Buddhism was insincere or shallow. As we shall see, its embeddedness in his thinking and manifestation in his action puts Nicola Shulman's belittling allegation, that Farrer's 'main reason behind' what she calls his 'conversion' was 'to annoy his family', into proper diminishing perspective.[66]

Farrer re-embarked on RMS *Ophir* and departed on the return journey on 26 March.[67] He returned to a cold reception at home at Ingleborough Hall, and amongst the extended family, because of his embrace of Buddhism. Osbert Sitwell's memorable phrase for the family's response is: 'a subdued polar shivering of disapproval', and Sitwell suspects that he, as a boy, was deliberately kept away from Farrer because of the religious question. As his relative Annie Farrer, herself an artist and distinguished botanical painter, put it, his 'unconventional and fresh approach to life was completely at odds with his stuffed-shirt family'.[68] From his tour of two months' duration in Ceylon came another outcome: Farrer's book, *In Old Ceylon*.

Notes to Chapter 1

1. Nicola Shulman, *A Rage for Rock Gardening: The Story of Reginald Farrer gardener, writer & plant collector* (2002; Boston: Godine, 2004), p. 8.
2. Farrer's father, James Anson Farrer, mentions surgical operations on Reginald in 1885, 1888, and 1896. See his 'Annual Narrative', which, however, only began in 1884: North Yorkshire County Record Office, Northallerton (NYCRO) Microfilm (MIC) 1756. 'Durham' and 'Bruce Clarke' are mentioned as two of the surgeons.
3. Rev. Paul Eyre, Newnham Rectory, Hook, Hampshire: see James Anson Farrer's 'Annual Narrative' for 1896. The entire Annual Narrative (which ends in 1923) is in NYCRO on Microfilm 1756.
4. *Journal of Botany (London),* 32, (1894), 344. See William T. Stearn, 'An Introductory Tribute to

Reginald Farrer', in *Reginald Farrer: Dalesman, Planthunter, Gardener*, ed. by John Illingworth and Jane Routh (Lancaster: Centre for North-West Regional Studies, University of Lancaster, Occasional Paper no. 19, 1991), pp. 1–7 (p. 1).

5. Stearn, 'An Introductory Tribute to Reginald Farrer', p. 1.

6. Letters of 1900, 29/3/1900, and 1901, in the Reginald John Farrer archive at the Royal Botanic Garden Edinburgh (hereafter RBGE): RJF 2/1/1.

7. J. A. Farrer, 'Annual Narrative' for 1902.

8. RBGE, RJF 2/2/1/1 Album 1: 1900–1908. The source is a photograph album, inscribed on the spine 'Round the World 1903'.

9. Reginald Farrer, *The Garden of Asia: Impressions from Japan* (London: Methuen, 1904) p. 62.

10. Ibid., p. 66.

11. Letter to Aubrey Herbert quoted without date in Shulman, *A Rage for Rock Gardening*, p. 19.

12. Ibid.

13. *Some Farrer Family Memorials: Being a Selection from the Papers of Thomas Henry, First Lord Farrer 1819–1899, on Various Matters Connected with his Life; together with Notes relating to some Branches of the Family of Greystoneley, Ingleborough, Abinger, between 1610 & 1923, made by his Son, Thomas Cecil, Second Lord Farrer* (London: Privately Printed, 1923), pp. 9–12, 15, 22, 29–30, 50–51.

14. Osbert Sitwell, *Noble Essences* (London: Macmillan, 1950), p. 15. The sister of Reginald Farrer's maternal grandmother (née Hely Hutchinson) had married Sir George Reresby Sitwell's father (Osbert, Edith and Sacheverell Sitwell's grandfather).

15. Shulman, *A Rage for Rock Gardening*, p. 20.

16. West Yorkshire Archive Service, Leeds, WYL 524/329.

17. *Country Life* contains correspondence about this. In March 1900, in reply to an enquiring letter, the editor denied that a modest gentleman's establishment could be kept on £500 p.a. (vol. VII, no. 166, 10 March 1900, p. 319). Two letters from readers printed on 24 March 1900 (168, p. 383) disagree with this conclusion and offer budgets in support.

18. Shulman, *A Rage for Rock Gardening*, pp. 14–15; Illingworth and Routh, *Reginald Farrer: Dalesman, Planthunter, Gardener*, p. 54.

19. John L. Illingworth, 'The Correspondence of Reginald Farrer', in *Reginald Farrer: Dalesman, Planthunter, Gardener*, pp. 72–80 (p. 75).

20. Letter quoted (without date) in Shulman, p. 21.

21. Undated letter to Aubrey Herbert, after 1903, Somerset County Archives, Taunton, DD\HER/38.

22. Letter to Aubrey Herbert, Nov. 4 [1907], Somerset Archives, DD\HER/38. The year is confirmed by James Anson Farrer's 'Annual Narrative' for 1907, mentioning the play. (North Yorkshire County Record Office, Northallerton: MIC 1756). The play, written by Reginald, was entitled *Hearts and Diamonds*.

23. *Some Farrer Family Memorials*, pp. 32–35, 185–87. An unmarried ancestor had also made £60,000 in four years as a lawyer in India, 1774–78, returning as a nabob and becoming M.P. for Wareham: pp. 183–84.

24. Sara Mason, 'The Ingleborough Estate: Home of Reginald Farrer', in Illingworth and Routh, *Reginald Farrer: Dalesman, Planthunter, Gardener*, pp. 81–88. John Bateman's *The Great Landowners of Great Britain* (London: Harrison and Sons, 4th edition, 1883) lists the Rev. Matthew Farrer's Ingleborough estate as 11,512 acres, with a gross annual valuation of £9,403. This seems healthy enough, but the clergyman had four children and two sisters, and the monetary figure is a valuation, not a profit. Real landed magnates, such as Sir Tatton Sykes, in the East Riding, the Earl Fitzwilliam in the West Riding, or Farrer's friend Aubrey Herbert's family, owned upwards of 30,000 acres of good farm land or even more valuable industrial areas.

25. Sitwell, *Noble Essences*, p. 14.

26. RBGE, RJF 2/1/2, letter addressed from Hotel de la Poste, Mt. Cenis July 27. Tentatively dated by Mrs. Joan Farrer, wife of Dr. John Farrer who owned the Ingleborough Hall estate 1952–2014, as 1910.

27. Sitwell, *Noble Essences*, p. 18.

28. Shulman, *A Rage for Rock Gardening*, p. 90.

29. Jane Austen, *Lady Susan, The Watsons, Sanditon* (Harmondsworth: Penguin, 1974), 'Introduction' by Margaret Drabble, pp. 7–31 (p. 16). *The Watsons* was published as part of an edition of Jane Austen's complete works in 1878 and it seems reasonable to assume that this is the edition Farrer read.

30. Austen, *Lady Susan, The Watsons, Sanditon*, p. 151.

31. Austen, *Lady Susan, The Watsons, Sanditon*, pp. 140–43.

32. Austen, *Lady Susan, The Watsons, Sanditon*, p. 151.

33. Draft or copy (in Farrer's hand) of a letter of 5/2/1908 from the Galle Face Hotel, Colombo, in RBGE, RJF 2/1/2.

34. The whole account of this ceremony is from Farrer's letter of 5/2/1908.

35. Letter of 5/2/1908.

36. Anne Blackburn, *Locations of Buddhism: Colonialism and Modernity in Sri Lanka* (Chicago: The University of Chicago Press, 2010), pp. 171–74, 176–80, 182–83.

37. Tamara Loos, *Bones Around My Neck: The Life and Exile of a Prince Provocateur* (Ithaca, NY: Cornell University Press, 2016), especially pp. 103–13.

38. Here and in the rest of the account of the day, my source is Farrer's letter of 5/2/1908.

39. Letter of February 28, 1908, dated from The Residency, Anuradhapura, RBGE, RJF 2/1/2/7.

40. Donald S. Lopez Jr., *Buddhism & Science: a guide for the perplexed* (Chicago: University of Chicago Press, 2008), p. 146.

41. T. W. Rhys Davids, *Lectures on the Origin and Growth of Religion as Illustrated by Some Points in the History of Indian Buddhism* (London: Williams and Norgate, 1881), p. 94, quoted by Lopez, *Buddhism & Science*, p. 146.

42. T. H. Huxley, *Evolution and Ethics and Other Essays* (London: Macmillan, 1894), p. 61, quoted by Lopez, *Buddhism & Science*, p. 146.

43. W. S. Lilly, 'The Message of Buddhism to the Western World,' *The Fortnightly Review* n.s., 78 (July-December 1905), 213. Quoted by Lopez, *Buddhism & Science*, p. 244. Lopez also cites an article in *The Literary Digest* of 1890 (p. 244).

44. I am using the terms 'statement' and 'discourse' deliberately, following their definitions by Michel Foucault in *L'Archéologie du Savoir* (Paris: Gallimard, 1969).

45. *The Times of Ceylon*, 6th February 1908, p. 5.

46. E. Harris, *Theravada Buddhism and the British Encounter: Religious, Missionary and Colonial Experience in Nineteenth-Century Sri Lanka* (London: Routledge, 2006) ebook, no pagination, accessed 26 September 2015.

47. Letter quoted by Illingworth, *Reginald Farrer: Dalesman, Planthunter, Gardener*, p. 73.

48. RBGE, RJF 2/1/2, letter of 16 April 1903 from Japan.

49. For a revelation of the clear, sympathetic, and intelligent interest in Buddhism worked by Kipling into the plot and characterisations of *Kim*, see Janice Leoshko, 'What is in *Kim*? Rudyard Kipling and Tibetan Buddhist Traditions', *South Asia Research*, 21, 1 (2001), 51–75.

50. For a detailed explanation of this important image, see Tenzin Gyatso, the Fourteenth Dalai Lama, *The Meaning of Life from a Buddhist Perspective* trans. and ed. by Jeffrey Hopkins, 1992 (Boston, Mass.: Wisdom , 2000).

51. Quoted in Lopez, *Buddhism & Science*, pp. 13–14.

52. RBGE, RJF 2/1/2/5.

53. Reginald Farrer, *In Old Ceylon* (London: Arnold, 1908), p. 9. Although in Farrer's day this hymn (265 in *Hymns Ancient and Modern*) was thought of as expressing disgust with the Ceylonese people, Henry Noltie draws my attention to the fact that the hymn was written before Heber went to Ceylon; and that Java was substituted for Ceylon in the hymn.

54. RBGE, RJF 2/1/2, letter of 6 February 1908.

55. Rather than keeping them nameless, I should reveal that both Farrer's mother, 'Bessie', and her sister Grace were daughters of Lieutenant-Colonel Arthur John Reynell Pack, of Netherton House, Newton Abbott, whose wife's maiden name was Catherine Hely Hutchinson.

56. Farrer, letter to Aubrey Herbert, addressed from 'Lunefield', Kirby Lonsdale and dated 'Sept. 7' [1902], Somerset County Archives, DD\HER/38. The Princess is sometimes known as Marie Louise and sometimes Louise Augusta. The year 1902 for the letter is confirmed by the fact

that in the letter Farrer eagerly anticipates the trip to Japan, which happened in the autumn of 1902.

57. On 5th January 1906 she had helped to open the Kandy Jewellery and Embroidery Exhibition. Sri Lanka National Archives, Kandy Branch, 18/34: Government Agent's Diary, Jan-June 1906, p. 1.

58. RBGE, RJF 2/1/2.

59. The 'Anson' I mention was Mary Louise Anson, daughter of the 1st Baronet, General Sir William Anson (1772–1847), therefore coming from the junior Baronet branch of the Anson family.

60. RBGE, RJF 2/1/2, letter of 4 February 1908.

61. The phrase 'and I guessed' is interpolated as an afterthought over the words of the first draft at this point in the letter.

62. Draft or copy of a letter to Aubrey Herbert, 28/2/1908, RBGE RJF 2/1/2/7. Another source reveals the lady's name as 'Mrs Bonham': RBGE RJF 2/1/2/4, letter of 8/2/1908.

63. Draft or copy of a letter to Mervyn Herbert, 26/2/1908, RBGE RJF 2/1/2.

64. The question will be clarified later, with respect to evidence from Farrer's expedition to Burma, and his novels.

65. *Oxford Dictionary of National Biography*, online version, updated since 2002 and 2010, accessed 11/3/2015.

66. Shulman, *A Rage for Rock Gardening*, pp. 27–28.

67. *Times of Ceylon*, 27/3/08, p. 9.

68. Sitwell, *Noble Essences*, p. 15. Annie Farrer, talk during the Yorkshire Gardens' Trust's Study Day on Reginald Farrer, Ingleborough Hall, 19 August 2009.

CHAPTER 2

Farrer *In Old Ceylon*, 1908

In Old Ceylon is not a normal travel book, though the travel account is its pretext. Nor is it an account of Farrer becoming a Buddhist, an event to which he only refers tangentially at the beginning of Chapter V. Over a hundred pages later he writes of Buddhists using the pronoun 'us' (p. 185). So his acceptance into the community is alluded to modestly and undemonstratively. The book is not a history of Ceylon, though it makes extensive use of historical material. The article about Farrer in *The Times of Ceylon* had written of the planned book that its author 'will confine his attention to what is artistic and picturesque, the chief object being the ruins of Anuradhapura and such other places. The book will be profusely illustrated.' The finished work is far more than a picturesque tour of Ceylon, and it is hardly profusely illustrated. There are sixteen photographs, two of which can be classed as excellent, the rest as disappointments. On one page, just before a 42-page section without any photographs, Farrer apologizes in a footnote: 'Alas, that all my photographs of Polonnarua proved failures!'[1] There is a question, therefore, about what sort of a book *In Old Ceylon* is.

In addressing this question, I wish to begin by specifying the dominant rhetorical tropes of the book; since I believe that what we call tropes are not simply limited to written or spoken verbal productions, but more properly describe the way we think and, to some extent, feel.[2] That is, tropes designate modes of thought, and if we can identify them we accomplish important analysis of the character of thought that informs and creates a work. Secondly I will sketch the structure of the book and its theme, before turning attention to the constituents of the narrator's sensibility. Finally, out of the very methods I shall use to investigate it arises the question of whether the book has any politics.

Tropics

As his ship approaches Ceylon, the narrator fills with anticipation: 'Everything heralds the approach of fairyland — of that beautiful dream-Paradise which is the very kingdom of heaven on earth — the land for ever consecrated to holy feet that never lighted there.' The bubble bursts rapidly: 'And so at last one rises, in the blazing morning, to the reality of sweltering Colombo. Colombo, city of small account, has no place in the existence of Lanka. Colombo is a modern ugly mushroom' (p. 1). The motif is Baudelairean and Nervalian, made most memorable in Charles Baudelaire's poem 'Voyage': over-eager anticipation is dashed by crude reality; Eldorado spied from afar resolves into a bare reef when viewed close in the morning light.[3] This use of the theme on the first page of *In Old Ceylon* effectively announces Farrer's book as literary, arguably Romantic, no matter how much its pretext or alibi is that of a plain account of travels. And the outset of the book has introduced paradox.

The paradox of the first paragraph, 'the land for ever consecrated to holy feet that never lighted there' is confirmed on the last page of Chapter I, when the narrator wakes the following morning in the Galle Face Hotel, looks out of the window and sees the mountain named Adam's Peak: 'It is the Peak, holy place of the world's three religions. It is the sacred mountain where Our Lord Buddha left his foot-print. And now, suddenly, we understand that the present is all a delusion. We are in old Lanka; in dead Lanka.' (p. 15). On the first page we are told that holy feet did not alight; on the last page that the Buddha left his footprint.

Oscar Wilde had used paradox as a form of complication of thought, in *The Critic as Artist* (1891), for example. It is a way of stirring the reader up, of inducing him or her not to rely too slavishly on a unisemic authorial *énoncé* (an immaculate narrative), of introducing the implied questions brought to the fore by focussing on the *énonciation* (the modes of telling) that paradox exemplifies.[4] It is also, of course, a guard against acceptance of a normal or received opinion, which is introduced only to be contradicted. This employment works for Farrer too, but in addition, perhaps even more fundamentally, he sees paradox as inherent in Lanka/Ceylon.

The narrator uses both of these names for the island. Lanka he uses as the name for the ancient island, mainly to be studied now from its archaeological remains (which is why, for Farrer, it is 'dead'). Ceylon, however, is an invention of colonialism (Portuguese, Dutch, and in Farrer's day, British). If Lanka is dead, Ceylon is an undead ghost that has never been alive, has 'never existed' (p. 45); it is the 'empty, soulless phantom of old Lanka.' (p. 48). So what can one call this alluring and disappointing island?

Fundamental to a sense of the island's identity, paradox becomes the dominant trope of *In Old Ceylon*. For instance, ruin has the effect of paradox: a lake becomes a plain or field, while the jungle around becomes a sea (p. 201). In the view from the rock in the centre of Ceylon at Dambulla,

> Far north, in film after film of one indistinguishable plain, stretches the vast *aequor* of the jungle; for, indeed, seen from here, the jungle is seen as a sea — one perfectly level tideless flood of green, stretching away, without eddy or crest, without a break, into the utmost distances until it only disappears with the curve of earth itself. Here and there from its unperturbed surface rise azure islands of hill [...] The effect is of a magic scene, where an archipelago of sapphire stands up from the unrippled levels of a sea that some magician has transformed into verdure [...] Impressive always, and even terrifying, is this flat unity of the jungle when you see it from any high point. But this view from Dambûlla Rock has the added force of surprise. It is unbelievable at first — too fantastic, too overpowering, too like a transformation scene, to be realized at the first glance. (pp. 117–18)

The last phrase is perhaps revealing. Farrer was in Ceylon for just two months: a first and only visit out of which the book was fashioned. Comprehending things at first glance was therefore of importance. Arguably this is one reason why panoramic views feature prominently in the book, since metaphorically they offer a way to take in a lot of information in a short time. For instance, from the top of Sigiriya rock, 'one commands all Lanka's history', Farrer writes (p.158). But a struggle is reported in the passage about Dambulla's view, revealing that Farrer is less interested in digging out historical or contemporary facts than in being true to the phenomenon (or phenomena) of viewing. Viewing, that is, in its literal sense of seeing, of enjoying a view, as well as in a metaphorical one of accumulating a set of opinions and forming an understanding. In this case the plain view of understanding is baffled by a vision 'like' a transformation scene. Transformation is very genuinely what Farrer sees here: the narrator is looking at the ruined Northern Kingdom, which fell during the time of the European Middle Ages, after which farmland and a huge and orderly irrigation system went to ruin, gradually but completely giving way to elephant-, snake- and leopard-haunted jungle.

On a more mundane level, for Farrer paradox is also characteristic of contemporary Ceylonese crafts, which demonstrate 'barbarity of design' and 'prehistoric immaturity of workmanship' (p. 323). At the Maha Bodhi Tree, 'Devotion here, as ever, is combining with tastelessness to disfigure the holy place' (p. 252). In making these statements Farrer was both agreeing and disagreeing, whether consciously or not, with contemporaneous judgements of Ananda Kentish Coomaraswamy, who had scolded Ceylonese of wealth and influence over the present neglected state of traditional Ceylonese arts and crafts in a variety of essays, such as his 'Open Letter to the Kandyan Chiefs',[5] and who was in England while Farrer was in Ceylon, completing his magisterial *Medieval Sinhalese Art* as a sort of last stand for traditional Ceylonese crafts. In Farrer's book, present Ceylon has 'no art', but the ancient chronicle of Lanka, the largely 6th century *Mahavamsa*, is a 'pre-eminent treasure' because 'readable', and because 'the personality of the compiler often emerges clear as we read — a man of sympathy [.. and] weighty sense of purpose and character' (p. 125). On the way to this judgement, Farrer likens the compiler to both Herodotus and Thucydides, the ancient Greek historians. The *Mahavamsa* exhibits a 'paradoxical merit' in comparison with the 'History of the Kings of Israel' (p. 126).

If paradox is the trope of Ceylon, as it were, the other dominant trope in the book belongs to Farrer himself, in the sense that it is characteristic of all his travel writing. This is *hyperbaton*, or *anastrophe*, disruption of normal word order, which he uses as a prime tool for descriptive passages. Given the prevalence of the trope, and its strong connection with description, it is worth dwelling, by way of introduction, on the topic of description in *In Old Ceylon* for a moment.

The first chapter of *In Old Ceylon* contains relatively lengthy passages about buying gems. The pretext is that of informing us about what to do in Colombo; but Farrer wants to get a good dose of materialism in early, because the book will later emphasize the spiritual. Questions of buying jewels lead the narrator to think about Bishop Heber, the first Anglican Bishop of Calcutta, the limitations of the churchman and of his hymn (p. 9). Heber therefore becomes a mere ramification of Farrer's main theme. There are pages of extraordinary descriptions of gems and their colours, of the hues that make up their colours, and how they change in differences of light. These passages show off Farrer's unusual abilities in description, and they also display his knowledge. The element of showing-off comes through too clearly at moments, such as when he writes that certain stones are 'cheaper than a syco-phant's praise, and quite as dull.' The simile is forced, over-lordly, a false note.

Despite such minor over-reachings, Farrer's descriptive powers are still valued: he is quoted in sources as different as a mass-produced guidebook for tourists,[6] and a scholarly labour of love about a wooded hill in Kandy.[7] In a book in which descriptions of places feature so frequently, almost every rhetorical division of description is used: from chorography and topography to *pragmatographia* (description of an action or event). His description of the ruined cities of Lanka as they were in their hey-days amounts to *topothesia* (description of an imaginary place), since the cities are in effect now non-existent. And a further prominent feature of Farrer's descriptions is constituted by his use of anastrophe, or unusual word order. This can be read to vivid effect in his description of the railway journey from Colombo to Kandy:

> Famous among the beauties of the world is this climb to Kandy; and justly so. Mountains jagged or bossy, jungle, cultivated land or tangled river-bank — all in the afternoon are clad in that almost opaque turquoise blue which never fails to glorify Cinhalese landscape at about three o-clock of a fine day. Away and away they unfold, those hills, sometimes easy and heavy in their lines, sometimes stringent and craggy — isolated pinnacles with some small shrine or fortalice at their summit. Far down the steep bank, up which the train goes winding, the terraced rice-fields descend like gigantic waved stairways, or like successive ripples left on the hill-side by some retiring sea. (p. 52)

Brought to the front in many of Farrer's sentences are words that he wishes to emphasize, or the reader to remember. It would have been more orthodox, for example, to write the first sentence quoted above as: 'the climb to Kandy is famous among the beauties of the world'; more orthodox and much more dull to read. Anastrophe serves emphasis, and the emphasis is most often on sense-perception or on emotion. At times the phrases enact perceptual processes, as when Farrer writes 'Far down the steep bank, up which the train goes winding'. This solution conveys vividly the contrast given by the railway between the climbing train and the land which often falls precipitously from the very edge of the track. By its dual function of privileging emphasis and sense-perception or affective response, anastrophe proves extremely suitable and useful for the communication of impressions; those basic but variable units of perception, the truth of human life, attention to and communication of which, following David Hume's work and especially in the nineteenth century, achieves considerable importance. Farrer's particularly vivid descriptive abilities are also, of course, related to his artistic sensibility and his love of plants.

Structure

Paradox is therefore inherent in the island and its culture, in Farrer's view. Embracing it gives him a way of disentangling certain themes by means of which he orders his narrative. One point of assuring readers that 'holy feet ... never lighted there' and afterwards telling us that they did, is to place the rational and the religious in relationship. We have already seen in the letters to Herbert that Farrer thought Buddhism to be a rational system of spiritual belief. A series of three oppositions orders the structure of ideas in the book:

modern ↔ ancient
material ↔ spiritual
rationality ↔ religious emotionalism

Farrer's thoughts about religion constitute the most serious theme of the book. Thoughts about holy relics are central to the questions of both religion and materialism. Farrer takes the view that 'material belief in a definite visible fact' is only for the uninstructed multitude in a religion. Discussing the alleged destruction of the tooth of the Buddha (arguably the most important holy relic in Sri Lanka) by the Portuguese, and its alleged survival as the relic presently housed in the Temple of the Tooth in Kandy, Farrer writes that: 'it is everlastingly the spirit of worship that counts, not the visible object of that worship.' He cites the Japanese term '*nazoraëru*' — substitution — as expressing the truth of religious experience (p. 80), and proposes the eucharistic Mass in Christianity as a prime example: 'eating bread in contemplation of the Divine, we are indeed assimilating the Divine itself' (p. 81). According to Farrer's idea of *nazoraëru* 'the worshippers' intention' is alone important; thus the actual material relics, their authenticity and even shape, matter very little in comparison with the devotion they can cause. The danger of the worship of relics is that with it 'comes materialism' (p. 232); but a beneficial side-effect of that has been that the need to house all the relics stimulated a flowering of Lankan art and architecture before medieval destruction and the colonial-era degradation of those pursuits (p. 233).

On his way from Colombo to the sacred archaeological sites, Farrer spent a few days in Kandy to see the greatest of relics, the Tooth relic. In his account of this the material and rational are balanced against the spiritual and religious. It also contains one of the few passages of comic writing in the book (which are far fewer than in *The Garden of Asia*: evidently becoming a Buddhist was a serious thing). Sri Sumangala had written a letter for Farrer to take to the chief monk of a local monastic community, asking for a view of the relic; but in the event Farrer waited a day in order to see the relic when the Crown Prince of Japan was also viewing it.[8] Two people had to unlock the shrine: a Government representative, and one of the local men of authority, the secular Kandyan chiefs. There was a lot of waiting: the first group of people to assemble included Farrer, and they all had to wait, in the small and stifling spaces of the Tooth Relic Shrine, for the Crown Prince and his followers. Then the whole group waited for the Kandyan chief to appear. 'There are whisperings,' writes Farrer, 'trottings to and fro along the corridor of the cloister, tappings at doors, inquiries, apologies. His Imperial Highness murmurs to his attendants, laughs, and grows impatient.'

> At last the chieftain emerges. No wonder that his preparations took time, for he is the most gorgeous spectacle. A magnificent old man, stalwart, tall, erect, portly, with a face at once beautiful and royal; serene, aquiline, with streaming beard of gray — the very face of Oedipus the King. And he is clothed in pantalettes of white muslin, ruched round his ankles like a ham-frill. About his middle is wound some six miles of similar muslin, starred and spangled with gold, until his figure has the shape of a bobbin or a peg-top. His shirt is snowy fine, and over it he wears an Eton jacket, very short, with puffed gigot sleeves. Its material is of some marvellous brocade, stiff and opulent, in which the ground colour, of hot rich salmon, glimmers and glows through a film of pure gold, shifting, changing, darkening, disappearing in altered planes and folds of the fabric as he moves. His cap or crown is a big flattened biretta, hard, four-sided, of crimson satin, hidden from sight with jewels and embroideries of gold. In state this commanding figure comes advancing down the cloister. (p.71)

Admiration for the man, as a figure, is uncomplicated. It gives way to an amazed incredulous irony about how he is dressed. Pantalettes and puffed sleeves were exclusively old-fashioned female items in contemporary Britain. Amazement at the chief's extraordinary garments also gives ground, in the end, to another underlying feeling. By the time we are reading about the colours of the jacket, and how the colours work, the upper layer allowing through the gleam of the lower layer's hue, we can't help becoming aware that Farrer, a bit of a dandy who knew all about jewels, would have liked to dress up like that himself. I have seen about ten photographs of Farrer. Three of them show him dressed up in far eastern garments acquired on his travels. This is a fairly high proportion.

Leonard Woolf was Office Assistant to the Government Agent of the Central Province during Farrer's visit, and thus the representative of Government whose task was to unlock the shrine. Farrer refers to him rather grandly but namelessly as 'the Government Agent's Viceroy' who met the party and conducted it round a corridor of the temple (p. 70). In his own memoir, Woolf names his partner in the unlocking, the imposing 'chieftain': 'the Manager or Guardian of the Temple, the Diyawadana Nilame, in 1908 a fine old Kandyan chief and Ratemahatmaya, called Nugawela'.[9] Writing fifty years after the events, Woolf forgets the Japanese Crown Prince, stating that he only unlocked the shrine three times: for the big annual festival where the Tooth is paraded about town; for the Empress Eugénie; and: 'once at the Nilame's request for Reginald Farrer, the Himalayan botanist, who had become a Buddhist.'[10] Perhaps the two Britons found some things to talk about: Woolf's scepticism about the authenticity of the Tooth is shared by Farrer (for whom, of course, inauthenticity is not important). The two men differed, however, about the value of Buddhism; at least to the extent that Woolf did not become a Buddhist during his years in the island.

The structure of ideas needed an armature around which it could be displayed. This support is given by the simple narrative structure of the book, which centres on a journey from Colombo to Mihintale (the 'Holy Hill'), where the book ends.

Beginning in Colombo, the colonial capital, Farrer journeys by train east to the flourishing town of Kandy, the last capital of an indigenous kingdom that lasted until the early nineteenth century. From there he goes north in a horse-drawn cart to Sigiriya, capital of a strange ill-fated and short-lived fifth-century kingdom, and on to the ruined city of Polonnarua, which was the capital of the north kingdom before the retreat to Kandy from Indian invaders, and was in Farrer's time still being disentangled from the jungle by the colonial authorities. From there he reaches Anuradhapura, the most ancient capital city and former Buddhist metropolis, now entirely in ruins, and finally he climbs Mihintale. There is no completion of the experience in the form of a return to Colombo. The trip is thus a journey backwards in time through ages of history to the beginning of Buddhism in Lanka, which is deemed to have begun with the conversion of a king on Mihintale. Farrer doesn't rely on a tour company such as Thomas Cook: he has already decided where to go. The newly-become Buddhist makes a pilgrimage around the holy sites of the island. The narrative structure gives Farrer the opportunity to describe a series of ecstatic panoramic views interleaved with description of details. We have already seen part of one of these, the view from Dambulla, and I shall leave a longer look at another until later in this section.

Theme

The theme, ramified as it is by the structure of ideas, is Buddhism; or rather, especially an account of moments in the life of the Buddha Gautama and the example he sets for followers of his way. This is a Western Buddhism, in the sense that it is a search for origins. In another sense, too: because Farrer does not stay in Buddhist communities with the monks, and seems to spend little time talking to indigenous figures. He stays instead in Government rest-houses and other types of official lodging.

One of the main ways in which the theme of Buddhism is developed in the book is by concentration on how it is represented in art. Architecture plays its part; but Farrer is particularly affected by ancient statues. He enthuses for pages over a plaster cast of a (famous) Gandharan statue of the emaciated Buddha that he finds in Jinavaravamsa's museum at the temple in Kotahena. He loves the standing statue at the Gal Vihara in Polonnarua, and the reclining Buddha in the first cave at Dambulla. He finds, though, that modern Ceylon has 'no art' and 'there is no taste for beauty in modern Ceylon'.

Then something rare happens. In the rock hill at Dambulla is a Buddhist temple-shrine: a sequence of caves painted and housing statues. In the Maharaja Vihara cave at Dambulla, contemplating late statues and eighteenth-century repaintings of earlier late-medieval decorations, Farrer has this to say:

> Crude, gaudy, and unconvincing are all these paintings — eighteenth-century
> refurbishings of the worn frescoes they copied. Simple, too, primitive, awkward,
> are the huge seated Buddhas and Bodhisattas. And yet their awkwardness, even
> the ugliness of many, make one realize anew, as one is ever realizing, not
> only in Ceylon, but in Italy, that awkwardness of treatment not only does not

damage the religious spirit, but even enhances it. It seems as if maturity of art
has the sad gift of ousting its indwelling spirit, as if only through the eager
efforts of primitive enthusiasts, groping awkwardly to express their ebullient
meaning, can the pure intensity of their fervour ever transpire. With certainty
of touch comes the delight in certainty of touch for its own sake. And this is
the final divorce between art and religion — the death of religious art. Even
as there is more Divine spirit in Giotto, Mantegna, and the best Byzantine
work than in the bland and self-conscious perfections of Raphael — interested
in the treatment, but quite uninterested and unconvinced by its subject — so
the gaudy crudities of Dambûlla have a rougher, more insistent conviction,
perhaps, than you might find in a more congruous, advanced, and dignified
art — not to mention that in the lurid twilight of the Maharaja Vihara the dim
dusk softens all crudities, until your gaze can only discern long seated lines of
calm gigantic figures, a great vague glow and glory of colour, on roof and wall
and alley, from end to end, from depth to depth of the cavern's tremendous
gloom. (pp. 122–23) (figures 2.1, 2.2)

The painting and the statues in the Maharaja Vihara stir up the Modernist in Farrer.
The sensitivity manifested here in his response to the art is, for the time, and the
place, extraordinary. The passage shows overt influence from the Pre-Raphaelite
movement in nineteenth-century Britain, with its reverence for the Italian
Primitives. A sacred spatial setting that displays: 'efforts of primitive enthusiasts,
groping awkwardly to express their ebullient meaning', conforms to John Ruskin's
and William Morris's passionately-held convictions about the worth of medieval
art, and feeling for ancient churches. And the concepts Farrer employs — praising
crudity, 'awkwardness of treatment', 'even [...] ugliness', 'primitive enthusiasts',
'ebullient meaning', 'pure intensity', and 'a rougher, more insistent conviction', all
exemplify the type of phrase employed in European advanced critical writing about
painting (especially contemporary painting) by the end of 1907.[11] In writing that
awkwardness makes better religious art, he is saying that it makes better art (the
subject is religious). Particularly in relation to the work of Cézanne, awkwardness
had been critically celebrated as a manifestation of the artist's sincerity.[12]

So Farrer responds to the painting at Dambulla as suitable to its subject-matter:
a unity between form and content. A unity not based, however, on the idea of
'correctness' — whether naturalistic correctness, or correctness of adherence to
classical forms, or other. Instead, unified form and content is based on 'ebullience',
'intensity', 'insistent conviction', or, in a word, feeling. Farrer the modernist, visiting
Ceylon, can recognize in eighteenth-century Kandyan painting the properties so
prized by advanced contemporary art critics in Britain and Europe. So here, at least,
one of Ceylon's paradoxes is reconciled.

Another example of Farrer's critical judgement comes when he visits what is now
called the Royal Pleasure Gardens, near Issurumuniya in Anuradhapura, and finds
there 'the finest piece of naturalistic sculpture in Ceylon' (figure 2.3):

Through a field of great lotuses wild elephants go trumpeting and plunging;
their drawing, their execution, their spirit, is no less vivid and faultless than
those of the elks and mammoths, drawn long since on bone by the first realists
in art, the nameless savages of the Tarn and Garonne. Delicate, fiery, skilful,

FIG. 2.1. Part of the interior of the cave known as the Mahavihara at Dambulla, Sri Lanka. Photo: author.

FIG. 2.2. Detail of the interior of the Mahavihara, Dambulla. Photo: author.

FIG. 2.3. Relief carving of elephants bathing, Issurumuniya, Sri Lanka.
Photo: Janice Leoshko, 2015.

this sculpture has every merit. Alas that it stands here, tragic and forgotten, open to the rains of ages, veiled with dead leaves that lodge in the deep lines of the work, corroded by the damps and lichen of the dell! (pp. 328–29)

The carving embellishes the 'forsaken bathing-place' of a queen, rather like the one Farrer had already encountered in China and evoked in a Wildean sentence: 'The holy lotus runs rank, and reeds grow thick in the bathing-place of queens.'[13]

While the theme of Buddhism and the Buddha's example is developed through Farrer's appreciations of art, it is also ramified, elaborated, through the book's structure. The theme of Buddhism in the book begins with the Buddha's footprint on Adam's Peak (p. 15), and an explanation of the Buddha's supposed visits to the island (pp. 16–19). There is a section on flower-sacrifice and why this is acceptable, closely followed by an assertion of Buddhism as knowledge and certainty (pp. 22–23). We are told what Buddhism is (compassion) and what it is not (cosmology) (pp. 23–31). The Gandharan statue of the Buddha and a narration of its subject occupies pages 34–38, and Farrer summarizes the Buddhist account of the remote future (pp. 38–42). He touches on the nature of Buddhahood (pp. 83,119) and gives accounts of the Buddha's passing into Nirvana (p. 197–200), and the coming of Buddhism to Lanka under the auspices of Ashoka's son and daughter (p. 227–50). Farrer defends

Buddhism against the western condemnation of it as a 'doctrine of misery' (pp. 240–41). He describes the Buddha's attaining of enlightenment at Bodhgaya (pp. 254–58) and sketches in the nature of the Buddhist 'church' (p. 262–64).

It is noticeable that the theme of Buddhism in the book does not focus on Farrer himself becoming a Buddhist. Chapter Two, entitled 'Initiation' does not describe Farrer's own initiation into Buddhism, as we might expect, not least from the assumed chronological progression of the narrative, but instead initiates the reader into Buddhism by means of the topics specified above as occurring on pp. 16–42. And yet, as everything quoted so far shows (not least the passage about the Nilame of Kandy), the whole narrative is, inevitably, refracted through a sensibility. Farrer declines overt discussion of his adoption of Buddhism while presenting strong opinions through his (far from neutral) descriptions.

Constituents of the narrator's sensibility

His view of Ceylon is constituted by three major factors.

There is geography: especially involving the placing of Buddhist establishments in the landscape. To anyone who has visited a number of Buddhist stupas and *viharas* (monastic establishments) in Sri Lanka, it becomes obvious that the art of siting such establishments, from the beginning at least until the eighteenth century, has been an art of landscape. In the choice of sites, rocks, cliffs, steep and difficult ascents, wooded and leafy surroundings, high bare places for the temple buildings themselves, but with some elements of gardens, such as plantings of the trees that give flowers for the altars, or small pools in which to grow lilies, views out, and streams of running water, were all desiderata. Little scholarship has been undertaken on this topic, but Gregory Schopen has clarified the dynamics of siting, as evidence for it survives in textual references to ancient Indian Buddhist sites, and in doing so he also relies on the work of Daud Ali about Sigiriya in Sri Lanka.[14]

Schopen elucidates that 'vihara', a word commonly used for designating a Buddhist monastery, means garden, or place of pleasure. Sifting carefully through the textual evidence he demonstrates the conception of a garden to be active in the arrangements, as well as the siting, of viharas. The ruined sites Farrer visited of course lacked the feeling of being gardens; but whether ruined or not, the places elicited from him lively responses to their landscape characteristics. At the still functioning temple of Gadaladeniya (the *stupa* of which was depicted on the cover of Farrer's book, Fig. 2.4) he is very sensitive to the landscape features: the steep slope up, the bare rock summit, the gnarled tree, which shows on a larger scale and in the tropics a kindred hardiness to Farrer's beloved alpines:

> Worn, rounded planes of rock are these, grey, dark, and very ancient of appearance, rough in grain, yet smoothed by the infinite course of years and seasons across the unprotected summit of the hill [...] then the slope ends [...] we stand beneath the shadow of a stout old temple-tree; its snow-white bark is gnarled and blistered with age; its growth grotesque, gnome-like, tempest-tossed [...] Rooted far down in some unguessed cranny of the rock, this aged offering thrives, with its fellows standing round, tossing wild knotted branches

FIG. 2.4. Cover of Farrer's *In Old Ceylon* (1908) showing the embossed depiction of the stupa at Gadaladeniya.

in a sweep to windward. Their stump-like sausage-fingers end all in a crown
of waxen flowers; the air is thick and brilliant with their sweetness, and on the
grey rock far and wide lie carpeted the fallen blooms, drifted, like creamy snow,
on level spaces. (pp. 89–90)

Farrer's enjoyment extends also to the architecture of the place, and the views out
it affords: 'in the interspace, very far away, pale and clear in the uttermost distance,
one soft blue jag of mountain stands up over many miles of hill and jungle' (p. 90).

Gadaladeniya is not an isolated occurrence: we have already noticed Farrer's
response to the views from the rock-cut verandah in front of the famous cave-
shrines at Dambulla. And at a secular site, his sensitivity to geographical and cultural
factors blends with a sense of history in a startling juxtaposition between charming
overnight accommodation and the 600 foot high vast overhanging crag on top of
which King Kasyapa the Parricide built his fifth-century palace at Sigiriya:

> Delightful and fairy-like above everything is this little rest-house of Sigiri [...]
> Clean, sweet, ineffably restful and delicious is this place [...] Perhaps the clear
> charm of Sigiri Rest-house, so rustic, so gentle, is due in part to the contrast
> of its view. There in full sight stands grimly up above the world that terrible
> monument of crime and terror and doom. Poised on its pedestal, the Lion Rock
> frowns out across the jungle, its rounded cliff all scarred and blackened with
> long trails of rain and tears from the dead centuries. From here the Rock —
> vast pebble from the shingle of a planet greater than the solar system — has a
> curious effect. (pp. 148–49)

A second constituent of the narrator's sensibility, equally exemplified in his
response to Sigiriya, is his understanding of history. Here he shows an uncritical
acceptance of the *Mahavamsa* and other chronicles as historically factual that would
be regarded dubiously by a professional historian. Much of the final eighty pages
of the book is occupied by stories from the ancient chronicle, which serve very
successfully to illuminate the acres of ruins that the narrator explores.

The third constituent element is the narrator's subjectivity itself, which is occasionally alluded to openly. There are references, for example, to his childhood
environment and activities, such as grinding chocolate in the kitchen, or playing
on the 'scar limestone' that extends from Ingleborough towards Pen-y-ghent. His
Modernist sensibility emerges very vigorously in the cave at Dambulla, as we have
seen. And his subjectivity is also partly constituted by his cultural knowledge,
emerging in a range of references: for example, repeated mention of the legend
of Sidonia von Bork, whose story, translated from the German by Oscar Wilde's
mother, became favourite reading of the Pre-Raphaelite circle, in which Sidonia was
painted by Edward Burne-Jones. Farrer's references to Sidonia (pp. 7, 143) effectively
suggest the narrator's sensibility to have been partly founded within that *milieu*.

On the question of subjectivity, what does *In Old Ceylon* show Reginald Farrer
to be, over and above what we know he was before he disembarked from the
Ophir? An obvious answer is that it shows he considered himself to be a Buddhist.
The description of Sigiriya shows him to be a poet (the rock is stained by 'rain and
tears from the dead centuries'). And then there is his evocation of the monastic
cells of Vessagiriya. This is a very ancient site near Anuradhapura, where a small

FIG. 2.5. Vessagiriya, where Farrer experienced psychometry. Photo: author, 2015.

community of monks had lived in primitive conditions with little but the huge boulders for shelter. Farrer saw it on the day he had also seen the bathing-place of queens in the Royal Pleasure Garden. Vessagiriya is a site which stirred up his liking for simple, unadorned intimations of primitive Buddhist piety antecedent to the later glories and opulences of the big abbeys. Huge detached boulders lie along a great ridge of exposed gneiss rock (figure 2.5). Under the boulders, in little caves, cells and shelters, lived in ancient times the community of monks. 'Strangely simple and impressive are these little dens,' writes Farrer; 'each cell is simply a cavity, with one smoothed length for a bed' (p. 318):

> Utterly silent now lies empty Vessagiriya; but not more silent must it have been in the bygone times when every cell was tenanted by some holy soul intent on highest aspiration and holiness. One feels even to-day that that aspiration haunts the stillness no less now than then; for though men may crumble, and Empires go to undecipherable ruin, aspiration, holy thought, kind wish, can never change nor perish, being part of the eternal, but hover for ever about the sphere of their activity, blessing the world insensibly long after their thinker has gone on to other activities [...] All these kind and sacred things that once were thought at Vessagiriya are still active, then, in the happy world around us, and one wanders buoyantly up and down amid the cells, feeling at every step the influence of a vanished but very present holiness — a happiness complete and unsurpassable, that once animated the silent devotees of every hollow in the rock. (pp. 319–20)

The material perishes. The spiritual remains, lives on in the world. This passage, emphasizing stored spiritual energy, takes us into rather unfamiliar territory. Farrer here approaches an occult belief, as expressed, for example, by Dion Fortune a few years later: 'It is well known to all psychics that the sites of ancient temples where mystery-rituals have been worked, are always potently charged with psychic force.'[15]

Farrer detects the psychic aura that lingers around Vessagiriya; the psychic reverberation, lingering on as a record of the past, that is detectable by the initiated: ancient spiritual resonance, comprehension of which was the goal of such practices as psychometry. But at this point we must obviously step back for a moment.

For further insight into *In Old Ceylon* we will need to turn to a way of thinking that has been combined with a set of exploratory practices; in which the psychological can unite with the psychic and with the riveting nature of space and place. The term 'psycho-geography' dates from the activities of the *Lettriste* personalities of the French-based Situationist International in the 1950s and 60s, and has been rejuvenated since the late 1980s by the activities of some British writers.[16] Its main activity consists of registering subjectively the effect of place and spaces on the emotions and actions of individuals. The psycho-geographer does not observe the effect of place on others (except sporadically): instead, he or she is the subject. Investigation proceeds by means of the planned journey (ideally on foot) with its unpredictable but almost inevitable drifts away from the plan. The term psycho-geography suggests some foundation in science or at least social science, but in fact there is nothing scientific about the practices of psycho-geography or the forms in which they are recorded or written up. To state only the most obvious point, the supposed findings are unverifiable. Psycho-geography is therefore a way of producing art; perhaps an art in itself.

In thinking along these lines about the psychological dynamics of landscape, we should disentangle ourselves from the mid-twentieth century and understand that poets have practised this type of activity for centuries. To go back no further than high Romanticism, one thinks of Byron in Venice and Rome (*Childe Harold's Pilgrimage*); Wordsworth in the Lake district; Goethe on his *Italian Journey*; Gerard de Nerval wandering along a psychological edge in the Ile de France, Italy, Austria and east of Cythera; Thomas De Quincy adrift in London; Charles Baudelaire's poet crossing La Place du Carrousel in Paris.[17] It was the Situationists who worked out and named the *dérive*, the 'drift', and who gave a particularly anti-capitalist character to psycho-geography. Nineteenth-century poets sometimes take on kindred characteristics, but not necessarily systematically. Nevertheless, what has been called psycho-geography's 'more-or-less gruelling investigations of the effect of place on human behaviour' is detectable as a prominent element in nineteenth-century literature.[18]

To regard Farrer's *In Old Ceylon* in light of psycho-geography can throw considerable light on his purposes and achievements. The book amounts to a psycho-geography of historical Buddhist sites in Ceylon. To begin to explain the operation of this, let us first give due weight to Farrer's geographical sensitivity, already outlined above. Psycho-geographic characteristics run throughout the book, are arguably the main point of the book, because they allow for the blending of geographical qualities of place, of history, and Farrer's subjectivity. This can be seen particularly clearly in the last section, when the narrator visits 'Mihintalé, the Holy Hill.'

The hill is holy (and still venerated now) because in the 3rd century B.C.E. the Indian emperor Ashoka's son, Mahinda, already a Buddhist himself, landed there after floating through the air from India. He met the Lankan king, who was hunting, and persuaded him to follow the way of the Buddha. The people in their turn followed the example of the king. So, according to the myth, Buddhism in Lanka began at Mihintalé. Farrer's description of exploring the hill must be quoted at length:

> You pass the crumbling dâgabas on the pavement that hold the ashes of forgotten abbots, you pass the grass-grown wall of the precinct, and so you come to the monks' dwellings beneath the rock, where, in the shadow of the cliff, their yellow robes, stretched out to dry after dyeing, make brilliant flares of orange against the darkness of cave and cliff behind. Thence a break-neck little path leads down the sheer slope of the mountain through a fertile little rocky ravine, rich with the heavy fan-foliage of banana and other lush herbage of the monks' gardens, on down a gully of shrubs, overhung by gigantic poised boulders that threaten at every moment to clash together like the Symplegades; and the path ends at last before the greatest of these — a rock, flattened, oval, as large as a church, just balanced on edge upon a pedestal of a smaller boulder, from which the hill-side falls sheer and far to the plain 1,000 feet below; and in the giant pebble is gnawed a small arched hole at its base, resting on the rock-slope beneath. To this one climbs over a huddle of fallen blocks by a small iron stairway, and there in that tiny cavern of draughts, open on either side to all the airs that blow, some saint, abbot, or hermit of the dead centuries once made his lair. The holy place is filled with a rectangle carved for a bed, and made smooth by many years of pious occupation. Sweet flowers are laid there to this day in reverence for the sanctity that sought meditation and enlightenment here. For legend has it that this hermitage was chosen by no less a personage than Mahinda himself, and popular tradition calls the place 'Mahinda's Bed.' Be this as it may, the anchorite who retired here had before his eyes a spectacle more illuminating than most. Through the arching frame of rock the eye looks insatiably out from that high place on the shelving cliff, over mile after mile after blue mile of flat forest, into the pale violet distances of the uttermost jungle far below, fading in plane after plane of amethyst, into the pale violet of the furthest horizon, where the wild and jagged mountain-ranges rise on the rim of the world, like islands towering from the smooth immovable level that seems to cover all the curving globe from here. Palaces and temples may fade from the memory; ineffaceably written on one's soul remains that enormous placid prospect, that vast and awful peace, implacable, impenetrable, imperturbable, which makes the mysterious and compelling sanctity of this view from the Bed of the Saint. It has a quality of perfect detachment, of superhuman exaltation; that high place hangs far above the world, and is not of the world. As one gazes, the feet of one's soul float free of the earth, and one's whole being achieves the miracle of levitation, soaring untrammelled in the ocean of eternity, where time and space and matter are no longer even words. (pp. 342–43)

Farrer persuades by the *energia* of his writing, its extraordinarily vivid description, which here achieves victory by obtaining belief.[19] It is important to register the trope of *energia* here, not least because, as we shall see, it constitutes the rhetorical foundation of Farrer's success as a writer. *Energia* is often translated as 'action' or 'animation'. In Aristotle it is vigorous description, a 'setting forth to the eyes' of a subject.[20] For Pierre Fontanier this effect appears under the name of *hypotyposis,* which: 'paints things in a manner so lively and energetic, that she puts them in some way before the eyes, and makes an image, a tableau or even a living scene from a narrative or description'.[21] In the face of Farrer's forceful assertions, who are we to demur from the idea of levitation? Not only the subjectivity of psycho-geography, but *nazoraëru* form up against our scepticism.

Farrer contrives to live not only in the unsatisfactory modern Ceylon, but simultaneously with the splendid and passionate dead in old Lanka. 'I really do', he wrote years later, 'live in the past and the absent more vividly perhaps than most people'.[22]

Another, and, as it turns out in the progress of the book, final view from Mihintalé draws elements of Farrer's theme together and resolves some paradoxes. The narrator looks out towards the heart of the ruined 'Sacred City' some ten miles away, and it becomes apparent that what he sees is the passage of time, as much as space:

> there is nothing but the stupendous and overwhelming plain of the jungle-sea, sliding away in shades of azure across the receding curve of the earth. Far, and far, and far — seeming illimitable as the apparently illimitable sea of Birth and Death — the great Northern Plain goes stretching from horizon to pale horizon, one undecipherable motionless ocean of jungle, broken only here and there by those sudden purple islets of mountain and pinnacle. Larger, wider, more infinite than anything I have ever seen, is that prospect [...]
>
> And there, full in the middle of the view, lies sleeping the Sacred City. From end to end its relics lie extended before us, and from their extent we suddenly realize that all this eternal sea of woodland was once crowded with a glory of building that its creators deemed to be no less eternal than we, to-day, conceive the unbroken silence of the forest. Anuradhapura lies far across the world from east to west. Anuradhapura now is nothing but a memory — a phantom dimly to be recalled amid the dense wilderness that holds its place [...]
>
> The whole purpose of the thing lies apparent from here — its whole history, its whole doom. Nowhere in the world is the utter grandeur, the utter ruin, of a city and a nation so apparent as when one looks from Mihintalé out across the interminable jungle that was once the gorgeous capital of Ceylon. Almost beyond guesswork the splendour has receded into the unfathomable past, and yet, in a way, its scanty bones, its very abandonment of hopelessness, enable one to feel more keenly than ever the splendid things that once were, by contrast with the jumbled tragedy of what now is. Rome of to-day is a mean thing... compared with the extended enormous ruin of the Sacred City — vast, resigned, silent, leisurely, with full consciousness of an eternity of desolation to face. Gone and vanished are the golden Kings and abbots; of their palaces remain but sordid, naked beams of hewn stone, lost in the grass, standing at drunken angles in forgotten gloamings of the forest, glimmering in the green depths of the jungle-sea like weed-grown wreckage of great galleons foundered

FIG. 2.6. 'Like drunken galleons' on the sea-bed: ruins at Anuradhapura.
Photo: author, 2015.

a hundred centuries since. [See figure 2.6.] Their ghostly life is now but the life of the forest; lizards flirt their tails in the blurred faces of the statues, and wise-faced apes go swinging foolishly from bough to bough of the Sacred Tree itself.[23] Only the holiness that made them and dwelt in them still lives, and lives for ever. For holiness and devotion are the immortal parts of life — are the only realities of life.

And so, as one gazes out over the waste of Anuradhapura, and repeats the invocation, 'Anicca, dukkha, anatta' — 'Impermanent, full of disappointment, without fixed personality' — one realizes also that in the higher sense these things, and all lovely things of good intent, *are* permanent, filled with perfect satisfaction, radiant with an eternal fixed personality that must outlast the stars and the universe. (pp. 345–47)

The theme of Buddhism provides a higher paradox that trumps one of Ceylon's main paradoxes. Farrer's structural sub-themes of ancient and modern, and of the place of art in the relation between the material and the spiritual, are brought to a climax here partly through the consistency of his view, established hundreds of pages earlier, of the jungle as a sea, as his narrative structure reaches its logical conclusion at the place of origin of Buddhism in the island. The narrator's sensibility is flooded with his Buddhist belief.

Ultimately, for the reader, the book communicates vividly the work, and play, of Farrer's imagination around the Buddhist sites of Sri Lanka.

Politics

My argument that the book is an outstanding example of psycho-geography might raise the objection that psycho-geography as it developed later is noted for its anti-capitalist politics, and that *In Old Ceylon* lacks any overt political discussion. Certainly we cannot expect Farrer to share the political aspirations of the Situationists, based as they were in France of the 1950s and 60s. At the same time, use of psycho-geography, containing as it does this well-acknowledged element, as a heuristic tool with which to investigate *In Old Ceylon*, rather demands or determines that we consider the politics of Farrer's book. We find some politics endowed on the book by its context.

The first point to make is that *In Old Ceylon* Buddhism is central. Other religious beliefs held by people on the island (Moslem, Hindu, Christian) are merely alluded to. This no doubt reflects Farrer's own preference, as well as his near total reliance on the Buddhist *Mahavamsa* and other ancient chronicles for his historical understanding. For the historian of Sri Lanka, John Rogers, it was George Turnour's translation of the Mahavamsa in the 1830s that paved the way for ideas of ethnic identity to become prominent in the island and institutionalized by the 1870s.[24] Of course, Farrer's stated view was that belief resides in the heart of an individual, rather than in the functioning of an organized cult, and becomes distorted or perverted by the activities of the institutions of a Church or Cult — institutions such as monasticism. He contemplates this question, stating that despite the shortcomings of monks:

> the Truth had such power as never to fail in the heart of the people; and the sacred gift of happiness and simplicity of life that the Buddha's doctrine, rightly learned, can never fail to bestow on a nation, has never passed out of the grip of Lanka, whatever may have been the avarice and untrustworthiness of its interpreters. (p. 93)

An implied contrast here is with the history of the Christian West, where people mutually slaughtered each other in the name of God or Christ, and where, in Farrer's time, 'happiness and simplicity of life' have been pushed aside in the pursuit of materialism. He then immediately makes a wishful assertion about the nineteenth-century Buddhist revival:

> And now that clouds in east and west are clearing away from the sunlight of the Buddha, a higher aspiration is dawning amid the monks of Lanka, stripped now, for the most part, of the splendid endowments and rich acres that made so deadly a trap for their souls. (p.93)

While *In Old Ceylon* makes no attempt to describe contemporary Buddhist life in any comprehensive way, it does occasionally allude to specific individuals and incidents. We are told about 'the gentle saint of the Peradéniya road' (the main road into Kandy from the west) who has opened the first Buddhist nunnery in the island to have been founded for centuries. This was, although Farrer doesn't tell us so, Sister Sudham Macheri, who was assisted in her effort by the Governor's wife, Lady Blake.[25] Later on, Farrer refers to a riot in Anuradhapura. A well-established problem there arose from the fact that under the aegis of colonial government, a settlement and bazaar had grown up on ground formerly sacred to Buddhism. There were butchers' shops and drinking-booths. The riot was triggered when an old woman on Buddhist pilgrimage was 'knocked down' by a 'native [Government] official' (p. 266). In Farrer's words: 'a mob of riff-raff had come up from Colombo for the lark of a row [...] merely in disorder and from no religious motives, [they] broke down the obnoxious bazaar, destroyed the buildings, and [...] went and sacked the Roman Catholic Church.' Farrer points to 'a certain demagogue' who 'had long been at the head of discontent', implying that the man incited the crowd. In fact, John Rogers identifies the underlying cause of the riot to have been: 'outrage in response to the use by the Public Works Department of stones taken from ancient sites.' He states that 'pilgrims from the maritime districts' constituted the main part of the rioters.[26]

The riot happened in June 1903, and is described by another modern scholar as 'a minor anti-Christian riot [...] during which [...] a Roman Catholic church was burned and a slaughterhouse destroyed.' The prominent figure involved in the riot was Walsinha Harischandra (1877–1913), Farrer's 'demagogue', who was subsequently tried for incitement and acquitted.[27] Harischandra was an associate of Anagarika Dharmapala, and a member of his Maha Bodhi Society; an organisation that promoted a certain militancy or aggression in attempts to re-possess ancient Buddhist sites (even as far afield as Bodhgaya in India) that had fallen into disuse, other uses, or had been appropriated by different groups. Dismissing Harischandra as a 'demagogue' does not prevent Farrer from relying on his book about Anuradhapura; in fact, citing his interpretation of the Lankarama (another ruined dagaba in Anuradhapura), and summarizing an incident that Harischandra recounts about it, when (1901): 'a Siamese monk went into retreat here, and the assembling crowds under his inspiration developed into a committee for the restoration of the holy place. Unfortunately a Government official came on the scene, and with rather unnecessary brutality quelled the whole scheme.'[28] The context surrounding Farrer's brief accounts of the 1901 and 1903 incidents, therefore, includes the activities of Dharmapala, Harischandra, even Sri Sumangala, in promoting assertive, even aggressive, Buddhist resurgence. Farrer's own hope for Anuradhapura is that 'some wise Governor of the future will move the whole settlement [...] to a less sacred spot [...] nearer the railway' (p. 267), which eventually happened in the 1930s and 40s.

A second, yet related, point to make about political interpretation of *In Old Ceylon* concerns the book's consistent anti-Christianist stance. There can be no doubt that this was motivated by Farrer's own convictions and beliefs. Spirited repudiation of Christianity is a feature of several of his other books. To say as much is not to disentangle Farrer from Ceylonese anti-Christianist politics completely. To the extent that Christianity was imported to Ceylon by the colonial powers (Portugal, The Netherlands, Britain) the rejection of it throughout the book could perhaps be taken as reflecting a political position. The context embraces the activities of a pugnacious veteran of the U.S. Civil War, Colonel Olcott the Theosophist, and of his protégé, Dharmapala, whose anti-Christianist activities were part of their pushing forward of Buddhism. Given the context sketched above of Buddhist resurgence, in an island divided by religion any anti-Christianist statements were potentially construable from that point of view — even involving a constitutional politics.[29] At the same time, Farrer's condemnation of Harischandra indicates his wish to distance himself from any such political movement.

The third point to make about possible relations between *In Old Ceylon* and Ceylonese politics concerns Farrer's antagonism to the planters (tea planters especially), already referred to in Chapter One. In his discussion of the damaging effects of the riot at Anuradhapura, Farrer describes the effect on Government officials (to which we shall turn in a moment), before directing his attention to the effect on the opinions of the planters:

> With the planters, of course, the situation is far worse. The official is a man of education, in most cases anxious to know something of the country in which he is working, and in all cases anxious to do the best work he can for it. To the average planter, though, it would seem that Ceylon is too often simply a conquered country of heathen, in which his only interest is to make money as soon as possible and then clear out. And while he is there, though, it is simply the waste land "east of Suez, where the best is like the worst, where there ain't no Ten Commandments, and a man can raise a thirst." There his concern with the island ends; of its history, faith, and civilization he too often has no thought. He makes his toy Surbiton at a toy Grasmere, [Nuwara Eliya][30] and is more or less unhappy in the pretence of English life. The native is simply his slave, the monk his pet antipathy, for whom no slander can be too foul or preposterous. Of the [Buddhist] Church he talks with the blank, uncomprehending rage with which Attila's men-at-arms must have spoken of St. Leo and his priestly escort. (pp. 268–69)

This damnation is comprehensive and, with the help of the quotation from Kipling's poem 'On the Road to Mandalay', wholesale. Nevertheless Farrer will have been able to talk to people, including Leonard Woolf (in addition to Princess Louise), about the planters, as well as to meet planters himself. Woolf reminds us in a horrifying parenthetical comment of the hardships faced by Tamil labourers on the plantations: 'No people in Ceylon starve', he writes, 'except a few Tamil coolies who are driven off or leave estates in Sinhalese districts.'[31] There is perhaps a basic anti-capitalism in Farrer's scorn for the planters, though he objects most strongly to the planters' attendant brutal cultural attitudes. He never refers at length to their economic exploitation. Since Farrer himself belonged to the land-owning group in Britain, there is possibly an anti-trade prejudice involved too, though since he was also a nurseryman, perhaps not. Yet planters were landowners too; so a liberal landowner condemns illiberal ones. But rather than resembling the large landowners of northern England, the planters are perhaps most like hard-hearted farmers.

A fourth element in the political context surrounding Farrer's visit and his book focusses on the activities of government officials. As we saw in his comparison with the planters, Farrer tries to be fair to the Government officials. After all they were providing or finding him accommodation, and sometimes transport. Neither Farrer himself, nor our study of the political context, however, can exculpate them from injustices. However fair-minded the officials may have striven to be, they were working for an exploitative system. A. Dissanaike's article, 'The Land Settlement Policy under the Waste Lands Ordinance in Ceylon', published in the journal founded by Coomaraswamy, the *Ceylon National Review*, condemns just one part of this system: the expropriation and privatisation, by the British, of land worked on a customary basis by Ceylonese families.[32] At stake were areas subjected to a slash-and-burn agriculture, cleared by the Ceylonese every few years for sowing a year or two's crops, and then left fallow to recover their fertility for several years. By a process rather akin to the enclosures of common land that had affected England itself in the period 1725–1850, and had caused great hardship to the rural poor, in Ceylon: 'large numbers of villagers in the Low-country as well as the Up-country have been ousted from their ancestral possessions.' Without protest and relief their condition will be 'reduced to one of utter depression and helplessness', resulting in 'increase of crime and the degradation of self-respecting peasant proprietors into a scorned and despised slavishness.'[33] This is convincing criticism. Just as shocking was the persistence of another old British landowners' custom associated with enclosures, but illegal in Britain since 1828: the use of booby-traps. During Farrer's visit a report noted that: 'In Upper Dambara a man has been killed by a spring gun set to kill pig or porcupine.'[34]

No condemnation of reprehensible government policy such as that in the *Ceylon National Review* troubles the pages of *In Old Ceylon*. Farrer limits himself to considering religious questions. The case of the 1903 riot at Anuradhapura laid bare a certain dynamic:

> the harm was done — a spirit of suspicious dislike encouraged in the Government, a certain feeling of wrong and injustice engendered in the [Buddhist] Church [...] From all this it is difficult for the officials to look with a very sympathetic eye upon the Church. It is far more easy to dislike and slander men when their views oppose yours, than to study their work and their opinions in the favouring light of truth. The officials [...] cannot avoid a certain bias, and are apt to take it too readily for granted, I think, that the monks are a lazy, shifty, feeble lot, simply because the assumption is easier and more comfortable for busy men who have no time to sift such matters. Quite possibly the monks may be all this: it is pleasanter to think that, quite possibly, they are not. Nobody, however, has made any solid attempt to find out the truth about them without fear or favour. One meets everywhere the accepted view, for which there is no more stable foundation than, indeed, for any favourable hypothesis.

The 'everywhere the accepted view' from which Farrer demurs was that of the British (Europeans, Westerners). The book suggests that, aside from Jinavaravamsa and a few other monks, Farrer did not spend a lot of time talking to local indigenous people. He continues on the subject of the monks:

> Their rights may be respected; their point of view is not considered. And their position is a difficult one. They are ecclesiastics and dignitaries, and therefore attached to the pomps and appanages of their Church; they represent an omnipotent force, which once owned all this city, and held the land in

undisputed sway. Yet now they are nothing. The bare shrines are left to them, and diminished endowments; but their power is gone. Christian missionaries invade their territory, and they exist on sufferance — simply licensed heathen, called 'priests' to make them sound more heathen still. It is impossible but that there should be saints among them; the whole multitude, however, is lumped by official opinion in the condemnation of the inevitable black sheep, and it is not from servants of Government that you can gain any really convincing view of the servants of the Church. (pp. 267–68)

The incident of the Siamese monk at Lankarama, introduced later in Farrer's narrative, serves to substantiate this claim. Government officials are guilty at least of prejudice, ignorance, and neglect.

For Farrer, though, the thoughts about ancient Lankan ruins are less motivated by the state of modern Ceylon than by the historian's task, here expressed by Stephen Bann: to recover 'the mythic wholeness from the *disjecta membra*'.[35] At Anuradhapura, where ruins of ancient buildings can still be measured by the square mile, rather than by a more modest measure, there are plenty of *disjecta membra*. The mythic wholeness that Farrer seeks will always be beyond the ability of this world's life to give.

Notes to Chapter 2

1. Farrer, *In Old Ceylon*, p. 162. Hereafter citation of page numbers for this book will be in the main text.
2. In this I am following the lead of Stephen Bann; see his *The Clothing of Clio: A study of the representation of history in nineteenth-century Britain and France* (Cambridge: Cambridge University Press, 1984) throughout for his insight into the nature of rhetorical tropes and figures.
3. This motif is too well-known to need particular elaboration here. There is a discussion of one ramification of it in Michael Charlesworth, *Landscape and Vision in Nineteenth Century Britain and France* (Aldershot: Ashgate, 2008).
4. These terms are borrowed from the French structuralist linguistician Emile Benveniste, *Problèmes de Linguistique Générale* (Paris: Gallimard, 1968).
5. Coomaraswamy, 'Open Letter to the Kandyan Chiefs' (Kandy: printed for the author, 1905; first printed in the *Ceylon Observer*, 17 February 1905).
6. *Insight Guides: Sri Lanka* (Singapore: Apa, 2009), p. 151, quotes his description of the Galle Face Hotel.
7. Nihal Karunaratne, *Udavattekälē: the Forbidden Forest of the Kings of Kandy* (Colombo: Department of National Archives, 1986), pp. 99–100.
8. The Government Agent's Diary for 1908 specifies the date as 7 February: Sri Lanka National Archives, Kandy Branch, diary for Jan–June 1908: 18/36.
9. Leonard Woolf, *An Autobiography, I: 1880–1911* (1960, 1961: Oxford: Oxford University Press, 1980), p. 224. 'Ratemahatmaya' translates as 'chief headman'; in this case of Kandy.
10. Ibid, p. 225.
11. Richard Shiff, personal communication, 8/7/2015. I want to emphasize that Farrer published *In Old Ceylon* two years before Roger Fry staged the exhibition *Manet and the Post-Impressionists* in London; an event that contributed to Virginia Woolf's notorious assertion that 'around 1910, human nature changed'.
12. Richard Shiff, *Cézanne and the End of Impressionism: A Study of the Theory, Technique, and Critical Evaluation of Modern Art* (Chicago: University of Chicago Press, 1984).
13. Reginald Farrer, *The Garden of Asia: Impressions from Japan* (London: Arnold, 1904), p. 84. The influence I am suggesting comes from Oscar Wilde's *The Critic as Artist* (1891), part of *Intentions*

(London: The Unicorn Press, 1945), pp. 77–170; for instance, in the passage in which Wilde conjures up the present state of Troy to compare with our imagining of it while reading Homer: 'On the mouldering citadel of Troy lies the lizard like a thing of green bronze. The owl has built her nest in the palace of Priam. [...] Yet, every morning the doors of the city are thrown open, and on foot, or in horse-drawn chariot, the warriors go forth to battle' (p. 105).

14. Gregory Schopen, 'The Buddhist "Monastery" and the Indian Garden: Aesthetics, Assimilations, and the Siting of Monastic Establishments', *Journal of the American Oriental Society* vol. 126, 4, (Oct-Dec 2006), 487–505.

15. Dion Fortune, *Psychic Self-Defence* (London: Rider and Company, 1930), p. 72.

16. In France, the most famous psycho-geographer was Guy Debord. In England, Iain Sinclair, Will Self, Patrick Keiller, Stewart Home, to name only the obvious.

17. Baudelaire, 'Le Cygne', The Swan, one of his *Tableaux Parisiens*. Almost all Nerval's poetry and creative writing qualifies as psycho-geographic.

18. Samantha Matthews, *Times Literary Supplement*, January 13, 2012, p. 30.

19. For Thomas Hobbes, 'the end of rhetorick is Victory, which consists in having gotten Belief': *A Brief of the Art of Rhetoric* (1637. In Buckley, *Aristotle's Treatise on Rhetoric*, pp. 273–346, see next note).

20. Aristotle, *Rhetoric*, 1411b 27+ (Book III Chapter XI). See Theodore Buckley, *Aristotle's Treatise on Rhetoric, literally translated from the Greek* (3rd edn., 1846: London: Bohn, 1853), p. 239.

21. Pierre Fontanier, *Les Figures du Discours* (1827; Paris: Flammarion, 1977), p. 390.

22. RBGE, RJF 4/1/1, letter to Ernest Gye of 24/9/1919. Farrer continues, '(is it not, in fact, a diagnostic mark of the Harlot?)'.

23. Compare Oscar Wilde: 'On the mouldering citadel of Troy lies the lizard like a thing of green bronze.', *The Critic as Artist*, p. 105.

24. John D. Rogers, 'Historical Images in the British Period', in *Sri Lanka: History and the Roots of Conflict*, ed. by Jonathan Spencer (London: Routledge, 1990), 87–106, esp. pp. 88–95.

25. See P. Carus and M. Verhoeven, *The Gospel of Buddha According to Old Records* (various editions before 1915; Peru, Illinois: Open Court Publishing Company, 2004), p. 309.

26. John D. Rogers, 'Historical Images in the British Period', p. 100.

27. Stanley Jeyaraja Tambiah, *Levelling Crowds: Ethnonationalist Conflicts and Collective Violence in South Asia* (Berkeley: University of California Press, 1996), p. 55.

28. *In Old Ceylon*, pp. 306–07. W. Harischandra's book that reports the incident is *The Sacred City of Anuradhapura, with forty-six illustrations* (1908; New Delhi: Asian Educational Services, 1985), pp. 60, 75.

29. See K. M. de Silva, 'Sri Lanka: National Identity and the Impact of Colonialism', in *Identity and Difference: Essays on Society and Culture in Sri Lanka*, ed. by J.C. Holt and P. B. Meegaskumbura (Kandy: Intercollegiate Sri Lanka Educational Program, 2006), pp. 1–26 for a broad and brief general view of the question of religion, including the British-Ceylonese agreement (1815) to provide government support for Buddhism, from which the British retreated in the 1840s at least in part because of evangelical Christian pressure, thus leaving Buddhism without State support.

30. For non-British readers: Surbiton is a middle-class suburb of London, and Grasmere a picturesque village in the Lake District. Nuwara Eliya is an elevated hill-station in the centre of Sri Lanka built by the British, much valued for its cooler climate.

31. Leonard Woolf, *Diaries in Ceylon 1908–1911: Records of a Colonial Administrator* (*Ceylon Historical Journal*, vol. IX — July 1959 and April 1960 Nos 1–4; published in book form by Tisara Press, Dehiwala, Sri Lanka: 1962; 2nd edition, 1963), p. 117.

32. A. Dissanaike, 'The Land Settlement Policy under the Waste Lands Ordinance in Ceylon', *Ceylon National Review* 9 (March 1910),130–32.

33. All quotations ibid., p. 132.

34. Goverment Agent's Diary, Kandy District, for March 3rd 1908. Kandy Branch Archives, 18/36.

35. S. Bann, *The Clothing of Clio*, p. 23. *Disjecta membra* can be translated as 'scattered parts' that once constituted an organic whole or even a living body.

CHAPTER 3

'Lovely flowers... made all worth while':
Biography, 1908–1920

I do not know how Farrer might have practised his Buddhism once home in Britain. His personal letters make no reference to it. A solitary recital of prayers? A literary pursuit — reading the *Suttas*? (As we shall see, and as the interview in the *Times of Ceylon* stated, he did read them.) Be that as it may, Farrer eventually made other trips to the far side of the world where Buddhism was practised: in 1914–1916 to China and Tibet, and in 1919–1920 to Burma. But between his return from Ceylon, in April 1908, and January 1914 there were no more round the world trips. In this middle stage of his life, foreign travel became Italy and France, Constantinople and Athens: at home the garden, the Craven Nursery, Liberal politics (he stood for election to the seat of Ashford, Kent, unsuccessfully in 1910) and life as a writer occupied him. Novels appeared in 1908, 1909, and 1912; his verse dramas were published in 1908 and 1913; books about gardens and plants in 1908, 1909 and 1912; his account of plant-collecting in the *Alpes Maritimes* and western Italy in 1911; and his book *The Dolomites* in 1913. This was an active life, but family tradition had been the Law. Perhaps from the family's perspective Reginald's activities therefore looked like those of a dilettante.

His family could annoy him about his Buddhism. On March 17, 1910 (obviously a bad year for relations between the family members), in a clinic for an operation on his stomach, he has been visited by a Christian clergyman (almost certainly sent by his mother). He rails against 'the canon's stupid and officious impertinence' and his mother's repeating it: 'he knows my religious views perfectly well, and so do you.'[1]

We might note at this point that, while he was extraordinarily energetic and hardy out in the field, Farrer's health was not robust. He had caught diphtheria in 1901. There was the abdominal operation in 1910. In August 1917 he's in London, anticipating an imminent operation to have 'most of my inside removed and some of it put back in.'[2] Three weeks later, in early September, despite having a job in London, he writes from Ingleborough Hall, so perhaps went there to convalesce.[3] And at the end of 1918 Farrer underwent another abdominal operation ('I am really in a nursing home, having had my inside removed', he writes).[4] The cause of his death has never been established, so we cannot say whether it was related to persistent problems with his digestive tract or not. In particular, Hardikar's Syndrome (identified in 1992) features cleft palate and cleft lip, together with any of a range of other symptoms, including kidney failure, intestinal obstruction and retarded growth early in life. J.A. Farrer describes the stomach operation in 1910 as caused by 'appendicitis' (Reginald entered the nursing home on 5th March, had the operation on the 25th, and returned to Ingleborough on the 4th April).[5] Both father and son are more explanatory about the operation of December, 1918. J. A. Farrer states that it was 'for the removal of adhesions resulting from his operation for appendicitis 8 years before', while Reginald wrote to a friend that: 'I am actually in a Knightsbridge nursing home, having had various knots in my inside unravelled, so as to confront the Burmese Alps with a straightforward skein.'[6] These two terse descriptions point to intestinal obstructions as a repeated problem for Farrer, which would mean that he exhibited at least three (perhaps four, if we count retarded growth) of the indicators for Hardikar's Syndrome.

Farrer had developed a personality that was not necessarily easy for people to like. In 1911 he stayed with the Herberts. His life-long friend Aubrey now had a wife, Mary, who described Farrer as: 'a malevolent gnome, with a wish to be fascinating but an ill-restrained bitterness of tongue.'[7] This comment, in which Farrer's short stature and odd appearance is used against him, makes Herbert's sister's comment seem mild by comparison: 'he is a cad, but an amusing one. I can't have him here every day.'[8] Evidently the sister, Vera, complained to the wife, who wrote: 'he really seems to have been poisonously insulting. It does make me feel rather annoyed, because though one is sorry for him, he has got the dwarfish ill-nature and canker about him somewhere that is very irritating and wounding.'[9] The reference to feeling 'sorry for him' makes one wonder whether Farrer had detected this attitude (of, from his point of view, being patronised and condescended to) and reacted adversely to it. A more dispassionate assessment than Mary Herbert's comes from Osbert Sitwell, who salutes Farrer's 'courage, character and persistence', and goes on to say that although his voice was 'at first as startling as the discordant cry of a jay or woodpecker':

> he possessed no hesitation in his speech [...] His manner was bland, but, albeit possessed of the capacity to be extremely considerate, he was impish by nature, and so, since he had also the power of identifying, with an intimidating speed and certainty, hypocrisy and pretentiousness, there were, even at his most clement, occasional sly digs and prods for all in his conversation. He was vain [...] and liked to air the contents of a well-stored and observant mind. [...] he had cultivated an intensely personal method of talk, in which he made evident his liking for effects, for epigrams and fireworks.[10]

Even through Sitwell's somewhat apologetic approach, we can recognize a demanding personality, competitive, not easy to relax with, 'even at his most clement.'

E. H. M. Cox, who accompanied Farrer in 1919 on the expedition in Burma, wrote later that Farrer:

> was forceful and dogmatic in his decisions [...] his was a nature that would not brook opposition [...] his enormous enthusiasm carried him through [...] All who knew him recognized his moods and, if they were wise, laid their plans accordingly. His learning was quite out of the ordinary.[11]

This appraisal was measured, compared with Cox's own diary entry from 1919, when he was travelling and living with Farrer on the plant-collecting expedition in Upper Burma. Their relations were sometimes not very happy, and for one moment Cox confided to himself that he would enjoy beating Farrer up: 'He has the superiority in brains but I can at least hurt him bodily & if I begin his face will be a fruity sight.'[12] With respect to the relations with Cox, Farrer himself reflected on them as Cox was returning home from Burma in January 1920. Writing to his close friend Ernest Gye of the Foreign Office, he regrets retrospectively his own behaviour with Cox, understanding that it had made the young man's position more uncomfortable than necessary. Farrer condemns his own 'unintimate pleasantness (or unpleasantness) very trying & provoking & refrigerating [... I was] grumpy and fratchy [...] cloaked in a maddening and perfectly transparent veil of assumed patience!'[13] Here Farrer, more clement after the fact, shows self-awareness and self-criticism of an unusual calibre. An earlier letter, from a rest-camp during the expedition with Cox, reveals his more acid mentality: 'Jumps' (Farrer's nickname for Cox) 'is [...] writing a novel. This is the latest stunt. Last week it was a sonnet, compiled of all the words he could remember out of Keats and Coleridge in the Oxford Book, and ending up with an appeal to the Irrawaddy to "flow on, thou stream".'[14] Luckily Cox was young, and able to bounce back after Farrer's 'refrigerating' treatment, to publish generous tributes to Farrer later. For example: '[Farrer] had the brains and the ability to advance far beyond ordinary mortals in anything which really interested him.'[15]

A different view of Farrer comes from three sources not hitherto mentioned in writings about him. One of the entries in the catalogue of Farrer's exhibition of water-colours of China and Tibet mounted by the Fine Art Society in 1917 adds a note about the painting in question (depicting a mountain): 'A long way after C. J. Holmes.'[16] Charles Holmes, painter, Slade Professor, later Director of the National Gallery, had met Farrer on a train in the autumn of 1912. His account is worth quoting at length, because it offers a view of Farrer at home, enjoying elements of an exotic civilisation. Sketching from the carriage window, Holmes tells us,

> I was startled by a remark from a plump little man with lively dark eyes, sitting just opposite. 'Excuse me: but you must be C. J. Holmes.' The acute observer introduced himself as Reginald Farrer, and started to talk. By the time we reached St. Pancras, we had discovered so many tastes in common that I promised to come and see him at Ingleborough in the following spring, and try for certain uncatchable trout in his lake. So there I found myself on a bitter March morning [...] Swathed in rugs and coats and scarves we then faced the elements in a little open car, driving round to Ribblehead by Stainforth [...] past a nobly snow-streaked Ingleborough, stopping wherever a subject for frozen fingers was suggested, and finally returning to the house, the lake and to sunshine. [...]   The next day was glorious, and we tramped over the hills from Troll Gill[17] to Sulber Nick, that miracle of desolation, chanting absurd verses in abuse of Sophocles, whom we both disliked, and behaving generally like schoolboys. Farrer, the professed Buddhist, loved to pass in a moment from the sublime to the ridiculous, to be as brilliant and as silly as he was learned in letters and in botany. His spirits and his good temper were inexhaustible, and

FIG. 3.1. C. J. Holmes, *Whernside* (1917). (Tate Images).

his consideration too. On our last morning he ran me down to the edge of his famous rock-garden and back, so that I could just say that I had seen it, without having to pretend to be interested. Indeed to me the garden looked just like the usual barren mixture of earth and stones, without a touch of colour, in which Alpine botanists discourse of glories to come; though the stones were larger and piled more grandly than any I had seen elsewhere. The one remark I made was unlucky. The mention of Clutton-Brock's garden in Surrey drew down a sudden outburst of the eternal disrespect of the man who does things for the man who writes about them.

Farrer, indeed, for all his lightness of heart and exuberance of language, was now preparing for another of his arduous expeditions to the highlands of China in search of new flowering plants. He introduced me to chopsticks, to tea made in native fashion, which exhilarates at the moment but leaves the mind afterwards a perfect blank, and to Chinese delicacies, like buried eggs, which resemble (when they are not mouldy) some ancient ethereal cheese. [...] Few men have impressed me more than this merry soul, whom I met so casually and knew so briefly, this lover of ease and civilized comfort, who sacrificed them, and ultimately his own life, to hunt in savage and dangerous places for the little flowers which now bear his name.[18]

During the drive out the two men were evidently sketching together: 'stopping wherever a subject for frozen fingers was suggested.' (Figure 3.1 shows an example of Holmes' landscape painting: Whernside, the mountain immediately north-west of Ingleborough).

The second of the sources comes in the form of a book in the Royal Horticultural Society's Lindley Library. This is a copy of Farrer's book about plant-hunting in the Alpes Maritimes and their Italian side: *Among the Hills: a Book of Joy in High Places*, extra-illustrated by its owner, Mrs. Alice Terry. Various photographs have been glued in, and inside the front cover a photograph of Farrer in his most characteristic pose, and a newspaper cutting (Fig 3.2). The photograph is inscribed in ink, 'Aug 3 1913'. The newspaper cutting reads:

> FARRER. – To the unfading memory of Reginald John
> Farrer, who passed into the Great Beyond, Oct.
> 16th, 1920.
> I shall remember while the light lasts, and when
> it is dark I shall not forget.   – Alice.

Underneath is pencilled the date '1921'. Terry had accompanied Farrer on a trip to the European alps in 1913.[19] And, as a final testimony that Farrer's friendship was valued, a group of affectionate letters from Farrer has very recently (September 2017) come to light addressed to Celia Noble. Their friendship had begun by 1914, at least, as she is mentioned in his Will of that year. Among many other things, one letter testifies to Farrer's advanced tastes in visual art. In it he tells Noble that he owns a work by C. W. R. Nevinson, and another by Henri Gaudier-Brzeska.[20]

In January 1914 the mercurial Farrer's 'merry soul' and sometimes trying personality had found his ideal travelling companion in William ('Bill') Purdom (1880–1921). Farrer had decided he wanted to go further afield than France and Italy in search of alpine plants. Purdom, a skilled plant collector working up from much humbler social beginnings than Farrer's, had already been in China finding plants for the nursery firm of Veitch for Sargent of the Arnold Arboretum in Boston, Massachusetts. He spoke Chinese. He recommended the extreme west of China, in Gansu, and the adjacent parts of Tibet, as potentially fertile ground for undiscovered alpines, and he evidently loved China, as he agreed to accompany Farrer in exchange for expenses alone.[21] The subsequent expedition the two made, with a small group of Chinese and Tibetan servants, provided the basis for Farrer's other major literary works in the genre of travel-writing, *On the Eaves of the World* (1917) and the posthumous *The Rainbow Bridge* (1921), which will be discussed in later chapters. Farrer dedicated both works to Purdom: 'through whom alone it was that these odysseys were made possible'. This was not an exaggeration.

The life of a plant collector in the hundred years or so before Farrer's expedition to China and Tibet could be very hazardous. The death of David Douglas in 1834 was the most spectacular: he fell into a buffalo trap (a camouflaged pit in the ground) in Hawaii, and a buffalo fell on top of him (though there is still doubt

FIG. 3.2. 'I shall remember': Inside front cover of Alice Terry's extra-illustrated copy of
Farrer's *Among the Hills*. (Royal Horticultural Society Library. Hereafter RHS).

about whether he might have been pushed).[22] Robert Fortune, to get his Chinese junk that was loaded with plants and seeds out of China in 1845, and armed only with a shotgun, had to fight off three attacks by Chinese pirate vessels. Richard Spruce in South America survived serious illness and several night-long vigils over loaded guns in expectation of attacks by thieves to die quietly at home in Coneysthorpe, Yorkshire, in 1892. Even in the early twentieth century dangers persisted: in 1910 Ernest Wilson, in China, was hit by a rock-fall, sustained a badly broken leg, refused to have it amputated and ended up with it becoming shorter than the other. George Forrest needed guns to brandish and fire when he blundered into fighting between Tibetans and Chinese in 1905. He was the last European to see the unfortunate Roman Catholic missionary, father Dubarnard, alive. Without Purdom, and if he had gone unarmed, Farrer would have been in serious danger in 1914–15. As it was, the expedition ran into real dangers, but with luck and bravado its participants survived.

Farrer travelled out to China — and returned two years later — along the Trans-Siberian Railway via Petrograd (St. Petersburg). The journey from London to Shanghai occupied thirteen days. Farrer's 1st Class ticket cost £45 7s 11d.[23] I will consider Farrer's published account of the expedition in chapters 7 and 10.

At expedition's end, in December 1915, Purdom decided to stay in China, where he eventually found work in the Forestry Department of the Chinese State Railways. Farrer returned home: to a vastly changed nation. Already, in late summer 1915, he had received a letter from 'a foolish female cousin' of his friend Collier's, accusing him of 'shirking' service in the Great War that had broken out in August, 1914, and demanding that he come home![24] First he had to get home: returning via Petrograd, where he visited the Herbarium,[25] and overland across Finland and Sweden to Bergen in Norway; thence over the mine-infested North Sea to Newcastle was no easy thing.[26] He wrote a note on paper from the Regina Hotel, Petrograd, as late as the 1st May 1916, expecting to return, via Sweden, by 9–10 May.[27] He seems to have gone first to Ingleborough Hall, from where he writes to his mother about being struck by 'the *smallness* of everything, — the country, the house, the hills, the whole scene.'[28] He thanks his mother for: 'the cheque & letter of cheer. I needed the one as much as the other, for I did not anticipate the horrible depression [...] which attends one's striking back'. The most depressing thing is foreseeing the destruction of 'incalculable multitudes of Chinese treasures' (i.e. plants), 'for lack of hands to tend them, or purses to afford them!' The letter can only be dated by virtue of Farrer stating 'the daffs are beginning to be over & the garden generally is in the transition stage between Spring & summer.' As he was in London by at least 19th May, this puts him at Ingleborough in the middle of the month.[29]

Farrer was thus dropped back into a nation nearing the end of its second year of war; and war on a larger scale than anything before experienced. There are signs that he was confused about the state of the country, so different from when he left in January 1914. The case of *Primula woodwardii* is an example. In March 1915 Mary Woodward of Arley Castle, Bewdley, had written to Professor Bayley Balfour, Director of the Royal Botanic Garden in Edinburgh an appreciative comment about Farrer: 'Mr. Farrer's notes are most graphic and make the plants almost alive before one already.' Balfour wrote back, 'Yes, Mr. Farrer does give you a picture of his plants. He has a wonderful gift in that way.'[30] Mary Woodward's husband also sent to Balfour, who was a personal friend, an account of their son's death at the Battle of Loos:

> He was struck by a shrapnel bullet in the right elbow in the morning which rendered his arm useless, so that he could carry no weapon. It was a veritable death trap. The German trenches had not been levelled or the barbed wire destroyed by high explosive. The concreted trenches were held by the Prussian guard. The whole area was swept by machine gun fire. The dear boy fell within a few yards of the German lines at the head of his platoon.[31]

In July 1916 Farrer had begun to talk about one of his new flower introductions by the name 'Primula blattea' but finds that it has been named by the Royal Botanic Garden *Primula woodwardii* in commemoration of the dead Captain Woodward. 'Cannot such deplorableness be avoided?' he writes to Balfour. 'Anyway, poor Woodward never so much as saw the plant I gather, except as from seed sent home. [It makes] *me* look a fool, with my P. 'blattea'. — Can't you strangle 'Woodwardii' secretly in its cradle?'[32] This is insensitive, to say the least: not only because Woodward had given financial support to Farrer's expedition, was a victim of the war, and his parents friends of Balfour, but also because it would have been Balfour who had decided the name. Moreover, Balfour's only son had been killed at Gallipoli in June, 1915. Farrer's attitude suggests that he cannot quite gauge yet the changed circumstances in the country that he'd left two and a half years before. Balfour wrote back with admirable efficiency: 'Of course it is open to you to name your plant P. BLATTEA and to maintain it is different from P. WOODWARDII'.[33] Balfour knew, of course, that for Farrer to do so would be to reveal himself as an insensitive fool. He therefore brushes Farrer off without having to show himself in any other way angered. Farrer replied apologetically.[34]

Balfour had in fact tried to warn Farrer about the changed situation. He had written to him in February 1915 about manpower shortage, especially in gardens:

> We are for the time on our beam-ends so far as gardening is concerned. Every one of my gardeners who is sound has joined the colours. One, I am sorry to say, has been killed — another permanently maimed — and several wounded [...] No less than sixty went from here [...] However nothing matters here but the war. A temporary set-back to our gardening efforts is nothing to the saving of our race from suppression — for that is the inwardness of the whole business.[35]

All of Farrer's great homecomings to Britain were thus vexed. The heroic young traveller from Japan, hiring a train to get home to Ingleborough to be met with indifference;[36] the Buddhist returning from Ceylon to a reception of 'subdued polar shivering' from his family, in Osbert Sitwell's phrase;[37] and now the return after a memorably successful trip collecting plants in the heart of Asia, only to find that many of his plants would have to be burned for want of care and a market for them. Returns were a lot more unsatisfactory than departures, but it was the being away that gave the real pleasure. May 1916, by which time we are certain that Farrer had returned, saw the Battle of Jutland, and the Military Service Act (conscription). His return in 1916 was to grimness, subdued pessimism, financial depression in the nursery trade, effort, work.

What, in wartime, should Farrer do, aside from lamenting the bottom falling out of the nurseryman's business? He no doubt felt that he had to repay for his life of privilege by helping in the war effort. He certainly replied explosively to a suggestion of his mother's, as his reply to her letter survives: 'You say it's "Christlike"(!!) to do nothing! *Faugh!*'[38] Various recent writers assert that Farrer was found unfit to be a soldier,[39] but his Certificate of Exemption under the Military Service Act 1916, states his occupation as 'Civil Servant', exempted from active service by the Foreign Office conditional on 'remaining in his present employment' as 'engaged on work of national importance.'[40] He had joined the Foreign Office by June (having political contacts even as high up as the Prime Minister, Herbert Asquith, whose son Raymond, a friend of Farrer, was about to be killed in the Battle of the Somme).[41] From there, as a talented travel-writer and novelist, he was seconded to the Department of Information, a boiler-house of propaganda, and worked for some of the time at least as secretary for its chief, the novelist John Buchan.[42] As Farrer had never worked for anybody in his life, we might surmise that he was not the most efficient employee Buchan ever had. But there is little documentary evidence of Farrer's life in 1916. He probably felt most himself when giving a lecture to the Royal Geographical Society on 20 November, which described the first year of Asian travels (1914). He gave a second, to the same society, on 11 March 1918, describing the second year of the expedition. The invader of Tibet in 1904, Sir Francis Younghusband, attended, and this was an acquaintance that, as we shall see, Farrer valued.

Having begun to learn to paint before 1914, in April 1917 Farrer had a solo exhibition of 101 of his water-colour paintings from the China-Tibet expedition staged by the Fine Art Society in its Bond Street gallery. In July of the same year his essay on the works of Jane Austen was printed in *The Quarterly Review*, and in August he had leave from the Department for his abdominal operation. September found him at Ingleborough Hall, presumably convalescing. Later in September and throughout October he was sent round the Western Fronts — the British, French and Italian fronts. From November 1917 to January 1918 he was on leave at Ingleborough Hall writing up the experience for what became his book *The Void of War*, his principal published contribution to the propaganda effort.[43] Also in October 1917, *On the Eaves of the World* appeared in two volumes, dealing with the first year's expedition in China and Tibet.

We know a little of Farrer's activities in 1918. In January he was sent to G.H.Q. (General Headquarters) in France, and led tours of visitors until the second week of March.[44] In March, as mentioned above, he was in London lecturing to the R.G.S. His note of 20th April to Aubrey Herbert describes him 'doing Secretary (inter alia et alias) for John Buchan' and thus in London, where he lodged with Jim Baird at 37 Queen's Gate — a household that had a profound and liberating effect on

Farrer.[45] And some time during the early spring he met his cousin Osbert Sitwell in Bath.[46] Whatever else he did during the summer of 1918, he found time to write *The Rainbow Bridge*.

Yet there was a deeper malaise: not emanating from Farrer, but in the nation. Most of the recent interest in the Great War focusses, understandably enough, on the fighting fronts, from Belgium to the Pripet Marshes to Gallipoli and Jerusalem in a great geographical triangle (while not forgetting Africa and the Mesopotamian campaign). But there were great difficulties on the home front, in England. Richard Aldington, the trench war veteran, poet and novelist, in his book *Death of a Hero* (1929), writes of 'the sinister degradation of English life in the last two years of the War.'[47] He recommends the twelfth chapter of D. H. Lawrence's novel *Kangaroo* (1923) as the best rendering of this. In Lawrence's novel, the protagonist, Richard Somers (a figure strongly reflecting Lawrence's own experience), remembers:

> in England, during the later years of the War, a true and deadly fear of the criminal *living* spirit which arose in all the stay-at-home bullies who governed the country during those years. From 1916 to 1919 a wave of criminal lust rose and possessed England, there was a reign of terror [...] the fear of the criminal public and the criminal government. The torture was steadily applied, during those years after Asquith fell, to break the independent soul in any man who would not hunt with the criminal mob. A man must identify himself with the criminal mob, sink his sense of truth, of justice, and of human honour, and bay like a horrible unclean hound.[48]

A little later, Somers remembers, 'When the Asquith government so softly foundered, he began to suffer agonies. But when the Asquith government went right under, and in its place came the *John Bull* government of '16, '17, '18, then agonies gave way to tortures.'[49] Lawrence characterizes the spirit of the time with Horatio Bottomley's bellicose periodical *John Bull*.

The entire passage therefore represents the spirit of the nation that Farrer walked back into from Asia in 1916. Intolerant bellicosity accompanied by the demand that everyone in the nation should share it, with suspicion and hostility against anyone who did not fall into line. The death of Raymond Asquith, the end of his father's government in December 1916, and a strangely poisoned atmosphere all affected Farrer too, who associated the atmosphere with a different newspaper rather than *John Bull*. Two years after the meeting in 1918, alluded to above, he wrote to Sitwell (who had served in the Guards) from Burma, reflecting on their wartime experiences:

> War is a wholly beastly irredeemable evil, let it be as defensive, as chivalrous, as all-the-rest-of-the-balls ever preached by the wildest war profiteer: at its very best, it is a doing of unimaginable harm in the theory that a possible good may result. It is fatal, then, in the course of such a crime, to look to right or left, to ponder reason, mercy and justice: the only thing is to make oneself deliberately drunk with the DAILY MAIL, in order to be able to live through the dreadful drunkenness of everybody else. If one stops to think of the utter sham one knows the whole thing to be, everything collapses, and one can't go on [...] No, one must [verb missing] shutters to all thought, admit only the maddening

and deafening clamour of the time [...] To keep stark in hate you have to go on making yourself drunk with it, the state being, fortunately, abnormal. Let no-one say I didn't do *my* little best. But *how* greatly I loathed myself, and life, and everything all the time: It was like going straight forward, desperately, along a tight-rope, over Hell.[50]

In Lawrence's case (and his protagonist Somers's) there was intimidation by hostile fellow-citizens, and harassment by the authorities, including the police. By a genuine heroism Lawrence/Somers did not give in and began to 'bay like a hound'. Farrer, differently placed socially and different psychologically (and unlike Lawrence, with no German wife to attract the suspicion of neighbours and authorities), effectively accuses himself of having given in. He asks, 'What is the use of fighting and raving? The only thing to do for a wise man, is to sit under the wall while the dust storm of mortal folly drives by.'[51] Had he not been a wise man, then, in 1916–1918? It might have been difficult for him to resist war hysteria, not having been able to watch the situation develop inexorably over the first two years of the War, and with close friends, Aubrey Herbert and Raymond Asquith, eager to do their bit in the war. In the same letter, he writes to Sitwell:

> You will be surprised at this outburst of peevishness against the claptrap and slumgullion of the world, when you remember how loyally I clung by just that very slumgullion during the war. But this was not done blindly, but of choice, knowing the claptrap and falsehood for what they were, but finding them the only possible drugs for a delirious disease. You cannot go on doing beastly things without buoying yourself up on beastly thoughts, wicked madnesses to match the madness by which you are driven.

Farrer excuses himself by recourse to the idea of necessity. Yet Lawrence put it differently, writing of: 'the collapse of the proud human spirit at home, the triumph of sordid, rampant, raging meanness.'[52] 'Men lost their heads', he tells us, 'and worse, lost their inward, individual integrity.'[53] Lawrence's protagonist feels alone, refusing to compromise and hanging on to his own soul; Farrer knows that he lost something, but hopes for forgiveness: 'But, out of the fantasmagoric nightmare of hysteria,' he continues to Sitwell, 'you do emerge to me as a possibly real person. [...] Neither of us, praise be, is to be judged and valued, I think, by our distraught selves of 1917–8.'

One other thing Lawrence writes provides some insight into Farrer's predicament: 'it was in 1915 that the old world ended. In the winter of 1915–1916 the spirit of old London collapsed; the city, in some way, perished, perished from being a heart of the world, and became a vortex of broken passions, lusts, hopes, fears, and horrors.'[54] This was just as Farrer was making his way home. From Ingleborough, feeling the 'horrible depression' of coming back, before he had seen London again, he wrote to his mother, 'I shall be quite glad to be back in town, where the chat of people may distract one.'[55] He arrived to find a city very different from the one he had known previously, and with very little time to take stock of his own choices. He elected to work for the war effort: this was to have been expected by his friends; in a sense demanded by his life of privilege. Perhaps not expected by his family, however. Farrer wrote to his mother in 1917: 'You say it's "Christlike"(!!) to do nothing! *Faugh!*'[56] Yet Lawrence has an insight into the compromised nature of work at this stage of the War: 'the industrialism and commercialism of England, with which patriotism and democracy became identified: did not these insult a man and hit him pleasantly across the mouth? How much humiliation had [Somers] suffered, trying to earn his living!'[57]

One of Aldington's points, in his novel, is that the mania and hysteria of the war years simply distilled, concentrated and made overt, tensions within British society of the pre-war period. There is consensus among modernist novelists of the time about this. Wyndham Lewis wrote to Aldington in 1929 about: '19th Century weaknesses and philistinism. (That produced one fair-sized War — who knows, it might produce another one?!)'[58] Ford Madox Ford had already imparted the analysis, on a grand scale, in his four-volume *Parade's End* (1924–1928). As the later novelist, Malcolm Bradbury, saw it, in the first volume, *Some Do Not . . .*, Ford

> establishes the world of 1912 as one of already conflicting and dividing principles, muddled history, colliding forces. Harsh machines contrast with organic life; subjective consciousness with public responsibility; literary interests with official duties; the old aristocracy with the rising mandarin class; sexual desire with moral code. [...] the world is growing increasingly chaotic.[59]

In the following volume, after the fighting has started, Ford also manages to keep his attention on: 'the world at home. Ford is concerned with the debasement of the ruling class, the false motives and selfish impulses, the "swine in the corridors" of Whitehall, the bungled political issue of the Single Command [...] the War [...] as society's purgatory.'[60] In his analysis of Ford's novel, Joseph Wiesenfarth adds that '[Tietjens, Ford's protagonist] learns that the code of gentlemanly manners that governed a supposedly civilized society has no place in a confrontation with death. Rather than a cure for savagery, such a code is the cause of it: "Middle Class Morality? A pretty gory carnival that had been for the last four years!"'[61]

Pre-war society, then, was riddled with contradictions, weaknesses, prejudices, overbearing class oppression, hypocrisies, ignorance, and barely suppressed violence that helped to cause the war and then exploded into the open in the war's last three years. Lacking Aldington's olympian vision (itself in part owed to a ten years' perspective, his novel not being written until 1928–1929), Farrer becomes a partial victim of these forces and tensions, rather than a dispassionate panoramic observer. But one of the points of my biographical sketch so far has been to show moments when Farrer called his society into question, and acted to escape or evade some of its apparatus. He had become a Buddhist. He had insisted on trying to make a living in accordance with his own values, rather than passively accepting the value-system of a corrupted civilisation. And he maintained and developed his early love of alpine plants as an alternative world exemplifying beauty in life and the heroism of survival despite harsh surroundings. Nevertheless, working in the propaganda unit named the Department of Information in 1917–1918 he was at one of the centres of dissemination of the lies, cant and intolerance condemned by the modernist writers.

8887.

FIG. 3.3. Lilian Snelling, *Viburnum farreri* (RHS Library).

Two compensations, at least, for Farrer emerge from these war years. There was the slow acceptance and celebration of many of his plant introductions, once the reduced staff of Edinburgh's Royal Botanic Garden had succeeded in raising and studying them. The other was the garden at Ingleborough Hall. In Edinburgh, Bayley Balfour and his staff were going through the process of confirming and naming the plants from the Farrer-Purdom expedition. Arguably Farrer's most successful plant introductions are three. *Viburnum farreri*, (often, but incorrectly, known as *Viburnum fragrans*) is a woody shrub that produces delicate pink flowers during the winter months on its bare stems (usually in very early spring; Figure 3.3). The flowers are beautifully scented, and for many gardeners the appearance of them holds promise of the more extensive pleasures of the summer to come. *Gentiana farreri*, a low-growing azure blue trumpet-shaped flower, was described by Balfour in a letter to Farrer as 'the Queen of the lot' (of blooming gentians); and he enthused (perhaps with the recent exchange about *P. woodwardii* in mind): 'One could wish for no better memorial than association of one's name with such a plant.'[62] Indeed, this sort of memorial Farrer recognized as enduring fame. For a short-lived period it looked as if he might have discovered a new genus, *Farreri*.[63] Farrer was careful to suggest that Purdom's name should be attached to some of the introductions, as a distinguished thanks and recognition of his part in the expedition. As early as 13 December 1914 Farrer wrote to Balfour from Lanchow, 'your very welcome letter of July 27 [...] arrived a week ago [...] [Purdom] 'is now among the many thousands beggared by this awful war! He is a propagator and a cultivator second to none, but above all a man of character and pleasantness impossible to overpraise.'[64] Balfour replied on 24 February: 'No. F 14' (this was the collecting number for one of the plants, including groups of seeds, sent back) 'which you suggest is a Leptodermis is really a dwarf Buddleia and we have named it Buddleia Purdomii.' Of a new species of Iris he writes, 'I have told [W. R.] Dykes to call it Purdomii.'[65]

The third of Farrer's more successful introductions is another Buddleia, *Buddleia alternifolia* (Figure 3.4). It has a shaggy habit of growth, yet its honey-smelling flowers grow along its stems and branches, which themselves grow straight, project outwards from the main trunks, and hang down towards the ground in a 'weeping' effect rather akin to a weeping willow. Farrer also introduced a vigorous and popular variety of the more common *Buddleia davidii*, called *Nanhoensis*.

While these official recognitions were taking place, Farrer also found time to undertake gardening at Ingleborough Hall. In his letter to his mother on his immediate return in 1916 he is pleased by the state of the garden, and he spent some time there in 1916 establishing Chinese 'treasures'. In 1917 there are letters from Ingleborough in May and September. He returned there on 8 November for an intense two and a half-month period of planting and of writing *The Void of War*. He must have planted and gardened during the daylight hours and written during the longer periods of darkness. He obtained seeds of various rhododendrons from Balfour, explaining that: 'I want to get each one established with my own hands in some chosen crevice or ledge of the Chinese Ghyll, which is really by degrees promising to become rather wonderful and beautiful'.[66] The Chinese Ghyll was evidently the gorge, or gully, of the Clapdale Beck upstream from the head of the

FIG. 3.4. *Buddleia alternifolia.*

lake (immediately to the head of the lake is the 'Black Ark', which is thus part of the Chinese Ghyll. The Ghyll extends north of the Black Ark for several hundred yards along the valley). Reaching each 'chosen crevice or ledge' is no easy task in this rugged site. Farrer's activity there lasted until early January, when he had to report back to the Foreign Office.[67] So the garden, and the plants, kept him going during 1916–1919; and now a new expedition took shape.

After the operation on his 'inside' of late December 1918, Farrer was also at Ingleborough in January 1919, on his way to Glasgow for embarkation on the S. S. Henzada to Rangoon in Burma (departure 31 January; arrival 18 March; £62 10s; Room 15, Berth 3).[68] He wrote to his mother on 20th that he was: 'particularly pleased with the massed banks of Potentilla and honeysuckle, though G[eorge] R[edman] has put the birches along by the lake in much too much of a line.' He exhorts mother not to do anything 'extreme' while he's gone.[69]

The trip to Burma was his only foreign expedition about which Farrer did not write an account that was published in book form. We are therefore presented with a completely different historiographical situation. For published sources, we must rely on Farrer's contributions to the *Gardeners' Chronicle*, and the books of E. H. M. Cox: particularly *Farrer's Last Journey: Upper Burma, 1919–20: Together with a complete list of all Rhododendrons collected by Farrer, and his field notes* (1926); but also

The Plant Introductions of Reginald Farrer (1930) and *Plant-hunting in China: a history of botanical exploration in China and the Tibetan Marches* (1945). Understandably enough, Cox's approach concentrates on the plants, and delivers a plain account of routes, timetables and finds. Farrer's own bulletins from the field are almost entirely about plants, and devoid of the anecdotal account of adventures that (as we shall see in a later chapter) distinguishes the published accounts of his earlier Chinese and Tibetan travels. So far as the archival sources are concerned, known sources before 2008 included some letters by Farrer to family, to Balfour, and to various friends, and Cox's diary kept until he left the expedition in January 1920.[70] Then, in 2008, the Royal Botanic Garden Edinburgh bought thirteen letters written by Farrer between May 1919 and September 1920 to his close friend Ernest Gye of the Foreign Office. These letters completely revise our view of the expedition, especially in its second year after Cox's departure. They are also enormously revealing about Farrer in general, and are written with a freedom and a delight that do not emanate as clearly from letters to any other correspondent. Without these thirteen letters our view of Farrer would be very significantly impoverished.

Farrer's Burma expedition has been described as an 'ill-conceived trip, generated by despair and shaped by compromise', with an implication that it was hastily planned.[71] Yet as early as May 1917 Farrer was corresponding with Balfour about a likely place for his next expedition. Balfour recommended Putao, 'our frontier station in Burma' as a base, and this is indeed the suggestion that was accepted.[72] Farrer planned to set off as soon as the War ended; the only question was, when would the end occur? Even on this question, Farrer's contacts at the Foreign Office would have meant that he had some advance notice of the likely date, so he could obtain his ticket, his permission to travel, and arrange funding for the expedition. The remaining question was who would accompany him? He hoped for Purdom again. Purdom's sister, Nell, had written from China in April 1918 saying that Bill continued there bored to death with nothing to do. For whatever reason, however, Purdom didn't join the Burma expedition. He seems to have loved China more than he did Farrer, and so was unwilling to leave.

So the only really hasty thing about the arrangements for the Burma expedition was the choice of Cox as companion. Cox was young; had met Farrer at the Foreign Office;[73] visited him as he was recovering from the abdominal operation, and agreed to go when Farrer suggested it. So Farrer set off for a very remote location immediately after the third operation on his intestines, when he must have known that the condition was chronic and trouble would inevitably happen again. This was an act of courage and of defiance of his physical disabilities. It was undertaken not out of nihilism but from a feeling of urgency. He wanted to live.

Far northern Burma was the area; undiscovered plants the goal. In a revealing letter to Aubrey Herbert two days before departure, Farrer complains about the rumoured climate (which was to prove much worse in the expedition's second year), and writes: 'anyhow, it'll be out of England: which, after all these years of strain and stress (now, in their cessation, just beginning to be realized) is the one thing psychically necessary for all of us. I start [...] on Friday, rather appalled at the vastness and difficulty of my new mission.' He laments that Purdom won't be with him, and adds that John Buchan thinks Farrer's *The Void of War* to be 'the finest thing yet written on that dismal subject [...] for all the balls and bunkum of its hyperbole.'[74]

In their chosen collecting area, human habitations were sparse, the jungle was thick, the going was extraordinarily slow, alpine plants were few, and rhododendrons relatively plentiful. The British authorities seconded two Gurkha soldiers from the Burma Rifles to look after the expedition, and some servants were picked up. Farrer writes in May 1919: 'Jumps [Cox] now presides in the kitchen. The fact is that the cook, being embottled, fell over a cliff and bust himself.' The same letter alludes to gay goings-on in camp between Farrer's 'younger Gurkha' and 'a boy'. 'The camp suggests an Abbey of Theleme', which Farrer doesn't seem to mind, and he's rather regretful about having to stop the goings-on by sending the boy away. He signs the letter, 'yr. loving Poppet', and adds a P.S.: 'The busted cook is better and back at work, though I am still cold to him. Never, in my wildest moments did *I* fall off a khud, were the bottell never so red.'[75]

This letter is to Ernest Gye.[76] Obviously, there is a completely different feeling suffusing it than in other letters by Farrer that we have already considered. This new sense is not confined to the happiness that is such a marked feature of it; Ernest Gye allowed a different part of Farrer to come out plainly onto the page: funny, witty, tolerant, self-deprecating and remarkably camp. Close friendship with Gye was one of the great benefits that the War happened to provide to Farrer. Gye allowed Farrer to reveal himself. At the end of July Farrer wrote,

> our frayed nerves have been enjoying a ten days rest here, after the unspeakable trials of a ten days trek down-country after a hypothetical Rhodo[dendron], during all which time it rained with passionate persistence. There are few things more conducive to modesty and moral stock-takings of the gloomiest description than to lie kept awake for hours through the black dark by the adamantine roar of the rain on a thatched roof overhead. I conceived the liveliest conviction of my sins. Two o'clock of a blind wet morning is just the moment to make one realise how old and cross and crusted one is getting, how unjustified in life, how congealed in sterile egoisms, what an unprofitable bit of jetsam rudderless on the chaos of existence. And all for the lack of some fleshy female and a brace of prattling babes to anchor and steady one with a sense of responsibility not purely for oneself alone. Tiresome, in fact, though the cure be, I have moments of believing the disease worse, and that for our age and temper, wedlock is the only thing to keep our minds and morals sweet [...] Rest, however, and Easton's syrup, have mitigated the extremity of my views and I am once more in modified charity with myself, Jumps and all the world. Send me out Cleopatra herself in a carpet and I would send her packing.[77]

Emotionally alone. Marriage. A tiresome solution. He would send even Cleopatra away. The implication seems clear; the thoughts induced by the elemental simplicity of conditions. However, the whole season wasn't rain and ruefulness. In early September they are back at camp in 'Hpimaw Fort' after

> a month of really wonderful camp-life, up in a high-alpine valley, in a beautiful open glade filled with golden anemones beside a babbling beck, with gaunt hungry-looking granite peaks aspiring overhead all round. It was a glorious

place, and I brought up the bag of Rhode's to 45: we go back in October for their seeds. The weather was amazingly kind, too, and has pointed its kindliness by raining passionately ever since we got back here.

Equally, though, it wasn't all sunshine and flowers. This is the letter that complains sarcastically about Cox writing a novel and a sonnet. The letter continues with meditations on the time of war:

> I suppose the anguish of coming out of a long nightmare is as bitter as revival from drowning. Reaction, release from the cohesive force of a common strain — it must all be dreadful, and as I long ago foresaw, much worse than the actual war, and with nothing to show for it either [...] It is very curious and interesting, from whole batches of letters, to get a uniform impression of utter fatigue, of the fatigue so acute that it can't find rest, of disappointment, old age, and general failure. Goodness knows what about, though: surely the Peace can't be called a bad bargain, by the most Osbertian pessimist.[78]

Farrer registers one of the most important and pervading feelings of the period: war-strain and war-fatigue; the feeling of futility and hopelessness that the war left. Three weeks later comes the letter (already quoted) in which Farrer reflects on himself: 'I really do live in the past and the absent more vividly perhaps than most people (is it not, in fact, a diagnostic mark of the Harlot?)' He says that Cox has told him that Deputy Commissioners (agents of Empire) are in 'a state of salutory terror' of Farrer — though heaven knows why, for 'a milder-nachered woman never breathed.'[79] This theatrical assumption of mock-innocence, based on the Dickensian character, Mrs. Gamp, is at odds with Cox's diary, which characterizes Farrer as 'querulous and abusive', as well as 'noisy and absurd', and says of dealing with the Deputy Commissioners that Farrer has 'an extraordinary bad way with him & frequently ignores the most obvious civilities [...] Everything is taken for granted & all done for us is his due, not act of kindness.'[80] No doubt in Farrer's view there was no 'kindness' but simply fulfillment of the duties of the Commissioner's job. What Cox, thirteen years younger than Farrer, and from a family in trade, might have seen and misunderstood in the latter's behaviour, were unreformed Victorian and Edwardian attitudes to class, in which officials were government workers and public servants who by definition belonged to a different social stratum than elder sons of landowners.

Farrer's letter continued with the news that Frank Kingdon Ward, 'a rival botanist from off an adjacent peak' had visited them: 'a queer little wild-eyed bird with a face like a haggard nut.' In fact Balfour had ensured that not only Farrer and Kingdon Ward but also the collector George Forrest were all working in adjacent parts of the Burma-China border close up against Tibet and Assam. He no doubt knew that Forrest and Kingdon Ward were collecting for science (so that every unknown plant was of interest) while Farrer would only bother with plants that held the promise of being good garden flowers or shrubs.

The same letter states that 'the Watsons' are firmly in possession of Ingleborough, and refers to the need to return to the previous Burmese site to collect the rhododendron seed: 'of these [treasures] I have already told you the gorgeous tale, and besides, for a dispenditure of sixpence, you can follow this fuller account in the Gardeners' Chronicle, unfolded in the Master's happiest vein of racy prattle, to the weekly Enthralment, I am told, of thousands.'

Some of the happiness that comes through in the letters to Gye is no doubt attributable to Farrer having put the Europe of the war years away from him. A letter to Aubrey Herbert emphasizes the literal truth of this in geographical terms: 'There's no post, no mails, no white man within a month's journey, nothing whatever to remind me of that distressful insane world of the West.'[81] Another letter to Herbert shows the same distancing in psychological terms, primarily through a reference to *The Void of War*. In January 1919 Farrer had still wished to impress him with Buchan's praise of the book. Now his attitude has changed: 'I'm glad you've done a war book', he writes to Herbert: 'Send it to me. And I'm glad you liked mine. It was but a poor thing and nobody read it.'[82]

The last letter to Gye before the return to civilisation in the autumn of 1919 muses on some non-threatening but unexpected hardships of the expedition:

> The landscape [of Hpimaw Fort] departs from art. It is too absolutely lacking in human interest or emotional appeal of any sort. The colours, of course, are beyond words. I couldn't make much even out of colour, unless some interest were also aroused. [The point is in the contrast with China]: China gave me odds and ends of buildings, temples, etc., to stimulate and appeal.

The letter then turns to his health:

> Very odd and unexpected . . wherever I have cut or scratched myself (as one is for ever doing) my sumptuous flesh, instead of promptly healing as its habit is, has developed large and perpetually pussiferous sores till now I'm a perfect Lazarus, my lovely legs like a professional beggar's. The worst of all was a maladroit attempt at violation by a bamboo, which has produced, on the apex of my (now) most prominent beauty, a gangrene that for weeks has impaired the majesty of my démarche and impeded the pleasure of sitting.[83]

Farrer the clown survived. Conditions may have been strange, but were not impossible. The ability to laugh at himself helps. Of aesthetic potential in his present location, the picturesque of China remains the ideal, valued over the more abstract picturesque (even non-figurational) of Burma.

The collectors came out of the mountains for the winter months, and with a return to civilisation the pace of life changed. In a letter of 23 December, the 'loving Poppet' who signs the letters writes that he has bought Gye 'a pair of very ample pantalettes of glacé silk [...] in incredibly sumptuous shades of opalescent rose and azure', which, he assures Gye, will cause envy at Queen's Gate. He adds a racy detail about his latest activity: 'I got off with a soldier-man this morning who seems to like coming with me, and like being a pleasure if he does.'[84] To 'get off with' (almost always used, as here, in the past tense) means to come to an arrangement with somebody about sexual activity; and to engage in sexual activity. There is also an obvious sexual pun in Farrer's use of the word 'coming'. On the face of it, this is evidence of Farrer's sexual activity. This was in Rangoon, where Kingdon Ward was spending Christmas with Cox and Farrer. Cox witnessed a heated row between Farrer and Kingdon Ward on Boxing Day. 'If I had been K-W' he told his diary, 'I would have hit him.'[85] We have already noted earlier one of Cox's pugilistic fantasies.

Eventually, Cox and Kingdon Ward left. Whatever the truth of the argument, the latter wrote later that Farrer was: 'a gifted talker, deeply read and widely travelled. The writer looks back on the days spent in his company in Burma as one of the most delightful of episodes.'[86] After they left, Farrer moved to a rented bungalow (The Oaks) in Maymyo, to spend two months 3000 feet above the 'grilling plain of Burma.'[87] He made a detour to the Arakan Pagoda in Mandalay, where he was able to view and handle a most precious relic. This was an 'oval crystal reliquary' bound with gold that contained some of the Buddha Sakyamuni's ashes. The relics came, Farrer reports, from the ruins of the 'Golden Pagoda in which Kanishka the Emperor enshrined them nearly two thousand years ago, in a Greek wrought casket of bronze.'[88] The site had been excavated in 1909–1910. For Farrer, this was: 'the one first-class relic in the world, of whose authenticity there cannot be a shadow of a doubt.' Cox had noticed that, as they journeyed through Burma, Farrer would 'whisper to himself and his lips would move for hours on end' and he assumed that Farrer was creating literature by doing so: 'he imagined conversations or concocted themes'.[89] Certainly Farrer worked (largely in 1920) at two books of fiction. As a Buddhist, however, whispering to himself he could well have been reciting Buddhist prayers.

By the end of February, preparing to go into the field again, Farrer reflects briefly to Gye on his own feelings about Cox leaving the expedition: feelings that are quickly dismissed to make way for more interesting thoughts: 'I felt quite sad and solitary; nor have my streetwalkings proved either persevering or productive, though the flesh has been most willing. A little man in the soldiers' band has smiled upon me, and that is the limit of my successes.'[90] Clearly feelings of sadness and solitariness are being linked to his failure to pick up men. There was also the problem of companionship on the expedition. A young man Farrer terms 'the beautiful boy' (Derick Milner) was supposed to replace Cox, but changed his mind.[91] Farrer writes with cross philosophy, 'sluts, unless they are ladies, are always apt to be nuisances.'

Then there was the problem of sheer geographical remoteness. The prospect of being alone (that is, without British or European companionship) in the back of beyond: 'challenges all the courage and cheerfulness that I've got. I almost wonder if there are points in our Poppet which do not wholly or invariably deserve the profound contempt that you and I so unstintingly apply!'[92] Farrer described the Burmese jungle as 'a vast palm-house, blind and dark and frightening and deadly silent.'[93]

With respect to the situation Farrer found himself in at the beginning of 1920, Nicola Shulman raises the question, why did Farrer not return home? She says that the letter to Herbert from about this time answers the question. Farrer writes:

> I can't very well go on living at Ingleborough while the Family rule and I
> haven't means or wish to live anywhere else in England [...] I do not see that I

can do better than make plant-collecting my business in life [...] I propose to be out here another year and then come back to England via Peking, early in 1921.[94]

Unlike Shulman, I can't see this letter as an expression of Farrer's fate being determined, as expressing a sense of him having nowhere else to go but the Burmese jungle. While he acknowledges lack of 'means', the emphasis should be on 'wish'; he didn't want to return; he makes the choice of plant-collecting (in his beloved Asia) as an act of free will over the determinism that Shulman applies when she asks, 'Why didn't he go home? [when Cox left]. Every fresh development urged it. He must have known [...] that most of the plants from the area would be unsuitable for cultivation in England. He could have [...] returned without dishonour.'[95] Her view sees a greater determinism (having nowhere else to go) beating the deterministic factors that indicated a return home. Yet Farrer had plenty of Asia still to discover, and as we shall see, a little later started to lay plans to get to Nepal or Tibet. To remain a plant-collector was a choice of free will, and Farrer himself wrote that: 'I can [...] be only thankful for the miraculous mercy that turns ones greatest pleasure in living into a possible livelihood.'[96] He re-dedicates himself to the lessons of pleasure learned as a boy on the slopes of Ingleborough. Farrer himself stated that he was happier in the second year of the expedition than the first, because free of Cox's depressing company:

> all my feathers are once more lying down comfortably, and I am enjoying this season, by myself, already a thousand times more than last year's, with dear good excellent Jumps, who had no joy, and who 'could not meet me in conversation, either serious or playful'.[97]

The new situation left Farrer in sole charge of the logistics. From Edinburgh, Balfour was obviously badgering him to get a move on. Farrer wrote back telling him to stop writing: 'as if it were only original sin on my part that debars me from going North. In fact I *am* doing so, as far as I can get. Only not even a Botanical explorer [...] is exempt from the human frailty of requiring food.'[98] As Shulman summarizes the exchange of letters,

> [Farrer] implored [Balfour], and his deputy, [William Wright] Smith, to scratch him up some more financial support. He expected considerable expense over the next year: the range of mountains he had in mind, about 120 miles north of Hpimaw, was a twelve-week journey, there and back, away from any possible base. He would need forty mules to carry "every atom of food, for me and all the staff, for the whole season". Unless more money came, he warned them, his position threatened to become quite unpleasant.[99]

Most of the plants Farrer collected and sent back from Burma came from a range of altitude from 11,000 to 13,000 feet. The mountains were high, slopes were very steep and covered in jungle, people were few, paths fewer, settlements capable of providing the comforts of a base — forts, frontier stations — very widely scattered. This was extremely difficult terrain.

Letters to Gye from this winter express Farrer's admiration for Somerset Maugham's novel, *The Moon and Sixpence*, which Farrer recognizes as 'essentially a biography of Gauguin'.[100] Quite apart from its literary quality, Farrer needed the encouragement of its plot about an uncompromising Englishman who leaves European civilisation to live with the natives in a remote and much simpler place: a place more primitive, in a non-pejorative sense. In his letter to Osbert Sitwell, Farrer wrote: 'I hate lies and humbug, journalism, Christianity, domesticity, dullness and European civilisation in general, with a fury that, if I let it, makes me feel quite ill.'[101] Maugham's novel, appearing in 1919, exemplifies a post-War fantasy of abandoning a corrupted and lethal civilisation to find a more authentic life living amongst people of a different race. Paul Gauguin's life might have provided the model, but the story was transposed to fictional characters, and the novel is one of a group of British writings published in the period 1918–1920 that reject the values of conventional European civilisation, the culture of the drawing-room (as Ford Madox Ford termed it); of clean respectability and the pursuit of materialism. In favour instead are the characters' attempts to lead more fulfilled lives. Another novel Farrer read that winter, Virginia Woolf's *Night and Day*, shares the same idea. Farrer admired both of Woolf's novels that had been published by that date, stating that *The Voyage Out* has more 'daemonic ebullience' than *Night and Day*.[102] I believe we can understand Farrer's enthusiasm for these three works as more than just a fellow-craftsman's appreciation for technique. A wish, turned into action, to find a way of life better than the one provided by the traditional and pietistic society of the British ruling class that he had been born into (with its prison sentences for the 'crime' of homosexuality, for example) had become for Farrer a two-decades quest. The idea of the rejection of conventional British civilisation in favour of an attempt to discover a way of life both simpler and more fulfilling was not just a literary theme of the time, but a lived experience for quite a large number of people. Farrer lived the last two years of his life at the edge of Empire among the natives of Upper Burma, with Assam to the west, the Himalayas and Tibet to the north-west and north, and China to the north-east and east. He lived through months of monsoon rain collecting plants that seemed likely to make good garden plants in Britain. He wrote, and continued his painting.

Farrer's sense of a new post-war start surfaces in a letter to Gye in which he considers a review by *The Times* of his own book, *The English Rock Garden*, published in two volumes in 1919 but written largely in 1913. This is his botanical monument: the single greatest claim to fame in the area of plant knowledge that he produced, an encyclopedia of entries on thousands of rock plants and alpines. He contemplates it from the perspective of the end of 1919: 'it is now 6 years old, and a mere compilation, and it wears its vast erudition (second hand) with an affectation of jocosity or preciousness that nowadays would make me feel quite sick. [...] the time for harlotries is over.' In this view he agreed with some of his more severe reviewers.[103]

Indeed, the sense of escape (and the necessity to escape) from the Britain of the war years remained strong for Farrer. In a letter dated 4 January 1920 he reports:

> All this year [...] my own brain has increasingly afflicted me with a sense of deliquescence and general fatuous futility exceedingly unpleasant to revolve during the long night-watches with the cast-iron roar of rain ravening overhead.

And I had been pessimistically attributing this to my own personal weakness [...] now, however, you give me hope that I'm merely dreeing the weird of all my kind, in our common reaction from war-strain — with more to bear than ever, yet with nothing new to show for it, and nothing left to do it with. From afar I look on the welter of European life with nothing but miserable nausea. I am frightened almost unbearably by the way in which everything one ever knew has crumbled. Did one ever have a mind, or what one called convictions, I wonder?[104]

'Dreeing the weird' is an interesting phrase. While 'dree' as an adjective in Yorkshire dialect means forlorn or sad, the word as a verb means 'to undergo', as in a long journey of some sort.[105] 'Weird', with obvious connotations of the uncanny and fantastic, in this phrase means 'fate' or 'destiny'. So 'enduring the fate' is a paraphrase. This letter suggests strongly that Farrer faces a test of character in his second year in Burma. Shulman has argued persuasively that he had faced one in the first year of the Burmese expedition — living with Cox and helping him to become a useful botanist — and failed it signally.[106] (And yet Cox did become a more than useful botanist, and like Farrer, a nurseryman). The second year's test was different. Could he endure and flourish in this remotest, most difficult environment without breaking down mentally or emotionally?

The experience with Cox preyed on his mind. We have already noticed the letter of December 1919 in which he reproached himself for his ungenerous and refrigerating treatment of Cox. In May 1920 he wrote to Gye, saying that he was happy because without Cox: 'the ineffable soothing of being without him' is a phrase he uses. 'How persistent a trial had been the company of one who always was a drag, wanting to do *just* a *little* less than was adequate, instead of rather more.' 'Poppet' then describes his own circumstances:

> In a preposterous little shack of bamboo-matting with neither comfort nor convenience [...] here impend upon me magnificently, in ranges of appalling black-granite needles, fantasmagoric dark nightmares, far overhead [...] in ecstasies of bliss I do be [...] let us hope this Arcadian state of things may continue [...] I am gone down to the bedrock of existence unadorned, and there [...] achieve a bare and barbarous glory of contentment.[107]

The letter also contains, however, a warning: 'one's only drawback here is the distance, and length of communication with the nearest outpost, at Kong-lu, 19 days away. It is 9 days, even, to the heliograph.' Remoteness became critical when Farrer sickened and died in October.

In June William Purdom sent a letter from Peking, saying that 'China is, and has been in the most hopeless state of confusion for at least two years [...] the whole country is divided up into little "kingdoms".'[108] This news no doubt reassured Farrer that further travels in China instead of Burma would have been out of the question, and deepened his thankfulness that he and Bill had accomplished their trip when they did. Farrer wrote to Gye, telling him that he has booked a ticket to Peking for 8th January 1921, to enjoy a fortnight in Peking, then 'straight home'. The Cox affair still troubles his conscience: he says that 'this year I am enjoying myself so infinitely more than last' because not responsible for Cox's happiness, which responsibility 'overstrained' him.[109] Farrer's letters to Cox from 1920, preserved by Cox in a beautiful chased leather cover with decorative endpapers, admit this point and Farrer's refrigerating treatment. The overall tone of them is cheerful and optimistic. He encourages Cox in his efforts towards individual self-definition in the teeth of expectations from Cox's parents that he will join the family jute business.[110] To Gye, Farrer adds good financial news: the Royal Geographical Society has bestowed on him their 'Gill Award', which brings £36; royalties from *On The Eaves of the World* bring in another £24. (These figures, while not representing wealth, were the equivalent of ca £6000 of today's hyper-inflated money).[111]

About this time Farrer wrote to Herbert, returning to a theme he had already rehearsed with Ernest Gye, but this time with more decision:

> On one thing I am determined, when I come home, for which I shall earnestly beg the enlightened help of Mary and yourself. For I am resolved, now at last, to do my duty and get wed: find me a fair one, please, not particular about looks; and assist my diffidence in the matter [...] as you know, such hotness as I can muster is always rather in such heart as I've got rather than in my blood [... but] I have now got quite a lot to give, in the way of happiness, if both parties play the game.[112]

He writes that he wants children, though he wishes there were 'more desirable methods of procuring them'. This is all rather surprising. Farrer — short, plump, narrow-shouldered, parrot-voiced, excitable and sometimes difficult, not yet come into his estate, fond of men, on the face of it had little to offer many women, even (for the time being) financially. He needs a woman who is 'not particular about looks' and who will 'play the game'. On the other hand, we should consider the historical circumstances: 800,000 Britons dead in the War, others maimed and mutilated; the death toll among the educated class proportionally as high as among the workers. This situation, together with Farrer's prospect of becoming proprietor of the Ingleborough estate, meant that it was not out of the question that he might have been able to find an obliging woman. With characteristic humour, the letter asserts that:

> Against all evidence, I hope by now that I am a trifle more seasoned and less selfish and silly than I've always been [...] I can't afford to waste any more years in mincing and mewing about and pretending grand passions.[113]

Self-knowledge and insight. It is particularly brilliant for Farrer to have adapted the traditional figure, 'mopping and mowing' — the description of ghouls or ghosts mocking and intimidating their victims — into 'mincing and mewing.' 'Mincing [...] about' is presumptively linked to the activities of campy gay men trying to draw attention to themselves by a particular mode of walking; while Farrer's love of cats — he owned several, with extravagant names such as La Reine de Sarawa and Princess Alice of Siam, and dedicated several of his published works to them, while several times referring to himself via a cat-related metaphor — makes the picture of him 'mewing about' highly pointed and effective, combining the charm and vulnerability of a kitten with a straightforward expression of need.

On a more direct and immediate level, though, he is telling Herbert that he is resolved to abandon his theatrical, histrionic, and hypocritical side. There remain obvious contradictions, however, between the idea of getting a wife and other things that Farrer was telling people he wanted to be and to do, such as continuing as a plant-collector, being in Asia, and avoiding ghastly Great Britain and Europe.

In July, addressing Ernest Gye as 'Esmé', he reports that he has been in a 21 days' 'blind drench' up the mountain: 'Day by day, all else being impossible, I could write a book or paint a flower.' The paints won't dry in the weather, though: 'the paintings had to be cooked at a bon-fire on one side, while they were being sopped with drizzle on the other.'[114] The haunting lesson of Cox is now distanced enough to be generalized: 'I couldn't have got through, though, had I not been alone. One's own discomforts one *can* disregard: to bear up those of somebody else also is too much.' In the end, '*lovely* flowers [...] made all worth while.'[115]

Farrer was in fact writing two books. One was another novel, *The Empty House*, and the other was called *Latter Ends*, case studies of women in literary history. In the next letter to Gye in August, he announces that: 'by this very mail shall the Empty House, in 2 tomes (loot from the Min. of Misinformation)[116] and some pinned sheets, start off towards you in the Foreign Office in a secure parcel.' He instructs the recipient to take the manuscript to 'Misses Beckett and Watts, of 77 Brompton Road [...] a brace of admirable women who have had the immortality of typing for the Master these many years past.' One copy is to go to A. S. Watt, Hastings House, Norfolk Street, Strand. The other copy to be sent to Farrer c/o Alston or Lampson in Peking. Watt is to 'place' the masterpiece. Farrer calculates it will reach Peking on 30th January.[117]

The loss of this, the only novel Farrer wrote in the post-War years, which presumably embodied his changed post-drawing-room attitudes, is a tragedy. In the same letter to Gye he alludes to it as what seems to be a *roman à clef*, with satire of John Buchan, 'Toby, Paddy and Everard, [and] Bottlebeak'. It seems to have been a camp novel. Of Toby, we are told that: 'the description of him powdering his nose at the mirror is a masterpiece of apparently servile appreciation.'[118] Farrer tells Gye that 'the following people' have 'lent features' to the fiction: 'Laban and Bica Schloss, Hereward Wakefield and his brother Minnehaha, Jasper Buckingham, Donwell Bishop and Ma Boozeleigh of St. Bees; Amelia, Rooty Bean, Mercy Bunnell, Primrose Perianth, Arabella Bottlebeak.'[119] Gye himself features in it as 'Lord Esmé Dalbrett [...] the one person who shows even the faintest and most intermittent gleams of pleasantness!'[120] In July he worked on cutting the novel: 'cutting out such masses of wit and wisdom that now I sometimes wonder if I've cut the balls from the body. The thing will probably never pass the agent, or reader or Censor. *Il y a des choses raides*.'[121] The novel grew out of Farrer's experience working at the Foreign Office and lodging with Jim Baird at 37 Queen's Gate, London: 'what a very curious three years it was: I do think it had to be written down, so unlike as it was to anything in the normal course of life. I'm still, perhaps a harlot [...] anyway, out of that astonishing louche world, did I manage to pick a pair of pearls': the pair being Gye and Cox.[122] After all, Farrer wrote of himself, 'In memory, if no longer quite in figure, I am [...] the [...] elephant.'[123] By September Farrer referred to the novel as 'the Empty Bidet', which he hopes will nevertheless slop a few drops on Gye.[124] Perhaps 'The Empty House' reached Gye. Perhaps he sent it on after Farrer's death (its legal status having changed pending probate) to Farrer's executor or parents. Perhaps they preserved it, unpublished, or destroyed it. The catalogue of the Reginald J. Farrer collection at the Royal Botanic Garden Edinburgh lists under 'RJF/2/1 Farrer Family Collection — written material 1880–2004' as Item RJF 2/1/6: 'Box 6 [...] including poem written by Farrer one week before his death "found in the pencil copy of the Empty House" ' which suggests that the manuscript reached Ingleborough Hall.

His fondness for Gye was great: in February he wrote using a nickname: 'Viper [...] I love you very much.'[125] Much of the letter of February 1920 is occupied by offering Gye advice and comfort about his relationship with 'Emily', sometimes known as 'Amelia': 'Her trouble is, that she *just* isn't a gentleman, that she piques herself on fantastic follies, and nourishes the Lie in the Soul.' I think we can take it that here, and elsewhere, female names and pronouns are being applied to men. If Emily had been a woman, the first part of the sentence would not make sense. The letters feature a particular slang: Emily's antagonism for 'Mercy Bunnell' is 'pure chi chi', meaning a lie or falsity; while pleasures are 'pots' and even 'poos' (Tangier, where Gye might be posted, is a 'pot-full' place 'with ampler resources to cope with them').[126]

The August letter to Gye contains the news that Farrer has just come off the mountain Moku-ji: 'I was also a trifle the worse for wear, as the whole party had walked into a bee-pit on the way down, and been most drastically reproved by the bees.' He plans to go up again: 'for two se'nnights [...] on the Chawchi, and then, my dear, for the whole of September I shall just sit here and do nothing whatever any more, except caress my bottom in comfort, until the last whirl of all begins.' This last phrase refers to the seed-collecting stage of the fieldwork (only possible, of course, after the seeds have set) after which the expedition can pack up and go home.

Moku-ji yielded new plants, including *Cotoneaster farreri*; the mountain of Hpawshi Bum supported *Omphalogramma farreri* at 12,300 feet. Hpimaw Pass (10–11,000 feet up) produced *Nomocharis farreri* (figure 3.5 shows one of its offspring, crossed with other species of nomocharis, which exemplifies a further value derived from plant introductions). In the Feng-Shui Ling Valley, which gives the arcadian translation of 'Valley of the Winds and Waters', Farrer found the now extremely rare spruce tree, *Picea farreri*. Then there were the rhododendrons. So the haul of Burmese plants was not bad.

On 13th August the Deputy Commissioner in Putao, J. Barnard, wrote an urgent note ordering Farrer and his party *not* to cross the Chinese frontier into the Salween watershed. It is doubtful whether this letter gained any real purchase on the situation. Farrer's own last letters all date from mid-September. From Nyitadi he wrote to Smith at the Royal Botanic Garden, reporting good health and spirits, sending details of plants, and managing a joke about the dreadful weather: 'I can't make out what's happened: the sun is shining!'[127] His last letter to Ernest Gye

FIG. 3.5. *Nomocharis findlayi,* bred from *N. farreri* and other *Nomocharis.*
Photo: author, 2012.

reflects on art (his own) and landscape:

> Art, alas, has forcedly been in abeyance, except as flowers are concerned. And
> these are bad for it. Anyhow, I almost despair of that loose, free, flowing style in
> which you and [C. J.] Holmes are my idols: but flowers put one absolutely out
> of practise for it, too, requiring, as they do, not niggliness, I hope, but certainly
> an attention to their detail which reacts unfavourably when one comes to aim
> at portraying a mountain in a wash, a splodge, and three splashes. Also, a vast,
> historiless unshadowed country, so crowded with features as to be featureless,
> baffles emotion and the creative impulse [...] But oh, yet again, for the curly
> corner of a Chinese temple, for the blues of China, the gigantic thronged
> atmosphere, the haunting sense of immemorial ages that is always setting one
> in a vibration at every corner of road or street.[128]

It would be pleasant to leave off this sketch of Farrer's biography at this point, with
his paean of love for China. It is conventional in biography, however, to describe
the subject's death. Our account comes from Bhanje Bhanju, Farrer's servant on the
expedition. Death came unexpectedly, quite suddenly and quickly. Farrer became
ill with a cough and pains in the chest in October. Bhanju made a remarkably
athletic dash to Konglu for medicines (a week's journey in three days, Shulman
tells us). His report, via a local scribe, says that on 14 October this 'breafvery and

honesty officer [...] discontinued to take his food except soda water, wiskly and medicines [...] but it has been unsucessful at least and without giving any pain and trouble to us he breathe his last on the morning of 17 October 1920.'[129]

Diphtheria was reported in the area. Or it might have been pneumonia. But it is as likely that his death came from complications associated with Hardikar's Syndrome (which as we saw can include both kidney failure and intestinal obstruction). In the archive in Edinburgh there is a scrap of paper on which someone has written notes in pencil. I believe Farrer's mother Bessie was the writer, and the notes reflect her search through the last few weeks of Farrer's diary for details of his life and clues about his death. In effect the notes are a type of selective, perhaps paraphrased, summary from the diary. There are notes of bundles of plants being sent off; urticaria from shrimp paste at luncheon; and 'Sep 12 Interior still feeling the descent. no remedy.'[130] Farrer wrote to Bessie on the 10th September, 'With the turn of the season one's stomach begins to turn a little also.'[131] It is just possible that these slight notes reflect Farrer becoming aware of problems with his inside that occasioned his death a month later.

The expedition party buried Farrer on a high place at Kwanglangphu or Kwanglanghpi (Figure 3.6). There is in the archive an undated cutting of a letter to a newspaper by J. F. Bowerman, Captain, Burma Military Police, describing clearing the grave of jungle and weeds. 'The grave is on a hill at the junction of the Akyang and 'Nmai Rivers,' he writes, 'a most magnificent view'.[132]

By now I hope I have conveyed the idea that any notion that Farrer cast himself away, drinking himself to death in the dark jungle out of despair, depression and gloom, a semi-suicide, is misguided. His most remarkable letter in September deserves to be quoted at length. It confirms that he was entirely in command of himself and in good spirits, beginning to plan the next expedition. The letter was written to Sir Francis Younghusband, who, when he heard of the death, sent it to Farrer's mother with a covering letter of his own. Farrer's letter, dated from Nyitadi, above Konglu, 'Sino-Burmese Alps' describes himself as Sir Francis's 'protegé' (presumably meaning within the Royal Geographical Society) and says that in 1923:

> I feel I may be ripe for another expedition. Now, could you, and would you, give me your help towards either Nepal or Tibet? I suppose though that an invitation, or a mission to Holy Lhas$a (I don't know how to spell the Holy City!)[133] *would* be quite out of the question, even for one of His Holiness's own flock? In Rangoon I had a long talk with the Venerable Bhikku Silaçara[134] (né Mr. McKechnie, of Hull: and you will agree that the change of name was felicitous): and he told me that not even he, professed religious of the Yellow Robe, would be allowed within sight of Lhas$a. But then, of course, he *is* of the *yellow* Robe and I don't suppose the Three Abbeys would stretch points for *him*:[135] whereas, with times and policies always changing, it *might* be that Authority at home might now be in favour of making *acte de présence* at Lhasa, by means of some unofficial person of quality, who by this time, I hope, has acquired a good reputation as a discreet and not unpopular traveller? My scheme may be wild: but it is not outside the bounds of human possibility, so I thought I would put it to you. The botanical haul would of course be prodigious: but fades into

FIG. 3.6. Farrer, 'The City of Kwanglanghpi', Burma. Watercolour on paper, 22 April, 1920. (Royal Botanic Garden Edinburgh. Hereafter RBGE).

^utter^[136] insignificance, even to me, beside the thought of setting my eyes on the inside of the böring, and the outside of the Potala! But Nepal would be a glorious second-best, and, as I see that you are lending your countenance to an expedition that once more aims at violating Gaurisankar,[137] I have hopes that you might do as much for me. I gather that neither Nepal nor its Maharajah are quite as intransigent about strangers as Lhas$a and His Holiness: nor, I think, would O'Connor, a friendly acquaintance of mine (I believe) be hostile to the scheme. In any case, there are tracts of time before us [...]

Farrer writes that he would go in 1922 if necessary:

to Nepal, certainly, and to Lhasa, probably, my faithful Myitkyina Gurkhas would, I know, be all agog to follow me [there are two, detailed to his service..] out of their poking little Battalion at Myitkyina. For *what* a life is this, of the hills: even in country so uninhabited as this, and so curiously inviolate of history and religion. Lonely, lonely, not so much dead, as never having lived: that is the impression one gets as one stands on one of these peaks and looks out northward, over an uncharted sea of undistinguished mountain ranges, broken only by two or three tremendous peaks, very far away indeed, up in Tibet, or away over East in China. One has two Empires in view, India and China's and the last two great theocracies of the world, Burma and Tibet. Not that the climate often allows so stimulating a prospect! It is, in fact, so foul that though I long to visit every one of these peaks and passes, I never really want to visit the Sino-Burmese Alps again. [... in jungle of 'Malayan' density] I have often given a sigh to the clear air of Siku, the roads, the facilities, the immemorial geniality of China.[138]

The idea of the irrepressible Farrer becoming a diplomat in Lhasa, and Young-husband, the invader of Tibet of 1904, helping to put him there, is an idea as surreal as it is unlikely. A more likely outcome of this initiative, had Farrer lived, might have been his attachment as expedition botanist to one of the mountaineering expeditions to 'violate' Everest that Younghusband helped sponsor in 1921, 1922 and 1924.[139]

★   ★   ★   ★   ★

This has been one way of putting it. A biographical sketch based on what we think we know about Reginald Farrer, who died as long ago as 1920. Most of the evidence comes, in the end, from Farrer himself: his letters to Herbert, his mother, Ernest Gye and others, preserved in English and Scottish archives. This evidence is leavened by testimony from some who knew him.

The rest of this study takes a different approach. It looks at the connections between his milieu, (the society around him, his environment) and the cultural artefacts he left behind: novels and travel-writing; plant introductions; garden design and writing about plants; paintings and photographs. He is recognized as a moderniser in his chosen fields of plant-writing and garden design. Questions that arise are: to what extent was he a moderniser in his other activities? And to what extent was his modernism determined by his Buddhism?

Notes to Chapter 3

1. RBGE, RJF 2/1/2. J. A. Farrer's 'Annual Narrative' gives the surgeon's name as 'Stabb'.
2. RBGE, RJF 1/1/61, letter of 13/8/1917. By 20th August he's had the operation: RJF 1/1/63.
3. RBGE, RJF 1/1, letter of 9/9/1917
4. RBGE, RJF 1/1/1, letter of 23/12/1918 to Prof. Bayley Balfour of the Royal Botanic Garden.
5. J.A. Farrer, 'Annual Narrative' for 1910.
6. Post card to Mrs. Terry, 28/12/1918, Royal Horticultural Society, Lindley Library, FAR Box 1. See also J. A. Farrer's 'Annual Narrative' for 1918.
7. Margaret Fitzherbert, *The Man who was Greenmantle: a biography of Aubrey Herbert* (London: Murray, 1983), p. 100.
8. Ibid., p. 49.
9. Quoted in Shulman, *A Rage for Rock Gardening*, pp. 48–49.
10. Sitwell, *Noble Essences*, pp. 16–18.
11. E. H. M. Cox, *Farrer's Last Journey: Upper Burma 1919–20* (London: Dulau & Co., 1926), p. xiv.
12. Diary for 12/9/1919, Quoted by Shulman, p. 97.
13. Farrer, letter to Ernest Gye, 19/xii/19, RBGE, RJF 4/1/1–13. 'Fratchy', a dialect word, means 'quarrelsome', after 'fratch', quarrel: A Native of Craven, *Horae Momenta Cravenae, or, The Craven Dialect, Exemplified in Two Dialogues between Farmer Giles and his neighbour Bridget, to which is annexed a glossary* (London, 1824), p. 75.
14. Farrer, letter to Gye, 4/ix/19, RBGE, RJF 4/1/1.
15. E. H. M. Cox, *The Plant Introductions of Reginald Farrer* (London: New Flora and Sylva Ltd., 1930), p. 3.
16. No. 21, 'Tibetanischer Matterhorn', in *Catalogue of an Exhibition of Water-colours by Reginald Farrer of Scenes and Flowers in Western China and Tibet* (The Fine Art Society, 148 New Bond Street: April, 1917), p. 8.
17. Holmes has misheard; the actual name is Trow Ghyll (the gorge encountered between Ingleborough Cave and Gaping Ghyll, all upstream for the landscape garden of Ingleborough Hall).
18. C. J. Holmes, *Self and Partners (Mostly Self): Being the Reminiscences of C. J. Holmes* (New York: Macmillan, 1936), pp. 297–99.
19. Royal Horticultural Society, Lindley Library, FAR/Survey/1.1.
20. Letter dated from 50 Ennismore Gardens (his parent's London house) on 8th January 1919. I owe great thanks to Nicola Shulman and Lady Vanessa Thomas for allowing me to see copies of these letters and refer to them here.
21. RBGE, RJF 2/1/3/1 Letter from Purdom 9/9/1913 suggesting the geographical base.
22. This, and all the other examples in this paragraph, are summarized in Charles Lyte, *The Plant Hunters* (London: Orbis, 1983).
23. RBGE, RJF 2/1/3/13.
24. Letter from Farrer to Aubrey Herbert, quoted in Fitzherbert, p. 163.
25. Farrer, *On the Eaves of the World* (London: Arnold, 1917), Vol. I, p. 306.
26. His route home is specified in a letter to his mother from Petrograd (RBGE, RJF 2/1/2, 1st May 1916) and confirmed in *The Rainbow Bridge*, p. 146.
27. Note to Balfour, RBGE, RJF 1/1/40, dated 1/5/16.
28. Undated letter, RBGE, RJF 2/1/3/13.
29. Letter to Balfour from London dated 19th May, RBGE RJF 1/1/47.
30. RBGE, RJF 2/1/3/5, letter of 23/3/15.
31. RBGE, RJF 2/1/3/3, copy of letter of 17 May 1915. Woodward, 38 years old, died as an officer in the 1st Battalion, South Wales Borderers.
32. RBGE, RJF 1/1/37, letter of 19/7/16 to Balfour.
33. RBGE, RJF 1/1/38, letter of 27/7/16, Balfour to Farrer.
34. RBGE, RJF 1/1/39, letter of 29/7/16.
35. RBGE, RJF 1/1/1/1–40, letter of 6/2/15. Balfour adds that labourers in the garden are appallingly badly paid on 22/- per week.
36. Letter to Herbert quoted by Shulman, p. 19.

37. Sitwell, *Noble Essences*, p. 15.
38. Farrer to his mother, 7/7/1917, RBGE RJF 2/1/4/1.
39. Shulman, *A Rage for Rock Gardening*, p. 88.
40. RBGE, RJF 2/1/4/3.
41. RBGE, RJF 1/1/50. Letter to Balfour announcing that Farrer is working for the Foreign Office.
42. RBGE, RJF 2/1/4/1, note from Farrer to Aubrey Herbert dated 20/4/18.
43. RBGE, RJF 1/1/78, letter of 30/11/1917.
44. Farrer, letters to Balfour, 31/1/1918, and letter of 5/2/1918. RBGE RJF 1/1/1–40 and 2/1/4/1.
45. RBGE, RJF 2/1/4/1.
46. Sitwell, *Noble Essences*, p. 18.
47. Richard Aldington, *Death of a Hero* (London: Chatto & Windus, 1929), p. 255.
48. D. H. Lawrence, *Kangaroo*, 1923 (Harmondsworth: Penguin, 1977), chapter 12, 'The Nightmare' (pp. 235–86), p. 236.
49. Ibid., p. 237.
50. Farrer's letter, undated but probably from late summer 1920, is in the Harry Ransom Humanities Research Center, University of Texas at Austin: Osbert Sitwell papers, Corr. 40:1 (E-L) Recip. The letter is quoted by Sitwell himself (op. cit., pp. 22–23) apparently entire, but in fact with omissions and changes to the text.
51. Ibid.
52. Lawrence, p. 241.
53. Ibid., p. 236–37.
54. Ibid., p. 240.
55. RBGE, RJF 2/1/3/13.
56. Farrer, letter to Bessie Farrer, 7/7/1917, RBGE RJF 2/1/4/1.
57. Lawrence, *Kangaroo*, p. 237.
58. Quoted in Christopher Ridgway's unpaginated 'Introduction' to Aldington's *Death of a Hero* (London: Hogarth, 1984).
59. Malcolm Bradbury, 'Introduction' to Ford Madox Ford, *Parade's End* (London: Campbell, 1992) p. xxviii. On this theme, see also Sara Haslam, *Fragmenting Modernism: Ford Madox Ford, the Novel, and the Great War* (Manchester: Manchester University Press, 2002) pp. 25–28.
60. Bradbury, 'Introduction', p. xxix.
61. Joseph Wiesenfarth, 'Death in the Wasteland: Ford, Wells and Waugh', in *Ford Madox Ford's Parade's End: The First World War, Culture, and Modernity*, ed. by Ashley Chantler and Rob Hawkes, (International Ford Madox Ford Studies, 13, Amsterdam: Rodopi, 2014), pp. 197–206 (p. 200). The quotation from Ford comes from *A Man Could Stand Up —* , the third volume of the novel.
62. Balfour, letter to Farrer 2/10/1916, RBGE, RJF 1/1/1/1–40.
63. In the plant list at the end of Farrer's *On the Eaves of the World* Bayley Balfour and Wright Smith named, but did not describe *Farreri pretiosa*, later realised to be a species of *Wikstroemia*, though, Henry Noltie states, the specimen has not survived.
64. RBGE, RJF 1/1/1/1–40, letter of 13/12/1914.
65. RBGE, RJF 1/1/1/1–40, Balfour to Farrer 24/2/1915.
66. RBGE, RJF 1/1/1/1–40, letter of 13/11/1917.
67. RBGE, RJF 1/1/1/1–40, letter of 2/1/1918 in which Farrer anticipates going off, 'worse luck' to 'G.H.Q. again in a week or two. For Goodness knows what and Goodness knows how long.'
68. RBGE, RJF 2/1/5/8.
69. RBGE, RJF, 2/1/5/1, letter of 20/1/1919. Redman was the faithful manager of the Craven Nursery.
70. Farrer's diary also exists. Apart from a few extracts published by Farrer's relative Ann Farrer in 'Farrer as Illustrator: The Diaries of Reginald Farrer' in Illingworth and Routh, *Reginald Farrer: Dalesman, Planthunter, Gardener*, pp. 64–71, the diaries have been kept sequestered by the Farrer family.
71. Shulman, *A Rage for Rock Gardening*, p. 91.

72. RBGE, RJF 1/1/1/ 1–40, letter of 19/5/1917.

73. Shulman, *A Rage for Rock Gardening*, p. 93. Cox was, Henry Noltie informs me, John Buchan's secretary.

74. RBGE, RJF 2/1/5/2, letter to unidentified recipient that mentions 'your Albanian comic Opera', 29/1/1919. The reference to Albania means that the recipient was Aubrey Herbert, who had been offered the throne of Albania.

75. A *khud* is a deep ravine or cleft in the hillside, derived from a Hindi word. H. Yule and A.C. Burnell, *Hobson-Jobson: The Anglo-Indian Dictionary* (1886: Ware: Wordsworth Editions, 1996), p. 481. Yule and Burnell state that the word is 'chiefly employed in Himālaya [...] in constant Anglo-Indian colloquial use at Simla and other Himalayan stations.'

76. RBGE, RJF 4/1/1, letter dated 29/5/1919.

77. RBGE, RJF 4/1/1, letter to Gye 26/7/1919.

78. RBGE, RJF 4/1/1, letter to Gye 4/9/1919.

79. RBGE, RJF 4/1/1, letter to Gye 24/9/1919. Farrer's writings are sown, as here, with various imitations of Mrs. Gamp, the character in Charles Dickens' *Martin Chuzzlewit*. Farrer calls himself a woman and imitates a very specifically awkward and eccentric (albeit imaginary) one.

80. Quoted in Shulman, *A Rage for Rock Gardening*, pp. 97–98.

81. Letter of July 1919 quoted in Fitzherbert, *The Man who was Greenmantle*, p. 223.

82. Letter, not dated, quoted in Fitzherbert, ibid.

83. RBGE, RJF 4/1/1, letter to Gye, 12/11/1919.

84. RBGE, RJF 4/1/1, letter of 23/12/1919.

85. Quoted in Shulman, *A Rage for Rock Gardening*, p. 98.

86. Frank Kingdon Ward, 'Reginald Farrer', *Geographical Journal*, 57, 1 (January 1921), 69–70, p. 69. This is an obituary notice.

87. RBGE, RJF 4/1/1, letter to Gye, 26/2/1920. David Marsh discusses Farrer's opinion of the botanical gardens at Maymyo in ' "An Amateurish Effort"? The Foundation of the National Botanic Gardens of Burma, 1914–22', *Garden History* 43, 2 (2015), 182–98.

88. Farrer's letter quoted in Cox, *Farrer's Last Journey*, p. 157.

89. Ibid., p. 161.

90. RBGE, RJF 4/1/1, letter of 26/2/1920.

91. Shulman, *A Rage for Rock Gardening*, pp. 99–100. Milner told Farrer that his sister had died and he needed to stay with a grieving parent: Farrer's letter of 28/12/1919, RBGE RJF 2/1/5/1.

92. The letter to Gye of 26/2/1920.

93. Quoted in Cox, *Farrer's Last Journey*, p. 162.

94. Letter to Aubrey Herbert from Hpimaw Fort, 9/X/19, Somerset Archives.

95. Shulman, *A Rage for Rock Gardening*, pp. 100–01.

96. Letter to Aubrey Herbert 9/X/19.

97. Letter to Aubrey Herbert from Nyitadi, 8/VI/1920, Somerset Archives.

98. Quoted in Shulman, *A Rage for Rock Gardening*, p. 100.

99. Ibid., p. 100. The rupee had risen steeply in value since the expedition set off in January 1919, which put Farrer at a disadvantage converting his pounds sterling.

100. RBGE, RJF 4/1/1, letter of 19/12/1919; the other letter that admires the novel is that of 26/2/1920.

101. This is the letter cited in n. 41 above.

102. RBGE RJF 4/1/1–13, letter to Ernest Gye, 26/2/1920.

103. For example, those quoted by William T. Stearn, 'An Introductory Tribute to Reginald Farrer', in Illingworth and Routh, *Reginald Farrer: Dalesman, Planthunter, Gardener*, pp. 1–7, reviewers quoted on p. 4. The relevant letter to Gye is that of 19/12/1919.

104. Copy of letter to unknown correspondent, RBGE RJF 2/1/5/3, 4/1/1920.

105. A Native of Craven, *Horae Momenta Cravenae*, p. 70.

106. Shulman, *A Rage for Rock Gardening*, p. 93.

107. RBGE, RJF 4/1/1, letter dated 6/5/1920.

108. RBGE, RJF 2/1/5/7, letter from Purdom dated 10/6/1920.

109. RBGE, RJF 4/1/1, letter dated 25/6/1920.
110. Thanks to Euan Cox's son Peter for this reference.
111. Letter dated 25/6/1920. For justification of my currency revision rate, see n.35.
112. Somerset County Archives, Taunton, DD\HER/38, letter of 8/6/1920.
113. Continuation of the letter quoted in Fitzherbert, *The Man who was Greenmantle*, p. 224.
114. Rainfall totals in this part of Burma indicate that in July and August, on average, 35 inches of rain falls in *each* month. Total rainfall for the year is over 150 inches, nearly half of which falls in these two summer months.
115. RBGE, RJF 4/1/1, letter dated 25/7/1920.
116. On 4th March 1918 the Department of Information, Farrer's employer, had become a Ministry under Lord Beaverbrook, with John Buchan its Director of Intelligence. So Farrer's comic and satirical use of this pre-Orwellian phrase has its basis in accuracy.
117. RBGE, RJF 4/1/12, letter dated 10/8/1920.
118. Letter to Gye of 25/6/1920.
119. Letter to Gye of 26/2/1920.
120. Letter of 25/6/1920.
121. Letter to Gye, 25/7/1920.
122. Letter to Gye, 10/8/1920.
123. Letter of 25/6/1920.
124. Letter to Gye dated 11/9/1920.
125. Letter of 26/2/1920.
126. RBGE, RJF 4/1/1, letter of 29/5/1919.
127. RBGE, RJF 1/2/3/27, letter to Wright Smith dated 13/9/1920.
128. RBGE, RJF 4/1/1–13 letter dated 11/9/1920.
129. Quoted in Shulman, *A Rage for Rock Gardening*, p. 106.
130. RBGE, RJF 2/1/6/3.
131. RBGE RJF 2/1/5/3, letter of 10/9/1920.
132. RBGE, GB235, RJF 2/1/6/4.
133. Farrer has written a double s, then crossed through one of the letters s. I have attempted to transliterate that to available symbols.
134. Bhikku means 'monk'. Farrer is referring here to a Yorkshireman who had become a Buddhist monk in Burma.
135. Farrer seems to be alluding here to doctrinal differences between Mahayana Buddhism, the Buddhism of Tibet, which became introduced to China and Japan, and the Buddhism of the south (Burma, Thailand and Sri Lanka), which is Theravada Buddhism.
136. Farrer inserted this word in superscript.
137. The name of a mountain 'long confused with Everest'; Wade Davis, *Into the Silence: The Great War, Mallory, and the Conquest of Everest* (New York: Knopf, 2012), p. 304.
138. RBGE RJF 2/1/6/3, letter dated 13/9/1920.
139. For these, see Davis, *Into the Silence*.

CHAPTER 4

Among the Personalities:
Garden-Writing and Garden Design

From Farrer's life I want to isolate two incidents that I understand to be paradigmatic: that is, to demonstrate the pattern of the larger whole. The first of these is Farrer's finding of *Arenaria gothica* (as it was then known) growing on Ingleborough in a new locality, only five years after its first discovery.

Handicapped, isolated, the boy Farrer seems to have found, in the alpine plants on the mountain, kindred spirits; mirror images of himself. Small beautiful living things surviving despite their own isolation in an unfavourable situation. We know, of course, that they survived on Ingleborough because they had been able to adapt to the conditions there, which thereby became hospitable to them; but if we set aside this ecological view and view them more naively, with a large amount of the pathetic fallacy, they can seem heroic. For the handicapped boy let loose on Ingleborough, perhaps the spectacle of these beautiful (sometimes fragrant) wild plants growing in seeming adversity really went home to him; a sort of reflection of himself. He wrote later of his favoured type of plant:

> The enormous majority of alpine plants, despite the peculiarities of their natural conditions, are quite extraordinarily easy, robust, and hearty in cultivation. They are also, by force of nature, dazzlingly brilliant and profuse in flower, cosy, compact and dwarf in shape; and they have (apart from their brave and blazing loveliness, and the charm of their sedate refined habit) a personal force of attraction such as no other plant can hope to rival — the attraction of their limitless courage, of their stubborn individuality, of their indomitable ingenuity against difficulty, far up in the grim and lonely places of the world.[1]

As Shulman put it, 'Farrer identified with alpine plants'.[2] She suggests that this is the reason he started to write of plants in his distinctive and highly influential way. But this plausible explanation that Farrer's view of plants was wholly subjective, intimately bound into the psychology of his early years, is not sufficient by itself to explain the views of plants represented in his writings. To this psychological explanation we shall have to add a cultural one.

At 14 years of age he accomplished something that was made up of several stages. He found something. He identified it (Yorkshire Sandwort) and understood it (that it was growing in a previously unrecorded place). To his natural enthusiasm, knowledge and liking he added a scientific comprehension. And he communicated the interesting fact to the rest of the world: that is, he wrote a letter to the *Journal of Botany* and had the exciting experience of seeing his own words in print. The boy who could barely make himself understood in normal communication (speech) had made himself understood by a wide readership. This experience surely set the pattern for Farrer's life from that moment: his plant-discovering, his botanical expertise, his written and printed communication that integrated his youthful love and enthusiasm with his presence on a larger stage, as it were, and even with the possibility of making a living.

The other paradigmatic event took place in Ceylon, when he became a Buddhist. This decision, carried through, freed him from much about the culture that had formed him. He was born and brought up into an ugly, inadequate, vulgar and arrogant society, and was marked by it, in attitudes and language. But he wanted to get out; he knew it wasn't right. Becoming a Buddhist meant renouncing a Christianity that had outlived its usefulness to him, but meant also renouncing the possibility of a completely secular state of life. He had to overcome the apparently racist attitude of the formidable personality of his friend Aubrey Herbert, speaking no doubt merely as spokesman for the British ruling class. Farrer had to brave his family's disapproval. The action involved him embracing a very important element in the cultures and history of Asia, and so set the seal on his openness to, and liking for, Asia that was originally formed during the trip to Japan, with the side-trip to Korea and China. Becoming a Buddhist was a step into freedom. The consequence was accepting a doctrine of non-violence, of the acquisition of merit by good karma as the means for getting 'off the Wheel', or defeating ignorance, desire and anger and understanding the Cycle of Dependent Origination that keeps us bound to the Wheel. Accepting also a compassionate view of other living things.

And this gives rise to a virtual contradiction which in the end complements and strengthens the psychological dynamic discussed above, of Farrer's attitude to plants. A Western man encountering Buddhism for the first time learns that if we commit and accumulate bad karma we might be sent round again for future lives in the Buddhist hells, or as a lowly form of earthly life, an insect or slug, rat or shrew. To such a person, especially if they are involved with the cultivation of plants, might well occur the question, what about plants? Can we be sent round again as plants? And whether or not we can, where does plant-life fit into the Buddhist view of things? Jains, members of a religious group strongly related to both Buddhism and Hinduism, do not eat root vegetables, for example. They refrain out of respect for the life in the plants. Where does this leave a gardener and alpine enthusiast? Where does it leave Reginald Farrer?

One of the books he published in the year after his return from Ceylon as an avowed Buddhist seems to provide a very direct straightforward answer. The first chapter of his *In a Yorkshire Garden* (1909) begins with an evocation of a chilly early Spring. This brings to the author's mind daffodils, and thoughts of a trip recently made to Cornwall, where he has visited some nurserymen. No matter how ironically he expresses himself, Farrer has clearly been disturbed. The nurserymen hybridize daffodils in the hope of making desirable new forms, and those bulbs that do not meet their expectations of excellence are burned by the hundred on bonfires. Farrer states his misgivings immediately, via a Christian parallel:

> It is [...] bad to be a specialist. But even worse for one's moral development, I clearly perceive, is to meddle with God's work, and become a hybridist, a maker of new species. For, in the arrogating of a Creator's function, it appears inevitable that the human being must develop the creator's callousness and high indifference.[3]

Developing this theme, Farrer reveals something of his own secrets:

> There are many plants I positively dislike, many that I admire without loving. But, towards all the plants I love, I do honestly affirm that I present an equal front, and make no account of novelty and rarity, but cherish the Wood-Anemone as heartily as any new Daffodil or Poppy from the roof of the world [...] Certainly I am a sentimentalist in the matter, I who loathe sentimentality [...] And, to be frank, I am not sure that the sentimentalist is not as true a gardener as the specialist. It really did horrify me, and make me feel physically ill, when I heard of all those Daffodils being doomed to the fire. In the first place, I hate the idea of burning a flower or plant, with a, perhaps, wholly sentimental and unreasoned hatred. It seems to me a horrible thing to do. In the second place [...] appeared the affront to decency and goodness involved in deliberately creating a thing, and then, because it did not exactly answer to some pre-ordained canon, sweeping it out of existence through an agonising gate of death. To create life for the mere fun of taking it away again afterwards, or with the thought that you will do so if it doesn't please you, must always be an evil thing in the eyes of any Buddhist, whether the life be that of beast or bird or plant.[4]

This is straightforwardly put. We shall have to return the question of why destroying a plant you've created but don't like is evil to a Buddhist, but first note that Farrer doesn't easily leave off this theme:

> the hybridist seems to develop, in fact, into a sort of Calvinistic God, predestining millions of his creatures quite happily to the fire. And therefore, I say, that unless he resists the temptation, he is putting himself in great danger of peril through spiritual arrogance.[5]

Farrer then worries away for over 3½ pages at the theme of what a gardener is to do with plants he or she doesn't like, before ending the chapter with a rousing paragraph:

> Only I will again proclaim my gospel: every flower in your garden is a personality to you, if you have any of the flower-soul in you at all — a tiresome personality, it may be, to you, perhaps even an intrusive personality, an ugly personality even. But a personality the whole time, a personality living and thinking and feeling just as you and I do, though on a scale infinitely reduced, of course. But there is the One Soul, more or less of it, in all created things, and the One Life abounding in us all. Remember, every time you hurt or bruise a flower you send up the temperature of that plant, and enfever it and make it miserable. That is a bedrock fact, minimise the suffering and the thought as much as your sensitiveness prompts. But we are brothers and sisters, every one of us, on stalks or feet — Colonel's lady or Judy O'Grady; never let a flower be

to you a mere colour, or a possibility of points;[6] and never, never let me hear of
burning Daffodil bulbs, or anything else at all with our holy life in its veins.[7]

Here is a plainly stated as possible the principle of Farrer's writing about plants.
'For him, plants had temperaments.'[8] In 1907 we find him beginning his book
My Rock-Garden with the statement that 'plants, no less than people, have perverse
individualities of their own.'[9] Indeed, they were even personalities. That word is
used six times in the first four lines of the last lengthy quotation, to differentiate
individual plants, but also for emphasis: to drive the point home. In *My Rock
Garden*, the plant *Saxifraga florulenta*, an ancient species making its 'last stand' against
'extinction', is a 'wonderful, tragic personality'.[10] This principle was also the key to
Farrer's influence on other garden writers, as we shall see.

An answer to the question of where this view of plants came from is indicated
above in Farrer's own writing, but it needs further discussion and elucidation. It
should be said that no evidence about this survives in Farrer's letters to friends
or any other part of the archival record, so we have to attempt to detect clues
in his published works. The idea of plants as being personalities, together with
a revulsion at the massed burning of bulbs, complement and reinforce Farrer's
early experience encountering on Ingleborough plants of 'limitless courage' and
'stubborn individuality.' The ideas strengthen the early passion, but owe a great deal
of their power to another source.

Why should the destruction of a plant you've created but don't like be abhorrent
to a Buddhist? Lambert Schmithausen has studied the Buddhist idea, which he
identifies as 'Far Eastern' (Japanese or Chinese), that plants contain 'Buddha nature'
(the capacity to become enlightened) and may become Buddha (that is, awakened).[11]
The concepts (themselves not uncontroversial) involved with this belief are rather
difficult. Fundamental is the idea that true reality (Suchness) is indivisible. From
this comes the realisation that all sentient beings must therefore share the same
Suchness as the *tathāgata* (a Buddha, an enlightened one) because Suchness is
indivisible.[12] Schmithausen explains that the Buddha-nature (*tathāgatagarbha*) is the
hidden presence of a reality that pervades all things and has to be developed and
realized in all things. *Tathāgatagarbha* designates the Buddha-'germ' or -'seed' (or
Buddha-nature) — the potential to become enlightened — that has to be developed
to come to fruition.

Does this idea occur in Farrer's writings? 'If you have any flower-soul in you',
he says in one of the passages just quoted, which reads strangely to a westerner
brought up in the Church of England. 'One soul' and 'one life abounding' in
'created things': these phrases could just take on a Christian inflection; but that
is not what Farrer intends, except perhaps as part of a strategy of trying not to
alienate his readership. Farrer tells us that the Buddha receives offerings of flowers
in temples with pleasure, because no animals have been killed: 'the flower being
of so low a grade of soul-consciousness that it cannot grudge martyrdom, as
might an animal.'[13] Farrer's phrase 'soul-consciousness' is almost certainly derived
(via someone else's translation, of course) from the Sanskrit term *ekindriya jīva*.
Schmithausen translates '*ekindriya jīva*', as 'living beings [jīva] with one sense-

faculty', meaning an intelligence based on sensory perception. Humans and animals have this in abundance, yet it can be discerned in plants too, which can be observed to be sensitive to light, heat, and humidity, for example.[14] The presence of *ekindriya jīva* is the determining factor for various Buddhist scholars of the past in regarding plants as having consciousness and therefore the potential to become awakened, or Buddha. And yet there is another way of seeing this whole question. At least one school of Buddhist thought went even further. Schmithausen quotes a 'Treatise on the Transcendence of Discrimination', produced by a particular strand in Chinese Ch'an tradition, an 8th-century product of the 'Ox-head School'. He summarizes:

> Grasses and trees are Awakened in the sense that they are always, from the outset, in harmony with the *tao*, i.e., with the true nature of things, because they lack deluded thoughts and emotions (ch'ing)[15] and have no [feeling of an] ego. Therefore, they do not produce thoughts [of displeasure, or revenge?] when injured. In a similar way accomplished persons, who are free from [the notion or feeling of] an ego and in harmony with the *tao*, regard their bodies as equal to grasses and trees and react like a tree (i.e. remain unconcerned and calm) when they are injured.[16]

It seems that Farrer was aware of some descendant of these ideas of plants having the potential to become awakened or even having succeeded in doing so. He seems to imply that plants are inferior: 'so low a grade of soul-consciousness'. Yet, if he equates 'soul-consciousness' with the idea of fixed personality or inherent existence (one of the things a Buddhist has to try to understand as delusion) Farrer's thinking about plants thus harmonizes with the view summarized here by Schmithausen. Being culled for sacrifice in a temple is a very different fate for a plant (serving a sacred purpose) from that of being burned because deemed substandard. The stalk and flower (which form the sacrifice) are also fundamentally different parts of the plant compared with the bulb, and can regenerate.

From which of his major experiences of living Buddhist cultures did Farrer derive this belief about plants? He may well have studied the matter in London in preparation for his trip to Ceylon. It is worth remembering that the Buddhist Society of Great Britain was founded in 1907 and that Farrer was a founding member; indeed, on the Society's council. We know little about the activities and learning of Buddhists active in Britain in the first decade of the twentieth century, and more scholarship needs to be done to elucidate the situation. In his book about Ceylon, however, Farrer quotes what he calls a Japanese 'proverb': 'All trees and grass, these shall also become Lord Buddha.'[17] Schmithausen cites two relatively ancient Japanese texts that come fairly close to Farrer's phrasing of the proverb: 'Annen (841?–c.890) asserts that grasses and trees may become individual Buddhas in their own right.'[18] Annen was an important thinker and teacher in the *Tendai* sect of Japanese Buddhism. In a later period the 'Japanese tendai master Hōchi_bō Shōshin (active 1153–1207)' also asserted the Buddha-nature of grasses and trees.[19]

The involvement of Tendai in producing the saying that Farrer printed as a 'proverb' is very interesting. Tendai grew up within Mahayana Buddhism, the Buddhism of the 'Great Vehicle' which became particularly strong in Japan (as well as China and Tibet). Closely related to the Chinese T'ien-t'ai tradition of *ekayana*

Buddhism, Tendai nevertheless became a distinct Japanese school and survives in the present time. It was very important in the development of Buddhism in Japan: 'As the "womb" from which were born the "new" religious movements of the Kamakura period (1185–1333), the Tendai tradition retains a special place in the history of Japanese Buddhism.'[20] In addition to Tendai, there is another tradition of Japanese Buddhism that is as significant in contributing philosophy about the individual sentience of plants. The *Shingon* master Dōhan argued that plants have 'mind' inside them, hidden below the surface, and it is only the covert nature of this that leads people to think that plants are non-sentient.[21] Thus plants are really possessed of individual sentience, and can, according to Dōhan, '*individually* resolve to awaken and attain Buddhahood'. This view accords with Farrer's view of plants as individuals — even quirky and awkward individuals, and so makes Japan the source of the idea that he relays in various ways as highly important to him; one might call it the foundation (or at least one of the twin foundations) of his view of plants as personalities.

On the other hand, Schmithausen concedes that the Theravada tradition of Buddhism (particularly strong throughout Southeast Asia and Sri Lanka) places a prohibition on the violent treatment of plants and seeds, implicitly conceding plants to be classed among sentient beings, and harmonizing, for our purposes, with Farrer's disgust at the spectacle of daffodil bulbs being immolated.[22] So could Farrer have derived the ideas that strengthened his own passionately-held views of the lives of plants from the Lankan religious tradition into which he was accepted in 1908? There is some evidence, but it is rather weak compared to the direct connection with Japanese Tendai and Shingon that we have just traced. A product of the northern Mahayana tradition, perhaps surprisingly, provides some important evidence bearing on this question. In the 1930s Gendun Chopel, a renegade Tibetan monk, discusses the idea he has come across outside Tibet that plants are sentient. 'Jains claimed that trees are sentient because they fold their leaves at night.' He also cites the flowers Sundew and Venus flytrap that eat insects.[23] Chopel writes, 'the Sinhalese scientists who are Buddhists say [the Buddha ...] prohibited [monks from] cutting plants.'[24] Donald S. Lopez states that this amounts to an acknowledgement among the Sinhalese that plants are sentient, and tells us that 'Gendun Chopel was famous in his youth [as a monastery debater] for having successfully upheld the Jain view that plants have consciousness.'[25]

Thus, once he had enquired, Farrer might have found confirmation in Ceylon of the idea that plants are sentient. There is however less evidence from the Sinhalese side that is expressed with the specificity of the Japanese utterances about 'trees and grasses'. Moreover, Schmithausen's view is that, outside Jain texts, it is only in Japan that plants are seen as endowed with *individual* sentience.[26] So we have to conclude that the main influence on Farrer's developed views of the 'One Soul, more or less of it' (the Buddha–nature) of plants was derived from his earlier experience of Japanese Buddhism.

Further indication that lessons learned from the Far East informed Farrer's thinking is provided by *In Old Ceylon,* where he states that: 'all forms of life are one; there is no essential difference between the life of a rock and the life of a man — no real difference in kind, though an incalculably vast difference in degree; yet it is the same spirit that possesses both.'[27] This seems a statement that would have been thought rather extraordinary by a conventional British readership of Farrer's book. In Far Eastern Buddhist thought, though, it is the omnipresence and the indivisibility of Suchness that provide for the belief that insentient things, such as stones and rock, also have the Buddha-nature. The Chinese T'ien-t'ai monk Chan-jan explained in the *Diamond Scalpel*:

> the mind and [Buddha-] nature of each sentient being are all pervasive and all-containing, like space, which means that at every moment my own mind as well as [that of] all the other sentient beings is equal to the mind and (because there is nothing outside the mind) the body and the environment (or 'field') of Vairocana, the Buddha in his actualized glory, [in such a way that] self and other are mutually interfused and interpenetrating. It is on account of error and due to their clinging to an Ego that sentient beings ignore their own and their environment's Buddha-nature and construe it as their individual body and its profane external world.[28]

In Japan, the 'Vairocana' concept (of the whole world being the Buddha's cosmic body) is particularly associated with the founder of the Shingon tradition.[29] The idea expressed by Farrer, that 'one spirit [...] possesses both' (the life of a rock and that of a man) seems in harmony with this concept as explained in the paragraph just quoted, and probably derived from it. The same may be said for his phrases quoted earlier, 'one soul' and 'one life abounding in created things'. The ancient Chinese Ch'an master Nan-yang Hui-chung (?–775) wrote what Schmithausen judges to be the 'most famous and most explicit' passage about how 'stones' and other insentient things 'expound the Dharma' because they have 'Mind and hence Buddha-nature'.[30] Japanese Zen-masters shared this view, which comes very close to Farrer's assertion: a recent article on Japanese aesthetics cites the 13th-century monk Dōgen as a prime authority: he indicated trees, grasses, streams and mountains as things that possess the Buddha-nature.[31] In my reading, Farrer's word 'spirit' might also equate with the term translated by Schmithausen as 'Mind'. Schmithausen also quotes Shōshin repeating the belief that 'sentient beings and insentient things are a single body [so] sentient beings becoming Buddha means that insentient things become Buddha.'[32] This seems quite close in spirit to Farrer's assertion that 'all forms of life are one'. The Buddhist goal is to realize this unity. So in this case of stone or rock it is the Chinese-Japanese Buddhist connection that provided the authority for Farrer's belief.

In the case of rock a set of Buddhist ideas, picked up via Japan, gives Farrer, a rock gardener since his teens, who knew and understood rock, at least from the points of view of its providing a habitat for his favourite plants, and its beauty, a spiritual framework that deepens and strengthens whatever feeling for rock he previously had. In his paper, 'Geographical Work in India for this Society', presented to the Royal Geographical Society in March, 1917, Sir Francis Younghusband thanks Farrer for teaching him about the beauty of rock, citing Farrer's book *Among the Hills: a Book of Joy in High Places* (1911) as the instrument of this learning. He also states that in the book Farrer declares that: 'gods [...] dwell in rock and cliff as in the oak or glittering water.'[33]

It is worth dwelling for a moment on the passage that taught Younghusband. Within a page or two Farrer regrets the ordinary utilitarian attitude to rock; the attitude that destroys it as an obstacle, or crushes it for roadstone, and he writes of: 'the idiosyncrasies and charms of different strata' of rock.[34] He celebrates the varied colours of Ingleborough limestone in different lights, weathers and seasons, the rock thereby 'conveying in its successive moods the impression of its personality'.[35] In the following paragraph he turns to thoughts about the difference in fertility between the granitic rocks, on one hand, and limestones, chalk and marble, on the other, made up as these latter types are of the skeletons of millions of small sea creatures:

> I can but feel that all the organic strata have more sympathy with the ways of the world than those grim primeval rocks that are congealed fire out of the time when no life yet was. [...] for those rocks that are built up of countless myriad myriad husks of existence, it seems as if the ghosts of their bygone component activities still linger in them, and make them one with the life that unceasingly flows on; and friendly, and understanding, adapting themselves to the purposes of the world, instead of resisting stupidly, like the granites.[36]

Farrer here takes us to the brink of a psychism which we have already seen in his descriptions of Vessagiriya and Mihintale in Sri Lanka. He is also implying that the 'friendly' characteristic of these rocks is linked to the fact they were once sentient beings. In a rare apologetic moment he concedes that his thought would not sit well 'in Jermyn Street' (in London, site of the offices of the Geological Survey). Yet he was not the only British writer to feel a sort of kinship with rocks. Writing about early fossils (trilobites) forty years later in her book *A Land*, the archaeologist Jacquetta Hawkes says:

> I see modern men enjoying a unity with the trilobites of a nature more deeply significant than anything at present understood in the processes of biological evolution [...]
> The nature of this unity cannot be stated, for it remains always just beyond the threshold of intellectual comprehension. It can only be shown as a blurred reflection through hints coming from many directions but always falling short of their objective.[37]

Hawkes is writing on the eve of the Festival of Britain, during a period of post-war reconstruction. An elegiac sense of the nation having survived two world wars informs her deep retrospection:

> The Indo-European aristocracy, renewed again and again by Celtic, Anglo-Saxon, Scandinavian and Norman conquerors, has held its ascendancy until recent times. I should say that so far as Britain is concerned it made its last stand with the guards regiments that were cut to pieces at Calais in 1940. What is succeeding it no one can as yet distinguish.[38]

Hawkes also shows that she is not alone in feeling a sense of connection with rocks akin to that of Farrer:

> Life has grown from the rock and still rests upon it; because men have left it

far behind, they are able consciously to turn back to it. We do turn back, for it has kept some hold over us. A liberal rationalist, Professor G. M. Trevelyan, can write of 'the brotherly love that we feel... for trees, flowers, even for grass, nay even for rocks and water' and of 'our brother the rock'.[39]

Farrer's exposure to Far Eastern Buddhism gave him precisely the element Hawkes says is missing from the unsayable feeling of connection with fossils and rocks: the 'intellectual comprehension' that might complement the feeling. A question about Hawkes, Younghusband and Trevelyan, not to be explored here, however, becomes: did their intellectual comprehension get beyond the geologically-inspired understanding that, in addition to the fact that rocks sustain the lives of plants through the nutrients released by their decomposition, plants have created rocks (coal); as has animal life (chalk, limestone, marble)?[40]

The evidence we have already seen provided by Farrer's own published writings implies an exploration by him of the sentience of plants, and an encounter with the far eastern Buddhist view of rock, during the period extending between his visit to Japan (which began in November 1902) and the publication of *In Old Ceylon* (October 1908). I believe that we can be fairly certain that, given his pre-existing emotional identification with flowers, Farrer sought out Buddhist explanations of the nature of plants at a relatively early stage of his interest in Buddhism. Ceylon possibly yielded a certain amount of confirmation for what Farrer had already heard in Japan. Farrer's *My Rock Garden*, of 1907 (before he set foot in Ceylon) is suffused by characterization of flowers as personalities, on nearly every page.

For Farrer, plants could be sulky, demanding, and have their 'flaggings and faintings';[41] a plant could even be 'a snob'![42] But they could also be trustworthy, generous and grateful. Referring to the use of such epithets, Nicola Shulman states the case for Farrer's arguably greatest single achievement, broadly and comprehensively:

> This trait of Farrer's resulted in a new language for horticulture [...] Nobody else wrote like this about plants at the time. Now everybody does, quite as a matter of course: Farrer's temperament furnished a vocabulary so expressive and pertinent that it was universally adopted as the natural language of gardening.[43]

Shulman prints twelve examples culled from five different writers.[44] Plenty of others could be added. When Christopher Lloyd writes of the plants in Derek Jarman's garden, for example, that Jarman: 'well understood which plants would like him under these extreme conditions [of Dungeness]', he is writing under the influence of Farrer.[45] Not 'which plants he would like' we note, but 'which plants would like him'.

Is Shulman's view correct, that Farrer did this singlehandedly: that he alone fashioned this new way of writing about garden plants for the anglophone world? After all, at least by 1899 the gardener Gertrude Jekyll had got as far as writing that plants 'look happy' in certain situations.[46] Luckily we have some corroborating judgements. In his obituary of Farrer in 1921, Clarence Elliott wrote that: 'As a writer of garden books he stood alone. He wrote, as a rule, from a peculiar angle of his own, giving queer human attributes to his plants, which somehow exactly described them.'[47] Elliott states very plainly that Farrer was 'alone', on 'his own,' evolving this mode of plant-writing. An anonymous obituary of Farrer in *The Garden* states that his books are: 'unlike any other gardening work in the personal note he managed to interweave into even a botanical description', explaining that: 'he was able to create a living interest in any plant he described, and to give to each an individuality of temperament such as he might to a character in a novel or a play.' The obituary concludes by celebrating Farrer's 'brilliant writing and invigorating personality'.[48] The eminent botanist W. T. Stearn admits that in 1928 he was inspired to scientific work by the 'alluring' and 'enthusiastic description' by Farrer of a plant Stearn had never heard of. Stearn writes that: 'No one will ever again enrich and enliven the literature of horticulture as Reginald Farrer did.'[49] This opinion about his writing in general was shared by E. H. M. Cox, who put the salient characteristic rather crudely: 'He always looked upon plants as human, and he invariably brought out this point in his writings [...] there is no writer on gardening who has made his subject live before our eyes as he has', and for Cox, Farrer's 'greatest influence on contemporary gardening was [...] as a gardening writer; and this influence reached far beyond the actual public that read his books.'[50] The evidence suggests that we can therefore with some confidence comprehend Farrer as a highly influential innovative moderniser of his chosen field, of writing gardening books. And we have to acknowledge that the foundation of that modernism was not simply Farrer's 'temperament' expressing itself, but also, and very emphatically, the influence of the Buddhism that he had wholeheartedly embraced.

Garden Design

Farrer believed in the personalities of plants. He believed the idea that plants take their place in a continuity of forms of life, from rocks to human beings, all of which have the Buddha-nature and some of which are striving upwards to the achievement of Buddhahood. These beliefs manifested themselves in his writings about gardens and plants. We can expect that they also determined his garden design and his designing with plants. Yet can we show explicit evidence? Was Farrer a moderniser in garden design? And can we show Farrer designing from, as it were, a Buddhist point of view?

The question admits of no very unambiguous answer. One thing we can show, however, is strong influence from a heavily Buddhist-influenced culture. In *My Rock-Garden* (1907), Farrer states his principle of design of rock-gardens, showing such design to be an art of landscape:

> Have an idea, and stick to it. Let your rock-garden set out to be something definite, not a mere agglomeration of stones. Let it be a mountain gorge, if you like, or the stony slope of a hill, or a rocky crest, or peak. But, whatever it be, it must have definiteness of scheme. It is, in effect, an imitation of Nature, and, to be successful, must aim at reproducing with fidelity some particular feature of nature — whichever you may choose.[51]

A GLEN IN THE OLD GARDEN.

FIG. 4.1. Farrer, rock-garden 'glen'; photograph from *My Rock Garden* (1907).

At Warley, he tells us, is a gorge-design: 'to my own personal taste, a trifle too violent to be altogether pleasant, but still a noble example of definite purpose definitely carried out.'[52] Along these lines, Farrer illustrates with a photograph his own creation of a 'glen' (figure 4.1). The sandy floor of the glen will have been just large enough to permit a gardener's access to look after the plants. Miniaturisation in representation of landscape is therefore a standard recourse in the creation of rock-gardens.

After the mention of Warley comes an encomium:

Of course the absolute masters of rock-garden, before whose names one must

go helpless to one's knees in adoration, are the Japanese. Not to plunge into
the bottomless sea of their mysticism and symbolism in design, the sight of a
Japanese garden is enough to bring tears of ecstasy to the eyes of any garden-
lover. No distortions, no abortion, no discords are there, but some corner of
landscape — a rocky gully, a view among islands — some famous corner of
landscape carefully copied to scale, with a sense of harmony and perspective
so perfect that in a cottage yard four yards square you will seem to have half a
mountain-side.[53]

While in Japan, Farrer had visited some of the famous historical gardens, and seen
many examples of smaller gardens, *bonsai* and tray-gardens.[54] Admiring the achieved
effects, however, might not have been so instructive to him as watching Japanese
workmen creating a garden for the house he rented, although he only describes this
very briefly: 'They built a pile of rock-work, and in precisely the right places they
planted fern and grass and asarum. They made for it a background of azalea and
striped daphne, till the whole had the air of a rocky clearing in a jungle. Then they
arranged a wilderness of daphne and camellia and azalea, and the thing was done.'[55]

In a later book, Farrer reiterates that the Japanese are masters of commanding
scale by means of 'an exact sense of proportion, and by care spent beforehand in
pondering the possibilities of the ground and the materials.' He now retreats a little
from the idea of a literal imitation of a scene in nature, stating rather that a gorge
or 'some high slope [...] should inspire you with a suggestion, as you begin to mould
your plans.' His next suggestion is probably directly related to things seen in Japan:
'often it will be some specially beautiful boulder that will insist on such and such a
position, and make you build up to it as the dominant point of your picture.'[56] In
Japan he had noted the 'vast importance' of particular stones and their shapes, as
well as certain designs in which a stone was the only feature.[57]

In contrast to all this Japanese excellence, Farrer finds that many British rock-
gardens follow the wrong principles of design. He sketched two bad examples,
above two suggestions of his own for better employment of the stones (Figure 4.2).
The Almond-Pudding system propped stones on end; the Plum-bun (together with
the Dogs' Grave he specified elsewhere) do not qualify as designs at all. In contrast
to this, Farrer stresses three things. The most important thing is to arrange the
stones in a way most favourable for the growing of alpine plants. He recommends
emulating the way strata of stones are found naturally (this is visible in both his
lower sketches), while ensuring that the stones are placed on a tilt, so that excess
water can drain off, rather than laid flat, in which case water would pool on the
stones and kill the roots of plants. This particular equation between the beauties
of designing with stones and suiting the needs of flowers is not derived from the
Japanese, who, according to Farrer, prize the rocks more than the flowers. Another
principle he follows is that: 'Very little stone indeed is needed; it is far easier to have
too much than too little: a lovely rock-garden is often made without any visible
stone at all. For the only essential part of stone, from an Alpine's point of view, is
that it should be buried under ground, so that one's roots may run gripping along its
sides, and penetrate underneath in search of the moisture that is always there.'[58] For
the garden historian Brent Elliott, this 'diminution of the need for rocks' is Farrer's

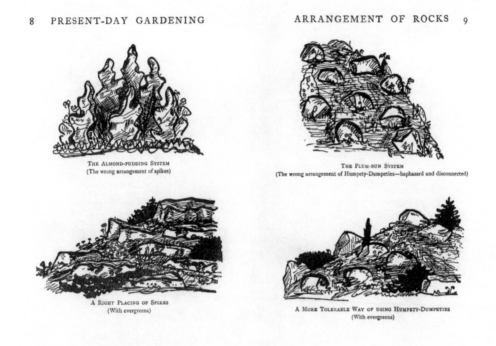

8   PRESENT-DAY GARDENING

ARRANGEMENT OF ROCKS   9

THE ALMOND-PUDDING SYSTEM
(The wrong arrangement of spikes)

THE PLUM-BUN SYSTEM
(The wrong arrangement of Humpety-Dumpeties—haphazard and disconnected)

A RIGHT PLACING OF SPIKES
(With evergreens)

A MORE TOLERABLE WAY OF USING HUMPETY-DUMPETIES
(With evergreens)

FIG. 4.2. Farrer, sketch of bad designs and good ones, from *The Rock Garden* (1912).

'originality' in rock-garden design.[59] The third principle of design of Farrer's is to promote the 'moraine garden': that is, planting in scree or decomposing rock, rather than in a combination of boulders and soil. The journal *Country Life in America* (1912) printed an article about Farrer under the title, 'A Wonderful New Kind of Rock Garden'.[60] The new kind of gardening was moraine gardening, and although Farrer is taken by the magazine as its inventor, Elliott traces its origin (at least as an idea) back to the 1870s.[61]

In 1912 Farrer contributed a volume, *The Rock Garden*, to a series of books on gardening edited by R. Hooper Pearson, the managing editor of the *Gardeners' Chronicle*. In the preface to Farrer's volume, Professor J. Bretland Farmer states that 'revolutionary advances' have come about 'within a few years' in 'Rock-gardening', because of: 'a keener study of natural conditions, and the consequent discernment of the principles which underlie successful practice.' He writes that 'No one has done more to bring this about than Mr. Farrer, who is everywhere recognized as a pioneer in the movement. [...] by the device of the moraine garden he has shown us how to grow with relative certainty and ease, many a plant that used to be regarded as difficult or impossible.'[62] Although these statements occur within the covers of Farrer's own book, they would not have appeared, and with the approval of Pearson, had they not been widely accepted or acceptable. E. A. Bowles, a friend of Farrer, describes him in 1914 as having arisen as: 'the prophet [...] the Moraine Magician' with a 'master mind'.[63]

SAXIFRAGA CAESIA IN THE OLD MORAINE.

*(Saxifraga Fosteri and Saxifraga thessalica to the left: Petrocallis in the foreground:
Edraianthus Pumilio beyond to the right: Saxifraga patens immediately behind
Saxifraga caesia.)*

FIG. 4.3. Farrer, moraine garden; photograph from *In a Yorkshire Garden* (1909).

In practical terms, what was a 'moraine'? Farrer describes his own:

> my toy-garden, my baby moraine, the particular pet joy of my heart. And this
> is built of four big limestone blocks, arranged in a square, with a deep well in
> the middle. Drainage burrs were put at the bottom of the well, and then the
> whole filled up with mere sheer blue limestone chips, with only the faintest
> possible dash of soil. And here do some of the most difficult plants go on and
> prosper in the most marvellous way *Campanula Allioni* -- yes, in limestone
> chips! [...] some of the rarest eastern Saxifrages live here [...] but I talk of it here
> simply as an illustration of our water-worn limestone, and its extraordinary
> decorative value. For those four blocks, set together and filled in, make the
> effect of one enormous boulder, into whose topmost crevices the plants have
> rooted.[64] (Figure 4.3)

Thus it is not the visual appearance of this type of landscape feature (a moraine)
that is striven for (though that would feature, albeit in second place), but the
moraine as a specific environment in which certain types of plant could best grow.
In energetically promoting moraine gardening, not only by making his own, but
also by writing about it with such enthusiasm, Farrer shows himself a dynamic
innovator: a modernist. Moraines assume an importance in at least three ways. They
are formally or visually innovative, because the flowers look as if they are growing
from a heap of small stones, rock fragments, or even grit. We have become used to
this effect by the early twenty-first century: Derek Jarman's garden at Dungeness,
where the plants apparently sprouting from bare beach pebbles constitutes a
cornerstone of the garden's aesthetics, furnishes a relatively well-known example,
and a similar effect is a feature of the 'xeriscapes', or drought tolerant gardens, of
the south-west USA. But in Farrer's time the effect was still new. The moraine
was also socially important because cheap: accessible to all gardeners because the
materials were not costly and making a moraine was possible without the labour and
equipment needed for moving boulders of great weight. Botanically, the moraine
was important because, as Bretland Farmer, a professor of botany, stated, it solved
the problem of growing even difficult plants. In a later book Farrer acclaims the
moraine garden as 'the most important discovery ever made as to the culture of
Alpine plants in England', and states that his own 'is on the lines of the Ko-niwa
-- box-gardens -- landscapes and seascapes all perfect in a pan eight inches across'
of Japan.[65] So Japan is invoked in this case, but not as the source of the idea (the
difference in scale makes this clear): simply as an analogy or comparison. The
common factor is representation of landscape. Farrer's moraine is a work of imitative
art, a synecdoche, in that it conjures up a fragment of natural moraine in which the
pattern and working of the whole is discernible. At the same time, it stems from the
impulse, not solely to imitation, but to provide the best habitat for 'difficult' plants.
Farrer's hierarchy of value is clear. Plants find themselves at the top.

While the Japanese are masters of design with rocks, they fall short, for Farrer,
with respect to flowers: 'the Japanese is not the lover of flowers in general.'[66]

> He is of no use as a practical gardener for growing normal plants in their normal
> health. He brutalises them, ignores their wishes, and harries them to death. On
> the other hand, he is unsurpassable when it comes to distorting, torturing, and

tweaking into fantastic byways the plain courses of nature. It is not the plant he loves. It is the effect that the plant enables him to attain. He touches the highest point of artificiality. But he must never be called a good gardener. The true gardener cares far less for the freakish or abnormal possibilities of a plant than for the plant itself, as an individual, requiring the closest attention, and brilliantly rewarding a loyal devotion. A true gardener is the humble slave of nature; a Japanese her contemptuous tyrant.[67]

So although his experience in Japan helped to convince Farrer of the sentience of plants, and their Buddha-nature, Japanese gardening contradicted Farrer's reverence for the individual lives of plants.

Nevertheless, Farrer urges his countrymen to learn, at least in general terms, from the Japanese: 'never think [...] that you can't get the noblest and grandest effects, just because your ground is no more than a quarter the size of a small bedroom. In spaces no bigger, any Japanese townsman will have at the back of his house some apt and perfect little valley or mountain dell.'[68] One lesson from Japan, then, is that no matter how small the garden, its design is an art of landscape. In such endeavours, Farrer emphasizes the extraordinary usefulness of 'small evergreens, if you want to make your garden a picture':

for these, if properly placed, have the most astounding power of giving space and composition. They can make any rock look high and low, natural or artificial, near or far [...] the proper arrangement of evergreens on a rock-work is quite magical in at once giving majesty and vastness to what might, otherwise, however well-built, have looked an insignificant hummock of stones, because there happened to be a blank wall, or a church spire, or a factory chimney just beyond; and nothing on the rockwork to set up a new, independent, and self-contained scale of values and proportions.[69]

Evergreens are included in Farrer's published sketches, so important is the way they complement the placing of rocks (Figure 4.2). He had seen the gardeners who installed his garden at the rented house in Tokyo employ the evergreen azalea and 'striped daphne' (probably *Daphne odorata* Aureo-Marginata) as a 'background' and daphne, camellia and azalea as a 'wilderness', and had no doubt observed more sophisticated examples of the use of evergreens to shape scale and space in the famous gardens of Japan.[70]

An example that evoked Farrer's wondering delight in the art of small-scale imitation came when he ventured to Ikao, a Japanese town 'of small, precipitous streets'. He made an excursion into the mountainside, and made a find:

At one point there is by the wayside a temple, enshrined richly among waving pines. It has a little rock-garden fronting the road. This is a territory of eight foot square, composed in a pebbly hollow. The bounding wall is a precipice with a jutting promontory of crag. Ivy drapes the uppermost pinnacles, and down the face of the rocks go drifting wreaths of creepers. From each fissure sprouts a bush of azalea cut into a rounded shape, whose pruning results in a concentrated ball of fiery blossom against the grey of the cliff. As for the floor, it is of white pebble, diversified with mossy stones. There is, about this small compilation, a magnificent delicacy of refined imagination, which has

FIG. 4.4. Farrer, photograph of a roadside garden, Ikao, Japan, 1903. (RBGE).

designed the limited space into a perfect proportion of mountain rock and dale. The illusion is pleasant and convincing. The tiny garden has, too, a kindly luxuriance not often permitted to Japanese creations. It riots with blossom and leafage. Yet, for all its masses of bush and flower, the effect of the whole is never injured. The conception remains unmistakable. Here is a tract of precipice, immemorially overgrown with shrubs; a steep place falling through woodland into the embrace of the sea. The garden is some high headland and craggy bay, at whose feet lap the passionate seas of Japan.[71]

Setting a standard; a place, embodying an approach to landscape design on a small scale, to try to emulate. The kind of sight that provided an aesthetic ideal when Farrer himself was making parts of the rock-garden at Ingleborough Hall. Luckily Farrer took photographs (albeit blurred) of this find (figure 4.4). In general, the subtlety and flexibility of his aesthetic enjoyments, shown by a comparison between his appreciation of this Japanese garden, revealing its 'magnificent delicacy of refined imagination', and his relish for the very different effect of the decoration in the cave at Dambulla, for example, is memorable. As a young man of 22, the weight of the impression on him of the Japanese skills in miniaturisation surely helped to form his own sensibility with respect to the tasks of design.

The design of rock-gardens in Japan had for a long time been strongly influenced by the famous activities of Zen masters and by the examples they had left behind (of which the raked garden at Ryoanji is the most famous). In thinking about possible ideas (as design principles) that Farrer might have admired and been affected by during his stay in Japan, we should concentrate rather more deeply on the question of Zen influence, but approach this by first drawing back for a moment to make a more general point about Farrer's own approach to explaining his Japanese experience.

Farrer does not 'plunge into the bottomless sea of [Japanese] mysticism', either here as quoted from *My Rock-Garden*, or earlier in *The Garden of Asia*. In espousing impressions, rather than facts, and avoiding mysticism, he probably had in mind, at least so far as gardens were concerned, the example *a contrario* of Josiah Conder's *Landscape Gardening in Japan* (1893); filled as that is with facts, and accounts of mysticism in design, and dull as the result is to read. In his own garden design Farrer employed no overt symbols of Buddhism (carved or engraved stones, for example; statues of a bodhisattva). He derived influence from Japan, especially with respect to miniaturisation, and the representing of natural scenes: glen, gorge, mountain top, saddle between hills. Miniaturisation was a feature of monastery gardens, with their famous use of boulders with raked gravel. Yet Conder prints a diagram of a 'Religious arrangement of garden stones' — 48 in all, and provides a key to the 'names of some Buddha or saint' that each rock bears.[72] There is nothing like this in Farrer's own garden design, where in any case, as we have seen, the plants are more important than the stones.

We have already established that Farrer's design with plants was dedicated to giving the plant the best possible conditions, and therefore to showing the flowers off best. These concerns we have shown to be partly, at least, determined by his Buddhist

A BOULDER IN THE OLD GARDEN, PLANTED WITH PINKS, SAXIFRAGES, CAMPANULAS AND HOUSELEEKS.

FIG. 4.5. Farrer, a planted boulder; photograph from *My Rock Garden*.

A LIMESTONE BOULDER IN THE OLD GARDEN.

FIG. 4.6. Farrer, another planted boulder; photograph from *My Rock Garden*.

FIG. 4.7. Wild plant community, Norber Moor, 2014. Photo: author.

belief. As he put it in *The Rock Garden*: 'the children of the wild hills [alpines] are to be made [to] play out their captive life [...] with the utmost brilliancy and happiness of which captivity is capable.'[73] They must not be crowded together by the hundred, not least because they are: 'plants whose personality has far more interest and charm than any bedding Annual.'[74] The photographs that illustrate *My Rock-Garden* show some of the ways in which Farrer combined plants into beautiful groups (figures 4.5, 4.6). They demonstrate his compositional skill; his mastery of *combination*, which has variety (of form, of habit of growth, of flower shapes and colours) as its principle and a pleasing natural-seeming grouping or mixture as a result. The art also comes from the creation of harmony with the variety. This involves avoidance of stark contrasts or contradictions, and the avoidance of vulgarity of form(s). It is also partly dependent on the timing of the flowers' blooming. In these small, elaborate and painstaking works Farrer achieved magnificent results in an art that sought to improve on and concentrate the effect of the natural places from which its visual conception was derived. Figure 4.7 shows my own photograph of a spontaneous group of wild flowers growing on the exposed carboniferous limestone strata of Norber Moor, only a mile or two from Ingleborough Hall, in 2014. The group includes Harebell, *Scabiosa columbaria*, *Pimpinella saxifraga*, and a species of *Hieracium*. It is difficult to resist the idea that such communities, found by the young Farrer, appealed to him by their wildness and by the apparent sociability of the groupings (different plant personalities enjoying, as it were, each others' company); and that this formed a strong element in his aesthetic imagination: contributed, that is, to the formation of an aesthetic ideal for his chosen activity of designing with plants and rock. My argument is that his achieved mature designs imitated the wild plant communities of the hills, adapting, concentrating and exaggerating their effect while retaining a feeling of random association and thus a recognisably natural or spontaneous element as an idea or an impression for the viewer.

Farrer himself expressed some of these ideas verbally (in addition, that is, to designing his gardens to embody them). His 'Preface' to his close friend E. A. Bowles' book, *My Garden in Spring* is usually discussed by writers on Farrer for the sake of the controversy it stirred up in horticultural circles, antagonizing the millionaire Sir Frank Crisp and his supporter Ellen Wilmott against Farrer and Bowles.[75] Setting that aside, however, we can understand the Preface as a statement of Farrer's values in design: values at least in part shared by Bowles. In this respect the dismissal of a certain type of gardening associated with plutocrats amounts to setting in a particular context Farrer's ideas so that the latter can be apprehended more clearly:

> Passion for display appears the ruling note in English horticulture of every kind and in every period: we want a show [...] the rich must have their money's worth in show; culture will not give it to them nor rarity, nor interest in the plants themselves [...] neither blending nor variety [...] nothing but colour, laid on callously in slabs as if from a paintbox [...] a mosaic [...] a glare of expensive magnificence.
>
> The soul of a real garden lies in the perfect prosperity of the plants of which it is the home [...] here the plants are lords, and the rocks take their dim place in the background. [...] the real gardener works with love and knowledge and personal devotion, and not with money and orders issued to a nurseryman.[76]

Farrer argues against being too neat and tidy, as constant weeding eradicates plants that may be interesting and that may help to form interesting groupings.

> The highest art is to conceal art [...] the good rock garden [...] should [...] look [...] like the unharvested flower-fields of the hills — effortless, serene, and apparently neglected [...] nothing is harder in any walk of art than to strike the perfect note of calm assurance [...] the really good garden looks [...] simple and unaffected and easy. [... In E. A. Bowles' garden] the plants are given free scope for enjoying themselves in the company they love, and rare difficult treasures are jostled into health and happiness again by the rough-and-tumble of life as they lived it in the hills.[77]

It would be invidious at this point to suggest that Farrer is being over-insistent, and that he is mixing up Bowles' gardening with his friend's philanthropic tendency to act as host to disadvantaged boys from the poorer areas of London. Rather than getting distracted by those possibilities, it is more valuable to concentrate on these passages as statements of Farrer's aesthetics of garden design (or designing with plants). A letter to Bowles provides evidence of this from a different angle. The letter discusses (in the form of notes, possibly composed after some glasses of wine had been taken) the criteria for a cup Farrer is donating to the Royal Horticultural

Society as a prize. Making his own prize is a way of instituting his own tastes. The prize should reward:

> Plants specially suited to the special attention paid to correctness of name, and to the ^quality of exhibitor's observations on each plant^ rock garden. Colour forms of well-known species included. Doubles excluded. Natural hybrids allowed; rarity, novelty, interest to rank above size of specimen [...] Cup open to amateurs and professionals alike, the Craven Nursery ostentatiously excluded.[78]

It is possible to conclude that Farrer's preferences in plants, and in the meta-culture of them, reflect his sense of self rather strongly. But we can see that *natural* spontaneous variety of colour and form are being prized above nurserymen's efforts ('doubles excluded'). Without speculating about cause-and-effect relationships, we can at least say that these views harmonize with Japanese aesthetics based on natural process (visible in Japanese pottery, for example). There is also in Farrer's specifications a valuing, in a factory-produced world, of principles that are fundamental to a humanistic outlook: 'rarity, individuality, and character'.[79]

In his works of art, we find a respect for each plant. We understand that Farrer had a belief in the Buddha-nature of plants, and even of rocks. This strengthened his earlier boyhood's instinctive attitude to flowers (his love of them). Yuriko Saito states that, in the history of Japanese aesthetics, an early 11th-century treatise urged attention to the native characteristics of each rock, 'as if each rock is requesting that its voice be heard and respected.' Thereafter:

> A further theoretical basis of this respect for each object was supplied by Zen Buddhism. The Zen identification of Buddha nature, or ultimate reality, with the thusness or being-such-ness of an object cultivates an attentive and respectful attitude towards the characteristics essential to defining its individuality. This Zen celebration of the thusness of each object encourages the artist to lend sympathetic eyes and ears to what the object is prepared to articulate and to assist in distilling its quintessential features.[80]

The objects, in the case of gardens, obviously do not need to be confined to rocks. They could be individual plants. In Farrer's case plants were the most important elements. The importance of this within my argument is that it takes belief into the domain of aesthetics, and the aesthetics of gardens in particular. Arguably this view, identified here with Zen, confirmed another of Farrer's pre-existing preferences: that for the display of individual plants rather than the massing together of large crowds of identical plants. Brent Elliott has described the controversy in which Farrer engaged about the question of the massing of plants in rock gardens. Having helped to defeat the massing of plants in carpet-bedding (an elite, because expensive, activity, as well as being arguably aesthetically crude) the venerable gardener William Robinson had defended the massing of plants for colour in rock gardens! Farrer pointed out the contradiction: 'carpet-bedding is bursting to life again in the midst of the very rock garden itself, of all places impermissible and improbable.'[81] He objected on various grounds: expense; obliviousness to rarity of the plants; obliviousness to the intrinsic interest of the individual plants themselves;

aesthetic vulgarity; no blending or variety. It is easy to see how Farrer's skills in combination, composition, variety and harmony lead to a clear championing of subtlety and individuality that contrasts with the use of massed flowers.[82] Lack of interest in the plants themselves as individual entities he also identifies as a cardinal error.

Three elements thus constitute Farrer's formation with respect to plants: early love; the deepening realisation based on understanding of their Buddha-nature; and a sense of how that can be used to form a new aesthetics of garden design (especially rock-garden design). The second of these stages was clearly Buddhist, especially perhaps Tendai and Shingon in tendency; the third, arguably influenced by Zen Japanese aesthetics.

So far as larger-scale design is concerned, Farrer did not work as a peripatetic garden designer like the somewhat older Thomas Mawson. Some gardens were no doubt influenced by his practice and principles, all accessible via his published writings. The Craven Nursery operated as a purveyor of plants, especially alpines and aquatic plants, together with rocks for rockwork. The garden at Crarae in Argyll, developed by Farrer's aunt Grace, Lady Campbell of Succoth, and his cousin, Sir George, featured a rock garden dating from the time of Farrer's greatest fame as a rock gardener (1912), and a steep glen or gorge planted with rhododendrons and azaleas when Farrer was engaged in planting rhododendrons at Ingleborough and sending others back from Burma (1918 onwards). It is striking how similar the topography of Crarae is to the glen named the Black Ark at Ingleborough; but whether all these similarities can be claimed as showing Farrer's designs, rather than just his influence, is a moot point.[83]

A fellow nurseryman, W. E. Th. Ingwersen, writing in 1932, paid tribute to Farrer's effect on several fronts:

> In no small part has his influence made the Alpine Garden Society possible [...] I need say little more about Farrer's influence on Rock Gardening in our country. There never has been, and I do not think there ever will be, another who will leave so vivid a mark of his passing on any single horticultural subject. [...] almost every catalogue on Alpine Plants contains conscious or unconscious quotations from Farrer's books [...] Every modern Rock Garden in itself with its moraine or scree is a memory to him who put the Dog's Grave, the Almond Pudding and the Devil's Lapful style of Rock Gardening to derision. If neither the moraine nor scree or the underground watered beds are Farrer's own invention, but the result of his wide reading on all matters apertaining to the subject so near our hearts, there can be no doubt that Farrer has had the widest and most impressive influence on Rock Gardening, and his works bid fair to become classics on their entrancing subject.[84]

Had Farrer's gardening at Ingleborough Hall been better known, Ingwersen would no doubt have written that his works had become classics *of* their entrancing subject.

Notes to Chapter 4

1. Farrer, *The Rock Garden* (London: J. C. & E. C. Jack, n. d. but 1912), p. 23. The emphasis is Farrer's.
2. Shulman, *A Rage for Rock Gardening*, p. 44.
3. Farrer, *In a Yorkshire Garden* (London: Arnold, 1909), p. 13.
4. Ibid., pp. 14–15.
5. Ibid., p. 16.
6. Points scored in a flower-show competition.
7. *In a Yorkshire Garden*, pp. 19–20.
8. Shulman, *A Rage for Rock Gardening*, p. 45.
9. Farrer, *My Rock-Garden* (London: Arnold, 1907), p. 1.
10. Ibid., pp. 103–04.
11. Lambert Schmithausen, *Plants in Early Buddhism and the Far eastern Idea of the Buddha-Nature of Grasses and Trees* (Lumbini, Nepal: Lumbini International Research Institute, 2009), p. 101.
12. Ibid., pp. 106–17, 253.
13. Farrer, *In Old Ceylon*, p. 22.
14. Schmithausen, *Plants in Early Buddhism*, p. 32. Thanks to Patrick Olivelle for confirming the consonance of the two translations with the meaning of the Sanskrit original.
15. Here Schmithausen puts a Chinese character that I have omitted.
16. Ibid., pp. 265–66. Here, and in other quotations from Schmithausen, the parenthetical words and phrases, employing two shapes of parenthesis, are Schmithausen's own. (In all other quotations my own clarifications occur in square brackets).
17. Farrer, *In Old Ceylon*, p. 25.
18. Schmithausen, *Plants in Early Buddhism*, pp. 294–95. Annen's transliterated text reads 'Shinjō sōmoku jō butsu shihi.'
19. Ibid., p. 247.
20. Hazama Jikō, 'The Characteristics of Japanese Tendai', *Japanese Journal of Religious Studies*, 14/2–3 (1987), 101–12.
21. Schmithausen, *Plants in Early Buddhism*, p. 305–07. Similar ideas are found in the 12th-century tendai text, *Kankōruijū*. (pp. 301–05).
22. Ibid., p. 26.
23. Discussed and quoted by Donald S. Lopez, *Buddhism and Science: A Guide for the Perplexed* (Chicago: University of Chicago Press, 2008), p. 111.
24. Ibid., p. 112.
25. Ibid., pp. 112, 124.
26. Schmithausen, *Plants in Early Buddhism*, pp. 322–24 especially.
27. Farrer, *In Old Ceylon*, pp. 24–25.
28. Schmithausen, *Plants in Early Buddhism*, pp. 260–62.
29. Ibid., p. 287.
30. Ibid., pp. 267, 169–70.
31. Yuriko Saito, 'Japanese Aesthetics: Historical Overview', in *The Encyclopedia of Aesthetics*, ed. by Michael Kelly and others, 4 vols (New York: Oxford University Press, 1998) 2, pp. 545–53 (p. 547).
32. Schmithausen, *Plants in Early Buddhism*, p. 278 n.844.
33. Lieutenant-Colonel Sir Francis Younghusband, K.C.S.I., K.C.I.E., 'Geographical Work in India for this Society', *The Geographical Journal*, XLIX, 6 (June 1917), 401–15, (p. 412).
34. Farrer, *Among the Hills: A Book of Joy in High Places* (1911; London: Swarthmore, 1927), p. 104.
35. Ibid., p. 105.
36. Ibid., p. 105.
37. Jacquetta Hawkes, *A Land* (London: Cresset, 1951), 'Preface', p. 1.
38. Ibid., p. 162.
39. Ibid., p. 100.
40. We now understand limestone and chalk to be partially precipitated chemically from water supersaturated with calcium carbonate, thus only partially formed from the bodies of small organisms.

41. Farrer, diary entry for 6th August, 1920, quoted by Ann Farrer, 'Farrer as Illustrator: The Diaries of Reginald Farrer' in Illingworth and Routh, *Reginald Farrer*, pp. 64–71 (p. 67).
42. Farrer, *Among the Hills*, p. 62.
43. Shulman, *A Rage for Rock Gardening*, pp. 44–45.
44. Shulman, *A Rage for Rock Gardening*, pp. 111–15. The writers are E. A. Bowles, a friend of Farrer; Marion Cran; Vita Sackville-West; Andrew Young; Edward Bunyard. The quotations cover the dates 1914–1950.
45. Christopher Lloyd, 'The Jarman Garden Experience' in *Derek Jarman: A Portrait*, ed. by R. Wollen (London: Thames and Hudson, 1996), pp. 147–52 (p. 149).
46. Gertrude Jekyll, *Wood and Garden: Notes and Thoughrs, Practical and Critical, of a Working Amateur* (London: Longmans, Green & Co., 1899), pp. 253–54. Jekyll often uses 'happy' in this way.
47. Clarence Elliott, 'The Late Reginald Farrer: an Appreciation', *The Gardeners' Chronicle*, 15 January 1921, 31.
48. Anon., *The Garden* Nov. 27th, 1920.
49. W. T. Stearn, 'Introductory Tribute to Reginald Farrer', in Illingworth and Routh, *Reginald Farrer*, pp. 4–5, 7.
50. E. H. M. Cox, obituary of Farrer, *Gardener's Chronicle* (Nov. 20 1920) p. 247; and *Plant Hunting in China: A History of Botanical Exploration in China and the Tibetan Marches* (London: Collins, 1945), p. 170.
51. Farrer, *My Rock-Garden* (London: Arnold, 1907), p. 8.
52. Ibid., p. 9. Warley was Ellen Wilmott's famous garden.
53. Ibid., p. 9.
54. Farrer, *The Garden of Asia*, chapters 3 and 4 (pp. 15–28).
55. Ibid., pp. 15–16.
56. Farrer, *The Rock Garden*, all these quotations from p. 11.
57. Farrer, *The Garden of Asia*, p. 20.
58. Farrer, *The Rock Garden*, p. 3.
59. W. Brent Elliott, 'Farrer and the Victorian Rock Garden', in Illingworth and Routh, *Reginald Farrer*, pp. 27–35 (p. 33).
60. Thomas Macadam, 'A Wonderful New Kind of Rock Garden', *Country Life in America*, v. 21, (April 15, 1912), p. 49.
61. Elliott, 'Farrer and the Victorian Rock Garden', p. 32. For a longer view of the effects of alpine plant horticulture on garden design in Europe, see Denis Lambin, 'From Grottoes to the Alps — A contribution to a history of rock and alpine gardens', *Journal of Garden History*, 14, 4 (1994), 236–56.
62. Professor J. Bretland Farmer, 'Preface' to Reginald Farrer, *The Rock Garden*, p. vii.
63. E.A. Bowles, *My Garden in Spring* (London: T. C. and E. C. Jack, 1914), pp. 104–06.
64. Farrer, *My Rock-Garden*, pp. 14–15.
65. Farrer, *In a Yorkshire Garden*, pp. 167, 169.
66. Farrer, *The Garden of Asia*, p. 21.
67. Ibid., p. 22.
68. Farrer, *The Rock Garden*, pp. 10–11. More recent examples of this Japanese tradition can be seen in (for example) Tatsui Teien Kenkyujo, *Garden Views III: Water and Stream Gardens* (Tokyo: Kenchiku Shiryō Kenkyusha, 1991).
69. Farrer, *The Rock Garden*, p. 15.
70. Farrer, *The Garden of Asia*, pp. 16–17.
71. Ibid., pp. 238, 240–41.
72. Josiah Conder, *Landscape Gardening in Japan* (1893: reprint New York: Dover Publication, 1964), pp. 43–44.
73. Farrer, *The Rock Garden*, p. 2.
74. Ibid.
75. Brent Elliott describes the rock garden controversy briefly in 'Farrer and the Victorian Rock Garden', pp. 30–33.
76. Farrer, 'Preface' to E. A. Bowles, *My Garden in Spring*.

77. Ibid.
78. Royal Horticultural Society, Lindley Library, E. A. Bowles Collection, EAB/2/3/5, letter dated October 1st.
79. This phrase is quoted from Alan Bennett's encomium on John Williams, and represents the values perpetuated by Williams in a way that Bennett found exemplary: see Bennett, *Untold Stories* (London: Faber and Faber, and Profile Books, 2005) paperback (2006), p. 223.
80. Yuriko Saito, 'Japanese Aesthetics: Historical Overview', p. 550.
81. Farrer, 'Introduction' to E. A. Bowles, *My Garden in Spring*, p. vii, quoted by Elliott, 'Farrer and the Victorian Rock Garden', p. 31.
82. Elliott shows how, in addition to Robinson, others were ranged against Farrer over this issue and as a result became his enemies: Sir Frank Crisp, whose garden at Henley-on-Thames, later owned by the Beatle George Harrison, featured a rock-work Matterhorn; and Ellen Wilmott, whose 'gorge' in her rock garden at Warley we saw Farrer admiring.
83. My knowledge of Crarae is derived from a visit there in August 2012, and conversations with the head gardener, Nigel Price.
84. W. E. Th. Ingwersen, 'Reginald Farrer and his Influence on Present-Day Rock Gardening', in *Reginald Farrer, Author, Traveller, Botanist and Flower Painter*, ed. by F. H. Fisher (The Alpine Garden Society: A Bound Edition of the *Alpine Garden Society's Bulletin*, Vol. 1, No. 10, 1932), pp. 34–38 (pp. 34, 37–38).

CHAPTER 5

Literary Impressionism:
The Garden of Asia

> If experience consists of impressions, it may be said that impressions *are* experience, just as (have we not seen it?) they are the very air we breathe.
> HENRY JAMES, 'The Art of Fiction', 1888.[1]

In becoming a modernist in garden design, Farrer applied lessons learned from the Japanese to the task of renewing practices and forms of gardening. After his return from Japan, he continued to run the Craven Nursery. At the same time as being a gardener and nurseryman, Farrer was engaging in literary activities. It is becoming obvious, by now, considering the quotations from Farrer already given, that he was literary; but before studying in this short chapter and at greater length in the two following chapters some of his literary works, I want to look briefly at two passages from personal letters in order to demonstrate how deeply he lived a literary form of psychological experience. This also serves as a reminder of his multiple interconnected interests.

The first quotation is from the letter to his mother in which he reports to her Princess Louise's warning against Ceylonese planters. He writes that: 'The planters form a close intolerant caste, hardened into a cast-iron crust of Englishry.' Here we see clearly the poetry of his written thought, even in a letter home: how language moves in him in a poetic way. The phrase features a dense combination of alliteration of 'c', 's' and 't' (joined in effect by the solitary 'd') in 'close intolerant caste, hardened [...] cast-iron crust' and joins to this an assonance involving the abandonment of the repeated 'o' sounds of the earlier part of the sentence, and domination by the 'a' sound 'planters ... caste, hardened ... cast ... crust'. In this little drama of sounds, this enacted struggle of phonemes, and its insistence on only four forms repeated dogmatically, the phrase enacts on the level of sound the closeness and narrowness of the world-view that Farrer condemns in the planters.

The second passage from a personal letter that I want to consider is Farrer's use of the phrase 'mincing and mewing about', applied to himself, in the letter from Burma in which he asks Aubrey Herbert to find him a wife. First we should recall how the phrase is used:

> Against all evidence, I hope by now that I am a trifle more seasoned and less selfish and silly than I've always been [...] I can't afford to waste any more years in mincing and mewing about and pretending grand passions.[2]

Farrer, as I stated, has adapted the traditional figure, 'mopping and mowing', with its ghoulish connotations, into 'mincing and mewing'. In fact the poet Shelley had used the combination of 'mincing' and 'mewing' in his description of women in hell/London, in his satire 'Peter Bell the Third':

> There are mincing women, mewing
> (Like cats, who *amant misere*)
> Of their own virtue, and pursuing
> Their gentler sisters to that ruin,
> Without which — what were chastity?[3]

This shows the density of historical knowledge, and the complexity, of Farrer's literary mind. The cats in Shelley are an analogy; in Farrer a metaphor. Farrer equates himself with Shelley's women, who are hypocrites. Chastity only exists because prostitution exists. Shelley provides a footnote to the word 'chastity':

> What would this husk and excuse for a virtue be without its kernal [sic] prostitution, or the kernal prostitution without this husk of a virtue? I wonder the women of the town do not form an association, like the Society for the Suppression of Vice, for the support of what might be called the 'King, Church and Constitution' of their order. But this subject is almost too horrible for a joke.

So we conclude that Farrer has been dwelling on questions of chastity, virtue and prostitution, as his repeated use in other letters from the same period of the word 'harlot' and 'harlotries', also shows.

These two quotations suggest such a thorough permeation of his thought, at such a profound level, with literary and poetic energies, that it might have been more surprising if Farrer had *not* become a literary figure himself. However, he did; and I will begin my discussion of his productions in this field by reverting for the rest of this chapter to his first such work, written in consequence of his travel to the Far East.[4]

At the beginning of *The Garden of Asia: Impressions from Japan* (1904), Farrer issues a warning to the reader: 'let no one take this work as a guide-book to facts.' Instead, 'it is a guide-book of impressions'; that is to say, 'devoted rather to accuracy of impression than to the soul-destroying form of inaccuracy which is known as fidelity to facts. My object has been to give true pictures rather than elaborate statistics.'[5] We note in passing the employment of paradox, which assumes greater prominence later in *In Old Ceylon*, and it serves the purpose of literary impressionism here. Farrer styles himself a modern artist of 'true pictures', because insisting on the subjective element as truth. Of impressions, Oscar Wilde had written that:

> the only civilized form of autobiography [...] deals [...] with the thoughts of one's life [...] with the spiritual moods and imaginative passions of the mind [...] [The critic's] sole aim is to chronicle his own impressions [...] for the highest criticism deals with Art not as expressive but as impressive purely.[6]

Wilde reinforces the lesson previously expressed by Walter Pater, in both *Studies in the Renaissance* (1873) and the essay on style in *Appreciations* (1889), and it is with Pater that literary impressionism, at least in English, begins. In his essay on 'Style' he had argued:

> For just in proportion as the writer's aim, consciously or unconsciously, comes to be the transcribing, not of the world, not of mere fact, but of his sense of it, he becomes an artist, his work fine art; and good art [...] in proportion to the truth of his presentment of that sense [...]
>
> — The transcript of his sense of fact rather than the fact, as being preferable, pleasanter, more beautiful to the writer himself. In literature, as in every other product of human skill, in the moulding of a bell or a platter for instance, wherever this sense asserts itself, wherever the producer so modifies his work as, over and above its primary use and intention, to make it pleasing [...] there, 'fine' as opposed to merely serviceable art, exists. [...]
>
> Such is the matter of imaginative or artistic literature — this transcript, not of mere fact, but of fact in its infinite variety, as modified by human preference in all its infinitely varied forms.[7]

It is important to note that Pater is not advocating the removal of facts, but the writing of facts according to the truth of their perception by the writer. Bearing in mind Farrer's defence of the 'true pictures' of his 'impressions', as well as his subtitle, we can take it that this is what Farrer has set himself to do. Building on the tradition of British empiricist philosophy, Pater had earlier shown that impressions are the last 'tremulous wisp' to which consciousness, our sense of 'what is real in our lives, fines itself down.'[8] This earlier view paves the way for Henry James's assertion that stands as the epigraph to this chapter.

Farrer offers an intimation that even French impressionism may be regarded as an influence or model. The very first sentence of chapter I reads: 'Across the waste of waters a mass of broken grey sketches itself dimly against the turbulent clouds.' The pictorial metaphor comes from watercolour painting or wash drawing, and suggests that description will be an important feature of the book, as indeed it proves, though mainly without the distinct flavour of visual art conveyed by this first sentence, which would have become too affected had it been applied insistently.

The Garden of Asia has some claim to be considered Farrer's best novel next to *The House of Shadows* (which will be considered in the following chapter). To the obvious objection that *The Garden of Asia* is not a novel at all, but an account of Farrer's first prolonged stay in the Far East, both external and internal evidence can be brought to justify the view of the book as a novel. In 1924 Ford Madox Ford stated that he and Joseph Conrad had agreed that non-fiction could be a novel:

> according to our view of the thing, a novel should be the biography of a man or an affair, and a biography, whether of a man or an affair, should be a novel, both being, if they are efficiently performed, renderings of such affairs as are our human lives.

Ford repeats the verb 'rendering': a key word in impressionism, extensively used by Ford, Henry James; and employed by Farrer in his own Preface about his descriptions of Japan. To 'render' carries strong implications of giving back: the impression has come in, and now the writer attempts to describe it. It also has connotations of translation into a different medium, as when Shakespeare employs a character to offer a battle 'rendered in music' (OED).

The internal evidence to justify the understanding of *The Garden of Asia* as a novel is ramified. The first thing to consider is that here we have a cast of characters. The cast is headed by Wataguchi, the small, wizened sixty-ish 'boy' in charge of the organisation of the household once the narrator has set up house in Japan:

> He had a genial manner of announcing an important visitor perhaps three weeks after the said visitor had come and gone, by which time Wataguchi had also succeeded in entirely forgetting the man's name, and the momentous message that he had left. When these proceedings roused our spleen, Wataguchi would face the efforts of our indignation with the happiest of smiles, regarding the whole affair, and especially our irritation, as a perfect triumph of quiet humour.[9]

With Wataguchi, the literary mode is humour, and this main servant is surrounded by a group of lesser servants, such as the cook (who moves with wife, baby and niece into the house rented by the narrator for himself), or 'Mr. Desire' the *kurumaya* (rickshaw-puller) who lives in a 'dog-kennel' by the front gate with his wife and noisy baby. The two other main characters are the geisha, Lady Little Willow Tree, who brings a love interest into the account; and the narrator himself. The people who do not feature at all in the book are the English companions who were in fact with Farrer in Japan: Aubrey Herbert, his friends Gerard and Eric Collier, joined at least for a while by Herbert's mother Lady Carnarvon and the Colliers', Lady Monkswell; and Gertrude Bell with her brother Hugo. There are occasional vague allusions in the first person plural ('we', 'our'), and an even rarer reference to 'our friends', so the effect is of ghostly company; but the narrator is central and the other characters mainly Japanese. Taking its tone perhaps from Wataguchi, the comic servant, the book in the main gives the effect of genial good-humour throughout.

The young narrator is not above rebuking himself and trying to learn from his mistakes. A significant example comes during an excursion in the cold of early spring to Inage. There is a view of Mt. Fuji, 90 miles away, and beautiful pine woodland, where 'man moves like the unreal ghost he is' (p. 42). There are dunes; a cliff-top with coarse long grass, where one can lie full length in a sunwarmed hollow, 'and listen to the bitter winds that whistle overhead, bearing over the sea to earth the sharp message of spring' (p. 43). The 'wanderer' picks camellia flowers ('that beautiful flower of death') from nearby bushes. And as his rickshaw pulls him away towards the railway:

> Suddenly, a shock-headed boy of fifteen leaps on to the road and holds out imploring hands. He runs along by the rickshaw's side, still with gestures of entreaty. He pleads with his eyes, and unintelligible words proclaim his wishes. But the wanderer sits bolt upright, and, remembering the golden rule that to succour beggars is to foster intemperance, hugs himself upon his virtuous denial and passes righteously upon his way. [...] So the wanderer regards the horizon stonily, and takes no heed. Then, at last, an idea flashes across him. There are no public-houses here. Can the beggar have had another idea than money? The wanderer looks back. Upon the wind-swept road the boy stands still.

The rickshaw passes a graveyard.

A small congregation of clustered tombstones marks the holy place, and on

the tombs of the bodies are flowers laid in tribute to the glorified souls. It
was in tribute to some dear thing dead that the boy had desired even one of
our glowing flowers of death. And the gift would have brought us merit. But
we denied him. So, at last, we recognise the truth of his entreaties. But our
comprehension comes too late. [...] The boy sinks wistfully back in the dusk [...]
The glory of day fades into the bitter cold of night. And in our hands the glow
of the death-flowers, too, has faded like a phantom. They are all bruised, and
their crimson crowns are fallen into the dust. Their death has been useless. And
still, against the dull glare of sunset, that dark figure watches tragically, unable
to understand our hardness of heart. (pp. 43–45).

So the narrator learns that what fits one culture does not help in another. Conventions of uncharity are not appropriate in a non-Protestant country. Attribution
of intemperance, contradicted by devotion to the memory of the dead, says more
about the character of the attributer than that of the potential recipient of charity.
Incomprehension and futility fill minds as a result. The narrator has the honest
confidence to admit — and at quite some length — his fault.

The Garden of Asia has two chapters on Japanese gardens, one on housekeeping,
another on shops and shopping. One chapter deals with Korea, and another renders
'Impressions round Peking'. Here the narrator finds an imperial garden at the palace
of Tangshan, deserted not long before by the Empress-Dowager. A chapter tells of
the first meeting with Lady Little Willow Tree (figure 1.3) in the 'Palace of the
Thousand New Delights'. There are descriptions of parties for the geishas. Another
chapter, originally printed in rather different form in the journal The Nineteenth
Century, discourses on the position of women in Japan, with special attention to the
tension between marriage and the geisha.[10]

One chapter describes a Buddhist temple service. Throughout the book the
narrator is strict against the faults of Christianity, and indeed of Euro-American
civilisation in general. 'In the eyes of all the Buddhas it is a pleasant and good thing to
give life and happiness', he tells us; 'whoever does thus acquires merit. The Buddhas
take delight in mercy; not, like the gloomy Moloch whom Christianity has adopted
from Judaism, in doom and sacrifice, and the smell of things slaughtered.' (pp.
128–29) Clearly, by the time of writing, Farrer has moved away from Christianity
and is turning, at least, towards Buddhism. In a later chapter the narrator visits
Kamakura and its famous statue of the Amida Buddha. 'Kamakura once was a high
and famous city [...] But it is now many centuries since Nitta Yoshisada marched
his troops in triumph through the streets, and the most gorgeous metropolis of the
East passed away for ever in a storm of blood and fire.' He finds the temple of 'Our
Lord Emma-O, the King of Hell. [...] Behind his altar crouches the god, writhing
for ever in the fury of his immortal rage against human sin and weakness. He is
terrible as justice, violent as righteous wrath. There are many Christians whose
gloomy theology might profitably adopt the image of Emma-O.' (pp. 220–21). The
chapter finally allows Farrer, in contemplation of the statue of the Amida Buddha,
to develop an affirmation that, though it bends the identity of the Amida Buddha
towards that of Shakyamuni, shows the bases of attraction that Buddhism exerted
on Farrer:

The Buddha is a Sakya-Muni in his love, his deep pity, his far sight across the fields of human error, and his unwearying helpfulness that watches and shows the way out of the wilderness. [...] the Master of Time and Things, before whom the years and sorrows cease to exist, who bids man face his life without cowardly appeal to divine responsibility, but with sure trust in the salvation that God has appointed for his achievement. [...] Here is the true Giver of Rest, the Comforter who teaches bravery and joy in life, through the knowledge that the root of all grief is disappointment, and the root of all disappointment desire. Here is one who cries for no feeble renunciation [...] but who promises rest from weariness, release from loneliness in pain, through the clear truth that God is just, a man's fate his own work, a man's sufferings the mere punishment of his selfish and inordinate demands. (pp. 224–25)

Emotion is paramount. The scientific Buddhism that we saw in Chapter One cited in the letter to Herbert (mentioning evolution, for example), thus came later. The employment in these two pages of Christian vocabulary and analogies ('God', 'giver of rest', even the quotation of 'come unto me all ye that labour and are heavy laden, and I will give you rest', p. 224, to encapsulate the message of the Buddha) indicate that Farrer is still at an early stage of his transition, as it were, from Christian to enthusiast for Buddhism. He also states here that the 'root of all disappointment is desire', an allusion to the Buddha's first teaching, whereas two years later in *The House of Shadows*, as we shall see, he has accepted (and puts into the mouth of a character) the view that delving deeper into cause reveals that the root of the other errors and sorrows is ignorance, which keeps desire in place.[11] Japan was the place where Farrer's devotion to Buddhism began. Figure 1.1 shows his photograph of a Buddha statue in the precincts of the 'main temple of Shiba Park', his visit to which is described in Chapter XIII of *The Garden of Asia*. The visitor by the back way, he tells us, can pass: 'beneath the eyes of [this] small Shaka–Buddha, whose compelling grace of smile remains a blessed memory of the Comforter who led the way to the Everlasting Peace' (p. 118). He describes a temple service for the once-great Tokugawa Shoguns: 'over their souls the love of the Buddha extends its hallowing majesty to this day, and for many days to come' (p. 124). It is love that, at this stage of Farrer's interest in Buddhism, is paramount.

Places able to release the feeling of such love exist all the more vividly by contrast with other regions. In the secular domain, the narrator visits Sapporo, a town built for the Japanese Emperor *ex nihilo* by Americans. It shows American values and 'genius': 'planted in the middle of nowhere [...] most pompously laid out, in rectangles [...] neatly intersecting streets on the most rigidly mathematical plan [...] constructed regardless of expense -- a useless mushroom [...] this inhospitable city of parade.' (p. 160)

After telling the reader a great deal about the culture of Japan, and something of China and Korea, and always the effect upon him of these Far Eastern experiences, the narrator finds himself at a climax when he departs for his homeward journey. And this is the moment in the book that makes clear the influence of Pierre Loti's *Madame Chrysanthème* (1888) on Farrer's *The Garden of Asia*. In fact Farrer mentions Loti's work three times in his book. When he first arrives, he writes of Nagasaki:

'Squalid and foul it is, with all the hedonistic opportunities that the simple heart of the European sailor craves. Here is the home of Madame Chrysanthème, that most un-Japanese of Japanese' (p. 2). Later, considering the geisha in general, he says: 'She is different indeed from the apathetic, unattractive creature whom Loti found brutalised by European lusts, and after a summer's experience, posed and painted exquisitely as a typical woman of Japan' (p. 205). Both these references are intended to enhance the idea that Farrer, whose stay was longer, had developed a better understanding of Japanese life than that acquired by Loti (and Farrer's book taken as a whole bears out this assertion). The third reference comes when dollars are applied as a salve to the grief of Japanese servants on having to part with their master, apparently successfully (p. 290). Farrer admits that this last example sounds like a borrowing from Loti, but asserts that it is in fact absolute truth.

Yet Loti's example cannot be brushed off so easily. In two ways, one large and general, the other specific, its literary influence is clearly discernible. The general point is that, in common with *The Garden of Asia*, Loti's book precisely combines autobiography, travel account, and novel. In other words, it creatively confuses genres of writing normally kept apart (and it led to an opera by Puccini in 1904). Loti's book is therefore a model for what Farrer attempted, which was also the combination of these three genres. There are major differences, of course. Loti's book also has the figure of the geisha at its heart, but the geisha in Farrer's book doesn't figure so centrally as in Loti's, and his narrator visits many more places (including China); so the travel account, where the individual consciousness renders its impressions of both physical and human geography, features more strongly. In combination with this, Farrer's book has much less of the feeling of a conventional novel: dialogue is kept very minimal, for example. Nevertheless, it is clear that Farrer learned from Loti's example. The more specific point of influence is discernible in the final scene, of parting, in Farrer's book. In contrast to Loti's central figure and narrator, who is a worldly, sceptical, and ultimately cynical sailor, Farrer's narrator is a young man, feeling tragic at the necessity of leaving what has become for him a 'fairyland' (p. ix). Wataguchi, his wife Snow-Lady, and Mr. Desire all present small gifts, and are to accompany the narrator to embarkation in Yokohama. At the railway station in Tokyo a crucial balance comes to the fore:

> Wataguchi, failing himself in the assumption of tragedy, for his wrinkled mask is only made for jollity and laughter, shifts the burden of the rôle on to his wife [...] proclaiming through brilliant smiles his extreme sorrow at our imminent departure, and the prostrating grief of Snow-Lady. 'My wife, she bery sorry,' exclaims the beaming Wataguchi. 'My wife, she bery cry. Last night I no sleep; all last night my wife, she bery, bery cry.' Unflattering truth compels us to own that on inspection Snow-Lady betrays not the slightest departure from her usual adamantine calm [...] Unless her husband had informed us to the contrary, we should have guessed her to be in the full enjoyment of her usual placidity. But, doubtless, he knows best. (p. 285)

As the narrator feels, 'It is cruel to imagine the whole display a matter of courteous routine, performed at the parting from every master, good or bad [...] No doubt [the servants] have made their percentages, no doubt they have cheated us and mocked at us; but now, at the last, let us hope that they really liked us just a little' (pp. 285, 286). This is more tolerant than is the cool response of Loti's narrator when he covertly sees Chrysanthème testing coins for genuineness rather than weeping with grief at imminent parting.[12]

But a more difficult ordeal, though similar in kind to that presented by the conundrum of Wataguchi, awaits *The Garden of Asia*'s narrator: 'Suddenly a startling sight perturbs our equanimity. There stands before us an unexpected agony.' It is, of course, Lady Little Willow Tree:

> beautiful in black silk of the quietest design. She is full of delicate loveliness, affecting a drooping sorrow at our going. She timidly presents a packet of notepaper, bedizened with flowers and devils and monsters of fairy-tale. We are to write to her from beyond the pallid immensities of the ocean (p. 287).

A central paradox of Japanese life comes to the fore as the narrator apostrophizes the geisha: 'You were a sphinx of delight. We found you exquisite and tender and brilliant in your triumphant gaiety [...] Her air simulates sorrow; she seems to weep, but half in burlesque' (pp. 287–88). The apostrophe comes to a climax:

> How often shall we remember your words across the infinite roaring waters! If only you feel the sorrow you affect — if only you feel the faintest echo of it! Can such a thing be credible? Why should a famous geisha regret our uncouth rubbish? Condescension enough if she pretend to regret it -- and yet, and yet, can it be all affectation -- that tender sorrow? (p. 289)

Lady Little Willow Tree waves the train away. As he watches carefully, the narrator's doubts accumulate: 'She stands, looking after the vanishing carriage with a soft smile; then, ere due time, we see her turn away, and shamble off on pattened feet among the densities of the crowd. [...] Does that smile fade with the moment of her turning away? This is not possible. But yet [...]' (p. 289). 'Ere due time [...] Does that smile fade?' Luckily servants are coming to Yokohama, where they say their final farewells, and Wataguchi again takes centre-stage in the narrator's mind:

> The thought of your cheery little smile, your caressing voice, your untiring willingness in service, will stand with us for ever as among the most beautiful things in Japan. You had faults, and we had more; but if we could feel as confident of the smile of the Amida upon our own lives as upon yours, we could front death without tremors. Who can do more than their best? And that you did, without reserve or jealousy [...] If you liked us, even a little, we have more than our reward [...] And yet, what is this? You were only a faithful servant. But [...] there is no nobler place for man to fill. As sermons unceasingly inform us, we are all servants. Very few of us, though, are faithful servants. (p. 291)

The apostrophizing of the figures of Lady Little Willow Tree and Wataguchi has a strong and memorable precedent in Loti's *Madame Chrysanthème*. There the narrator also makes a final apostrophe in words never actually spoken to Chrysanthème:

> Well, little mousmé, let us part good friends; one last kiss, even, if you like. I took you to amuse me; you have not perhaps succeeded very well, but after all you have done what you could: given me your little face, your little curtseys,

your little music; in short, you have been pleasant enough in your Japanese way. And who knows, perhaps I may yet think of you sometimes when I recall this glorious summer, these pretty quaint gardens, and the ceaseless concert of the cicalas.[13]

The style is identical: one would say a complete continuity between Loti's and Farrer's. The tone is very different: Loti's narrator, still indignant that the checking of money has driven out any grieving, is patronizing to a great degree; within a few pages he decides that Japan has jaded him; while Farrer's young narrator relishes Japan to the last.

The view of Wataguchi gives way to the spectacle of Mt. Fuji as Farrer's ship makes way. The narrator looks ahead to his return via North America:

> The air has a chill, the sea a ghostly pallor, the deepening twilight is full of sombre tones. Dull gloom descends, obliterating the watery plain that is our Sorrowful Way from the land of all delight to the land of hustle and hideousness [...]. The days are cursed. (p. 295)

In keeping with all the rest of this final chapter, the last phrase quoted here strikes exactly the right note: a sort of Arthurian curse, a young man's despair at having to leave an enchanted land and get back to dull reality. In the contrast between the severity of the utterance and the severity of the problem we have the ironic situation. Farrer sees himself ironically; but with a gentle, indulgent irony.

What is revealed as the narrator ponders the question of whether servants and geisha really feel any of the prostrating sorrows they profess, is the fact that he loves the exaggerated expression of emotional responses in Japanese speech, accompanied as this is by no real uneasiness about the emotion in question. The polite convention is aired, while the alleged emotions don't really grip their professors. Farrer found an innate theatricality in Japanese culture that greatly attracted him.

Farrer's account succeeds triumphantly in applying Pater's recommended approach. We derive a lot of information about Japan, communicated to us with Farrer's own sense of it, his impressions. Farrer's ability and willingness to communicate his impressions becomes a feature of all his travel writing. At the same time the strong parallels with *Madame Chrysanthème*, even the positive influence of that slightly earlier book, endow Farrer's book on Japan with something of a turn-of-the-century quality, mitigated and modernized though that certainly is by Farrer's urbane and lively narrator (who succeeds in not taking himself too seriously).

The Garden of Asia won the reviewers' approval. Thirty-eight papers and journals, from *The Field* to the *Montreal Star*, from the *Literary World* to the *Church Family Times*, produced highly enthusiastic or approving reviews.[14] The *Singapore Daily Post and Mercury* asserted that: 'We have read many books on Japan [...] this of Mr. Farrer, in its versatility of subject and fairness of comment, appears to be one of the very best.'[15] For the *Pall Mall Gazette*: 'Mr. Farrer' demonstrated 'brilliant use of his palette [...] remarkable talent [...] his style is as effective as it is carefully artistic.' The reviewer only demurred over two things, use of the phrase 'the wanderer' to designate the narrator, and use of the third person historic present tense.[16] The

Westminster Gazette found that, among the many books about Japan at the time, Farrer's had 'sufficient individuality to give it distinction.'[17] For the *Observer* the book was a more welcome travel book because 'unconventional', while the *World* found it 'a beautiful piece of literature'.[18] The only journal to produce a negative response was the *Athenaeum*, whose sour review disliked Farrer's writing and demanded a simple style. One or two other papers protested mildly against his style while still liking the book.[19] *Punch* was irritated by the style at first, but then found it 'amusing', and decided that the book's merits include 'keen observation, sub-acid humour, poetical fancy, and picturesque writing'.[20] The magazine also approved of Farrer's comments on the adaptive capacity of the Japanese with respect to other people's inventions. To have scored so favourably and so widely with the reviewers gave Farrer the best possible start to a literary life.

Notes to Chapter 5

1. Henry James, 'The Art of Fiction' (1884, rev. ed. 1888), in *The Art of Criticism: Henry James on the Theory and Practice of Fiction* ed. by W. Veeder and S. M. Griffin (Chicago: University of Chicago Press, 1986) pp. 172–73.
2. Continuation of the letter quoted in Fitzherbert, p. 224.
3. P. B. Shelley, *Poetical Works* ed. Thomas Hutchinson, new edition (Oxford: Oxford University Press, 1970), p. 351.
4. I am discounting here the student spoof tragedy, *Herod Through the Opera Glass,* that Farrer published in 1901.
5. Farrer, *The Garden of Asia: Impressions from Japan*, pp. ix–x.
6. Oscar Wilde, 'The Critic as Artist: I' in *Intentions* (1891: London: The Unicorn Press, 1945), pp. 75–117 (p. 110).
7. Walter Pater, 'Style' (1888), in *Appreciations, with an Essay on Style* (1889; London: Macmillan and Co., 1927), pp. 6–7.
8. Walter Pater, *The Renaissance: Studies in Art and Poetry, the 1893 text,* ed. Donald L. Hill (Berkeley: University of California Press, 1980), 'Conclusion', pp. 186–90 (p. 188). The 'Conclusion' was first published in the first edition, 1873.
9. Farrer, *The Garden of Asia*, p. 31. Page numbers hereafter in the main text.
10. Farrer, 'The Geisha: a Faithful Study', *The Nineteenth Century*, LV (April 1904), 630–36.
11. The Buddha's first teaching is described in Edward J. Thomas, *The Life of the Buddha as Legend and History,* 1927 (London: Routledge and Kegan Paul, 1975), p. 87.
12. Pierre Loti, *Japan (Madame Chrysanthème)*, trans. by Laura Ensor (New York: Frederick A. Stokes Company, n.d.), pp. 319–21. This translation was published in London in 1897.
13. Loti, *Japan (Madame Chrysanthème)*, p. 323.
14. All reviews mentioned in this paragraph were collected by Farrer himself and are in RBG Edinburgh, RJF 2/1/6/4.
15. *Singapore Daily Post and Mercury*, 28/12/1904.
16. *Pall Mall Gazette*, 26/9/1904.
17. *Westminster Gazette*, 17/8/1904.
18. *Observer*, 24/8/1904; *World*, 1/8/1904.
19. *East Anglian Daily Times*, 22/8/1904, *Investors' Review* 27/8/1904.
20. *Punch*, 1/9/1904.

CHAPTER 6

'A suicidal job':
Novel-Writing

In 1904 and 1905 Farrer wrote drama criticism for *The Speaker: the Liberal Review*, in November, 1904, for example, reviewing George Bernard Shaw's *John Bull's Other Island* under the subtitle, 'Salted Pap'.[1] 1904 saw the publication of the novelistic *The Garden of Asia*; and in 1906 he started to publish more conventional realist novels.

The questions that I posed earlier about Farrer's work in general (to what extent is he a modernist, and is his modernism dependent on his Buddhism?) will need to be revised, in relation to his novels, at least, in order to become more sensitive to current conditions when he was writing. During Farrer's lifetime literary impressionism was not confined to travel-writing. It took hold in prose fiction, especially the novel, and formed one slice of a cake of innovatory techniques which only later, Max Saunders states, began to be referred to as literary *modernism*. Practitioners of the time saw themselves as realists, impressionists, vorticists, futurists, even cubists. Farrer himself complained in a letter of 1919 to Ernest Gye that some English writers 'tend to go a-whoring over-much after [...] Cubist dislocations'.[2] In poetry, advanced poets became imagists, starting in 1908. Farrer practised impressionism in his travel-writing, as we have seen in his books about Japan and Ceylon. A prime question that comes up about Farrer's novels, therefore, is: can we regard them as examples of fictional impressionism? A positive answer to this question would put Farrer at the very vanguard of innovation in prose fiction. Addressing the question, however, makes it plain that the answer is not simple, and we might not legitimately be able to assign Farrer such an advanced place.

In fact, in the opinions of many garden writers it is hard to assign Farrer's novels any place at all. They have been universally disparaged by writers about gardens and plant-collecting since E. H. M. Cox started the trend.[3] Geoffrey Taylor reinforced this view in 1951 by insulting Farrer's fiction in *Some Nineteenth Century Gardeners*. Anthony Huxley, writing in *Country Life* (1980) actually celebrates the fact that the novels have 'vanished into a generally merciful limbo', quoting Taylor with approval.[4] Taylor's dismissal is also quoted approvingly by Basil Morgan in the entry on Farrer in the *Oxford Dictionary of National Biography*. Ursula Buchan in 1986 agrees to find his novels 'unreadable'. So does the eminent botanist W. T. Stearn (1991) and for the journalist Nicola Shulman they are 'dreadful' (2002).[5] It hardly needs saying in the face of this chorus of disapproval that none of his novels has been reprinted since his death, and at the time of writing they are not even available in cheap print-to-order editions on the second-hand market.[6]

Luckily a very important figure can be introduced to contest this chorus of disparagement and dismissal. Farrer's first published novel, *The House of Shadows*, (1906) was reviewed for the *Times Literary Supplement* by Virginia Stephen (who on her marriage to Leonard became Virginia Woolf).

The story features a landowning squire, Tempest Ladon, whose Italian wife has died many years ago. His naive son, St John, marries a middle-class, beautiful and passionate woman, Barbara. Father-in-law and daughter-in-law dislike each other cordially. The squire falls victim to a painful, hereditary, and terminal disease that deranges his previous equanimity. He wants to die, but his Christianity forbids him from self-murder. He tries to persuade St John to kill him. The son refuses. Much of the novel is concerned with Tempest Ladon's bitterness and the soured relations between the three main characters. In the end, love-letters of the squire's dead wife, which he thought were addressed to him, turn out to have been written to an Italian lover who is St John's real father. If this becomes generally known, the squire's 'son' will not be able to inherit the estate and any future son of the daughter-in-law will also be disinherited. The danger of this to her husband's happiness convinces Barbara that she must administer the necessary poison. The old man vengefully assumes that she will break down and confess and thus spread unhappiness throughout the household. He dies. The daughter-in-law, strengthened not only by the material inheritance but by the knowledge that her own son will not inherit its putative grandfather's awful disease, instead destroys the letters and resolves to preserve her secret.

In this plot Farrer's call for renewal is clear, and it is a call that extends very emphatically to renewal in religious belief. Christianity, in this view, emphasizing the dangers of hell-fire and divine retribution, cannot help people in their human and material (physical) dilemmas. The book is also concerned with strong-mindedness in women.

In her review, Virginia Stephen makes a series of judgements:

> In many novels [she begins,] the situation seems to have been suggested by the author's desire to introduce certain characters; in others the writer seems to have conceived his scheme first and to have made his characters its creatures. Mr. R. J. Farrer [...] has written a novel under the stress of an idea; and although his method has certain drawbacks it has undoubtedly produced a book remarkable for its force and continuity.[7]

Farrer is, of course, one of those who make his characters the creatures of his 'scheme'. Stephen continues:

> The drawback of the concentration which is the result of the scheme of the book is naturally that the characters are always seen under some sort of distortion, and that at intervals the idea behind comes too prominently and crudely to the foreground.

Stephen notes that as the plot thickens, 'the situation verges on the melodramatic':

> but the reserve and humour with which it is treated keep it in proper

proportions. The same purpose, that is, links all the chapters together, and each adds something of its own to the single impression. And that impression is so consistently gloomy that it is possible to resent the power with which it is expounded.

This comment seems to qualify Farrer as an 'impressionist'. If so, it is in the general terms put forward by Henry James in his essay 'The Art of Fiction':

> A novel is in its broadest definition a personal, a direct impression of life: that, to begin with, contributes its value, which is greater or less according to the intensity of the impression. But there will be no intensity at all, and therefore no value, unless there is a freedom to feel and to say.[8]

Farrer's *The House of Shadows*, with its painful story, its 'power', qualifies thus far, according to Stephen. Its limitations, she writes, 'are the limitations of a remarkable book, and in some degree spring from its strength.[...] Mr. Farrer is clearly a writer to be remembered.'

Other critics were less perceptive, though some noticed the power of the novel. For the *Standard*, Farrer's is 'Better constructed than nine novels out of ten'; the *Nottingham Guardian* found that 'the whole scheme of the book is marked out with great skill.'[9] A review in *The Athenaeum* concurs about the strength in Farrer's novel:

> There is a certain grandeur in Barbara's final act, upon which a quite other price is set when the dying man realizes the secret of St John's birth and that the hereditary taint can go no further. The characters are drawn with a vivid touch, but not one is genuinely agreeable.[10]

The last point made here also bothered a less generous reviewer. The anonymous contributor to the *Academy* suggests that Farrer shares the characteristic of naivety with his younger male character, and is an insane thinker:

> Mr. Farrer is, let us hope, a very young man whose omniscience may be modified by experience of life.[...] There is not a lovable character in this unpleasantly morbid book, if we except the nebulous Dean and Lisa the cat; but it is clever enough to make us hope that, when Mr. Farrer has read more widely and thought more sanely, he may yet do good work.[11]

No doubt Farrer was dismayed by such a review. Yet reviewers' objections to disagreeable characters are completely unfair. They stem from the reviewers' sentimentalism (the Dean being the most compassionate character, Lisa arguably the most innocent) and Farrer's lack of sentimentality in his creation and anatomisation of the characters. All three major characters are varied and divided personalities. Barbara and her father-in-law spend much of the book at loggerheads, trading sarcasms and half-covert insults: but their moment of conciliation (pp. 195–97) when both are worn out by their anxieties is genuinely moving. So is St John's stout defence of his beloved wife against his beloved father's tyrannies. Working within the constraints of his 'idea', to use Virginia Stephen's word, Farrer has created plausible and convincing characterisation.

The book is a minor classic. It benefits from the unity of its plot and the simplicity of its place (divided between London and Ottemer, the northern house of the

Ladons). It is a variant of the country house novel (in the sense at least that St John's loyalty to his home becomes a crucial issue as the plot builds to a climax). The book also contains elements of the Sensation Novel. The sexual assault by Tempest Ladon on his daughter-in-law is genuinely shocking, and the subsequent moral degradation it works in her painful to observe. All this suggests a novel the literary loyalties of which belong in the nineteenth century, alongside Wilkie Collins, perhaps; and some of the book's other virtues are similarly traditional. The minor characters are vividly realized: Lady Morland is wonderfully vulgar; she and Mrs. Bolpett are well distinguished by characteristics of their speech. The characterisation is subtle and convincing about how people's moods change, often in response to small seemingly insignificant actions (such as those of Lisa the cat); sometimes in response to fatigue, hunger and other physical conditions within the subject. Out of these insights Farrer builds three major characters who are divided against themselves. They have divided consciousnesses, split selves, ascending to mutual sympathy and compassion for a moment, plunging to mutual incomprehension and scorn for a while. Here is Tempest Ladon in a hotel in Leeds ('that gloomiest of cities', p. 157) on his way home from London, where he has learned of his fatal illness:

> Once more he was filled with good resolutions, and, as often happens, his good resolutions were tinged with bitterness. He determined definitely to keep a locked mouth on his evil prospect, to spare St John and Barbara any knowledge of his impending agony; to bear his burden all alone, without bowing young shoulders prematurely beneath a share of its intolerable weight. Enforced by Pride, by Good-feeling, by Generosity, these honest and noble resolutions admitted also Spleen and Jealousy to the council that ratified them. When all motives everywhere are pure and unmixed, then, and then alone, may we mortals fairly blame or praise. But now, in the highest is always a germ of the lowest, as in the lowest there is always some little infinitesimal glimmering of the higher. Pride and Self-reliance bade Mr. Ladon bear his trouble alone; but Pride was angry, as well as self-righteous, and declared viciously that "nobody cared," and that therefore nobody should be given an opportunity for wearisome hypocrisy. "What does it matter," said Mr. Ladon's jaundiced Pride — "what does it matter to St John and Barbara whether I die to-day or to-morrow -- in pain or in peace?" Therefore they were to be barred from his gruesome confidence. Jealousy, too was spiteful and active in giving of the good advice. "St John and Barbara are so wrapped up in each other that it would be cruel to sever them even for a month by intrusion of a sick man's sufferings." Thus Jealousy artfully stabbed herself with an air of sacrifice, and rubbed the wound red, until Mr. Ladon found himself thinking in mournful triumph that one day the inseparable pair would be sorry, when they knew all too late. (pp. 153–54)

The narrator's tone is ironic, and the turn in Mr. Ladon's feelings is charted convincingly, not least because the passage shows, without overtly saying it, that he is emotionally immature. Yet it might be objected that to employ a group of personifications to do the work is rather old-fashioned. But Tempest Ladon is an old-fashioned man, adhering to the past, to tradition, priding himself on his family's long possession of land. The personifications would be recognisable to his ancestors.

The rigidities of his thinking, as the novel unfolds them, determine his immaturity. In any case, *prosopopeia* is not a predominant trope of the novel; elsewhere the work of showing the turns in mood is performed by conversations or free indirect discourse.

A modern element is provided the Dean, Mr. Gordon-Wentworth. He is introduced as a child of fiction: the grandson of 'Admiral Sir Frederick Wentworth and of Anne his wife, an Elliott of Kellynch' (p. 190) — the protagonists of Jane Austen's *Persuasion*. Through invoking this work by his most revered novelist, Farrer is light-heartedly announcing the Dean's reliability and probity. The Dean turns out to be a remarkably modern and ecumenical churchman. In a lengthy conversation with Tempest, he acknowledges the need for renewal in the Church. He quotes a Buddhist 'proverb' and condemns 'anger and intolerance' (p. 212), having previously stated that 'ignorance' is arguably 'the only real sin in the world' (p. 210). While this last thought was, for Farrer at least, Buddhist,[12] a character in Rudyard Kipling's *Kim,* Colonel Creighton, utters a similar thought: 'There is no sin so great as ignorance.'[13] The same idea happens to be pre-figured by the character Machevill, pronouncing the Prologue in Christopher Marlowe's play *The Jew of Malta* (1590): 'I [...] hold there is no sin but ignorance.'[14] This thought was taken up and adapted almost exactly three hundred years later by Oscar Wilde, in *The Critic as Artist*, where there is this exchange between Gilbert and Ernest: 'Gilbert: "People cry out against the sinner, yet it is not the sinful, but the stupid, who are our shame. There is no sin except stupidity." Ernest: "Ah, what an antinomian you are!"'[15] This level of intertextuality, the multiple allusion, helps to remind us how strange, even revolutionary, the Dean's discourse to Tempest might have seemed in 1906, and how there is an element of antinomianism in it, as the Dean strives to loosen the mental grip on Tempest enjoyed by a literal interpretation of the Thirty-Nine Articles and the Book of Common Prayer of the Church of England, while Tempest, even as he listens to the Dean, adheres to them. Tempest is not ignorant of the doctrine of the Church, but about Buddhist belief his ignorance is complete. The question becomes, is he stupid to adhere to his fundamentalist position? The Dean uses elements of Buddhist thought to create a Higher Christianity, in which, for example, the immortality of Christ is a way of figuring the spiritual belief that 'Perfect Goodness knows no death' (p. 217). He mentions 'Shakya-Buddha', condemns desire and denies that death exists (pp. 218, 221). Trying to coax him out of his rigidities into faith in God's forgiveness, the Dean tells Tempest the story of the burning house (pp. 207–09), stated by the novel's narrator to be 'an old parable'. Not old, though, in the experience of the average Christian in 1906, since it comes from chapter 3 of *The Lotus Sutra* (*Saddharmapundarika Sutra*). That Farrer not only knew, but had been thinking about this ancient and important Buddhist text, pondering how to make it an element in a Higher Spirituality, by 1906, testifies to the seriousness of his interest in Buddhist beliefs even before his trip to Ceylon.[16] *The Lotus Sutra* was particularly important in China and Japan. It taught:

> the Ekayana, the One Vehicle, or the one form of Buddhism that subsumes all forms of Buddhism. This doctrine is explained in the form of a parable in the

third chapter. In order to entice his deluded and rebellious sons out of a burning house in which they were happily playing, a wise man offered each his favourite beast-drawn cart: a goat cart, a deer cart, and a bullock cart. When the children were safely outside, he gave them instead one great cart which was better than the other three. The burning house signifies the mundane world, filled with suffering and decay; the wise man is the Buddha; and the children are representative of foolish and ignorant mankind. The carts symbolize the three traditional forms of Buddhist practice [...] The One Great Vehicle, represented by the Lotus Sutra, is the latter-day teaching, [...] subsuming all previous teachings and divisions of Buddhism, and is therefore the most comprehensive, profound, and compassionate of doctrines.[17]

Farrer, or the Dean, alters this parable somewhat, emphasizing the innocence of the children and the urgent drama of the fire, referring to 'toys' rather than carts, and making them stand for the 'beauties and ceremonial of religion': that is, the part supplied by an organized Church. More important than that is the 'path', which, according to the Dean, Tempest has forgotten. We can note in passing that the Dean calls the Buddha not by his usual designation, but 'The Best Friend of All the World'. This episode in the novel was characterized by the review of the book published in the *Madras Times* as: 'well worth reading, as expressing the views of an extremely liberal-minded churchman on orthodoxy, ritual, and the true spirit of Christianity.'[18]

Unlike his novelist, however, Tempest rejects the Dean's 'strange, monstrous ideas' and says: 'No thinking or bothering over religious questions for me. The Thirty-nine Articles give me all I need. I don't need to stray into Romanism and Heathenism and Dissent so long as I have *them* before me.' (p. 219). The irony is that Tempest had approached the Dean in the hope that the latter would be able to convince him that suicide will not lead to an eternity in hell-fire.

In a later passage the narrator generalizes from the example of both the Ladon males:

> your man of solid sense has neither power nor wish either to understand or to pardon. To see a sin is enough for him. It is a sin; it must be punished. That is sufficient. He has no concern with its origin, the person who engendered it, the distraction of the person who committed it; the bare, hard fact is all he asks to see. And thus the judgments of the sensible man are brief and easy; his life is simple, plain, obvious. He is spared all the complicated worries that beset unlucky people who try to understand their world. Surely a good deal of stupidity, a great deal of intolerance, an almost incredible amount of wooden-heartedness are not too heavy a price for the average man to pay for his blessed privilege of being able to live through life without the inconvenient disturbances of thought, intelligence, or sympathy (pp. 283–84).

The irony deployed against the 'sensible' man is effective; we might also note in passing the gendering of 'fact' (suitably 'bare, hard'). As a condemnation of stubbornness this is enjoyable. It is also quite close to Gilbert's view in Wilde's *The Critic as Artist*. Expounding his belief that 'the artistic critic, like the mystic, is an antinomian always', Gilbert says:

To be good, according to the vulgar standard of goodness, is obviously quite easy. It merely requires a certain amount of sordid terror, a certain lack of imaginative thought, and a certain low passion for middle-class respectability [...] If one contemplates the ordinary pulpits and platforms of England, one can but feel the contempt of Julian, or the indifference of Montaigne. We are dominated by the fanatic, whose worst vice is his sincerity.[19]

This would do quite well to characterize the two male Ladons. The novel's narrator says of St John's response to the situation:

That his father, alone and helpless, on the verge of the bottomless pit, which is despair, could be resolved into a mere cyclone of emotions, restrained by no considerations of morality or tradition, never for a moment occurred to the young man, serene in his confidence that, whatever happened, a gentleman would always remain a gentleman, and that nothing on earth could either explain or excuse the violation of a gentleman's code. [...] To a man of St John Ladon's type, a given action is the sole offspring of a given thought; it never occurs to him that one thought, besides its legitimate offspring, may have a hundred bastard children in other mansions of the mind, and that no action stands sole, but ramifies directly and indirectly through every district of the being, till the soul becomes a roaring loom of many threads, where no strand can be touched without at once involving half a hundred others. [...] A new idea had come to him in his father's case, and in its train brought a dim terror that required instant extinction, without consideration of his anger or his compassion. (pp. 284–85)

It is in dramatizing that 'roaring loom' successfully that one of the novel's main strengths lies. But as a combination of 'a certain lack of imaginative thought', a 'low passion for middle-class respectability' and some 'sordid terror', this state of mind of St John Ladon qualifies perfectly.

There are therefore certain continuities between Farrer's novel and late nineteenth-century advanced thinking. The House of Shadows' ingredient of twentieth-century modernity comes from its discussion of religion, and particularly from its inclusion of elements of Buddhist teachings. One cannot help thinking that the lack of a better response to the novel by reviewers reflects the book's reliance on recognition of Buddhist ideas. Kipling's Kim had appeared, but the Buddhist thought informing it had not been generally recognized. In other words, it is possible that success with reviewers of the novel was hampered by its very raison d'être. On the other hand, Farrer's father reported that the novel 'sold quickly'.[20]

Farrer's next novel, The Sundered Streams: the history of a memory that had no full stops (1907) is the most explicitly Buddhist in its story and plot. As such it deserves some detailed attention. The epigraph is Japanese, strongly Buddhist in tendency, and translated by Farrer: 'There is no shore to the bitter sea of Birth-and-Death; even the touching of sleeves in passing is the result of some connection in a former life.'

The father of the novel's protagonist, Kingston Darnley, is born with the name 'James Dadd'. Then, as now, the word 'dad' functioned as a short and informal word for 'father'. Creating this pun allows Farrer some broad private humour in the early pages, which obviously had his own father, James Farrer, as its target. Five generations of Farrers had borne the name James.[21] In the novel Kingston's father is 'James Dadd the Ninth'. Amidst some fun Farrer has with the petty-mindedness of isolated small-town society (there are allusions to Gaskell's Cranford and *Emma's* Highbury), we are told that the Dadds know their place:

> Their clan, like all the others in St. Eldred's, was magnificently complacent in contemplation of its own position. No Dadd was ever heard to aspire to more giddy worlds, no Dadd was ever known to show any hankerings after wilder flights, after new courses, after original thought or action of any kind. [...] A Dadd could be trusted to avoid giving offence, a Dadd could never be ostentatious.[22]

The novel soon abandons its coarse satire of Farrer's own family, and of small-town life involving the Dadds.[23] Kingston is a naive young man because of the absurd way his mother has brought him up. He turns out prudish, over-fastidious, virginal in the years before marriage, having 'an inordinate sensitiveness to impressions' and 'an excessive personal daintiness' (p. 44). He marries Gundred, a woman obsessed by her own social position and status who has grown up vain, and small-minded about her standing in the eyes of others. She has 'stiffened into a rigid piety' (p. 51) and plays to 'an invisible audience' (p. 61). She is the last member of an impoverished ducal house. The old duke is slowly succumbing to insanity. We are, the narrator asserts, 'the reincarnated spirits of very many dead ages' (p. 78), which suggests Farrer to be pushing Buddhist perspectives closer to the idea of inherited family or racial characteristics, since Gundred possesses 'the inherited blood of the Mortimers' (p. 79). Incidentally, Farrer himself had good reason to think himself a descendant both of Mortimers (through his Anson grandmother) and Plantagenets (through his mother, Bessie).[24] After Kingston and Gundred's marriage, the novel provides a convincing passage about how misunderstandings, offences and frigidities can dry up feelings between people against their good instincts (pp. 88–100). In its concern for emotional health, vitality and instinct, Farrer's fictional writing, at its best, anticipates, in a more limited way, that of D. H. Lawrence (one of Farrer's disadvantages being a complete lack of interest in the working class).

Into this situation steps trouble and the promise of liberation, in the form of Gundred's cousin Isabel, 'a young barbarian from New Zealand'.[25] She changes the discourse rapidly. Meeting her for the first time, Kingston has a feeling of 'renewed acquaintance'. Isabel, who shares this feeling, suggests a previous meeting on the astral plane 'in a dream', or that metempsychosis might explain it. Gundred confuses the latter with 'evolution' (pp. 112–13). There is mention of Kingston's uncle, who left England many years before to become a 'Buddhist Abbot or Bishop' in Japan (p. 123). Gundred's suggestion that Kingston take up shooting game again provokes a narrator's sneer against 'the usual tender-hearted woman's ambition that her husband should destroy innocent lives as lavishly and enthusiastically and successfully as fashion demands' (p. 124). Isabel asserts that 'Very few people are great and holy enough to die. Nine people out of ten just change shapes and go on again. [...] It is a far leap into Nirvana.' Kingston replies that he expects 'that a vast number of quiet good people reach Nirvana [...] They go on living obscure, kindly lives, and then, at the end of everything, they just gently slip away and cease, and enter Nirvana without any splash at all.' (pp. 126–27) In her reply Isabel provides an analogy for the loss of the ego required for the achievement of enlightenment:

> Ah, those are people who go on the great journey without luggage. But the average person takes any amount of packages and parcels with him, all kinds of fears and fusses and hopes and terrors. [...] He thinks they are his individuality, just as a decent woman thinks that her clothes are hers. [... People think] that the bundles are an essential part of themselves; whereas it is not until one has gradually shed all one's bundles that one can hope to arrive. (p. 127)

On a Yorkshire mountaintop occurs an emotional climax between Kingston and Isabel. Kingston moves towards physical embraces; Isabel wants them too, holding out her arms to him. For Kingston:

> This was the one woman in the world. He had known her since the beginning of time, been with her since the creation; now at last she threw aside her veils, and stood before him, no longer a stranger, but the lost part of his own soul — that lost part for which he had so long been vainly seeking. [...] 'Old friend,' she whispered, smiling into his eyes. (pp. 169–70)

At the crucial moment, however, Kingston remembers his wife. His passion swerves and diminishes. 'For the sake of Gundred, of himself, of Isabel — for the sake of his love and hers, he must live as clean as might be. The struggle was a martyrdom, though, the shock of self-mutilation a grinding, lancinating anguish.' (p. 176) The narrator's language changes: 'To go further into that ghastly labyrinth was impossible. Joy was unattainable. Only duty could be pursued. And for shirking that there could be no excuse.' (p. 176) Generations of Dadd ancestors work through Kingston: he does not make this effort to overcome desire for reasons of Buddhist conviction.

Isabel, understandably, accuses him of giving in to 'middle-class superstitions' and calls him 'a bloodless prig' (pp. 177, 180). A summary here can hardly do justice to the effectiveness of this scene and the successful ways in which intense struggles between the characters and within Kingston are conveyed. Afterwards, Isabel more conciliatory, the episode has given them 'a blessed consciousness' (p. 199) and 'their secret glory' (p. 210).

On adultery 'of the heart' [i.e. not the body], the novel tells us that: 'The marriage of heart with heart is a matter outside the reach of law; the world and its laws are only concerned with external and visible manifestations; it can be valued by no damages, absolved by no divorce'. (p. 188) This is antinomian: the life of the emotions is freedom.

Alas, Gundred's house, in which the married couple live (and the situation of which, perched on its own on a cliff overlooking the sea on a western coast, carries an echo of Culzean Castle on the coast of Scotland, just as the Yorkshire mountains that feature in the novel's rapturous and beautiful landscape descriptions are portraits of Ingleborough and Pen-y-ghent) catches fire. Isabel has a broken leg; Gundred faints. The broken leg is a working-out of fate: it occurred in a carriage-accident; Isabel was in the carriage because Gundred, worried and jealous of her husband's time and attention, was trying to monopolize Isabel to keep them apart.

So both women need to be carried to safety. Isabel tells Kingston to rescue his wife first. As a consequence of this compassionate impulse, she dies alone in the fire (pp. 228–29). We have just been told of Isabel's terror of pain and death, and her fear of being punished 'for something one has done hundreds of years ago' (p. 222). During this conversation, Kingston has said: 'before one can attain the perfect happiness [...] remember that one has to lose the desire for it. After ages and ages of purification, one leaves the last trace of desire behind — even the desire for good' (pp. 223–24). The couple are clearly talking from Buddhist perspectives without using the name.

As for Kingston: 'The soul passes in a moment from youth to manhood through the door of a great sorrow' (p. 229). He finds Isabel's skull in the ashes of the burned wing. He tries spiritualism in an attempt to contact her. Five years after Isabel's death Gundred gives birth to a son. Kingston remains obsessed by Isabel. Twenty years after her death, Kingston's uncle returns from the east a Buddhist sage, so that Buddhist ideas feature explicitly in his conversation with Kingston (pp. 269–84). He says to Kingston: 'You are suffering the penalty of bygone folly, you are chained in the bond of a bad Karma. You have loved something, and you think you have now lost it. Worst of all, you long to recover it, you long to rivet round you again the fetters of desire and sorrow.' The uncle explains what has happened to Isabel:

> In one tremendous moment the woman rose far above all the false desires in which she had bred herself. She gave her life for the truth. She sacrificed utterly that false self of hers which was the thing that your false self had so loved through the ages. And for her great merit it must be that she must reap great rewards, — not rewards apportioned by a personal providence, but rewards that spring naturally out of her action. She has shaken herself free of the links that bound her to you. The Buddha enwombed in every mortal Karma has torn away many of the veils that shrouded him in that woman's heart. Because, in her last moment she loved the true better than the false, and followed rather the higher love that led upwards than the lower love which would have kept her at your side — therefore she is released. The streams are sundered on the rock of parting. That bondage of hers has passed away — weak and erring and desirous, perhaps, she still may be — faulty and human, but at least that one chain of desire which held her is snapped and broken utterly. You go on hunting for her through all the fields of your earthly life, and she, in an instant, was cured of all vain longings. (pp. 279–80)

A contemporary scholar of Buddhism explains the belief that Farrer is here weaving into his plot:

> a single complete action, performed in this life or any previous lifetime, comes to the fore at the moment of death and serves as the primary cause of the entire next lifetime. Thus, the state of mind at the time of death is critical in Buddhism, with the recollection of a virtuous deed and an attitude of calm said to bring about a happy rebirth.[26]

Unhappily, Kingston refuses to be warned. Having forgotten everything he said to Isabel about the need to relinquish or overcome desire in order to attain 'perfect happiness', he is consumed with a thirst to find her again. The old Buddhist leaves, disappointed: 'Gently he gave his hand to Kingston. "Very far apart are we two," he said, with a whimsical smile of his dried lips. "We speak in different languages, across a barrier of worlds".' And he warns that Gundred will also pay a penalty.

Kingston finally meets Isabel again, this time sent round in the form of a young man, Ivor Restormel (a near-anagram: I'm lover restor). He was born twelve hours after Isabel's death. Ivor has a great fear of fire, and suffers even seeing women smoke. Kingston desires Isabel within the young man, who, however, does not reciprocate any interest. Kingston's floundering attempts to rouse interest spark the suspicion of Gundred, who retreats into Christianism, resolving to fight the 'Evil One' (p. 365) in Ivor the 'Amalekite' (p. 381). Kingston and Gundred's son and Ivor are killed by a flood while descending a cavern (modelled on Ingleborough's Gaping Ghyll). Gundred could have prevented the accident by raising the alarm, but, hating the young man for his hold over Kingston, and not knowing that her son was also in the cavern, she deliberately refrained. When told of the disaster she succumbs to her inherited tendency to madness.

Catastrophe thus strikes the protagonist because of his inability to be free of desire (the struggle between this aim and an inability to act upon desire is a rub or crux in Farrer's novels). Farrer sets bodily desires/material sexual impulses against Buddhist virtue quite deliberately. Through the effectively communicated strength with which the characters feel their desires, this opposition is quite genuinely painful. Kingston is admonished by his Buddhist uncle:

> Hell is nothing more than the dominion of passion that we establish over our lives — of passion and all the hellish torments that passion engenders. We make our own hells by dwelling obstinately in the world of false desire [...] Desire is hell. And that hell we build and stoke and kindle for ourselves — go on kindling from life to life, in our fancy that the fire we endure contains the ultimate pleasure our souls can taste [...] Because of that fire of false desire that you had fed in yourself for so many existences, you suffered anew the hell of your own making — the hell of loss and loneliness. But kill such false desires, and you kill the false miseries of this life that men think real. You stand at a point where you might strike upwards towards the heaven of peace; the curse of your love had nearly wrought out its completion, and passed away. But by nourishing as you do the fever of longing for the dead, you are binding yourself anew with the chains that were beginning to weaken and drop. (pp. 278–79)

For the uncle, there is such a thing as 'true desire, the desire of those things that are real' (p. 278) according to Buddhist belief. But most of these ideas have already been expounded by the narrator nearly fifty pages earlier, in a meditation on the death of Isabel (pp. 229–37), and without the help of any Buddhist character or any explicit reference to Buddhist texts or ideas. Some of the conversations between Isabel and Kingston manifest the same element. This shows that Farrer was trying to write a Buddhist novel, in which the workings of realism and plot correspond to a Buddhist reality, rather than simply a novel the denouement of which depended on a Buddhist character's explanations. In Buddhist belief, only the Buddha can remember past lives, though Hindus often believe that young children have some memories of a former life that are lost as they grow older.[27] Farrer is therefore pushing belief to the point where it can more clearly animate his story and plot. *The Sundered Streams* is not a book with a happy outcome — but because of the protagonist not following the Buddhist Way. In Gundred, motivated by anger, ignorance and her own desires for her place in society and her son, Farrer shows Christianity aiding ignorance and stoking anger (she believes that the flood that will kill Ivor is God's punishment).

In this novel, the unfolding delight of finding a soul-mate, and the extraordinary pain of losing loved ones, are both rendered with exceptional power. Critics in general seemed quite pleased with the book, though it seems doubtful that many of them understood its thrust. *The Evening Standard* wrote: 'A book of strong originality and striking outlines. The blending of the absolutely normal with the thrillingly mysterious makes the book what it is. For the style, it is good, with many vitriolic thumbnail portraits, such as the description of the 'modern woman, who is perfectly virtuous, except in dress, manners, and mind.'[28] The novel bemused the reviewer in *The Register*, a newspaper of South Australia, who wrote, under the heading 'Puzzling Plot', of 'psychic puzzles' and 'occult manifestations', but who sees 'possibilities of pathos, and even of tragedy, in Gundred — the young wife devoted to her husband, but unable to show the affection really felt.' The reviewer feels that later, though, the novelist treats her with persistent 'malice' and 'derision'. The 'mysterious uncle from Japan, who has become a Buddhist abbott [...] holds forth [...] on the dangers of the way and the bondage of the wheel in a manner weakly reminiscent of Kipling's Llama [sic] in "Kim".'[29] The protagonist, Kingston, however, is 'not particularly interesting'.

In the U.S.A., Charles Welsh Mason, himself a novelist, writing in the *Brooklyn Daily Eagle*, was much more appreciative. As his review, Mason took the opportunity to write a lengthy essay musing about the nature of love, entitled 'How Else Can You Account For the Mystic Rapture of Love?' At the outset, he recognizes that whether the novel is 'of unusual fascination, or unusual dullness' depends on the reader's 'partiality'. Mason, who had spent a considerable time in China, understands that the plot depends on 'Buddhism, or reincarnation'. Farrer, he tells us, goes some way beyond Marie Corelli in using this as a device of the plot. He identifies Farrer's underlying attitude: 'Love, [Farrer] explains, is a sin — in the sense that pain is the offspring of desire.'[30] And he is enthusiastic:

> the application of metaphysics to the mystification of fiction is entirely justi-fiable and the best novelty left to the psychological novelist. That is the way Mr. Farrer handles the reincarnation myth. He has written a marriage novel, and decorated it with the zest of the mystical by way of urging a change on the stereotyped phraseology of the emotions.
>
> Quite apart from metaphysics, "Sundered Streams" appeals to the cultured reader by the excellence of the character study of society women, and by a treatment of heredity at once scholarly and amusing. Mr. Farrer's real intimacy with the traditions of two great strata of English society — the middle class and the old aristocracy — is quite above the ordinary claptrap of the novelist "outside." His satire is keen and droll; but it is not caricature.

Mason suggests that Farrer's novel will appeal to readers who want to think, and not to readers who merely wish to 'feel'. So it took an exposure to Buddhism, through Mason's years in China, to begin to understand the thrust of Farrer's novel. Other critics simply took the explicitly Buddhist passages of the book as literary intertextuality (an influence from Kipling's *Kim*) or failed to comprehend them at all. Mason has an inkling of the radically different approach taken by Farrer as he attempted to place Buddhist realism into the mould of the realist novel. Indeed, in general, with few exceptions such as this, one is struck by the superficial approaches taken by most reviewers of all Farrer's novels. While reviewers might have been bemused by them, the plant-collector (and writer) Frank Kingdon-Ward, at least, understood the novel's key. Alluding in his obituary of Farrer to the years ca 1902–08, he wrote that this was the period in which: 'some of his best novels were written, and the mystic vein which runs through them may be attributed to the fascination the Buddhist religion had for him.'[31]

In March 1908 appeared Farrer's *The Ways of Rebellion*. This novel concerns two central characters, the childhood friends Michael and Elinor, who both rebel against their upbringing. Michael Halliburton comes from the land-owning elite: as he goes home from university for the holidays:

> so many things seemed wrong. Even as he drew up from the station it seemed snobbish and misplaced of the villagers so to touch their hats and make obeisance [...] it was conforming to rules Michael had begun to suspect.[...] Was he wiser, or honester, or kinder? Was he more heroic or trustworthy in great crises?

Michael feels that there was nothing in history to make 'the long line of Halliburtons worthy of the entailed respect and veneration that they extracted from county and village alike'.[32] In this, Michael is refracting Farrer's own experience. According to a local historian of Clapham, Reginald's mother: 'demanded respect from the lower orders. Woe betides any man or boy who did not doff his cap as she passed in her carriage or car.'[33]

Michael gives away his wealth and becomes a political activist on behalf of the poor:

> He grew to understand that the world to which he himself had belonged was, indeed, in perpetual terror of the great dumb beast that it tried to hold in leash by charity bazaars and endless hysterically-smiling assumption of friendly interest.[...] The landowning party is anxious to do anything and everything for the working classes, except allow the working classes to develop lives of their own, to have a real voice in the government of the country or their own existences, or any training in the great art of using that voice.[34]

This is splendid stuff: William Morris, even Karl Marx, might have approved. Unfortunately Farrer (son of a Liberal landowner) commits a huge error when he tries to divert this class-based view onto party politics, blaming the Conservative Party (p. 115). Yet perhaps Farrer is simply trying to dramatize the confused consciousness of his character, Michael, and these views do not align with his personal conceptions. In any case, the argument of George Dangerfield, in his *The Strange Death of Liberal England* (1936) can help to reveal how the socio-political context may have felt to Farrer while he was writing. Dangerfield found that the landslide victory of the Liberal Party at the elections of 1906 inaugurated a struggle between 'two doomed powers: between the middle-class philosophy that was Liberalism and the landed wealth that passed for aristocracy.'[35]

Elinor's rebellion, meanwhile, takes the form of embracing materialism and social status: 'I want room to grow, and a beautiful garden to grow in', she says. 'Otherwise my buds will never open properly.' (p. 74). Consequently she makes a hasty and bad marital choice (an ancient widower-baronet). Some time later she appears at Michael's dowdy lodging and asks to have a love-affair because she's unhappy; rather priggishly he sends her away uncaressed. The titanic argument they have about this is impressive, but rather overwrought and melodramatic. Partly this is because it is seen entirely from Michael's point of view. There are no pages devoted to the building-up of Elinor's frustrated feelings, for example, such as Lawrence would have provided. Farrer himself sensed the melodramatic effect, since at the end of the chapter devoted to this visit, with self-reflexive irony Elinor says, '"Unhand me, villain, or I scream!" she laughed, in the classic words of melodrama.' (p. 135).

Lucilla, a friend of Elinor's who has to make a living, sells hats. Elinor and her friends 'buy' the hats at Lucilla's hat show but no-one bothers actually to pay Lucilla, who is therefore forced to sell herself as a mistress to a rake. After some years Elinor's husband dies and she marries a younger man, John Brandon. Michael has become a revolutionary and an ascetic. A doctor diagnoses tuberculosis. Michael sticks to his guns:

> Even supposing death came down on him today, and the Halliburtons triumph over him tomorrow, nothing in all of this could logically affect his course of conduct, nor make it right or reasonable for him to act against the clear orders of his conscience — of that Buddha shrined in each mortal Karma, whose words have supreme authority above every dictate of prudence or desire. (pp. 235–36)

This is the only sign of Buddhist thought in the novel, and it represents the author rather than the character (Michael not being a Buddhist). The Buddha is used as a figure for conscience, and it is not entirely clear whether the Buddha, or the concept of conscience, is the greater power. In any case, G. E. Moore had just shown that conscience is an unreliable guide to ethical conduct, which makes this authorial intervention more unfortunate.[36]

After various other plot disturbances, Elinor discovering that Michael only has three months to live, the two depart together to a house on the Italian coast, where they live happily, consummating physically their loving friendship. Then one sunlit morning Michael says to her, 'we have known life', and dies (p. 308). Elinor writes to John, who takes her back, though she is socially ostracized by former friends. Thus both characters consummate their rebellions by rebelling against their own earlier decisions. Elinor breaks the marriage tie, the mechanism she chose to serve her social climbing, and thus will climb socially no more; and Michael acts on his need for human love for himself, rather than doggedly pursuing to the end his selfless acting for others.

In London, none of the critics seemed to understand that the novel is about ethics and free will, about characters rising above their determining conditions. *The*

Spectator and *Punch* took almost diametrically opposite positions about *The Ways of Rebellion*. *The Spectator* accuses Farrer of failures of psychological realism in terms of narrative cause-and-effect: 'The author of this book will hardly succeed in making his readers believe in the final flight of such a woman as the heroine, Elinor, with Michael Halliburton at the time when he is dying of consumption.' The reviewer dislikes the character of Elinor, who is called 'an absolute egoist [...] far too worldly and cold-minded a personage'. The short review concludes with the thought that 'It is difficult to believe that even so self-centred a person as Elinor could have treated her friend Lucille in the way represented. That the cruelty of thoughtlessness could be carried so far is hardly credible.'[37] The reviewer is trying to have it both ways, though, since he or she has just criticized the credibility of Elinor when she feels compassion and love for the dying Michael, her old childhood friend.

Punch, on the other hand, rather likes both Elinor and the book. Elinor, we are told,

> married *John*, and went off with *Michael*, simply because she felt she must. *Michael* died, and *John*, well satisfied when she told him all about it, took her back, and loved her all the more for her honesty. Personally, I think that is rather revolutionary too, though it doesn't actually count among the author's 'ways' [of rebellion] because he takes a great deal of trouble with his psychology, and succeeds very cleverly in making *John* plausible. Indeed, he makes all the characters plausible, from that dignified, quaint little figure, *Princess Anne Komnena* and the rest of the host of clearly drawn minor persons, to the ascetic *Michael* and beautiful, majestic *Elinor* herself, who is quite a dear, in spite (or perhaps because) of that light-hearted carelessness of hers, which to her own surprise does incalculable harm to people who don't deserve it.[38]

With *Punch*, of course, there is the question of how far the irony is intended to go. If the 'Learned Clerk' from the magazine's 'Booking-Office Staff' praises the plausibility of the characterisation, are we to suppose that he or she means that the characters are implausible? In this case I think not, because the characterisation of John Brandon is not as two-dimensional as *The Spectator* would like us to believe. *Punch*'s reviewer clearly signals in his or her plot synopsis the view that the story is implausible; and from that position concedes some merit to Farrer's successful creation of character, thereby indicating where the novel's weakness and strength, for this particular critic, lie.

One weakness of the novel is succinctly stated by *The Spectator*: 'The book would have been more interesting had the author given more prominence to Michael Halliburton's work and life after he has surrendered his fortune; but these are only alluded to in general terms.' This criticism, much more than the hesitations about plausibility, is entirely fair; and it indicates a huge hole in the novel that erodes the work's interest and credibility. This lack indicates a limitation in Farrer's commitment to the plodding work of a realist novel; or a lack of interest in his part in the dynamics of social improvement.

Virginia Woolf (more properly Stephen, until marriage in 1912) returned to Farrer's fiction with a short review of *Ways of Rebellion* in the *Times Literary Supplement*.[39] We find her on the side of the *The Spectator* with respect to the idea of the plausibility of the story, and she ends her review by characterizing Farrer's fiction, albeit very broadly, against the literary productions of the time. Most of the review consists of a synopsis; the second half reads:

> The story would run its course with all the directness of a tract were it not for certain unaccountable episodes, introduced, presumably, to enliven the way and drive home the moral; but very much at the expense of the consistency of the different characters. Elinor, for example, proposes to elope with Michael; he refuses, naturally; and she sends a house party to break up one of his meetings. The shock almost kills him; she nurses him, and they run away to the South, where his passions revive with his strength, and they live as husband and wife until, suddenly, he falls down dead. Bewildering as this is, the final solution is still more difficult to accept, for the patient husband comes out to find his wife, hears her story, and will only say that her 'soul is straight' so that they can start life together again happily. Mr. Farrer can write with vigour and originality, nor do those gifts wholly desert him here, but it is disappointing work compared with 'The House of Shadows', for it has so much more in common with the ordinary novel.[40]

Stephen's disappointment is plain. She no longer writes of 'the impression' of the work. Nor does she reiterate her earlier judgement that Farrer is a writer to be remembered. Should we take this review, by the great modernist, written just before her own first novels, to be a final indication of Farrer's failure as a modernist novelist? The judgement is damning, and seems incontestable. Other reviewers, though, concur that his writing is interesting, sometimes vigorous. In the *Liverpool Daily Post*, the review states that 'Mr. Reginald Farrer is cleverness itself, and once more he dazzles us by his brilliance. There can be no other description of "The Ways of Rebellion".[41] *The Pall Mall Gazette* emphasized the political dimension when it considered the novel 'An extremely ingenious and thoughtful piece of work, merciless and contemporaneous in its exposure of the weaknesses, follies, and pettinesses which, as the author finds or imagines, infect the class we dub the Upper Ten.[42] There is a hint here that critical opinion might have been partly inflected by party-political loyalty, especially as Farrer had clumsily realigned his class analysis in the novel with party-politics.

An exasperated review in *The Athenaeum* deserves to be quoted in full, as it shows the limits of adventurousness in social and psychological views that dominated British public discussion during the period, while conceding to Farrer some merits:

> If Mr. Farrer were not so clever, we should not feel irritated and disappointed, as we do, by his perversity. This novel is sadly perplexing. It contains such a knowledge of human nature in parts, so much shrewd philosophy, and withal so vivid a sympathy, that we are not prepared for the remarkable divagations towards its close. The conduct of the heroine there described is either hysterical or lunatic; it belongs to nothing in sanity. The behaviour of her husband is almost equally marvellous. Indeed, we are sure he is an impostor [sic]; for could such a plain, reasonable man as he is suddenly become the unintelligible person of the conclusion? Mr. Farrer's gifts of observation, satire, and wit are considerable, but do not show to advantage in these semi-mystical themes.[43]

Clearly, contemporary views of masculinity found it hard to accept Elinor's headstrong behaviour in 'eloping' with Michael, her childhood friend and object of her frustrated sexual feelings. Equally hard was it for reviewers to accept the patient, forgiving and confident masculinity of John Brandon, Elinor's husband, in being content to take her back after Michael's death. And yet Farrer is granted an unusual 'knowledge of human nature', cleverness, ingenuity and thoughtfulness; originality, and (by *Punch*) success in making all his characters plausible, if we can take that tribute at face value. If patient husbands were in short supply in 1908, the 21st century sensibility might be less bothered by that aspect than by the obvious shortcuts that Farrer has chosen to take in the writing, especially the omission noted by *The Spectator*; but there is also the matter of the uneven pacing of the book, which grinds very slowly through a tedious hat show, and speeds recklessly up at other places. *Ways of Rebellion* also doesn't have so much as his first two novels of the 'rough primary emotion' that he invoked in *The House of Shadows*; but perhaps *Ways* gives precisely a lesson in how modern life (that is, social preoccupations — philanthropical or marital) occludes that raw emotion.

Undeterred by the absence of a really triumphant review, Farrer kept on writing. Perhaps he found that an occasional novel was a useful way of getting £55 out of a publisher. That, at least, is the figure mentioned by Agatha, a secondary character and jobbing novelist in Farrer's novel, *Through the Ivory Gate* (1912). £55 was about the equivalent of half a year's pay for a skilled labourer. 'Novel writing', Agatha says, is 'a suicidal job'.[44]

All Farrer's novels consistently employ the traditional omniscient third person narrator, blended with excursions into Free Indirect Discourse, in which the narration suddenly adopts the character's perceptions, with no overt distanciation of narrator from character.[45] *Through the Ivory Gate*, the last novel Farrer published (though not the last he wrote), is no exception, except for a few pages (pp. 76–84, 130–39) which adopt the epistolary form, and are, in my view, the best parts of the novel, as the characters have to write in the first person.

The novel concentrates on the consciousness of John Trevannion, its protagonist. On page 7 John believes that 'dreaming is an end in itself, and its own reward.' This is a reminiscence of Oscar Wilde's *The Critic as Artist*. We may take this together with an echo of the famous conclusion of Walter Pater's *Studies in the Renaissance* on a later page: the narrator writes (closely adhering to John's sensibility): 'For each soul lives out its earthly life apart, in a cell of its own building that none can break' (p. 59). Pater had used the metaphor of a 'prisoner'.[46] John is thus defined as an Aesthete. He frets over the ideal vs. the real in women, wondering whether he could marry Atalanta and not be put off by the ugly way she does her hair. His friends and family expect an engagement, but 'all that was a damper' (p. 11). His self-contradictions are laid out in the early pages.

In Chapter 2, when he has arrived at a house-party in Atalanta's parents' home, 'Gayclops', he exclaims about how 'beautiful' his cousin Bruno is: beautiful in evening dress, or 'naked', or 'in a butt', or 'on the ridge of the "Schreckhorn"' (pp. 13–14). He tells Agatha that he likes Bruno better than anything in the world (p. 28).

She replies that John is 'a kind of old woman inside an ordinary man' (p. 30). His cousin Janet dares John to say whether he prefers Bruno or Atalanta (p. 37). Bruno tells John that John 'prefers men to women' (p. 51–52) and rails against Platonic relationships with women. Later, in London, John dines with his old friend Bernard Lorme, with whom, in occasional moments of communion, for John 'the joy was poignant, exceeding the utmost poignancy of women' (p. 108–09). All this suggests Farrer's deliberate deployment of a strategy:

> Queer inscription privileges subversion, slippage, and metaphorical language of deviation and substitution [...] homoerotic desire is often refracted or produced through a specific practice of dissimulation [...] nowhere figured mimetically [...] because [...] authors often disguise their representation of queerness, we must look for it in textual places that expressly demand that we become adept at multilayered readings.[47]

The queer approach apparently adopted here by Farrer amounts to one of several signs that he intended the novel to be deliberately racy. John thinks about the process of conversing (merely) with Agatha: 'one could be so splendidly undressed with Agatha [...] one's nudities so dispassionately pleased her' (p. 28). John, unsuccessfully proposing to Atalanta, fights 'with souls' (rather than bodies), 'and now his psychic orgasm was dying' (p. 62). There is a moment intended as mordant comedy when the real name of Bruno is revealed to be Reginald — 'a dreadful name' (pp. 21–22). Names are significant: there is an Atalanta, an Althea, and we are told that John's mother considered christening him Meleager! John meets his baleful object of desire, Althea, whom he has known disastrously before the novel opens, again at Bonchurch (the poet Algernon Charles Swinburne's sometime home that gave its name to the 'Bonchurch' edition of his works that was being published at the time Farrer was writing). The personal names come from Swinburne's most famous work, his verse drama *Atalanta in Calydon* (1865), and his poem 'The Garden of Proserpine' is misquoted, unattributed, on an early page (26). Why is Farrer so obviously signalling the influential significance of Swinburne as an important energy in the novel? Perhaps because in *Atalanta*, as Ian Fletcher writes, Swinburne announces the 'tyranny (and death) of the family'. There is also Swinburne's view of 'woman as an emblem of the unattainable'.[48]

  Althea proves unattainable for John, with disastrous consequences. His decision to perpetuate the family by making Atalanta his intended wife also proves futile. He is the last remaining part of his family with the exception of a dull aunt and uncles in Scotland. As the aesthete of the first third of the story is shown to be not strong enough to deal with the problems of life, the book begins to be about his inability to conquer desire. Disaster accelerates for John when he again meets Althea, towards whom he conceived a strong and unresolved desire several years before. He thinks, quite erroneously, that his mild interest in Atalanta has driven out this futile passion for Althea. A self-deceiving liar (p. 61), and also an egomaniac: in striving to persuade Atalanta to accept his proposal of marriage he says, 'My belief in your power to give *must* give you the power to give, don't you see? People become what one believes them.' (p. 62). John is partly propelled to meet Althea again by Atalanta's rejection of his proposal of marriage.

The conversation between Atalanta and John, on a mountain-top, is one of the successes of the novel. It has moments suggestive of some of the techniques of characterisation of D. H. Lawrence:

> 'Mr Trevannion,' said Atalanta, 'have you been in love before with anyone else?' She studied him with calm eyes, and his pain was sharp. The big enveloping love-feeling of him could find no outlet: and he remembered how wholly different had been the acrid insanity of his passion for Althea West. Often had his soul leapt out to strangle her with sinuous hands, strain the lovely life out of her, absorb her wholly in his male force. A little more, very often, and for sheer love he could have killed that other woman in a spasm. But this one, he could only crouch before, in a sentimental adoration, like a tamed beast. (p. 64)

Neither attitude to the women inspires any confidence in John's knowledge or emotional resources. Appearance of the word 'sentimental' reminds us of Swinburne's contemptuous rejection of that ubiquitous quality of Victorian domesticity.

After Atalanta rejects his proposal, John, thoroughly bored and exasperated by a few weeks with his aunt and uncles, rushes off to Bonchurch to see Agatha and encounter Althea again. To find her he proceeds down a 'thyme-walk' (p. 121). This is a minor point, but Farrer's friend Clarence Elliott had promoted thyme rather than grass as a surface for garden-paths. Althea is discovered in clothes that suggest the impassibility of a geisha: 'a straight Mandarin robe of sapphire silk' decorated with gold dragons, and later a kimono of gold (p. 135). She's also, perhaps like a geisha, small, dark-haired, with a small face and features. She leads John on, never quite rejecting his professions of love, never wholly rejecting the idea that she wants to see him, but usually ending her letters with the thought that it is Agatha who wants to see John (the implication of this is not understood by the stupid John). The climactic conversation between Althea and John occurs in the woods near Misurina, in northern Italy. There the teasing Althea is forced to go through a series of defensive positions. She denies that she will suit John as a wife. She says she has nothing to give him, and that she tried to prevent him from making a mistake (when she allowed him to make advances). She denies she is clever and pretty enough. She says their politics are different. She distracts attention towards his 'talking beautifully'. She denies she loves him. She hides behind the allegation that it was Agatha who wanted him to visit them. She doesn't understand how he has misunderstood. She says that she's sorry, and stupid, and bursts into tears. She says he's impertinent in attributing to her the motive of getting him to come to Italy and propose marriage. Finally she threatens him with the prospect of upsetting Agatha. By this terminal vulgarity John is set free from desiring her (pp. 188–98).

Returning to London, John takes to the bottle. Then he tries visiting prostitutes. A brothel leaves him feeling merely fastidious, but he takes a mistress. John's inability to conquer desire drives the plot, which means that Buddhism motivates the plot, and John proves unable to struggle against the cycle of dependent origination that keeps us here, in the Buddhist view, living innumerable lives. A little bit of Buddhist thinking (though not the word) has already been introduced into the book via the very secondary character of old Lord Kingsdale, a former Viceroy of India, who states that: 'there *is* no solid unchanging self to realize [...] when you have really grasped transience you have arrived at the end of sorrow' (p. 142). Buddhist thought takes the view that the self has no inherent existence. Kingsdale also talks of the need for 'perspective' to enable one to make sense of life, and judges that John has no sense of perspective (p. 143). The word 'perspective' recurs in the late stages of the book, when John reflects on its lack, a lack that allowed a 'chain of disasters' to follow from 'that very conception of himself as a thing permanent and permanently gratifiable — that was the source of his error' (p. 280).

So the character John struggles towards some self-knowledge. And here one has to acknowledge a division in Farrer's purposes. The story, motivated by the interaction of characters, in the end deviates from the plot, which is motivated by the author's Buddhist beliefs. John gains the above painful realisations after having become the lover of a strange woman, Theodora Clare (pp. 250–80). She is a liar, and psychotic: to gain the freedom for a long weekend of sexual congress with John in Brighton she bludgeons to death, in a public lavatory with a brick, her own ten year old son. Yet for John she has great attraction and the narrator endows her with dignity, too. To 'the world', people like her, he tells us as she is hanged, are 'strangers' here, 'from a dark planet' (p. 276).

Struggling out of this trauma, John finally gains useful self-knowledge. At that very moment Atalanta asks to see him, and opens the door for a possible engagement. So the interaction of character, no matter how strange that has been in this novel written within the realist mode, points towards a happy ending. Here Farrer intervenes. Returning rather dazed and happy from his reunion with Atalanta, John sees Althea coming out of the National Gallery, understands that he will never be free of his self-destructive desire for her, so returns home and kills himself. Farrer's imposition of a Buddhist element in the plot is at odds with the destiny that his characters are working out.

This reading of the novel can be related to Virginia Stephen's comment about *The House of Shadows*, that some novels are written for character interaction and others 'under stress of an idea', with Farrer's novels qualifying for the latter category. But let us draw back for a moment, and attempt to identify a different type of unity on a rather different level of analysis. In fact we could read the novel with respect to the major psychological models in place during the first decade of the twentieth century, and simultaneously bearing in mind the small quotation from Queer theory that I introduced earlier to throw into relief the care Farrer took to indicate homoerotic feelings in his protagonist John Trevannion. It is not, I trust, to reduce nascent psychoanalysis to caricature to say that by the end of the nineteenth century the ego was often seen as fundamentally dominated by unconscious desires and repressed passions: that the rational thinking self could be overwhelmed by irrational impulses. To read the plot with this in mind means that John, homoerotic in his most passionate feelings, deliberately ensures that his courtship of Atalanta — true, straight, and desirable — *fails*. He doggedly pursues Althea, who he knows will offer him nothing, because his unsayable love for Bruno is doomed by being outside society's conventions and laws, as well as by Bruno's heterosexuality. John's aim, directed by his irrational impulses, is self-destruction (hence his strange attraction to the mysterious, no doubt insane, child-murderer

Theodora Clare). This aim is abruptly fulfilled by self-inflicted death. According to this interpretation, *Through the Ivory Gate* manifests considerable psychological astuteness; indeed, does so in excess of Farrer's ability to make it entirely apparent to jobbing reviewers (trammelled as that ability is by the tabooed nature of his subject and the need for Queer indirectness).

In the *Evening Star*, a newspaper in New Zealand, the reviewer writes:

> Like all Mr. Farrer's work, this book is clever but unequal, and is Henry Jamesian in style. It is a chasse croise of women, followed by an essay on the psychology of drink. The hero, who cannot find peace with any of the heroines, attempts to console himself with venal amours, and finally goes out into the darkness. His final adventure with a murderess is dramatic, and well told. The reader will gather from this that the story is rather incoherent, but it is undoubtedly intuitive and distinguished by knowledge of the world.[49]

At the antipodes of this, Farrer's novel gained an equally appreciative review, signed 'F. G.' in John Middleton Murry's modernist little magazine, *Rhythm*. F. G. tells us that

> The earlier part of the story is told mainly in clever psychological conversations, entertaining enough as fancies, but not very true or important. There are also statements such as this: 'It was a dark-blue voice, a voice like a sapphire, velvet, or, a moonless night with stars' — which has the stamp of objective truth, but seems rather irrelevant. Later, the conversations peter out; the author tires a little and falls back on psychological narrative which moves forward with an impatient acceleration to the end of the book. The climax is orgiastic rather than dramatic. Yet the cleverness is undeniable and omnipresent. Sometimes the tone is high and dry and dignified; at others emotionalistic and wallowing. On the whole, a book which might titillate readers of *Rhythm* on their holidays. For the rest, it should prove a potent instrument of self-torture among maiden aunts, and in suburbs, universities, and other abodes of sexuality unduly deferred.[50]

The 'smart' tone of this is unmistakable. Both critics enjoy Farrer's cleverness, psychological insight, and the energy of the story, but both are bemused. F. G. wants the author to brace up and to stick to the point; the *Evening Star*'s reviewer will settle merely for coherence. It seems that, whether writing for fellow-Buddhists and for a Queer readership, Farrer pitched his novel at a different level from that of reviewers' expectations, and a level that he cannot quite make accessible to the critics' by no means hostile sensibilities.

Through the Ivory Gate is thus about a) the inability to overcome desire (and so make progress in an attempt to free oneself from endless rebirths); b) inadequacy of the Aesthetic attitude; c) the lie that romantic love is the great redemption for humans (esp. pp. 188–98, 203, 208, 226–27); d) alcoholism (pp. 209–17); e) prostitution (p. 224 onwards); f) the need for sexual activity; g) the disaster of sentiment (Althea is inauthentic, desiring to live by social convention, unthinking piety, family, materialism); h) the folly of hanging on to the idea that the self is inherently existent, and i) queer tragedy. Of these themes a) and h) are clearly Buddhist and g) heavily inflected by Buddhism.

Farrer's novels in general suffer from a certain laziness in their author; from technical errors largely to do with control of the narrative, and adequate distinction between the characters and the narrator. Farrer is not always able to distinguish between the narrator and the author (partly this fault is induced by persistent use of the third person omniscient narrator). His most riveting character is Tempest Ladon in *The House of Shadows*; and he never created a similar dominant old man again. Otherwise, it is his female characters who remain in the memory as having a fuller and livelier presence than the males: Mrs Bolpett, Lady Morland and Barbara; Isabel and Gundred; Elinor.

The novels' strengths are their concentration on the spiritual lives of the characters, and on their emotional lives; the view that emotional lives are an incomplete index of health; and the registration of peculiarities in society at the time (in general; and with sharper focus through specific characters: through Gundred in *The Sundered Streams*, for example). Perhaps most crucially, the novels present two themes simultaneously: 1) the vividly expressed yearning for physical sexual loving felt by the central characters (Kingston and Isabel in *The Sundered Streams*; Michael and Elinor in *The Ways of Rebellion*; John Trevannion in *Through the Ivory Gate*). This theme is presented with enough urgency and pathos to suggest that Farrer's deepest feelings were involved with it. 2) His Buddhist conviction that such sexual loving union is not enough, and has, as a form of desire, to be conquered. As Charles Mason put it in the *Brooklyn Daily Eagle*, 'Love is a sin — in the sense that pain is the offspring of desire.' The struggle between these two impulses or convictions motivates many of the tensions and energies of the novels, however crudely, suddenly, and seemingly wilfully resolved in some of them that struggle might be.

The main point to make, however, after this brief account of four of Farrer's novels, and in summary and defence of them, involves the question of realism. The nineteenth-century realist novel is 'realist' in the sense of evoking an idea of the material reality of a contemporary, usually British, or European, setting, and so broadly Christian (or even atheist), life going on around and sustaining the characters. Farrer's novels retain most elements of this, but they pour into the mould of the realist novel a background of a Buddhist reality. In other words, the spiritual background within the reality conjured up for the characters to inhabit, accept, and exist within corresponds to Buddhist ideas of what existence consists of, rather than the more conventional Providential, Christian or atheist background of other novelists.

In his review of *The Sundered Streams*, Charles Mason wrote that: 'In style and psychology [the novel] puts the author in the small, choice class of Meredith and James.' We should pay attention to the invocation of George Meredith's fiction, not least because Osbert Sitwell, from the standpoint of 1950, stated that in his novels Farrer employed 'a complex, sub-Meredithian style'.[51] The comparison with Meredith when the latter was at the height of his reputation (around his death in 1909) was no doubt intended by Mason as a compliment; by 1950 we can discern in Sitwell's comment rather more reserve. No writer's reputation has plummeted more absolutely and rapidly than that of Meredith, so to bracket Farrer with him, as it were, as we must do, will not enhance the conviction that Farrer was working in a way recognizably twentieth-century modernist. Perhaps the sinking of Meredith has dragged down with him Farrer, the infinitely more forgotten novelist disciple? Yet even to demonstrate in specific terms the affiliations between the two itself poses some problems, not least because Meredith's variety of narrative styles defies easy summary. 'Ah! Meredith! Who can define him?' mused Oscar Wilde: 'His style is chaos illumined by flashes of lightning. As a writer he has mastered everything except language'.[52]

One thing the two novelists share is a habit of making abrupt jumps from third-person narration into Free Indirect Discourse (FID), in which the authorial voice becomes a voice giving the inner thoughts or feelings of one of the characters. In Meredith, here is Clara resisting the attentions of 'the egoist', Sir Willoughby:

> 'I am very tired today,' said Clara.
> His arm was offered. She laid two fingers on it, and they dropped when he attempted to press them to his rib.
> He did not insist. To walk beside her was to share in the stateliness of her walking.[53]

In his description of the workings of the mind, Meredith is capable of writing sentences of an incredible awkwardness that Farrer would not have wanted to emulate. Towards the end of one novel, we are told:

> Often did Nesta conjure up to vision the palpitating form of the beloved mother with her hand at her mortal wound in secret through long years of the wearing of the mask to keep her mate inspirited. Her gathered knowledge of things and her ruthless penetrativeness made it sometimes hard for her to be tolerant of a world whose tolerance of the infinitely evil stamped blotches on its face and shrieked in stains across the skin beneath its gallant garb. That was only when she thought of it as the world condemning her mother.[54]

Effects more common in poetry invade the narrative, most obviously in the form of alliterative metaphor: 'shrieked in stains across the skin beneath its gallant garb.' However, in this example it can be doubted that they add anything coherent or telling to the description of a psychological state. And the final sentence in the paragraph quoted adds bathos as clarification.

In general terms, Farrer is more modern in his diction and both less staccato in hopping from one narrative approach to another and less long-winded than Meredith. Yet he has his moments when a kinship with the drawbacks of Meredith's approach is clear. For instance, the first appearance of Isabel in *The Sundered Streams* occasions an absorbed description that is Jamesian in its length and obsessive details (pp. 105–10). Relatively early in it we are told that Isabel is 'one of those woman who can never keep a hat straight':

> Their headgear is aimless, uncongenial, offering a perpetual suggestion of irrelevance. And, as the hat is symptomatic of the woman, the rest of Isabel fulfilled the dire promise of her headgear — immense, shapeless, foolishly waved and undulated, of limp, coarse black straw, with the big bow of cheap

satin that did not seem to belong to it [...]. Isabel, throughout, was flimsy, loose and flaccid in design. [...] Her figure was long and elastic. Only a certain arrogant untidiness of carriage could save her from the reproach of lankiness. She walked with a free unconventional swing from the hips, with a sort of bounding spring that might have been more pleasantly noteworthy had it not set her hat mopping and mowing afresh at every step. At every step it jauntily jumped, up and down, and from right to left, until the attention was concentrated on its antics rather than on any beauties that might have been found in the gait which compelled them. [...] That she wore no stays was very evident, and the flapping freedom of her legs suggested that her nature had been built for breeches rather than for petticoats. (pp. 105–06)

The poetic figure of taking the hat for the woman simply becomes grotesque, as if the human being is 'immense, shapeless, foolishly waved and undulated' and made of straw. It is with some effort that the reader remembers that all this is FID, intended simply to show Kingston's unfavourable reaction. Poetry invades: confining ourselves to alliteration only, we may note: 'flimsy and flaccid, jauntily jumped, flapping freedom, built for breeches'. As an evocation of legs, 'flapping freedom' seems particularly maladroit. Meredithian style may have its 'flashes of lightning', but it also has its periods of 'chaos'. It must be noted that another source of seemingly uncontrollable alliteration in prose (and verse) is the work of Swinburne, which, as we have already seen, Farrer knew well.

Pervasive influence of Meredith, with poetic effects affecting narrative (often impeding its clarity and drive), and sudden hops into FID, indicate a novelistic sensibility rooted in the nineteenth, rather than the twentieth, century. None of Farrer's novels exemplifies the formal experimentation that is one way of defining the modernism of the early twentieth century. That is to say, they do not experiment with new literary forms for the representation of the feeling of being alive. In relation to this, the *Academy* reviewer's use of the word 'omniscience' alerts us to a possible limitation about Farrer's approach. The reviewer is ironic, intending by the word to criticize Farrer's callowness: his limited knowledge of social habits and mores; but to establish the precise dividing line between such limitations and a more general constraint introduced by Farrer's use of the third-person omniscient narrator might prove difficult. Ford Madox Ford's view of impressionism in letters, which differs considerably from that of Henry James, is relevant to this point. Ford's novel *The Good Soldier* is taken to exemplify in the most successful way achievement of modernism in the novel through Fordian impressionism; and this impressionism is dependent on the story being narrated in the first person, with all the forgetfulness, invention, concealments and other unreliabilities of the all too human narrator, the definitely non-omniscient John Dowell.[55]

This leads me to the central point that I want to make about Farrer's novels and their relationship with his travel and garden writing. Any comparison between Farrer's novels, on one hand, and his travel- and garden-writing, on the other, must be struck with how much more liveliness and freedom his non-fiction work contains. In comparison with *The Garden of Asia,* or *On the Eaves of the World,* any of Farrer's novels after *The House of Shadows,* even *The Sundered Streams* or

Ways of Rebellion, have a conventionality, or a ponderousness, a solemnity, which make them less enjoyable to read than his non-fiction. Partly this comes from the constraint of his narrative voice. He is fully himself, in his element, in a first-person narration. In contrast a third person narration drives him into conventionality. It is as if he is not quite experiencing a complete 'freedom to feel and to say', to put it in Henry James's words. Why did he never venture into first-person narration in fiction? Probably because Jane Austen, his mentor in the novel, used third person omniscient narrative, Austen providing, according to Farrer's essay about her, the example of a supremely reliable and omniscient narrator. Presumably such an approach was taken by Farrer to be the novelist's responsibility.

I mentioned above that none of Farrer's novels manifests the formal experimentation that has consistently been taken as the hallmark of literary modernism in English. Yet to adhere too closely to such experimentation as the sole criterion of modernism risks being too materialist and essentialist.[56] Surely there are other concerns that allow writers who use traditional forms to qualify as modernist? Sara Haslam assembles several. She emphasizes the centrality of fragmentation; modernist terror lurks in 'nearness to an edge, dissolution of the self'.[57] This terror is certainly discernible biographically in Farrer's post-war letter to Osbert Sitwell, and in the world of the novels through the waywardness of Theodora Clare and John Trevannion, followed by the latter's suicide, in *Through the Ivory Gate*. The Buddhist inflection of that novel would have made the abandonment of the ego, if rightly conducted, a major step on the road to freedom that is never taken, though, by the protagonist.

Haslam cites the historian David Cannadine on the political question that contributes to modernism. For Cannadine the struggle between Liberal and Conservative dates back to the 1870s and: 'contemporary turmoil and fragmentation of the social system'. The decline in fortunes of the landed aristocrats began in the 1870s with the collapse of the economy of agriculture in Europe, the rise of plutocratic fortunes and extension of the franchise.[58] Ian Fletcher writes of 'the materialism, vulgarity, inflexibility and hypocrisy in morals of the age which took its name from [Victoria]' and confirms the new monarch Edward VII's 'closeness to the plutocracy'.[59] While Farrer's *Ways of Rebellion* is his most political novel, which deals most directly with the Liberal vs. landowner issue, these views of the period are highly relevant to a reading of *The House of Shadows*, where Lady Morland represents the vulgar and uneducated new rich, the ossified past is the enemy, and the novel dramatizes the shift from the nineteenth to the twentieth centuries.

Haslam quotes Edith Kurzweil to the effect that 'loneliness, self-doubt, hypersensitivity, perversities of all kinds, estrangement from the community' existed during the period as common neuroses and became 'themes of modernist literature'.[60] These feelings of alienation are felt acutely by Kingston Darnley in *The Sundered Streams* and vividly (and disastrously) by John Trevannion in *Through the Ivory Gate*. Haslam also brings up questions of sexual radicalism, fear of women, and debates about 'woman's true place'. In Farrer's novels we see women trying to hold on to family respectability and social position (Gundred, together with Kingston's mother), yet threatened by a new woman from the freer environment of the colonies (Isabel; *The Sundered Streams*). In *The Ways of Rebellion* Elinor makes an understandable mistake, we are made to feel, in choosing the path of material comfort and wealth, and her sexual appetite disrupts the lives of both Michael and John. Barbara, in *The House of Shadows,* a product of upbringing in the new vulgar society, disastrously destabilizes the landowner Tempest's quiet life. Farrer's themes include the need for social revolution that does not exclude personal fulfilment (*The Ways of Rebellion*) and a study of stress on, and eventual destruction of, the self because of society's incompatibilites and sexual rigidity (*Through the Ivory Gate*). In *The House of Shadows* the dogmatic brutal certainties of Tempest's world are founded on a deception. The product of that deception (St John) is innocent and worthy of love and respect. Should he be turned out of his beloved home for the crime, unbeknownst to everybody, of being the son of a different father? Or is it the institutions of society that need to change? The final question that can be posed about Farrer's novels is: does he qualify for the 'proud position' specified by Ford Madox Ford of 'historian of his own time'?[61]

An endnote on impressionism

Farrer wrote a novel about Anne Boleyn and Henry VIII: *The Anne-Queen's Chronicle* (1909). This historical novel is very different from his other novels, and is awkwardly pageant-like in its staging of its characters and their words. In his 'Prefatory Essay' to this work Farrer tries to adjust the balance between impressionism and historical fact: 'Assuredly, every man sees universal facts through his own spectacles, and may fairly read them accordingly; but fairness and historical value both depart if one deliberately shuts one's eyes to a truth, or deliberately sees it crooked, or accepts a hallucination of one's own as an honest or objective thing seen.'[62] As an explanation of historical method, this is valueless, as the novelist is trying to have it both ways. Farrer goes on to tell us that: 'a recent writer, in his wish to sanctify Katherine Howard, has found himself forced, for instance, to transform Jane Parker, Lady Rochford, Anne Boleyn's sister-in-law, into an almost imaginary person, tremulously doting and anile (instead of merely cowardly).' He has also made her Anne's 'cousin', distorting the historical fact of the legal relationship.[63] This foolish anonymous author was, of course, Ford Madox Ford, whose *The Fifth Queen* novels are remembered with much greater respect than is Farrer's *Anne-Queen's Chronicle.* Farrer's assault is made in order to defend the truthfulness of his own novel as compared with Ford's alleged 'perversion of fact which must necessarily damage the historical value of any such monograph.' Farrer has got himself onto a terribly high horse here. He himself has merely invented a character, 'Francis Wyatt', who is used to dramatize Anne's 'dialogues with her supposed lovers', and changed dates of actions, condensing months of negotiations into three pages of dialogue.[64] In other words, both novelists have used the historical material to build works of fiction.

A different personality would have reasoned that Ford was an influential figure in literary circles with interests overlapping Farrer's own, and thus a good person to know and to get on one's side. More often generous than otherwise, Ford might have been intrigued by Farrer's novel. Farrer shows himself prideful, defensive, and also a lingering Protestant: attacking a Roman Catholic convert's book about a Catholic Queen as an attempt to 'sanctify' her! This is not tactful or subtle.

Farrer was something of a snob. It took friendship with Bill Purdom, China and Tibet, the War and Burma, to get that out of him. So he enacts in his own person the divide/rupture between post-war straightforwardness and pre-war drawing-room culture with its petty hostilities, rivalries, divisions, confusions of mind. Farrer's cohorts before the War (the people he mixed with and sought out for personal or professional friendships) were friends from university (Alfred Gathorne Hardy, Raymond Asquith, Aubrey Herbert, Nobby Argles, Harold Brewer Hartley), selected ladies (Alice, Countess of Bective, Sara Anderson, Elizabeth Blanche Dugdale, Violet Asquith) or friends and acquaintances from the world of gardening (Clarence Elliott, E. A. Bowles). He had no time, or no inclination, to seek out literary figures such as Ford, who might have helped him with advancement or at least advice. Perhaps this provides another reason why his novels have become so forgotten.

Notes to Chapter 6

1. *George Bernard Shaw: The Critical Heritage*, ed. by T. F. Evans, pp. 134–35. Farrer reviewed drama in 1904 and 1905.
2. RBGE, RJF 4/1/1–13, 7, letter of 19 December 1919.
3. E. H. M. Cox, *The Plant Introductions of Reginald Farrer*, p. 8.
4. Anthony Huxley, 'Reginald Farrer', *Country Life*, 23 October 1980, pp. 1454–55, 1454.
5. Ursula Buchan, *An Anthology of Garden Writing: The lives and works of five great gardeners* (London: Croom Helm, 1986), p. 46; Stearn, 'Introductory Tribute to Reginald Farrer', p. 4; Shulman, *A Rage for Rock Gardening*, pp. 21–25.
6. I obtained a copy of one of them, Farrer's *The Ways of Rebellion* (1908) via Inter-Library Loan from Wellesley College. The due date slip at the back (the first to be glued in) has never been used. Nevertheless one sign suggests that the copy has been read, as the remains of food were adhering to p. 8.
7. *The Times Literary Supplement*, Friday 9 March 1906, p. 84. Anonymous review (the TLS's habit in the period).
8. Henry James, 'The Art of Fiction' (1884, rev. ed. 1888), in *The Art of Criticism: Henry James on the theory and practice of fiction*, ed. by W. Veeder and S. M. Griffin (Chicago: University of Chicago Press, 1986), pp. 165–96, 170.
9. Both quoted in a publisher's inset at the end of Farrer's *Ways of Rebellion*.
10. Anon, *The Athenaeum*, 17 March 1906, p. 324.
11. Anon, *The Academy*, 28 April 1906, p. 406.
12. See, for example, His Holiness the Dalai Lama, *The Meaning of Life: Buddhist Perspectives on Cause and Effect*, 1992 (Boston: Wisdom Publications, 2000), trans. by Jeffrey Hopkins, esp. pp. 60–62, 'Ignorance as the Root of Suffering'.
13. Rudyard Kipling, *Kim* (London: Macmillan, 1901), p. 169.
14. Christopher Marlowe, *The Jew of Malta*, l. 15, in *The Complete Plays*, ed. by M. T. Burnett (London: Everyman, 1999), p. 461.
15. Oscar Wilde, 'The Critic as Artist: II', in *Intentions*, 1891 (London: The Unicorn Press, 1945), pp. 121–70 (p. 165).
16. 'perhaps the single most influential text in the history of Buddhism', sent by Brian Hodgson from Kathmandu to the Société Asiatique in France in 1837 and translated by Eugène Burnouf: Donald S. Lopez., Jr., *Buddhism and Science*, p. 168.
17. John M. Rosenfield and Elizabeth ten Grotenhuis, *Journey of the Three Jewels: Japanese Buddhist Paintings from Western Collections* (New York: The Asia Society, 1979), p. 70.

18. RBGE, RJF 2/1/6/8 (Farrer's book of press cuttings).
19. Wilde, 'The Critic as Artist', pp. 165, 164–65.
20. J. A. Farrer, 'Annual Narrative' for 1906.
21. In addition to Farrer's own father, there were his great-uncle, his great-grandfather, and two more direct ancestors of the next two generations back; Sara Mason, 'The Ingleborough Estate: Home of Reginald Farrer' in Illingworth and Routh, *Reginald Farrer*, pp. 81–88 (p. 81).
22. Farrer, *The Sundered Streams: the history of a memory that had no full stops* (London: Arnold, 1907), pp. 6–7. Page numbers hereafter in main text.
23. It has to be said that a reading of *Some Farrer Family Memorials: Being a Selection from the Papers of Thomas Henry, First Lord Farrer 1819–1899, on Various Matters Connected with his Life; together with Notes relating to some Branches of the Family of Greystoneley, Ingleborough, Abinger, between 1610 & 1923, made by his Son, Thomas Cecil, Second Lord Farrer* (London: Privately Printed, 1923) gives the impression of generations of Farrers leading rather quiet lives.
24. See The Marquis of Ruvigny and Raineval, *The Plantagenet Roll of the Blood Royal: The Mortimer-Percy Volume. Being a Complete Table of all the Descendants now living of Edward III, King of England. Containing the Descendants of Lady Elizabeth Percy, née Mortimer* (London: Melville & Company, 1911), p. 553, entry for 'Anson'.
25. Anonymous review of the novel, *The Register* (Adelaide, Australia), 6 April 1907, p. 9.
26. Donald S. Lopez, Jr., *The Scientific Buddha*, pp. 54–55.
27. Oliver Freiburger and Jishnu Shankar, personal conversation with the author, 2/3/2016.
28. Quoted in a publishers' advertisement in *The Academy*, March 9, 1907, p. 228.
29. Anonymous review, *The Register* (Adelaide, Australia), 6 April 1907, p. 9.
30. Charles Welsh Mason, 'How else can you account for the mystic rapture of love?' *Brooklyn Daily Eagle*, 2nd May 1907, p. 29. All quotations are from this page.
31. Frank Kingdon-Ward, 'Reginald Farrer,' *Geographical Journal* 57, 1 (January 1921), 69–70, p. 69.
32. Farrer, *The Ways of Rebellion* (London: Arnold, 1908), p. 40.
33. W. R. Mitchell, *Reginald Farrer: At home in the Yorkshire Dales* (Giggleswick: Castleberg, 2002), p. 29.
34. Farrer, *The Ways of Rebellion*, pp. 113, 115. Page numbers hereafter in main text.
35. George Dangerfield, *The Strange Death of Liberal England* (London: Constable & Co., 1936), pp. 29–30.
36. G.E. Moore finds that 'It is as certain as anything can be that very harmful actions may be done from conscientious motives; and that Conscience does not always tell us the truth about what actions are right': *Principia Ethica* (1903; New York, Prometheus Books, 1988), p. 180. The whole of Chapter V, 142–82, is relevant to this point. We might note in passing Moore's reliance on *prosopopoeia* to drive home his point.
37. Anon, *The Spectator*, 16 May 1908, p. 24.
38. Anon, *Punch, or the London Charivari*, 6 May 1908, p. 312. It is *Punch*'s habit to put all names in italics.
39. Woolf (Stephen) is identified as the writer of the unsigned review in B. J. Kirkpatrick, 'Virginia Woolf — unrecorded TLS reviews', *Modern Fiction Studies*, 38:1 (1992), 279–301 (p. 279).
40. *Times Literary Supplement*, 12 March 1908, p. 86.
41. Quoted by a publisher's advertisement inserted in *The Saturday Review*, 21 March 1908, p. 383.
42. Quoted by a publisher's advertisement in *The Athenaeum*, No. 4197, April 4, 1908, p. 429.
43. *The Athenaeum*, 4198, April 11, 1908, p. 445.
44. Farrer, *Through the Ivory Gate* (London: Palmer, 1912), pp. 79–80. Subsequent page numbers will be given in the main text.
45. On the varieties of this, see Dorrit Cohn, *Transparent Minds: Narrative Modes for Presenting Consciousness in Fiction* (Princeton: Princeton University Press, 1978).
46. Walter Pater, *Studies in the Renaissance* pp. 187–88. The passage in Wilde's 'The Critic as Artist' relevant to my earlier point is in *Intentions*, p. 167.
47. Laura Doan and Jane Garrity, 'Modernism Queered', in *A Companion to Modernist Literature and Culture*, ed. by D. Bradshaw and K. J. H. Dettmarr (Oxford: Blackwell Publishing, 2006), pp. 545–48.

48. Ian Fletcher, *Swinburne* (Harlow: The Longman Group for the British Council, 1973), pp. 5 (woman), 32 (family).

49. 'Books and Bookmen', *Evening Star*, 10 August 1912, p. 10. Accessed through the extremely useful website < https://paperspast.natlib.govt.nz>, last accessed October 2015.

50. *Rhythm*, VII, August 1912.

51. Sitwell, *Noble Essences*, p. 18.

52. Oscar Wilde, 'The Decay of Lying', 1891, *Intentions*, p. 19.

53. George Meredith, *The Egoist: A Comedy in Narrative*, 1879 (London: Penguin, 1968, reprinted 1987), p. 124. I am looking at a library copy, in which a previous reader has penciled in the margin at this point, 'his ridiculous FID'!

54. Meredith, *One of Our Conquerors*, 1897 (New York: Charles Scribner's Sons, 1899), p. 431.

55. For recent articles on this very famous novel, see M. Saunders and S. Haslam, eds., *Ford Madox Ford's The Good Soldier: Centenary Essays, International Ford Madox Ford Studies* 14 (Leiden: Brill, 2015). See also Ford's essays on impressionism, included as appendices to the Oxford World's Classics edition of his *The Good Soldier*, (2012).

56. Jesse Matz cleaves to this older view in 'The Novel', in *A Companion to Modernist Literature and Culture* ed. by Bradshaw and Dettmar, pp. 215–16, even citing Virginia Woolf's claim that 'about 1910 human nature changed': a claim as dubious as it is memorable.

57. Sara Haslam, *Fragmenting Modernism: Ford Madox Ford, the Novel and the Great War* (Manchester: Manchester University Press, 2002), pp. 2–4.

58. Cannadine's argument quoted in Haslam, p. 16, n. 42.

59. Ian Fletcher, *W. B. Yeats and his Contemporaries* (New York: St. Martin's Press, 1987), p. 117.

60. Haslam quoting Kurzweil, p. 7. Kurzweil and Phillips (eds) *Literature and Psycholanalysis* (New York: Columbia University Press, 1983).

61. Ford quoted by Haslam, *Fragmenting Modernism*, p. 42.

62. Author's proof copy of *The Anne-Queen's Chronicle* (London: Alston Rivers Ltd, 1909), 'Prefatory Essay', p. xxiv. Copy in the Harry Ransom Humanities Research Center, University of Texas at Austin.

63. Ibid., p. xxv.

64. Ibid., p. viii.

CHAPTER 7

❖

Master of *energìa*:
On the Eaves of the World

When Farrer set off on the expedition he had planned and organized to far western China and far eastern Tibet, on 3 February 1914, it was, his father wrote, 'much against our wishes'.[1] Yet it had been wished-for and planned by Farrer for years; he had found the perfect co-expeditionary, William Purdom, a plant-collector trained by Kew; and the results of the expedition set the seal on Farrer's reputation as a plant-collector, alpine specialist, traveller, and writer. The three volumes he published to describe the expedition were together praised by the *Times Literary Supplement* as 'a classic of travel'.[2] This chapter will discuss the 2-volume work published in October 1917 as *On the Eaves of the World*; Chapter 10 will examine the final volume, *The Rainbow Bridge*, while Chapter 8 will consider Farrer's paintings from this expedition and his Burmese one.

In Asia, before the expedition to China and Tibet of 1914–1915, Farrer makes his way through a mythic geography. Korea is dead. Lanka is dead, and Ceylon horrible in its colonial aspect (yet in other ways attractive too) but it gives the opportunity for a psycho-geography of historical Buddhism and a re-telling of historical and Buddhist legends. Japan is largely sacred, otherwise comic and quaint. He evinces no political interests. In none of these countries is Farrer very interested in human geography; and he ignores economic geography. To put it broadly: his interest lies largely with the past, and he perceives places in mythic and horticultural terms almost exclusively.

With the Farrer-Purdom expedition of 1914–1915, the circumstances of travel change completely. In his earlier Asian travels Farrer had not been hunting for, and collecting, new plants. The different purpose and nature of the China-Tibet expedition (lower standard of living; searching from economic necessity for flowers) meant that the geography he was now moving through was emphatically real in a more urgent sense, while still mythic at the same time. It was also remote from centres of population, and much of the expedition's work was conducted in the wild, beyond even cultivatable regions, and thus conveyed on rudimentary transport. In his written accounts of the journey, Farrer uses the fact that they are in search of things in order to blend narratives of tension, setbacks, doubts, achievement, lucky finds, instinctive successes, and frustrations. To this extent his accounts differ from pure travel writing such as he had managed in *The Garden of Asia*: that is, travel for its own sake in order to look carefully at native life. In other Asian journeys he had been privileged, living largely in comfort with other British people (Herbert, the Colliers, and others in Japan; the human infrastructure of Empire — governors and district officers — in Ceylon). His books about those travels barely mention other people at all. In the account of China and Tibet published in book form as motivated narratives of quest (*On the Eaves of the World* covers the events of 1914, and *The Rainbow Bridge* deals with 1915) there are far more other people who feature as minor characters; not only the expedition personnel, but such characters as the 'comely' female inn-keeper, Mar-Mar Tanguei, who 'fondles' and 'strokes' Bill Purdom; or even a very minor introduction, nameless, who nevertheless is vividly seen and is described with considerable vigour. She comes into a Chinese town to help nurse a woman who has had a nervous breakdown:

> a magnificent old jolly Tibetan lady from Lodanee, in baggy blue trousers and a sort of Bretonne blue linen coif, with her hair plaited into two enormous long tresses looped almost down to her heels with coins and charms, while in front, almost to her toes, there swung and swayed a glittering cascade of successive silver chains, with charms and turquoises to match those that hung on huge silver rings at her ears. There was quite a music and a glinting when this powerful person came striding up the yard, her big face a-twinkle with smiles.[3]

This vivid description conjures her up. We have seen Balfour and Mary Woodward testifying to Farrer's descriptive powers, and (as we shall see) the novelist John Buchan was to do the same. To put it in rhetorical terms, Farrer was a master of *energìa*: vivid description that brings something to life for the reader.

The realisation of Farrer's exceptional powers in this regard, in conjunction with their employment in a book of travel in remote places, brings up a question. *The Garden of Asia* was, while not fictional, highly literary; even novelistic. Do we need to be careful about the authenticity of Farrer's account of travels in China and Tibet in *On the Eaves of the World*? Taking the two volumes together, the sheer cornucopia of details throughout the narrative persuades us that the account is real.[4] The narrative is loose, dependent on the progress and regress of the expedition. There are back-trackings in the expedition's progress, criss-crossings of their former paths, meteorological frustrations, and far too many clearly seen characters for the accounts to rely on invention for the particularities of their narratives. While the narrative is subjective, the subject himself directs his attention outwards, and only a small percentage of the narrative conveys only his feelings and thoughts. He is more interested in the life of Asia going on around him. Farrer's observation is quick, intense, detailed, and undertaken with feeling.

We readers also want to suspend disbelief because Farrer makes his narration so enjoyable. He wins us over by rhetorical means. The narrator is always optimistic and good-humoured: even when Reg loses his temper and berates the expedition's persons,[5] we see this distanced (we are told by Farrer that he gave them a piece of his mind: in other words the narrator himself appears for a moment as just another character). The account of Reg falling into a river and being swept away towards his death is funny, and shows the narrator able to laugh at himself.[6] Farrer is also cheerfully prepared to be what we would now call politically incorrect, for example expressing a liking for the mincing gait of Chinese women whose feet have been mutilated by the practice of foot-binding; although he also likes the 'free and bold' stride of Tibetan women.[7] He abominates *feng-shui*, for its determinism and economic exploitation: 'wind-and-water doctors... a set of scoundrels who dictate every detail of your life... With endless opportunities for illicit gains... the pardoners and indulgencers of China.'[8]

Good-humoured approach, honest preference, frank denunciation, intense observation, vivid description, all suffused by emotion or feeling: these are all parts of the overall rhetoric of the account, helping the narrative to gain our belief in its fidelity to the reality that the expedition lived. The speaker's goodwill is established; preference and denunciation testify to his sincerity; and observation-description appeals to the reader's imagination. Farrer builds his *ethos,* that element by which a speaker gains the trust of an audience; and thus he induces us to believe in his reliability as a guide to the facts. A skilful comic writer travels through remote Asia in search of flowers, scattering *obiter dicta* about Chinese and Tibetan politics and culture.

To pursue this line of thinking about fidelity and narrative authenticity for a little while is to detect, in addition to the rhetorical approach sketched above, other semiotic devices in the book that contribute to the same goal, and also allow the narrator some disguised revelations, as well as some concealments.

The trace of other narratives

Farrer uses the traces of other narratives in ways which implicitly bolster his claims to transparency and reliability. The most direct of these concerns the falsification of official reports. In Farrer's example, a Tibetan monk bribed a Chinese General to report that there had been no violent skirmishes on the border: 'no Tibetan incursion, no fighting, no wounded Chinese, no operation performed by the foreigners.'[9] Farrer has already described all these events, having taken part, as one of the 'foreigners' in the surgical 'operation' on the wounded foot of a junior Chinese officer (a comic masterpiece of reporting). He reflects about the bribery that: 'the episode gives a notion of the difficulties under which the Viceroy of a Chinese province labours in his efforts to ascertain the real state of affairs in his jurisdiction.'[10]

A second source of other narratives is the Christian missionaries who live in the Tibetan-Chinese borderlands. Other than those of the Church of England, Farrer abominates the Protestants, whom he excoriates for ignorance, stupidity, arrogance and craziness.[11] Self-induced ignorance is one of many faults. The dissenting Protestants have an 'assumption of being too celestially and evangelically occupied to have any time or interests left over for the wonderful world in which they live. [...] they learn nothing [...] and when asked questions reply with conscious pride that they have "no time" for such matters'.[12] The Catholics and Anglicans are better: he mentions 'Mr. Christie' by name as extremely helpful, and even exempts from condemnation, 'apart from his predications, kind old Mr. Ridley at Sining [who] is always straying out upon the paths of botany and entomology with an innocent and childlike delight', before regretting that, for information 'on any point of Chinese or Tibetan natural history, geography, and so forth, it is to the Catholics you must go if you want a sound, sensible, and workmanlike answer.'[13] This rather puts in perspective the Count de Lesdain's claim that Mr. Ridley possessed a thorough knowledge of the region.[14] Farrer also attacked the missionaries in an article published after his return in 1916:

> When you see the Protestant dissenters up against the fastness of Tibet, bringing their ignorance, their intestine disputes and divided counsels, their lack of learning, sense, or experience of life to bear upon the impregnable citadel of Tibetan Vaticanism, the spectacle becomes merely pathetico-comic...

And in a thought in keeping with one of the lessons learned earlier in Ceylon, he wrote: 'it is not from missionaries, nor from travellers fed entirely from missionary sources, that a fair appreciation of Lamaism can reasonably be expected.' ('Lamaism' is a way — itself not sympathetic — of designating Tibetan Buddhism).[15]

These same missionaries gave Farrer some trouble when they created rumours of scandal involving the expedition's most senior servant, Mafu. The scandal was stirred up by the expedition's cook, who couldn't cook:

> From first to last this wasp-waisted little person, so elegant in his murrey-coloured jersey and blue tights, had proved nothing but a failure, neither able to cook nor caring to try, waspish in tongue as well as in figure [...] and concerned, himself, with nothing but to go out into town in all his smartness and drink tea with his friends, suspicious people whom he indemnified with gossip. [...] one of his victims now proved to have been the little missionary at Jo-ni, who began to bombard me with volumes of denunciatory tattle about the Mafu, based on what he had picked up from the meat-woman and the cook and the milk-boy in the course of those kitchen confabulations which are bound to be the solace of these lonely souls in exile, with nothing to think about, and sometimes not much to do it with if there were.[16]

It is important to note that this final imputation of stupidity is aimed not at the natives, but at the western missionaries. Farrer wrote back remonstrating, and defending Mafu; and he reports that: 'it was with a gasp of delight that I found [the missionary's] answering letter hailed me as a "friend of Satan."'[17]

So rumour becomes an example of false narrative, having the effect, aside from the analysis of its working that Farrer provides, of validating by contrast his own account. The chief concealment is that the nature of the scandal is never mentioned. This is perhaps not surprising, given that gentlemanly or educated codes of behaviour of the period would reject the retailing of scandal.

The final point to be made with respect to the aligning within Farrer's account of other modes of narrative as a way of building up the reliability of his own, is that Farrer mentions in an aside that Jo-ni abbey has a printing-press, unique in the Tibetan world outside Lhasa, he writes (I, 106). Control of the press contrasts implicitly with the very system within which Farrer's own account freely appears.

The System of Photographs

Farrer's published books about the expedition are illustrated by photographs, which testify to the authenticity of the narrative by their effect of the real. Thus verbal references to 'developing plates' (and even to Reg painting) help build confidence in the reliability of the narrative by gesturing to potential cross-reference with other signifying systems. In the published volumes, wherever a photograph is used, almost every case has the photograph printed on the page before the object, place or person it shows is referred to in the written account. The articulation is thus very systematic. In *On the Eaves of the World* only in one section of volume II does this systematic use fall down. The 'Tibetan Yak-Boy' facing p. 222 is not mentioned in the text at all; the 'Little Bear' Aster (p. 232) has been mentioned hundreds of pages before; the Stone Mountain Heights (p. 242) are not mentioned in adjacent pages; and the caption on the photograph facing page 276 refers the reader to p. 163, which is clear, but uncharacteristic of the system as a whole.

Even the famous photograph of Bill in disguise, without his customary moustache, ready to undertake a seed-gathering mission into a hostile corner of Tibet, contributes to this effect of honesty. His disguising is frankly admitted; the reasons for it are given; and Reg's pleasure in the process of disguise (and in Bill's good looks) is not concealed. So the episode performs a balancing function: while it transgresses the code of openness of the expedition, it serves to show and confirm the code of openness of the text. In fact the major concealment with respect to the photographic system is that the majority of the photographs were taken by Purdom, but the volumes make no overt acknowledgement of this.

At this point we need to turn from this mainly semiotic approach to the volumes, in order to explore the dynamics of Farrer's achievements through a consideration of the overall shape of events in the tale of the journey. Later we can return to important general conclusions about Farrer's strategy and cultural attitudes in his account of these two years of his life.

The first volume of *On the Eaves of the World* sees the little expedition leaving Beijing and proceeding west through Xian, a city of the dead (pp. 64–65). Plant discoveries begin (*Buddleia Purdomii*, p. 118, *Buddleia Farreri*, p. 148). The writing occasionally betrays the fact that Farrer sometimes tries too hard: 'It is no commodious road, this, for armies and the forces of law and order. As easily may a camel go through a needle's eye.' (p. 118) A brigand, warlord or rebel leader named the 'White Wolf' is pillaging the far west of Gansu with an army. Sometimes by luck, and at other times by judgement, the expedition dodges this hazard, all the more important because they are carrying with them their whole money supply for the two years, converted into silver bullion. They cross arid lands: 'high gaunt ranges bare and brown and hard as charity [...] on which the one flower is the Asphodel, like the reminiscence of a dead flame.' (p. 159) In one region there had been no rain in four years, and half the population had died of starvation, in an 'aridness that suggested Aden' (pp. 159–60). Retreating into Tibet to avoid the White Wolves (while also trying to avoid 'robbing Tibetan tribes' of 'Black Tepos', p. 236), they are driven out at gunpoint by irate villagers, stirred up by a monk, who believe the expedition to have brought down a hailstorm that destroyed their crops. At this point Bill and Reg begin to think seriously about retreat into safety. They choose the mighty city of Siku, in China, the name of which means 'Western Strength'. In Siku they will be safe. Siku will see them right. Has Siku fallen to the Wolves, though? Rumour says so. Will they even be able to reach Siku? Rumour has it that the bridge over the River Blackwater at Nain Dzai has been destroyed. The expedition sets off anyway, and reaches Siku without trouble, incidentally showing how unreliable rumour is.

In Siku our view of the city changes. Although we are warned by being shown 'the vast and spacious derelict courts of the military Yamun', it is chiefly through the perception of a local man that our ideas about Siku are forced to change. The place is governed by a civilian Governor, Great Lord Jang, and a military commander, Great Man Pung. This latter person has had 'a varied life':

> In appearance he is like a small and wizen Robespierre, with an active manner and a smile that reveals the twisted wisdom of Machiavelli combined with a certain pathos in his own lot. He has travelled in almost all the provinces of the Empire, and has intimately known European customs in Shanghai and Peking. He has been in the train of the Amban to Holy Lhasa, and stood face to face with the Sovereign Pontiff; and he was also in the escort of the Grand Dowager when their Imperial Majesties fled to Sian.
>
> And now he ends up here, embittered and broken and helpless, in this rude little wild country town at the farthest back of beyond, and on the last edge of nowhere in the heart of the inhospitable hills, where the dour population of refugee criminals from other provinces make no case of him or his office, and remain fixed against all awakenings in the immovable methods of bygone ages.
> (I, p. 259)

Pung lives in a 'tiny' courtyard of the military Yamun; there 'dreams out the long summer days over the opium pipe.' In allowing Great Man Pung's point of view to do the work of transforming the reader's perception of Siku, Farrer employs a great deal of novelist's or dramatist's skill. This is a literary achievement. Although we are told that it has the characteristics of a time-warp, and, rather than being an impregnable city, consists of about a thousand inhabitants (Farrer told Herbert that it was 'a dear little place, about the size of Austwick', the next village east of Clapham)[18] nevertheless Siku has strong ramparts, upon which the expedition pitches its tents to help deter a Tibetan invasion with the suggestion of troops camping in the town.

Volume II opens in Siku, amid the need to discover new plants and the pleasure of doing so (p. 16). The effect of climbing on the heart is noted, as is a 'beautiful' young man (p. 42), and the path along the gorges of Nan-hor suggests Chinese landscape painting (p. 52). Another place brings to mind C. J. Holmes' work (p. 68). Naked soldiers on a raft are encountered, and a terrain like the landscapes of Cima da Conegliano (p. 77).[19] Farrer is obviously enjoying himself a great deal. The missionary Farrer likes, Mr. Christie, describes how his household escaped from a visitation of the White Wolves during the sack of Tao-jô. The end of the Wolves came after their pillage, rape and extermination of the people of the town of Tao-jô, when supply failed, they could not eat the silver they'd pillaged, and they melted away, many score drowning in the Tao River (p. 101–05).[20] One evening the Wolves became increasingly boisterous demanding the mission's women, until the household's 'sewing woman' gave herself to the Wolves in exchange for them not bothering the European women. She survived, and returned to the household in time to participate in their escape to the hills. After the adventure was over and the Wolves destroyed, she returned demurely to her job (p. 75). So the narrative jogs amiably on, with Reg's hilarious near-drowning, exciting plant discoveries, until, in the later part of the volume, the difficulty and stress of seed-collecting is emphasized. The narration forms a dense weave of landscape description, description of flowers, evocations of people and personalities met by the way, analyses of the politics of the border, and some geological and geographical thoughts.

   In the last eighty pages or so the style relaxes. For the most part before then it has been delightful, vivid and entertaining, albeit written for rhythm as well as meaning and description; but there have been obtrusive lapses detracting from the overall effect and success.[21] An example comes when Farrer describes *Meconopsis Prattii*:

> For all the shingles are full of the Celestial Poppy, tight and massive, and unvaryingly blue (in these parts) as the sky of a frosty morning, quite unnatural in its shrill crude loveliness of living light, as the spikes stand stockily up in bristling independence all over the huge desolation of the scree. (p. 174)

This is too careful, and in the middle too meaningless. Tight, quite, light, spikes; shingles, shrill; blue crude huge; loveliness of living light; spikes stand stockily bristling; all the alliterations and assonances become too heaped up, and accumulation of effects floods out meaning and erodes clear description. Only the final clause of the sentence works well. Moments such as this disappear in the last quarter or so of the book. A comparison can be made here between the description of the Celestial Poppy just quoted and a later description of autumn colour on a mountain slope:

> Dark rose the masses of Armand's pine amid a blaze of colour indescribable, up and up the heaven-high ascent, with splashes of gold and scarlet unbearably brilliant above the general brilliancy, like special flashes in the heart of a furnace; and the wild pears and mountain ashes stood up here and there in incandescent pyramids of a soft vermilion that seemed to throb and pulsate with its own intensity of light. (II, p. 248)

I would defend this later passage. In it we sense a lot of work being done by three linked groups of four words each:

$$\text{Dark — Armand's — scarlet — heart}$$
$$\text{masses — splashes — flashes — ashes}$$
$$\text{blaze — furnace — ashes — light}$$

Here the description is, as it were, thermal. It is a better description, because more relaxed; and the assonance, alliteration, pacing-out of meaning, both obvious and subliminal meaning, is more controlled, extended and successful. Alliteration and assonance extend metaphorical suggestion across the syntagmatic chain. 'Masses [...] splashes [...] flashes [...] ashes' all contribute to the overall effect of fire and heat that is established by 'blaze of colour' and reinforced by the use of 'incandescent'.

The relaxation in Farrer's descriptions coincides with more open appreciation of male beauty as something to contemplate and mention. This begins with the troublesome 'wasp-waisted' cook who is sacked. His successor is just as physically interesting to our narrator:

> a neat and charming little person with long black hair flowing round his shoulders (as in the Quattrocento) [...] I used to watch this exquisite small person, spotlessly tidy, and of an almost girlish delicacy of charm, perpetually smiling and cheerful and hard at work, in conditions of cold and snow and wet and discomfort which must have been as perpetual a keen anguish to him as plodding through cold mud to a clean little cat (pp. 231–32, 271).

The new cook is also taken up onto his horse by Reg, to sit in front of him as they jog along. Purdom's looks are extolled; once when dressed up by Reg in ancient armour in the military yard at Siku ('Magnificent and Norse he looked in his fair handsomeness', p. 245); once by observation of his effect on Mar-Mar Tanguei; and once when made up by Reg as part of his disguise for the seed-collecting trip in hostile territory ('former jovial beauty [...] now [...] most villainous and magnificent [...] daunting stature [...] flashing blue eye', p. 253). Then there is another 'kitten' to whom the reader is only introduced as he leaves:

> farewell to the strapping son of China who had joined our caravan at Jo-ni, and proved the most indefatigably delightful of all our staff — a rose-cheeked Adonis in the flush of sapid youth, so stalwart and nobly built that I always suspected him of Tibetan blood, playful and curious and happy-tempered as a kitten, with something about his rocketing gaiety of heart, his easy and gentlemanly bonhomousness of outlook, that strangely recalled the *jeunesse dorée* [sic] of Balliol in those far off days, for ever present, when "there were men in college." [...] So it was with a real feeling of parting that I watched his stately blue-clad figure swinging out into the brown distances and dwindling to a speck. (p. 301)

In the middle of this increased amount of interest in male attractions, Reg himself becomes an object. A Tibetan abbot:

> so freely heartened himself with the bottle that his holy person titubated deplorably round the court [...] As these moods of His Holiness flowered principally in a quite embarrassing degree of admiration for my personal beauty — a point on which only Tibetan wine in quantity could carry conviction to my most fervent admirers — I hailed at last the transference of his devotional energies. (p. 260)

Clearly at this mature stage of the narrative queer interest cannot be concealed and is forcing itself into the open. There may also be an effect from the time of writing. Farrer tried to complete the book while still in China (during the winter in Lanchow, and in Peking at the expedition's end).[22] The almost uncanny recall of detail, and the freshness of description, owe something to this, which is a little analogous to a landscape painter completing a painting on the spot rather than at home in the studio. But the end might have had to be written after his return to Britain, after the beginning of his employment at the Foreign Office and his meeting with Ernest Gye, Jim Baird, and some kindred spirits. The second year's account, *The Rainbow Bridge*, was only written in 1918. Having a job, for the first time in his life, will have given Farrer greater confidence than he had ever enjoyed before, and a feeling of independence; and as we have seen, Gye's friendship brought greater freedom of expression. The War, having shaken up staid conventions in Britain, was in itself liberating (as it proved for a lot of women, for example, also employed, and in responsible jobs for the first time). My suggestion is that the evidence of *On the Eaves of the World* (and of the letters to Gye) shows the quality of Farrer's writing improving as he allows his homoerotic preference to emerge more.

From West to East

One of the reasons Farrer takes so much care to persuade us of the reliability of his account, by building up his own *ethos*, and by showing, apparently casually, other narratives, and narrative sources, as unreliable, is to prepare the reader to accept one of the conceptual thrusts of his book. The bourgeois norms that Farrer is trying to get away from (and, in life, it appears that Purdom was), are represented in the book by the much-abominated missionaries, and by another plant-collector who appears late in the narrative, the Dutch-born American, F. N. Meyer. Through these presences on the Tibetan-Chinese borderlands, the despised norms become spiritual and racial in character. The question is no longer, to what extent is Farrer's modernity dependent on his Buddhism, but comes closer to the question that Jill Didur raised and that I referred to briefly in my Introduction: the question of Farrer's relations with local people, his acceptance of or fitting in with local cultures. To what extent does he deepen the victory over himself and over British culture that he won when he bowed before Sri Sumangala and Jinavaravamsa in Ceylon to become a Buddhist?

Meyer was 'travelling in search of economic products on behalf of the Agricultural Department of the American Government' (II, p. 276). This official support of his expedition would no doubt have stirred envy in Farrer, who had been obliged to round up private patronage for his own, and with whom Purdom had come for no pay at all. But Meyer has made a mess of relations with his servants. Arrived in Siku, he throws his interpreter down the stairs, and punches a 'coolie' on the nose. The little town, scandalized, bridles against him. Bill and Reg: 'meditated lending him rifle or revolver for immediate needs, until we discovered that he already had both, loaded and ready to discharge at any moment on any provocation, this being the proper White Man attitude in respect to the "damned yellow scum".' (II, p. 280) The point is that Farrer and Purdom hate the stupidities of this attitude, and Farrer's condemnation is plain enough, though his published account is delicate. But in a letter to Balfour he wrote that 'Mayer [sic] is a vaporful but specious person [...] he came [...] in bad trouble with his servants [...] he *hates* China and the Chinese ostentatiously.'[23]

Bill and Reg nevertheless treat Meyer with kindness, using their good relations with the town and its governors on his behalf to rescue his expedition, and Mafu found a guide for him. Eventually Meyer left the borderland: 'Mayer, praise be, was baffled by difficulties, and went off home with a pocket-full of walnuts off the street!'[24] Meyer is the consummation of dynamics Farrer has detected in himself and warned against in Volume I, p. 121: the difficulty of not knowing the language, combining with the bad effect of European education, to create impatience and contempt. The episode sets Meyer's more typical western attitude against Bill and Reg's immersion in local life and difficulties (they had helped to defend Siku against the Tibetan threat, operated in public on the Chinese officer's foot, exchanged formal visits with governors), their good relations with their own expedition servants, and the consequent trust in them demonstrated by the local inhabitants. The view of Meyer that we derive is Farrer's own, of course, designed to point up his own commitment to local culture. It cannot be taken to be complete evidence about Meyer as an actual person.

In telling contrast to Meyer and what he stood for, Reg had also practised 'equalizing and switching of self and other', recommended by the present Dalai Lama as a means of overcoming feelings of superiority.[25] Farrer writes about a day in Siku when he was wearing his Chinese clothes:

> I went out in my silken robe and Chinese string sandals to get seed of *Sophora viciifolia*, and to quest vainly for lingering germs in the gaping blackened capsules of the grey flannel Buddleia. And even so [...] a posse of small gamins attached itself to my heels with jokes and laughter, which caused me to proceed with nose-in-air majesty and a stiff consciousness that I was being made a public mock. There was no dislodging the little people. On my heels they jested and trotted, and a firm blankness was the only weapon possible. Until I reached the grave-coppice I imagined I was feeling the exact sensations of a Chinese dogged, helpless, by urchins in a London street with shouts of rudeness. I was soon to learn my error, for when I got to my bushes and set to work, feeling that the general amusement would now redouble, I found that all my twittering crowd of sparrows wanted was to help me at my task. And the grubby little paws went so busily at the business, and so industriously, that in a trice my basket was full of the bubbly-looking pods, and I next proceeded with my escort up on to the down to look for the fairy Leptoderm and the golden willow Daphne. Imagine such a crowd of European urchins going out after a fantastic stranger only to offer him help and stick to his toil! (II, p. 234)

Reg and Bill have already equalized and switched in another fashion, when, in order to satisfy local curiosity, they staged themselves as the sort of tableau that other races performed in European and U.S. *expositions universelles* (I, p. 123). The later episode with the *gamins* goes beyond such a staging, though, and is part of the way in which Farrer begins to feel that Chinese civilisation is in many respects better than European. Meyer's 'white man' attitude is more of a convention that the contemporary reader might have expected from accounts of travels in remote Asia; instead, Farrer wears Chinese clothes by preference (not for disguise) and practises equalizing and switching of self and other. The missionaries are people that a conventional reading public might rely on for supposed dependable accounts of remote parts of the world. Not so, says Farrer. In Siku in 1914 Farrer is developing his rejection of European civilisation, Christianity, and the White Man's attitude, in favour of embracing local native culture.

Although I have understood it as part of a rejection of the West and embrace of the East, one additional note that we must make about Farrer's adoption of Chinese dress, however, reveals a sub-text to his liking for it. It answers his liking for dressing-up, which in its camp manifestations can be a feature of queer life, born out of queer men's need for concealment and simultaneous wish to break out; the need to hide their true natures from a hostile outside world. Farrer, sending from Burma the 'ample pantalettes of glacé silk in incredibly sumptuous shades of opalescent rose and azure' to Ernest Gye at Christmas, 1919, tells him that they will be the envy of Queen's Gate (that outrageous menage presided over by Jim Baird and commemorated in 'The Empty House').[26] And Chinese clothing had an added appeal too, exemplified by the always comic character of 'Great Man Pung' in Siku, who arrived one day to summon Bill and Reg as honoured guests at a feast: 'resplendent in a bowler hat, silvery satin skirt, and crimson bodice'. (OEW II, p. 235) Dressing in Asian clothes would allow Farrer to wear, if he wanted, garments that he thought resembled those of women in western society, adding some of the fun of cross-dressing (that is, in his own imagination: not in the view of Chinese society around him) to the normal pleasures of dressing-up.

To return from this theme to politics: the travellers' safety depends on the politics of the border. Not all power is with the westerners. In Wen Hsieh, to preserve his status, Reg visits the Yamun on horseback (I, p. 157). This dignity contrasts with the indignity of the expedition being driven out of Chagola at gunpoint (I, pp. 178–89). The travellers need to be careful not to 'openly flout the harassed and anxious Governor' on the borderlands, as he may report them to the 'viceroy' of a province, who in turn might decide that they need to be escorted back to Peking with their passports revoked (I, p. 154). Indeed, Farrer doesn't even want all power to reside with the westerners. Bill and Reg negotiate patiently, endeavouring to adopt Chinese customs (founded on patience, we are told), demonstrating an attitude that contrasts strongly with Meyer's later actions. There is, Farrer tells us, 'a straight and direct chain of responsibility for our safety' from village headman up to the 'Emperor of China' (I, p. 205). This gives the expedition certain ways of exerting pressure to get what they want; but they have to operate within the limits of recognized authority.

Farrer's strategic view of the borderlands is that the Chinese empire alleges dominion, but hasn't the power to assert it consistently, although it can do so intermittently. In the meantime, the Tibetan abbeys of the border (Jo-ni, Tien Tang, Chebson, and the larger ones of Gumbum and Labrang) are theoretically under allegiance to the Dalai Lama in far-away Lhasa, though Lhasa is so far away that the abbeys tend to act as independent entities of power. There is also a 'Prince' at Jo-ni who likes to think of himself as independent. Therefore much depends on the relations that can be established with the monks. The monk at Chago stirred up the villagers to the point of violence against the expedition, despite Reg having played the Buddhist card (I, pp. 178–89, 230–31). The expedition escaped, probably because some more peaceful monks pointed out that murder would bring down on them the wrath of Empire.

So there is a politics, right down to the personal level. Bill and Reg rescue their Tibetan friend the Shang-yu of Satanee (the village headman) from gaol in Siku by paying his fine, which is the annual tribute alleged by Chinese authorities to be due from his village (II, p. 250). Cutting across this Tibetan-Chinese divide is the question of muslim Chinese, active in the White Wolf rebellion (and who, under their own warlords, ultimately attacked and occupied the Labrang monastery in 1917). Farrer gave a talk on 'The Mahommedan Problem in China' to the Central Asian Society in April 1918. He stated that the Mahommedans and Labrang abbey sometimes join forces in 'brewing trouble for the Chinese'.[27] Farrer's fear was that 'German intrigue should foment a new Mahommedan cataclysm (hard, anyhow, to avoid) in Western China.' The context was British apprehensions about German influence in the Muslim world, so memorably represented by John Buchan's adventure novel, *Greenmantle* (1916).

As reflected in *On the Eaves of the World*, spiritual life is a very important element in the borderlands and their politics. Tibet looms large, and represents the unity between the real and the mythic. When the expedition first crosses into Tibet, Farrer is impressed, but with reservations. The relevant passage will have to be quoted at length, since it shows him determined to be sceptical and even sardonic:

> For suddenly overhead, in the painted gateways of the road, you look up and salute the Lords Buddhas and Bodhisattvas smiling down benignantly in glory, and know that now you are indeed in the precincts of the sacred and mysterious land, which no doubt, if not so difficult and remote, would prove no more sacred and mysterious than any other. But here they sit, the Holy Ones; and between them, in the central space of the roof-beam, is a vane like a turbine, painted with emblems, and perpetually revolving the words of aspiration to every breath of the wind. Left behind is the dry and sensible materialism of China, and here you enter the grip of the most tremendous mysticism, and the most materially organised, of any that still holds the fettered imagination of man. Salute, then, as you pass under their gateway and into their territory, these strange legendary shapes, these indefinitely multiplied mysterious forces, whose very presence here, and whose almost every function in the creed they have coagulated, is an insult to the memory of the Wholly Perfect One, and to the Truth that they have darkened through the ages with a multitude of counsels. Yet it is a moment of note, this, of entering upon a land where truth is apprehended at all, though no longer naked indeed, but disguised with load upon load of multifarious trappings. (I, p. 163)

This is an apprehension of power, even though Farrer seems to want to repudiate that power, or at least see it as mistaken. Yet beyond the sardonic mind there is an intimation of compromise. Truth may be disguised; but it is abroad in the land. The man who embraced Buddhism as a religion not at odds with the concept of Evolution, will have his view of his own faith tested by practical evidence of the sort of society and the sort of people produced by Tibetan Buddhism. One place where this comes out clearly is when Farrer meets the Living Buddha of Nalang, then in Jo-ni abbey. Living Buddhas are reincarnations of previous Buddhas, who are also bodhisattvas. Reg is prepared to meet this one with a respect that matches his dignity. And he finds that:

> The Sacred Body, it was evident, had for its tenant a wise and sound being [...] its whole presence radiated rather learning and balance and kindliness than that extraordinary emanation of impregnable felicity which one only meets with once or twice in one's life — if [...] at all — and which, wherever met, in whatever country, sex, or creed, is the unmistakable sign of that happiness incarnate which is the Buddhahood, the perfected wisdom that stands for ever beyond reach of sorrow or uncertainty. (II, p. 112)

His holiness is interested that Reg has visited the eight sacred places of Ceylon and possesses leaves from the holy tree of Anuradhapura. They talk of Labrang, where the 'dominant Buddha' is 'good' but 'in the hands of a Chapter full of wickedness, ambition, and rebellion.' (II, p. 113) The Living Buddha condescends to show Reg to the door. (II, p. 114) For the next ten pages Farrer reflects on this meeting. He is sceptical about Living Buddhas. The process of finding one (the child, just before being recognized as a Living Buddha, recognizing its former possessions): 'offers many opportunities for fraud and jugglings', we are told, 'especially when some wealthy clan desires to have a Living Buddha in the family, and is ready to pay accordingly.' Then Farrer reveals a limit to his scepticism: 'On the other hand, to deny all validity to the test is to limit very arbitrarily the possibilities of memory, and the nature of being.' Here the Buddhist, and the author of *The Sundered Streams*, makes himself felt. The explanation continues, though, not with respect to spiritual mysticism, but focussing on the conjoining of religion and politics:

> The Living Buddhas are not incarnations, but manifestations through the flesh of aspects of the Supreme Holiness. The idea of these revelations was born in northern Buddhism long after the dissolution of the Perfect One, and has never met with a trace of favour in the purer school of the South. In the Buddhism of the Great Vehicle [*mahayana*], however, which prevails over China, Mongolia, Tibet, and Japan, the dogma of continued consciousness has been expanded into the basis for a new Pantheon of quasi-divinities, which has led to so important a politico-ecclesiatical institution as the Living Buddhahood. Quite early the State also saw the extreme importance of this development, and laid its hand on some of the more eminent manifestations. (II, pp. 115–16)

Farrer states that Buddhahoods can in effect be sold by 'Church' authorities to wealthy families. Both the families, and the wealthy abbeys, benefit. He contemplates some model examples:

> in such a mixture of sham and truth, diplomacy and the inspirations of memory, the Living Buddhas are of all sorts, from the Sodden Sovereign of Mongolia [i.e., a drinker] (who usually has to be held propped on his grubby old feet) and the supreme Pontiff of Lhasa, the most audacious and able of political ecclesiastics, who has appeared for long past in East and West, to the towering sanctity of the Tashi Lama, and of many another manifestation of truth lurking unsuspected in the enormous folds of Tibet. (II, p. 117)

There follow pages of attack on the Christian missionaries, and a relating of the ironic moment when the Living Buddha of Garan exorcized the 'devils of folly and prejudice' in the missionaries' own compound. 'Absurdities and minutiae of religious etiquette' surround and encumber the Living Buddhas (II, p. 121). Lamaism is equated, or made analogous, with Roman Catholicism; but the Protestant dissenting missionaries, 'up against the fastness of Tibet' are merely absurd: 'pathetico-comic' being one of Farrer's adjectives. 'There is no doubt', Farrer assures us, 'that the chain of Lamaism lies heavy over Tibet'; but the spiritual and the material are united and: 'the Tibetan gives every sign of being happy in' his faith. The contemplation ends with a comparison with Christianity. Someone else will have to decide, writes Farrer: 'on the extent to which material acts, if sincere in intention and sufficiently intense in purpose, can react on the spiritual world. [...] no creed can claim a monopoly on magic. We are still in no position to throw stones at the "superstitions" of Lamaism.' (II, p. 123)

The imputed unity of the material and mystic is ultimately what Farrer wants. After his return to Britain in 1916, he wrote a typescript, 'One of the Allies', about how the Dalai Lama had decreed prayer for the British and allied casualties in the Great War, and explaining the significance of that decree.[28] Spiritual matters were a life-long interest for Farrer. With respect to Tibet, in a magnificent denunciation he accused the British of hypocrisy:

> Worshipping as we do, above all, material success in this world, the capacity for slaughter, and that merciless Moloch, Efficiency, we fall foul of Lamaist monasticism in Mongolia because 'emollit mores, nec sinit esse feros,' reclaiming a wild and bloodthirsty people into a meekness and mildness that we ourselves despise as enthusiastically as our Gospels praise it. And yet, when we meet the same monasticism producing exactly the contrary effects in Thibet, and hardening a hard mountain race into yet further courage, audacity and fire, we have no better word than 'obstinate fanaticism' for our angry verdict on a frame of temper that may not suit our own purposes so well as the contemptible meekness or lethargy of the Mongolian.[29]

The British, in this view, are not spiritual but materialist, and ferocious. They practice one form of hypocrisy about Mongolia, and another about Tibet. To state as much, and in this way, was part of Farrer's process of rejecting the English and European civilisation of the West.

Farrer continues, in the same article: 'For my own part, deploring altogether the wide divergence of Mahayana Buddhism in all its branches from the pure traditions of the South.' This statement, while it accords with his sardonic view of the many Buddhas and Bodhisattvas of Tibet, is nevertheless simply not true to Farrer's own experience. The implication of the sentence is that southern Buddhism, more 'pure', is better than the divergent and ramified northern Mahayana. To assert as much is one of Farrer's self-contradictions, stemming from a difference between what he has been told, by fellow British buddhists as well as Ceylonese and Thai ones, and his own experience. Among other things, such sources will have told him that the Theravada tradition was earlier and purer than the northern tradition: an argument that appealed to people brought up in countries dominated by Protestantism, with its fetish for ideas of purity and privileging of textual fundamentalism over developed practices.[30] Yet it was a form of Mahayana Buddhism that had first awakened Farrer's interest in the religion, in Japan. We have already seen in Chapter 4 Farrer stating his belief that there is 'one Spirit' and 'one Life' in all things. Was this classed as a Theravada or Mahayana belief in Farrer's day? The original edition of Olcott's *The Buddhist Catechism* contained the assertion: 'There is but one All, of which we and every being and thing are but parts.' In his corrections of this text, made, obviously, in Ceylon in accordance with Theravada orthodoxy (and published in 1908) the High Priest Sri Sumangala eliminated this statement; but an editor of the *Ceylon National Review*, reporting his corrections and revisions, added this note about the assertion: 'N. B. This latter statement is, however, true according to Mahayana, "the All" being the Dharmakaya.'[31] The *dharmakaya* is the Buddha's body after the achievement of enlightenment. It now encompasses all things. So Farrer relayed this Mahayana truth in his *In a Yorkshire Garden* (1909) in his passages about burning daffodil bulbs and both rock and human life having within them one spirit. He did this after first becoming interested in Buddhism in Japan, and he continued to be interested in Mahayana Buddhism and sympathetic to it in Tibet. We have seen how he was planning to reach Lhasa at the time of his death; and when he arrived at the Pink Temple, in the mountains above Siku, during a plant-collecting foray, and was invited to stay the night there, he reported the experience as enchanting:

> It was afternoon before we reached the pinnacle of the Pink Temple and ensconced ourselves in that charming place. The attendant priest even invited me to pitch my bed in front of the Buddhas and Bodhisattvas, and was only induced to relegate me to the side-chamber set apart for guests by the protests of my servants [all Chinese], who feared that my nerves and brain might not prove strong enough to bear such manifestations as those holy presences would certainly provide through the dark watches about midnight. Myself, I think I could have borne them. They could only have been beautiful, for never in my life have I found a place so wholly filled with a sense of peace and holiness as that wee shrine, so high over the dusty world of the Blackwater. Our Lady of Mercy smiles out from rockworks surrounded by doves and angels and departing discomfited fiendlets. On her right sits an image of the Wholly Perfect One draped in a cope of scarlet silk. In front is the tiny courtyard, where no cat could swing, with lesser shrines on either side, one of which contains sad derelict deities collapsing amid dust, and the other a brace of cupboarded dolls in superimposed cloaks of silk, behind whom stand big statues on guard, and in front iron porringers full of incense silt, which are rung at evening, and give a sound as sweet and lingering as any bell. The court is closed by the block of Lilliputian rooms where the priest has his home, close to the great bell on its platform, while back to back to the main shrine of Our Lady is another, facing down towards the gate, where a benevolent old person sits throned on a reclaimed tiger cat; and in between are yet other minute houses of holiness, with the pine-trees murmurous all about them, and then the sheer fall of the cliff away on either side, and that wonderful feeling of being poised on space.
>
> It is certainly a very kindly and holy place, that little Pink Miao on the pinnacle, and the summer evening comes very sweet into its courts. As dusk descends, the priest begins his rounds. He is a dark shaggy creature, model

for any of the saints and martyrs you may see frescoed on the wall of Our Lady's shrine depicting her miracles ['Our Lady' is Guan-yin, a form of Avalokiteshvara, saving all from mundane and spiritual perils]. With arm outstretched from heaven she plucks them out of the fire, or, uprising from the water, she lifts them from drowning, in a series as naïf and passionate as any you may see in France or Italy, commemorating the interventions of that younger Madonna who rules over the heart of Christianity. And round he goes in the balmy twilight at his service. In the first blue moment of dusk the sticks of incense shine like stars before Our Lady and before the swathed figure of the Perfect One; the brocaded dolls in the cupboard of the wee lateral chapel get theirs also, and their bowls, sweetly smitten, give out a long ringing quivering tone that floats far in its vibrations through the twilight before the next stroke is rung.

And then the Angelus begins, and the great bell booms out its message of peace over the world down beneath the feet of this holy place. Deep and velvety and comforting as peace the vast and violet tone hangs reverberating in the air after each blow, and seems to ripple through the infinity of the air in a rhythmic procession of force. Far out above the darkened valley it haunts and floats, and the city hears its message of calm outstretching like a gesture of blessing over the troubled earth. And so the night draws her cloak across the unfolded world beneath, and sapphire darkness fills the courts of the Pink Temple. Still the incense ascends through the stillness in spires of unwavering sweetness, and the deep soft memories of the bell throb through the silence. (II, pp. 202–04)

Written in European wartime, the passage unequivocally celebrates the sense of peace he derives from Buddhism. There is none of the sardonic tone of the account of his first entry into Tibet that we quoted earlier. A benign, tolerant acceptance suffuses the whole passage. He has progressed beyond his earlier condemnation.

Notes to Chapter 7

1. J. A. Farrer, 'Annual Narrative' for 1914. NYCRO. 'Our' wishes being implicitly those of both parents.
2. *TLS*, November 10, 1921, p. 729.
3. *On the Eaves of the World*, vol. II (1917; London: Arnold, 1926), p. 46. Hereafter *OEW*.
4. Roland Barthes, 'The Reality Effect', is the classic exposition of this now-obvious point. Barthes, 'The Reality Effect', in the *Rustle of Language* (1984: Editions du Seuil; English translation by Richard Howard, New York: Farrar, Strauss and Giroux, 1986), pp. 141–48.
5. To distinguish Farrer from his figure as he appears in the books, and Purdom from his, I shall refer to them as they feature in Farrer's published narrative as 'Reg' and 'Bill'.
6. *OEW*, II, pp. 142–45.
7. *OEW*, II, p. 295.
8. Ibid., p. 273.
9. Ibid., pp. 238–39.
10. Ibid., p. 239. One might suggest that this tendency to falsify official reports, persisting at least until the 1960s, contributed to the catastrophe of the 'Great Leap Forward'. See William Hinton, *Shenfan: the Continuing Revolution in a Chinese Village* (New York: Vintage, 1984), pp. 234–49, 247–49.
11. Farrer's energetic diatribe against missionaries (of all denominations) occurs in *OEW* II, pp. 85–95.
12. Ibid., p. 94.

13. Ibid., p. 94

14. 'The rev. Mr. Ridley, of the China Inland Mission [...] gave us interesting details of the country, which he knows through and through.' The Count de Lesdain, *From Pekin to Sikkim Through the Ordos, the Gobi Desert, and Tibet* (London: Murray, 1908), p. 142.

15. Donald S. Lopez Jr., ' "Lamaism" and the Disappearance of Tibet', *Comparative Studies in Society and History*, 38, 1 (Jan 1996), 3–25. The quotation from Farrer comes from his 'The "White Wolf "in Kansu', *Quarterly Review*, (April 1915), 353–69, p. 356.

16. *OEW*, II, p. 229.

17. Ibid., p. 230.

18. Somerset Archives, DD\HER/38, letter from Farrer of 1st June 1914.

19. No. 18, 'The Four Little Trees' in Farrer's Fine Art Society exhibition, is explained in the catalogue as 'After Cima da Conegliano'.

20. This account was given to Farrer by Mr. Christie. Current thinking has the White Wolf rebellion driven back from Gansu by attacks of Chinese Muslim troops and Tibetans.

21. Written for rhythm: Farrer apologizes in a footnote for using a split infinitive (unprecedented, he claims, in his work) but states that 'the exigencies of rhythm and meaning really do compel me': *OEW*, II, p. 145.

22. Letter to Balfour from Peking, 13/12/15. RBGE RJF 1/1. Farrer was still in China on the 22nd February 1916 (RBGE RJF 3/1). As he was in Petrograd by 1st May, he probably left Peking in March or April.

23. RBGE RJF 1/1/15, letter of 13/12/1914.

24. Letter to Balfour, 24/3/1915: RBGE RJF 1/1/26.

25. Tenzin Gyatso, the 14th Dalai Lama, *The Meaning of Life: Buddhist Perspectives on Cause and Effect* (Somerville, MA: revised edition, 2000), p. 101.

26. RBGE, RJF 4/1/1–13, letter of 23/12/1919.

27. Farrer, personal letter to A. C. Yate. Yate's article, 'The Russian Débâcle and the East', *The Nineteenth Century and After*, 83 (May 1918), 1062–77, p. 1075, is the source of information about Farrer's activities here and quotes the letter.

28. The material in this typescript was incorporated into *On the Eaves of the World* (II, pp. 112–24, 258–59).

29. 'The White Wolf in Kansu', pp. 356–57. The Latin phrase, from Ovid, means 'it softens behaviour, and does not allow it to be fierce.' Ovid, *Epistulae ex Ponto* II, ix, 47.

30. An important article on this is Gregory Schopen, 'Archaeology and Protestant Suppositions in the Study of Indian Buddhism', *History of Religions* 31:1 (1991), 1–23.

31. *Ceylon National Review*, 7 (August 1908), 305.

CHAPTER 8

Painting (and Describing) Flowers and Landscapes

In addition to the published books, the expedition was also documented and conjured up in Farrer's paintings. The purpose of the expedition was to find new garden flowers and shrubs. These were photographed (mainly by Purdom), and photographs sent back from the field to Bayley Balfour in Edinburgh.[1] The plants were preserved on Herbarium sheets. They were also described by Farrer in words. An astonishing thing about his life is that he wrote thousands of descriptions of flowers (hundreds in *On the Eaves of the World* alone), and he very rarely repeats himself or produces a stale dull evocation of a plant. Given the volume of examples, it is not surprising that an occasional lapse such as that made about *Meconopsis Prattii* can be found. Frank Kingdon Ward (himself a plant collector and travel writer) wrote of Farrer that he had 'an insurgent style' that 'not only conveyed vivid impressions of scenery, but made the plants which he described rise up and live before his readers.'[2] Farrer was a master of *energìa* in prose. There was arguably a special quality about this in his writing about plants. If we take the description of *Cypripedium farreri*, (figure 8.1) for example, we find:

> Here and there she arose amid herbage, a small delicate person, recalling the Lady's-slipper of the alps, but far more graceful and slight in habit, with elvish pointed segments, quaintly twisted, of greenery-yallery tone, striped with solid lines of maroon. Her lip, however, was her outstanding beauty, being of a pale and waxy cream-yellow outside, and striped internally with maroon that faintly transpired. It was of the strangest bottle shape, too, constricted below the mouth, which expanded again in a row of vandykes so hard and glossy as to glitter to the light. (OEW I, pp. 302–03)

In moments like this the intense observation and concentration seem suffused by another form of longing. We might interpret the strong desiring sensuality of Farrer's response to flowers as a sublimation of sexual feelings defined as criminal by his society. As gay men had to reject both the law and social expectations in order to live more fulfilled lives, they had a position in the forefront of people struggling for social and political change, no matter how concealed their activities may have been (absolute concealment being impossible). This gives another value to Kingdon Ward's use of the interesting word 'insurgent' about Farrer's writing; a value that acknowledges his choice of a word with connotations of rebellion and desire for change.

FIG. 8.1. Farrer, *Cypripedium farreri* (RHS Library).

A black and white photograph, at least to an early 21st century viewer, can some-times seem a form of visual representation less than adequate to the needs of the plant and the expectations raised by Farrer's verbal descriptions. Farrer's paintings, rarely on public view, cannot normally be used by readers to validate the written descriptions. Although the text, as we shall see, sometimes validates the paintings, it is more rational to see the two systems as mainly separated. Farrer wrote briefly about his general approach to painting on two occasions. Early in 1917 he tried to persuade Balfour, in Edinburgh, to visit his exhibition of watercolours at the Fine Art Society. Of the flower paintings, he assures Balfour that many of the 'plates' (as he calls the watercolours) are 'original icons of known or of new spp. [species].' He goes on:

> Without being scientific plates, I have been careful to keep all the diagnostic points that the observing eye can detect, and the brush record. This, together with essential concentration on the growing character of the plant, and its natural surroundings.[3]

This will give us something to go on when we look at Farrer's paintings. His other comment came in a letter to Ernest Gye from Burma:

> Art, alas, has forcedly been in abeyance, except as far as flowers are concerned. And these are bad for it. Anyhow, I almost despair of that loose, free, flowing style in which you and Holmes are my idols: but flowers put one absolutely out of practise for it, too, requiring, as they do, not niggliness, I hope, but certainly an attention to their detail which reacts unfavourably when one comes to aim at pourtraying a mountain in a wash, a splodge and three splashes.[4]

Here Farrer reveals a fundamental difference in painting technique between the depiction of an entire landscape in a 'loose, free, flowing style' and the more controlled focus used to show the small individual constituent parts (the flowers) of the greater landscape scene.

This comment by Farrer confirms what we can see in his painting of *Trollius pumilus perfectissimi*.[5] It is important to remember that Farrer was an amateur painter, who had possibly taken some private lessons, and learned from the example of friends such as E. A. Bowles and C. J. Holmes, but who had never been a student in an art college or school. His painting of this flower (figure 8.2) exemplifies his most polished work. The flower is clearly seen, crisply delineated in a naturalistic way, the painting of it being a faithful and unambiguous portrait. This is the result of tight control of Farrer's materials, and tight self-control. Any impulsive energy has been denied. The painting is correct and vivid. Nature itself has done enough and simply needs to be portrayed carefully.

Or rather, nature has done most of the work, but another factor has also made itself felt. For this is a flower that should have been golden-yellow in colour. Farrer attributed this unique white form to the fact that it was growing next to a spring of water made sacred by the picture of the Buddha painted above it. The flower had responded to the holy presence. This belief of Farrer's is inscribed in the words on the painting itself, as well as next to a blurred photograph of the site in his album, and was also published in *The Rainbow Bridge*.[6] So Farrer includes in his painting the

Fig. 8.2. Farrer, *Trollius pumilus perfectissimi* (RHS Library).

spring ('well'), the rock-face above it, and the Buddhist painting, as his depiction of the flower's natural surroundings. His painting of all this context is more open, relaxed, loose and approximate, than his painting of the flower itself. The well, its rock and painting, are 'rendered' (to borrow a word from the discussions of impressionism that were being had at the time) with greater freedom. The painting of the Buddha is depicted by Farrer as mystical, with the halo of yellow/green around his head extending over his shoulders and down his chest. Turquoise water contrasts with red-painted rock; rounded forms of the painted rock contrast with the blue/grey spike below. Ancientness and erodedness of the rocks contrast with the Buddha's young face. At the top right there is a glimpse of valley receding up-stream. Seven flower or star-burst forms are around the Buddha; highlights on the hand, and parts of the cloak.

So this painting as a whole works by contrasts that are harmoniously combined. The painting of the flowers, while not qualifying as top-flight botanical depiction, is nevertheless technically rather good, and that success has correctness and control as its governing principles. The more impressionistic painting of the rest connotes freedom, even impulsivity (the red highlight on the hands is created by a single touch or dab). Of this contrast in contributing factors we might say that Farrer could make decorum work for him, but on its own it was not enough.

Botanical artists need to depict plants in a way that ensures the plants can be accurately recognized from a professional botanical point of view. The correct number of stamens needs to be accurately depicted, as do the modes of attachment between parts of the plants. The result should be easier and quicker to understand than a verbal description and sometimes more accurate as well, in the sense of being less approximate than words sometimes are. Nevertheless, an additional sense, of the plant as a whole living thing, is also sometimes striven for by advanced botanical artists, to judge by the comments recorded on film about a recent visit to Nepal by artists currently attached to the Royal Botanic Garden in Edinburgh. Concepts such as the 'essence', 'character' and 'quality of presence' of a plant were used to evoke this further elusive subject desired for depiction in addition to the important taxonomical information.[7]

Farrer never practised strict botanical illustration such as the example included here for comparison, Lilian Snelling's painting of *Viburnum farreri* (figure 3.3). The painting is clear, clean, explanatory, but has no atmosphere. In such plates often the whole plant, from roots to seeds and flowers, is included. Farrer never painted the roots and never produced a work that gave the same impression of hypnotic, obsessive attention to detail of a professional plate. His watercolours of flowers could be very careful, as he claimed to Balfour, but they also tried to set the plant in its native context and give a clear idea of its habit of growth (a sense of the overall shape of the whole plant, as well as the basic information as to whether it is clump-forming, a climber or rambler, mat-forming etc.). In the case of *Stellera chamaejasme,* he felt obliged to write on his (rather inadequate) painting, 'Stems should be stiffer and the plant forms a perfect domed bush.' The painting, rather in the manner of a botanical study, shows five individual stems of the plant, and Farrer has put in a depiction of the tufty whole of the plant (constituted by many more than five stems) in miniature in the middle distance of the picture.

Figure 8.3, *Incarvillea grandiflora*, records information about the steepness of the slope the flower was found growing on, the overall form of the whole plant, its short stems, floppy crimson petals and the pursed lips of its trumpet. No roots, stamens, anthers, seed pods, however. In fact, looking at the painting, do we get the impression that *Incarvillea grandiflora* looks a little *vainglorious*? That its heavy-looking floppy flowers are too big for their short stems? And in the case of F.883, *Fritillaria* sp. (figure 8.4) do we get the impression of an untidily dressed old man bustling away from us down the slope? Or *Primula viola-grandis* (figure 8.5): do these flowers in Farrer's painting look cross, as they struggle up a slope to the left? Are their eyes frowning? (They each appear to have one). Or have I taken leave of my senses to perform a horrendous 'reading-in' of the kind that has traditionally plagued art history and art criticism (and still does, not least in the cases of Minimal and Conceptual art)?

In the case of *Primula viola-grandis* Farrer had this to say:

> Now, all along the Himalayan borders, and up the very far-off southern Marches of Tibet, there lives a strange race of Primulas that are hardly Primulas at all [...] They are like nothing else we know [...] Before the leaves unfold to their full development spring up the sturdy fleshy stems, each one of which unfurls one solitary huge flower of rich purple, with a prognathous profile and a throat of quite ridiculous length. The group is a small one, and no member of it occurs farther north than Yunnan. Accordingly, it was with a jump of joy, as for something quite unhoped for, that I now saw an obviously new species of this paradoxical cousinhood flaring violet at my feet amid the grass — a grotesque rare glory, with the upper "petals" lying flat back on the tube like an angry cat's ears, while its lower ones stood straight forward like an angry child's pout.[8] (OEW I, p. 223)

He goes on to describe this plant's relative inaccessibility, writing that the flowers: 'seemed to mock me with the golden twinkle of their central pointil of stamens, which adds so much expression to that already elfish countenance.' The 'countenance', he explains, first opens small and flat, 'then swells and expands and retorts and protrudes until it has developed the full pouting eccentricity of its clear purple maturity.' So Farrer paints the plant seen and conceived of in accordance with his Buddhist-influenced, Japanese-influenced comprehension of it as a little personality, a characterful being, that we discussed in Chapter 4 with respect to his writing about garden plants. Kingdon Ward wrote that in Farrer's writings, the plants 'seem to rise up and live'. To this we can add that in his paintings too, they seem to come alive, emerging three-dimensionally from the paper. Another plant I mentioned above, *Incarvillea grandiflora,* 'sprawled' on a hot bank, 'so floppy and flimsy in the overdone magnificence of its enormous flowers' (RB p. 99, figure 8.3). And yet, if we compare his painting of the Primula with the photograph of it included on its herbarium sheet (Fig 8.6), we can see that he has, in the painting, captured the appearance of the flower. However animated the painting (and the description) it is not fanciful, in the sense of that word as meaning a deviation from fact or truth.

FIG. 8.3. Farrer, *Incarvillea grandiflora* (RBGE).

In comparison with orthodox botanical painting, Farrer's paintings tend to look amateur, rough, dirty, provisional. Like botanical paintings, they seem committed and dedicated. To criticize his paintings as bad botanical art is all very well. But scientific painting might not have been his goal. After all, he didn't collect plants as an exercise in scientific botany: he chose only plants that he thought might make good garden plants. That is why the number of introductions he made is small (c. 1900) compared with the tens of thousands of Forrest, Wilson and Kingdon Ward. Trying to coax his friend E. A. Bowles to persuade the Royal Horticultural Society to subscribe to the China-Tibet expedition, he wrote: 'the quantity may be small, but, oh golly, think of the quality! I'm not out for Wilsonian weeds!'[9] His painting was undertaken in the same not very scientific spirit; to render his impression of a plant, not simply the Linnean essence.

His defence of *The English Rock Garden*, his greatest work about garden plants, rests on this impressionist philosophy. In its Introduction, he wrote:

> It has been my endeavour, all through the book indeed, to preserve the vivid and personal note, at any cost to the arid grey gravity usually considered necessary to the dignity of a dictionary; not only so the work may perhaps be found more readable and pleasant, but also that other gardeners, finding their best-beloveds, maybe, here slighted or condemned, may be able to mitigate their wrath by constant contemplation of the fact that opinions are but the *obiter dicta* of a warm-blooded fellow-mortal, not the weighed everlasting pronouncements of some pompous and Olympian lexicographer, veiled in an awful impersonality that admits of no appeal.[10]

Farrer becomes the anti-Johnson. To be human is to have opinions and to make mistakes; but to be personal means being open to appeal, and therefore revision of views. In other words, it is important to admit of doubt.

Without being in any way pompous, conventional botanical painting aims to be the last word, as it were, at least for a long time, about the plants depicted. In other words it aims at a definitive way of depicting the plant. In contrast to this, Farrer's impressionism, which we have already noted in relation to *The Garden of Asia, The House of Shadows,* and *In Old Ceylon,* is also to the fore in his painting. He is being consistent. Thus in the case of *Trollius pumilus perfectissimi* he studied the flower intently: this painting of it is not a first impression. But he didn't study the well and the painted rock with the same close attention. He noticed that the painted image had some Tibetan or Chinese characters around it, but he didn't bother to record them, and he just gives an idea of them here. He conjures up rather than documents the water and the stones it flows around. The whole painting is therefore about how the place, and its botanical find, seemed to him.

Farrer's paintings were made to depict the actual habit of growth of actual plants growing in real places — their colours, forms and shape; and made as a memento of his first encounter with them, because the real plants were reduced to herbarium specimens, in which a dried example of the plant is fixed to a sheet of paper, accompanied by terse verbal notes and often by a photograph; or packed in boxes for transport, or next encountered having set seed after flowering, or recorded only

FIG. 8.4. Farrer, *Fritillaria* sp. (RBGE).

Fig. 8.5. Farrer, *Primula viola-grandis* (RBGE).

in monochrome photographs. But the paintings were also made, presumably, to persuade others about the potential value of the plants.

Conventional botanical painting has some of the properties of the diagram (sometimes an actual diagram forms part of the data within the frame). While diagrams involve spatial distortions, some things cannot be distorted, including 1) the proportions of the plant — the relative size or length of its parts in relation to other parts — need to be respected and 2) hue and value of colour need to be entirely accurate, which is one reason why botanical painting survives in an era of colour photography. A botanical painting is an *isomorph* of the depicted plant. Farrer's paintings can't be taken as reliably diagrammatic. Because his mode of painting is rough, approximate, imperfect, and sometimes incomplete, it lets the viewer have a way in to contemplate his process. We can see, and think about, how he set out to depict a flower. A reciprocity begins to form between painted and real flowers. The touches of paint are impressionistic; but they get us to look carefully at the blooms in the world next time, and to do so with a view informed by the painter's looking: careful, attentive, and with the question of the match, or otherwise, with a painting, whether that painting be hypothetical or real, in mind. For a perception under the influence of botanical or flower-painting, real flowers can begin to seem painted, just as painted ones strive to look natural: strive for verisimilitude or lifelikeness. Painting rhododendrons and primulas in Burma in the summer of 1920 was no doubt for Farrer a consolation in rain and solitude.

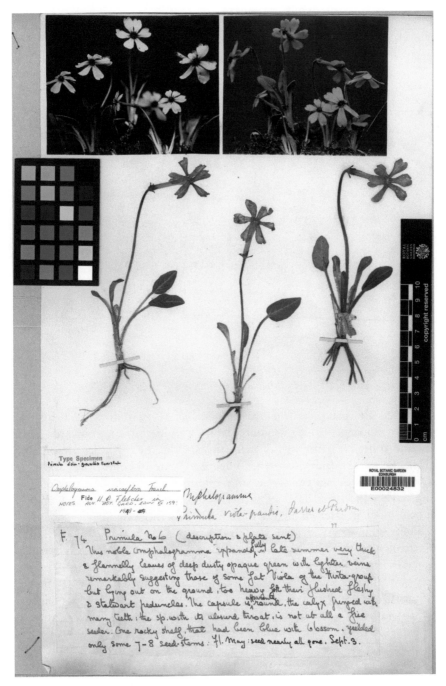

FIG. 8.6. Herbarium sheet for *Primula viola-grandis*, now known as *Omphalogramma vinciiflora*, William Purdom's photographs. (RBGE).

FIG. 8.7. Farrer, *Primula valentiniana* in Burma (RBGE).

Figure 8.7 sets the primulas (*Primula valentiniana*, F. 1723) in a landscape context recognizably modern in both its abbreviation and its tendency towards geometry. At the same time the painting is bizarre in its scale: the primulas are giants there. The paintings of rhododendrons become more careful, more 'botanical' (figure 8.8). The paintings depict twigs and single stems in the orthodox way of botanical painting, rather than the habit of growth of the whole plant, which in any case would be a much greater challenge in the case of a rhododendron.

No doubt such an effect of reciprocity between the real and the painted fades. Yet it is stronger with Farrer's paintings precisely because the question that might be stimulated by a real flower, 'how to paint this?' is answered in botanical painting by the very conventions imposed. Farrer, in contrast, produces a new attempt almost every time. Questions become, how do the plant's forms seem? How does the plant occupy a volume of space and air? One might go so far as to say that it is what cannot be painted — the air around a plant and between its stems — that becomes one of the prime subjects of his painting.

One of the weaknesses of Farrer's painting happens when the parts of his composition appear to detach themselves from each other. Farrer was aware of his limitations as a painter. He wrote to Ernest Gye from Burma:

> Even in landscape I have been assiduous: but for the fact that I can neither draw nor colour. [...] If I am stirred by an atmosphere or a mood, of mist or mountain, I can generally say *something,* though it is never [...] what I want: whereas, if I

FIG. 8.8. Farrer, rhododendron in Burma (RBGE).

ever sit down to paint a mere record of facts, dullness of the most dreadful is
the only result.[11]

His landscape painting is as uneven as his painting of flowers. He painted the
Burmese village that he later happened to be buried near (figure 3.6), and while
the painting is therefore of exceptional biographical and emotional interest, we
can see that it lacks conviction and polish. Its coherence is weak, in the sense that
the parts that constitute it seem separate from each other. The strong saturation of
the colours appears to overbalance the effect. The major influence on Farrer for
painting a mountainside as a continuous variable (though sometimes opaque) wash
was the work of C. J. Holmes (see figure 3.1). Figure 3.6 is, however, to borrow
Farrer's own description of an earlier painting, 'a long way after' him. The parts
have trouble cohering, which might not matter so much in a rough notation from
the field, but the painting aspires to be rather more than that.

In Farrer's worst efforts, he has assembled all the elements of the syntagmatic
chain, the objects, but can't make them work together. But not all his paintings are
about his struggle with his materials. His best paintings go beyond the successful
dramatization and integration of their array of objects and become successful
vehicles for the viewer's imaginative projection. Figure 8.9 shows a landscape on the
Chinese-Tibetan borderland. I believe that this might be the painting listed as: '21.
"Tibetanischer Matterhorn" (in the Swiss tongue). A long way after C. J. Holmes',
in the catalogue of his Fine Arts Society exhibition of 1917. It shows a village
and a mountain as if encountered in a dream: conjured up as an entire visionary
experience; the viewer travelling over a plain so parched it seems that little of the
rain-shower above it will reach the ground. Farrer has brushed in the falling rain
as a series of brown streaks, made with a brush carrying a small amount of dilute
brown hue, and enhanced by some scraping-out and sponging-away.

There is a formal balance to the painting. The tree growing between the two
short towers is directly aligned with the mountain-top, and this balance extends
to the guard-tower on the right and the tree on the left, balancing each other but
not symmetrically arranged. This form becomes three-dimensional as the left-
hand tree is related to the two distant trees on the left; thus with the guard-tower
they triangulate the middle ground. The horizontal triangle thus formed complements the vertical eroded or irregular pyramid of the main mountain, while the
oblongs of the man-made structures contrast with, without trying to conquer, the
mountains' natural forms. In particular, the mountains' contrast with the asym-
metrically arrayed main building is satisfying without being tactlessly obvious. The
constrained palette of browns and greys, leading to the grey-blue mountain and
trees, contributes its harmony of tones too. The tones have been arranged to throw
a halo around the main peak, imbuing a romance not just to it, but throughout the
painting as a whole.

The foreground, occupied by a trackway leading the viewer into the scene and
towards the settlement and mountain, provides a crucial psychological invitation
into a space of doubt, forbidding perhaps, yet exciting and not entirely devoid of a
potential for hospitality: yet it is ambiguity that rules, rather than direct promise.

FIG. 8.9. Farrer, landscape of the Tibet-China borderland (Private Collection).

Farrer's use of mist for spatial recession, and fainter horizon-lines behind the main subject, are entirely successful both in projecting space and augmenting the sense of mystery and potential. At the same time his handling of light and shadow works to integrate the whole, drawing the scene together with complete conviction. The dark grey clouds floating transparently over the mountain slopes in the centre-right have been evoked by him with great subtlety. The strongly three-dimensional feeling of the main mountain is suggested less by line and colour than by variation of tone: that is, the application of areas of wash and their modulation; a traditional technique.[12]

The tree growing in the citadel is in the centre of the horizontal reach of the painting; the areas of greatest psychological interest (entry to the depicted space on the foreground track, citadel, and mountain top) are aligned down the centre, but the composition is asymmetrical enough, and simple enough, parts subordinated to the overall effect, for this device not to be obtrusive or ugly.

Another landscape, this one from Burma, makes a surprising use of the tone of the paper in the large middle section of the painting, showing brightly through a very pale or tremendously faint brown wash depicting mist (figure 8.10). The foreground trees, shredded or reduced to stumps, suggest a nearby settlement. Here as in the distant mountain-tops Farrer employs abbreviated, approximative touches. There is a clear compositional line (a doubled line) from the tops of the two stumps on the extreme left, through the two shredded trees in the centre to the shoulders of the mountain on either side of the peak. This is crossed by a secondary compositional line involving the tops of the three tallest trees and the subsidiary peak in the upper left. The boldness of the central blankness is readily apparent, and shows the artist being influenced by Chinese landscape painting. He wrote about painting in

Fig. 8.10. Farrer, Burmese landscape (RBGE).

FIG. 8.11. Farrer, *Lloydia alpina* (RHS Library).

Burma to Gye: 'This country helps me, by giving wonderful colour, and also by trailing rolls of white cloud about in the depths, which entitles me to make full use of Chinese and Japanese convention.'[13] A passing indication of his familiarity with Japanese art comes from his 1917 catalogue, where no. 69, his painting of *Lloydia alpina,* is captioned: '"A Fairy's Child." After Kano Tsunenobu' (figure 8.11).[14]

Notes to Chapter 8

1. RBGE RJF 1/1/13.
2. Kingdon Ward, 'Reginald Farrer', *Geographical Journal,* 57,1 (Jan 1921), pp. 69–70.
3. Letter from RF to Balfour, 7/2/17, RBGE RJF 1/1/52.
4. RBGE RJF 4/1/13, Farrer's last letter to Gye, 11/9/1920.
5. The *Trollius farreri* described by Otto Stapf in 1928.
6. *The Rainbow Bridge* (London: Arnold, 1921; 3rd edition 1926), p. 218.
7. The films formed part of the exhibition, *Flora of Nepal,* John Hope Gateway, Royal Botanic Garden Edinburgh, 6/8/2016 until 6/11/2016.
8. This plant is now known as *Omphalogramma vinciflora.*
9. Letter to Bowles, 15/12/1913, RHS Lindley Library, EAB 2/3/5, folder 2.
10. Farrer, *The English Rock Garden,* 2 vols. (London: T. C. and E. C. Jack Ltd., 1919), vol. I, p. xxvi.
11. Letter to Gye 6/5/1920, RBGE RJF 4/1/1–13.
12. See Charlesworth, *Landscape and Vision in Nineteenth Century Britain and France,* p. 134, discussing the work of William Hodges (1744–1797).
13. Letter to Gye 6/5/1920.
14. In the letter to Celia Noble (8th January 1919) already cited in Chapter 3, Farrer reveals that he owned a work by Kano Tsunenobu.

CHAPTER 9

A Buddhist Visits the Trenches

After the end of the expedition with Purdom, Farrer sailed back into Britain in May, 1916, via an overland journey from Peking to Petrograd (St. Petersburg) and then through Scandinavia to the Norwegian port of Bergen. He walked back into a nation engaged in The Great War. Eager to do his bit, like his friends Alfred Gathorne-Hardy (who was already dead), Raymond Asquith and Aubrey Herbert, by June he had obtained employment in the Foreign Office. We know next to nothing about his activities in the second half of 1916, with the exception of his lecture to the Royal Geographical Society about his first year in China and Tibet. By 1917, however, as an experienced novelist and skilled travel writer, he was involved with the government's Department of Information.

The Department of Information, formed in February 1917 and subsuming a previous entity, Wellington House, meant propaganda. The novelist and journalist John Buchan was in charge. The Department became a Ministry under Lord Beaverbrook in February 1918. Before this happened, Buchan commissioned Farrer to write a book about the Great War. Buchan presumably knew that the large published output of his department's sponsoring could not be on one note: different works had to find and persuade different sorts of people. Farrer's book, with its seemingly pacifist or anti-war title, *The Void of War: Letters from Three Fronts*, would intrigue people who were disaffected or disillusioned. The tactic employed by the book would be to persuade readers into condemning the Germans and Austrians and thus endorsing the war. The fact that the book was published in both Britain and the U.S.A. suggests that its prime target audience was American: that its purpose was to keep Americans behind the war effort.[1]

It is important, in coming to grips with Farrer's *Void*, to understand the situation in Britain with regard to propaganda in 1917. Some of the following evidence will corroborate my statements in Chapter 3 about the unpleasant divided atmosphere of the years 1917–1918 that were drawn from work by D. H. Lawrence and Richard Aldington. Sue Malvern's summary of the situation is very useful. Against a background of unrest among the troops themselves, 'More covert and ultimately more repressive than ham-fisted and generally unsuccessful attempts to whitewash the horrors of war was a wide-spread, officially sponsored and escalating campaign [...] to counteract pacifism.'[2] Among other incidents, A. R. Orage's journal *The New Age* was banned from export, as it was 'said to "have a Socialist hatred of Capitalists".'[3] Buchan's Department lacked the resources for increased work on the home front, so the National War Aims Committee was formed in August 1917 'to counter-act war weariness and defeat pacifism.' It identified 'socialism with anti-patriotic interests'.[4] A stated intention was to 'encourage unity and stifle party and class distinctions.'[5] To push these aims to their logical conclusions for a moment in order to gauge what kind of nation they promoted: if successful, they would make it impossible to be a pacifist; impossible to be a socialist and yet love one's nation; impossible to be anti-capitalist, as if the war was a war for capitalism; and they would enact a stifling imposition of 'unity' over difference in thinking, even difference in thinking that simply reflected the truths of class distinctions and party politics. Thus untruth became a goal. In pursuit of these surely profoundly un-British aims, '38,000 "dossiers" on people suspected of hostile acts' were assembled,[6] while '5,246 persons suspected of pacifism, anti-militarism etc.' were investigated between June 1916 and October 1917 alone.[7] Under these circumstances, it is small wonder that D. H. Lawrence wrote: 'the industrialism and commercialism of England, with which patriotism and democracy became identified: did not these insult a man and hit him pleasantly across the mouth?'[8] These were some of the pressures of the historical moment during which Farrer's *Void* was written.

After his intestinal operation in August 1917, Farrer was sent round the British, French and Italian Fronts in the second half of September and the whole of October, and he wrote the book at Ingleborough Hall from November 1917 to late January 1918, where, as we have seen, he also spent his time gardening. The resulting book puts the reader with some suddenness into the middle of things. One peculiarity is the lack of framing devices that would relate the book to a larger situation or to the circumstances under which it came to be made. The dedication, to Buchan, tells us that we shall be reading letters, and the text is divided into 17 larger sections, each termed a 'Letter'. The only other framing device consists of a three-line epigraph. As this is simply a general evocation of war, and comes from Farrer's own verse drama, *The Dowager of Jerusalem*, it tells us nothing. The first Letter is entitled: 'First Impressions: Kemmel'. The book thus begins with the author already in France. A correspondence address is inserted on the upper right, as if in a real letter, and the Letter itself is divided into 7 short sections, each with its own title, and averaging perhaps a page long: '1. Difficulties. 2. The Gas-Mask. 3. Rural Tranquillity. 4. Enter Soldiers. 5. From a Hilltop. 6. Hills and the War. 7. Death's Hunting Park.' The sections are all narrated in the first person, and no name of the writer is given, so the assumption is that they are written by Farrer himself and constitute urgent reports from just behind the lines.

One of the reasons that I put the matter like this is that an earlier draft of the text was not so straightforward in apparent approach. Buchan wrote to Farrer in December 1917 about a draft of the first four Letters of the book: 'The description of the Somme battlefield is the best thing that has been done on that battlefield by a long way [...] whenever you describe you are first class.' However, criticism follows:

> Henry James has affected maleficently your light-footed style. For example, in
> your over-done impersonality of narration, the use of 'one' instead of 'you' or

'I'; and by the over-use of 'quite' as a kind of extra adverb tacked on to two others [...] do use a better name than John Trevanion, which sounds like one of those ghastly heroes of bad modern novels who are always defying destiny from some cliff in Cornwall.[9]

Buchan then encourages: 'I congratulate you warmly on them. They are real literature, and will do much to make people realise the bigness of the whole show.'

This letter gives us plenty to consider. Farrer's 'Letters' were not, evidently, composed in the 'Château de Noère, Somewhere in France' which is their 'address' given in the published book. In retrospect, the word 'Noère' is probably Farrer's ghastly pun, conveying the English word 'nowhere'. The whole effort becomes very much more literary and less of an urgent report from the Front. To do him credit, Farrer accepted Buchan's objections. The final text shows that he has done away with 'quite', pruned back his adverbs, and made his text more direct by using the first and second person pronouns rather than the awkward 'absent' person, 'one'.[10] He also made the book more subjective and personal, warming and breaking-up his initial 'over-done impersonality of narration.'

Buchan's letter also reveals that Farrer's initial strategy in the book had been to mask his own identity with that of John Trevannion, the character borrowed from his last published novel, *Through the Ivory Gate*. This move suggests rather strongly that Trevannion in the novel exhibited characteristics of Farrer himself. That is to say, it allows us to contemplate the idea that Trevannion in the novel, as was the intention no doubt in *Void*, could be largely identified with Farrer, rather in the way that Parson Yorick figures as an *alter ego* of Laurence Sterne in *A Sentimental Journey through France and Italy by Mr. Yorick*, having been a character in Sterne's *Tristram Shandy*. This possibility is biographically interesting, given the character Trevannion's difficulties with women, warm feelings for men, and despair; but in *Void* Farrer simply excised Trevannion altogether, rather than changing his name as Buchan recommended. The removal leads to greater directness of expression, the kind of directness characteristic of Farrer's travel writing and garden books, as opposed to the greater and rather baffling impersonality of his novels' narrators. It also removes an unnecessarily cumbersome intermediary level.

In fact it is a remarkable, a very bold move, that Farrer based the form of his book of war propaganda on a peaceful work by a fellow Yorkshireman: Laurence Sterne's *A Sentimental Journey* (1768). Both works begin abruptly: Sterne puts us in the middle of a conversation, and reaches France in the middle of his first paragraph, while Farrer writes that it is 'very difficult to begin,' but is (within the assumed time of the book) already in France as he writes that. Both works are built up from short sections of narrative, anything from half a page to half a dozen pages, as the incidents of travel or sights of the journey demand, and each section has a heading or title. Sometimes Sterne's headings indicate where his characters are: ('The Remise Door, Calais') and sometimes a thought he has: ('The Rose, Paris'). Farrer's follow the pattern laid down by Sterne: 'Difficulties', 'Rural Tranquillity' and 'Death's Hunting Park' are redolent of internal mental judgements, while the later 'Arras' or 'Delvile [sic] Wood' simply designate place, albeit places of traumatic events. The first seven of Sterne's headings (to compare with Farrer's) are: Calais; The Monk Calais; The Monk Calais; The Monk Calais; the Desobligeant Calais; Preface in the Desobligeant; and simply 'Calais' again. Every page of both books describes mental judgements; but Farrer introduces few other characters, and spends much more time describing the strange terrain that he traverses.

Farrer may well have been reminded of the potential usefulness to him of the example of Sterne's literary form by the imminent 150th anniversary of Sterne's death in 1768; he had just commemorated the centenary of Jane Austen's death by writing his article about her novels. Sterne's *Sentimental Journey* is also a classic contribution to the literary genre of travel-writing (that is, travel-writing as a *literary* genre) which the eighteenth century had created as a literary form, and to which Farrer made such celebrated contributions. Sterne's book is also, perhaps primarily, a defining contribution to the eighteenth century cult of sentiment, that we associate also with Jean-Jacques Rousseau (especially his *Julie: ou, la nouvelle Heloïse*) and Henry Mackenzie's *The Man of Feeling*. Sentiment or feeling was natural to Sterne's Mr. Yorick, in *A Sentimental Journey*, who meditates on it frequently and easily. Farrer's book, too, can be thought of as an unusual form of travel book, a wandering without set purpose, and has feeling at its heart. Seeing the battlefields and reporting how they make him feel seems the entire point. The text states no other aim. Coming late to the cult of sentiment, however, and having learned (from Swinburne, for example) to distrust it, Farrer is worried about whether he feels genuine emotion. In a section titled 'Emotional Staggers' he writes at the end of one Letter:

> I do not think I shall go on. The emotion of the thing takes hold of me so: and I do not yet quite know where emotion leaves off and emotionalism begins. But I hope in time I may grow strong enough to laugh at our characteristic dread of emotion. All *that* was the armour of weakness [...] Anyhow, do not expect me to tell you this tale of mine without emotion. But I want to be sure that what I am giving you is the real thing, not worked-up slop. So, as I am tired and dazed by now as not to be quite certain of myself or my balance any longer, I shall leave off here.[11]

Farrer returns to the subject just two pages later. He obviously feels his belatedness, having to engage with an area of life so distrusted by his lifetime as to have become unfamiliar. Swinburne had warned against false sentimentality in his novel *Love's Cross-Currents* (1905). A character exclaims against: 'this dolorous kind of verbal virtue and compromised sentiment — this tender tension of the moral machine, worse for the nerves than the headiest draughts of raw sensation!'[12] Farrer wanted to avoid 'worked-up slop' while having to deal with the irony to which Swinburne, Samuel Butler and others had subjected Victorian sentiment. His defence against irony is sincerity; the straightforward subjective address, and self-revelation, of the passage.

Mr. Yorick's main sentimental encounters are with women. Farrer's are not; they are with his own people, the Chinese labourers he unexpectedly finds looking after British tanks, who seem 'all old friends really', and who provoke in him a very honest emotion:

> Abruptly, violently, I was back upon the northern plains of China, jogging
> along from dawn to dusk over the loess lands of Shensi or Kansu, and through
> grey little walled cities filled with just such twinkling, ruddy faces as these. [...]
> I did so fiercely want to be once more out of all this, and away into the peace
> of Asia. (p. 11)

Or they are with the spectacle of a naked Tommy washing himself 'under a spout
of water':

> And the beauty of that tiny frail fair thing, vividly white in the sunshine
> upon that enormous background of emptiness and dun-coloured monotony of
> moorland was something so enormous in itself, that it went straight through me
> like a violent lance of pain. [...] to have made the earth such a place of horror,
> and itself, incidentally, in the making, a thing so infinitely great. Certainly, a
> lone man, bare as he was born, on a lone landscape bare as it was made, stands
> out at once as the climax of creation, the most beautiful thing in the world,
> the most wonderful, the most terrible. [...] his contrast of utter feebleness
> and immeasurable power, and all the boundless wonder of his endurances
> and heroisms, bounded physically in that strange, small engine of lusts. [...] I
> was really seized and shaken by the beauty of the mere mortal body, and the
> abominable wickedness of spoiling it. (pp. 99–100)

This section is entitled, 'Gloria Mundi'. There is also a sentimental encounter
with a Canadian private who strolls up out of desolation near Vimy Ridge,
whose garrulousness masks sheer fright at being in trenches for the first time, and
embodies his simple need for someone to talk to. Farrer at first is standoff-ish, but
then through the babble hears: 'the silence inside, and the deadly cold.' 'Yet what
can one do?' he asks. 'Uttermost loneliness is the place where we all live' (pp.
161–62, 'The Void of Fear').

As Farrer wanders over the former battlefields, approaching and retreating from
the front line itself, he meditates on objects in what seems a fairly random way. Some
of his meditations seem conventional, or at least precedented. At Arras he writes
of the 'massacre' and 'murder' of houses as a 'blasphemy' (p.22); this calls to mind
Ford Madox Ford's poem, 'The Houses of Flanders', subtly anthropomorphizing
the houses, and published in BLAST 2 in 1915. As Bruce Bairnsfather and others had
before him, Farrer emphasizes the unknowableness of the altered geography, and
finds that map-reading on these battlefields can't save you from getting lost (pp. 91,
81. See figure 9.1).[13] Trenches in chalk confuse Farrer particularly:

> their blind labyrinths are so baffling that one gets dazed and stunned and stupid
> [...] You cannot see out or over, of course: you lose all sense of direction —
> especially as no trench ever goes straight for more than a few yards. They zigzag
> through the ground [...] so as to minimize the damage of concussion, in case
> of a shell-burst. All intelligence and observation go to pieces in their viewless
> mazes; and all emotion too. You become merely a mechanism. (p. 122)

Farrer's burst into blank verse in the penultimate sentence above, 'All intelligence
and observation | go to pieces in their viewless mazes;' surely contains a distant
echo of Childe Harold in Rome, in Byron's *Childe Harold's Pilgrimage*.[14]

Meditating on camouflage, 'a perfect futurist masterpiece' (p. 67), Farrer becomes

FIG. 9.1. Bruce Bairnsfather, 'Modern Topography' from *The Bystander*, 1917.

a true prophet, concluding that: 'the only logical outcome will be to have no camouflage at all' (p. 68) since what is at issue is deception rather than concealment. The *doyenne* of British photo interpreters from the Second World War, Constance Babington-Smith, found that:

> In 1943, the Germans had made a habit of plastering camouflage paint over their dispersal factories, which was a great help to us, because we could then see at a glance which plants were being used for war production. But the [Albert] Speer regime evidently realized that when you convert buildings from other uses the most effective camouflage is no camouflage at all.[15]

There are plenty of moments in *Void* which remind us of Farrer's later judgement of his book as being full of 'balls and bunkum of its hyperbole'. The narrator sees: 'a new England [...] a whole huge people, methodically at work on a job it hates [...] a gallant grimness [...] indescribably reassuring and exalting'. (p. 29) There is a 'tremendous exaltation' that 'underlies' the soldiers' 'weariness and grumbling' about their horrible task (p. 39) and this point leads to a passage in which sentiment verges on occult registration:

> feeling is a far surer guide than knowledge. [An army of 2 million] energizing in unresting storm and stress, is bound to diffuse its emotions in waves incomparably vaster [than the audience in a theatre]; the sensitized plate of one's mind receives those waves with an almost agonizing vividness of impression. [...] I feel it so, I feel it vibrating in every fibre of me day and night. (pp. 39–40)

What are at issue here are psychic reverberations similar to Besant and Leadbeater's 'thought-forms', or to those Farrer detected at Vessagiriya in Sri Lanka, except now emanating not from the dead but the living; a psychic force that 'has a powerfully stimulating effect upon the psychic centres and stirs up the subconscious forces' according to one expert.[16] Or registers, in this case, on the photographic plate of Farrer's mind.

The Chinese labourers encountered by Farrer lead to thoughts of China as a nation, and the idea that China and Britain are the 'two anti-militarist empires' (p. 33): a conclusion that would have surprised the Ashanti, the Zulus, the Tibetans, the Boers, Burmese, Afghanis, and any of the other peoples attacked by Britain or China over the previous few decades! As an employee of the Foreign Office seconded to the Department of Information, to fulfil one of his official propaganda functions of combatting pacifism, while personally trying to avoid slipping into militarism, Farrer employs the sublime tactic of arguing that the ordinary British soldiers are true pacifists and non-pacifists at the same time:

> I find, in fact, in the achievements and existence of the New Army, not the triumph of militarism in England, but the hardest blow that militarism has ever had. Indeed, the triumph of real pacifism. For this army is an *ad hoc* army, doggedly and dourly devoted to the odiousness of war, for the sole sake of peace. [...] Unredeemed horror is the whole thing, a horror that breaks up the soul of man into a gibbering wreckage. Black and crimson, the knowledge has been written deep into the inmost heart of the New Army. And that is why the New Army is really pacifist in the genuine sense of the word; that is why it will never be the dupe of either 'pacifist' or junkers back at home, wailing

for a premature or inconclusive peace, to save their caste or their pocket. (pp. 36, 37–38)

So far, so implausible; and given that Farrer's father had resigned as president of Skipton Liberal Association over the issue of British refusal to make peace with Germany in 1916, so pointed.[17] And a ration of 'balls and bunkum' of hyperbole to follow: 'I tell you, it is something quite staggering and amazing, the sense of determination out here, that carries one up in a sort of cyclone of enthusiasm, entirely unguessed in England' (p. 38). Although he tries to deal with pacifism, Farrer never directly attacks Socialism, but he probably intends an attack on it when, on the French front, he objects to the word *égalité* in the motto of the French Republic: 'you can never have *égalité* unless you are all sovereigns or all slaves' (p. 208). He seems to have economic equality in mind, whereas the use of the word in the Republican motto more importantly intended equality under the law: a fundamental function of a self-respecting modern nation and conspicuously absent under the French *ancien régime*.

In his book that includes topographical descriptions of the ruin and wreckage of the battlefields, Farrer achieves something different, in verbal art, from Paul Nash's landscape paintings, exhibited in May 1918 under the title *Void of War*. In the section of his book entitled 'The Void of War' (in the middle of Letter XI), Farrer explains that the title means: 'these places completely battered and smashed and apparently quite lifeless and abandoned: yet really with military life buzzing in them indefatigably' (p. 148). This new topography is what Nash, too, had represented so well. Yet for Nash the void was total, and his paintings amount to condemnations of the war and the world that the war seemed to be creating. Farrer no doubt senses this new cosmic order of destruction that was being fashioned by the war; but his propaganda purpose leads him in a different direction, and ultimately his book differs markedly from Nash's wholesale condemnation of the war. To structure his topographical descriptions, Farrer has recourse to describing views from high places as a form of orientation. The view from Kemmel comes at the beginning, there is a cluster of such views in the middle, and more on the Italian front at end.[18] It is during his view of the battlefield described in 'The Void of War' section that the rot begins for Farrer, ultimately far more serious for him than anything to do with British propaganda aims. 'The Void of War' section comes towards the architectonic centre of the book (pp. 148–49 in a book of 303 pp.). Farrer is watching shellfire:

> Overhead go wailing our own shells, and in a little while a cloud of white or dingy smoke breaks up in Lens, now in one point, now in another. [...] And all the time the Boches were plugging big stuff into the ruins at the foot of the hill, hunting for the batteries. Thud and thud and thud into Vimy and Little Vimy they kept coming, and huge tawny mountains of smoke burst up.

The spectacle stirs feelings in him. 'Our' shellfire goes over: 'and you suddenly feel a real ill-will of your own going with it. [...] our own fire began to liven up: and I rejoiced in the endearing scream of the shells passing overhead.' This might not seem like much, but it is the thin end of a wedge. In fact an abyss is opening under Farrer that threatens all his futures. For he is a Buddhist visiting the trenches; and until this moment he has managed to avoid overt signals of satisfaction about the possibility of killing the enemy.

To explore what happens from this point, I want to start with a panoramic view from one of the Italian mountains that comes late in the book. On Monte Santo, known to Farrer from his plant-collecting forays before the War, but now blasted by war, easy to defend and impossible to attack, he writes of the view: 'there is nothing more in front of you whatever except, so to speak, all the kingdoms of the earth and the sea, unfolded beneath as if they were on a chart.' (p. 254) 'Kingdoms of the earth' is an interesting phrase for Farrer to have used. It might seem to suggest the Temptation of Christ in the books of Matthew and Luke in the New Testament of the Christian Bible; but the situation of temptation does not fit, and the phrase employed there in the Authorized Version is 'the kingdoms of the world.' The book of *Genesis* comes equally close (and equally misses) when God says to Abraham, 'in thy seed shall all the nations of the earth be blessed.' (22, v. 18). If Farrer intends an allusion to this, it is an ironic one, given that at his time of writing the nations were trying to slaughter each other. Nor is Farrer's phrase to be found in another obvious possible source, the poetry of John Milton, though *Paradise Lost* comes closest when the Archangel Gabriel takes Adam to a high place 'to show him all earth's kingdoms and their glory' (XI, l. 384). *Paradise Regained* employs three uses of 'the kingdoms of the world' within 47 lines.[19]

In fact the source of Farrer's phrase is in Christopher Marlowe's play, *Dr. Faustus* (1616 version). At the beginning of Act 3, the Chorus tells us that Faustus has departed for a ride on a dragon's back: 'He now is gone to prove cosmography, | That measures coasts and kingdoms of the earth, | And, as I guess, will first arrive at Rome'.[20] So Farrer is equating himself with Faustus after the latter's hellish agreement with the devil via Mephistopheles. Here is a clear intimation that all is not at peace in Farrer's mind about his relationship with the Department via Buchan. To push the implication to its furthest point: he feels he has made a Faustian bargain, and sold his soul for knowledge and (through the book) influence. A Buddhist visiting the trenches, he had entered a world that tested his belief. Finding graves in Delvile Wood, he meditates on 'The Undying Dead':

> I cannot see these graves as genuinely holding anything. [...] Where is the use of sentimentalizing falsely over graves and their inmates? There is nothing sanctifying, in itself, in the mere fact of having become defunct. No doubt a number of these dead would have been extremely tiresome people in life [...] Then what is so wonderful about John Jones dead that there was not about John Jones living? And why does he grip hold of me, in a quiet place like this, with such a sense of wonder and awe and envy? For it is no mere physical tragedy that his grave makes me think of; mark that. That side of things is mysteriously transcended by something remote and calm and grand, away behind all this. (pp. 76–77)

It is noticeable that what might be termed the normative approach to this problem at the time — to suggest that good lives have been consummated, or indifferent lives redeemed, by willing sacrifice to nation, or king and country — is here completely avoided: indeed, rejected. Farrer's attitude does not contradict the attitudes to death in northern Buddhist regions, as summarized by Rob Linrothe, the art historian of Tibet and Nepal:

> An embedded sense of cyclical time and recurring incarnation engenders an understanding that persons are not just "then". The beings whose forms are traced in photographs may in one sense be no more, but within a few years are believed to be back in the "now" in another form.[21]

To return to Farrer: at the notorious Butte de Warlencourt in the Somme battlefield, he discovered first 'a piece of pelvis', then a German corpse:

> there is a sodden twistage of grey mess which is trousers, and a loose little scatter of browned old bones, and a skull with tiny ants swarming across its dome. And among these, two enormous black Wellington boots: in their depths there is still a wet breccia of socks and feet. That is all that is left. (p. 85)

The skull is 'absurd', because so 'neat and so round and so small': 'There is a certain grimness in the thought that a thing like that, or hardly bigger, once held Bismarck, and all the accumulating evilness of the world. Or, on the other hand, might just as easily have held a Buddha.' (pp. 85–86) While it is not without a distant reminiscence of Hamlet, this moment, as well as Farrer's noting elsewhere of ribs and bits of skull grubbed up by his boots as he walks around, resembles somewhat a contemplation of the human body as something vile and filthy, a standard part of Buddhist meditation designed to break up one's love of one's own body and, through that, desire for other people's bodies.[22] As such it would be the antithesis of the 'Gloria Mundi' section that celebrates the naked private soldier. Such meditations also help to diminish fear of death and horror at bodily dissolution: 'one finds liberation by confronting death and encountering it as an existential reality.'[23] The point is to engender equanimity by immersion in close contemplation of bodily rottenness. Part of the Buddhist canon, the Middle Length Discourses, contain sections about contemplating bones, as in the *Satipatthāna Sutta*, so I think we can assume that Farrer was familiar with such 'charnel-house meditations'. As Tamara Loos has revealed, his acquaintance in Ceylon, the Prince-Priest Jinavaravamsa, had practised just such an austerity, leading an ascetic existence in the company of skulls and a skeleton on a small islet (Chulalanka) just off Sri Lanka in 1904; and Princess Louise had visited him on this little island at the time.[24] Perhaps she had told Farrer about this when they'd met and she recommended Prince Prisdang to him. Similar meditation habits characterized Tibet. Spending two years in China and Tibet might have even given him the opportunity to observe disposals of the body according to local customs there. At any rate, Farrer's encounter with the rotting jumbled remains of a human corpse shows that to an extent his Buddhism can comprehend the war.

The following section is entitled 'The Building of the Bodhisat', and is metaphysical:

> 'I do know now, though, why I had to say that the place seemed full of wings. [...] I can fairly tell you, that when one is up there, lonely among the unimaginable lonelinesses of the Butte, one does somehow cease to be alone, and cease to be one's self. One is swept away into an annihilating unity which

answers the riddle of the war and its millions of apparent dead. For, as you sit there, it is almost literally as if you could hear the drumming of a heart, the pulses of a Buddha booming up towards his birth. (pp. 86–87)

Farrer explains this optimism: 'Even as heat, growing in intensity, is bound at last inevitably to break into visible flame, so a Buddha is the ultimate visible flame of humanity's increasing glow. He is the periodical incarnation of the world's universal upward drive' (p.88). So the war, in this view, intensifying humanity's need and yet offering the chance of humanity getting away from the iron grip of the past, seen so clearly from the vantage-point of the Front's 'Golgotha' (p. 84), accelerates the coming of the next Buddha. In the ensuing section, 'The Birth of the Buddha', Farrer looks forward to the 'Manifestation of Maitreya', the 'Comforter' prophesied to be the next Buddha. The belief that he advances here corresponds to a Buddhist orthodoxy, enshrined, for example, in the revised edition of Colonel Olcott's *The Buddhist Catechism* (1908): 'a Buddha is developed only at long intervals of time, and, seemingly, when the state of humanity absolutely requires such a teacher to show it the forgotten Path to Nirvana.'[25] Referring to Maitreya, Farrer writes in 'The Birth of the Buddha':

> what I realize now, out here, is that our children or our children's children may actually see the Comforter in the flesh. [...] the pace of the world's development has furiously increased [...] needs and hungers, too, in these four years, have intensified to starvation point, and such a demand engenders its own supply [...] and that supply is the Comforter, the Buddha [...] We are making him every moment, at an increasing rate: and the significance of these dead who are not dead is that the things they did and the things they bore and the things they were, and are, are all combining now in the blood-beat of the imminent Comforter. Every grave out here strikes off so many years of delay before his birth. (pp. 88–89)

So Farrer's Buddhism, tested by the Front, survives and is even optimistic. There is a strange effect, or an unusual kind of redemption, in all those deaths.

In such ways Farrer's Buddhism, challenged, nevertheless accommodates the war. Not the least value of *The Void of War* is the way in which it shows a Western Buddhist attempting to live his Buddhism. And starting with the view of the shelling of Lens, something begins to go wrong for him. He loses control over his feelings. The experience of being shelled himself paradoxically induces euphoria: 'For now again my spirits towered and swelled inexplicably into a huge general serenity of exultation with everything and everybody. All was for the best in this most radiant of possible worlds.' (p. 138) We can take this at face value: a description of the absurdity of war, extreme personal danger paradoxically inducing empty-headed euphoria. At the same time, the echo of Voltaire's *Candide*, and specifically of Dr. Pangloss's ridiculous conviction that everything is for the best in this best of all possible worlds, indicates the need to find another interpretive level for Farrer's passage beyond the dysfunctional euphoria — a level that allows, through its extreme irony, for an inner disgust with the predicament he finds himself in, as a flower-loving Buddhist sent to write propaganda about an industrialized war vast in scale. By employing a variant of Pangloss's phrase Farrer creates a heavy irony about the absurdity of his position and, by extension, that of everybody involved in the war. He hates the awfulness of his job and he turns his text, in one sentence, against the purposes of the Department that employs him and the War that causes the situation. The condemnation may be distanced, but it is wholesale.

A visit to Ypres, on the other hand, stimulates other feelings in a section entitled 'Hardening Hate' (p. 172): 'Did I tell you how one gradually develops a personal baresarkness of own's own against the Boche? Well, it grows and grows on me [...] I have come to a real, keen pitch of personal desire to see him being lessoned. Nothing short of it satisfies me.'[26] He confesses to wishing to be: 'taking a hand in the good work' (p. 173) of 'driving the Boche back and back.' What he is admitting to is a wish to try to kill the enemy. In other words, Farrer finds himself succumbing to anger and hate. He confesses to: 'a moral decline — as I suppose some people might call it — in myself', and explains frankly that: 'I found myself quite definitely longing to see the Boche hammered, quite acutely longing to take a part in the hammering myself.' (p. 155)

But what does it matter though, from a Buddhist point of view, having hostile feelings and thoughts, so long as one doesn't convert them into actions that harm other sentient beings? In fact it is easy to think of at least five reasons why such thoughts are to be avoided. Firstly, they are explicitly condemned in Buddhist texts. The Buddha Shakyamuni warns against them in a speech to Rahula. The Dalai Lama of Tibet lists the 'ten unwholesome actions' that are 'committed under the sway of disturbing emotions': four of these are actions of communication (verbal); and three are purely mental, not even communicated to others.[27] Second, there is a risk that having such thoughts will induce us to commit actions based on them. Third, as the Dalai Lama emphasizes, they interfere with the development of 'the Awakening Mind' that pledges itself to compassion for all sentient beings. Fourth, if communicated to others (as Farrer was doing by writing and publishing them) they risk inducing others to perform harmful actions; and fifth, there is a risk that one might die while occupied by such a negative thought or feeling and thus jeopardize future rebirths (this risk is understood quite plainly by Farrer as the *a contrario* fate of Isabel in *The Sundered Streams* makes clear).

Here we can see a very good reason for the obvious unease Farrer later felt about his wartime work, and that he expressed in his letter to Osbert Sitwell. 'Slumgullion' he called it, and said that he knew: 'the claptrap and falsehood for what they were, but finding them the only possible drugs for a delirious disease. You cannot go on doing beastly things without buoying yourself up on beastly thoughts, wicked madnesses to match the madness by which you are driven.'[28] This is all very well as a *post facto* justification, but Lawrence put it differently: 'Men lost their heads, and worse, lost their inward individual integrity.'[29] The point to make here is that, even within the pages of *Void*, Farrer indicates that he understands that he is trying to live a contradiction. Reviewing the book, the *Times Literary Supplement* takes exception to a phrase from this section of the text. A passage of Farrer's is quoted: 'When at last a few rare shells of our own did begin to fly, my whole heart leapt savagely out with them as they went, and I watched with panting eyes for their burst over the blurred hazy levels of Lens.' The reviewer comments: 'This attitude of watching with "panting eyes" is typical of all these letters, and its description takes up too much space. [...] the process of his apprehensions is a trifle fatiguing.'[30] The reviewer decides he likes all the obviously propagandistic parts of the book, such as the idea of the British soldier being essentially pacifist, and dislikes all Farrer's personal writing, summed up for him in the phrase 'panting eyes'. 'Panting eyes' could be defended as a hypallage, in which an attribute or quality of one thing is applied to another; as when a thirsty person receives 'a grateful drink'. So it is part of Farrer's plentiful rhetorical supply. But it can be better defended on other grounds. Perhaps the expression is absurd; and perhaps Farrer meant it to be absurd, because it comes in a passage describing him accumulating bad karma by wanting people (the enemy) to be hurt and killed.

In general, of course, it can be said that various sections of the Buddhist community believe that it is permissible to fight to protect the *dharma* (the teaching or doctrine) against those wishing to destroy it; though whether that would be a legitimate interpretation of the character of the Great War struggle is another matter. Equally, a classic of South Asian poetry that, according to his interview in the *Times of Ceylon*, Farrer might well have read, the *Bhagavad Gita*, provides a lengthy justification for participation in war provided that the subject does not desire the 'fruits' of the conflict.[31] Such a thought might lie behind Farrer's defence of Britain's New Army as not enjoying the task of fighting, but being determined to do it nevertheless (of being essentially pacifist). Nevertheless, on a personal level, 'a moral decline' is the phrase Farrer used; and he senses that it is absurd to have got himself into that position.

Compulsory bellicosity — bullying people into being bellicose — was undoubtedly one of the problems of the time, and Farrer played his part. In the French sector of *The Void of War*, he suddenly turns on the conscientious objectors, exclaiming against:

> the full miserableness of those wretched creatures who have let their own self-righteousness and their own selfish consciences cut them off from all share in carrying the white man's burden. The superhuman egoism of it is what so appals me; that anybody should trouble about keeping the lily-white hands of his own soul, as he thinks, clean, when there is a question of damming back this unspeakable tide of filth in which the Boche is trying to submerge the world. (p. 200)

In a thought that he obviously forgets to apply to himself, Farrer damns conscientious objectors: 'Self-righteousness is its own damnation.' At least he draws the line at some things that were done to the objectors: 'Their noxiousness, of course, does not excuse their persecution' (p. 201). But he then derides people who buy books 'that whimper over the "martyrdom" of some brave hero who either would or would not put his breeches on, or take them off, at the behest of some brutal commanding officer.' All this is not pretty on Farrer's part, condemning those who have, as their dignified memorial in London's Tavistock Square puts it, 'established the right to refuse to kill.' To cap it, Farrer invokes the Buddha himself: '"Hard it is," said the Buddha, "to put up with folly"' (p. 201).

Farrer the Buddhist pours contempt on those who refuse to be conscripted into the war effort and to kill. To quote Lawrence again: 'A man must identify himself with the criminal mob, sink his sense of truth, of justice, and of human honour, and bay like a horrible unclean hound.'[32] A serious consequence from a Buddhist point of view is that Farrer surely performs bad karma by thinking and writing thus. Of the ten unwholesome actions listed by the Dalai Lama, we can see Farrer committing 'divisive talk' and 'harsh speech' (albeit printed and read rather than spoken), and 'harmful intention'. For Farrer to have committed 3 out of 10 all at once is rather unfortunate. Writing of 'the law of karma' and of rebirth, the Dalai Lama says: 'As a result of engaging in these ten unwholesome actions we will be projected into miserable states of existence, for example, as animals'.[33] Farrer's own involvement in the war effort probably reflects his conviction that 'People who deny responsibilities cannot claim amenities'. (p. 202) Nevertheless, acquiring bad karma in such a spectacular way gives extra weight to things Farrer wrote in letters after the war, that we have already read, such as (to Sitwell): 'To keep stark in hate you have to go on making yourself drunk with it [...] Let no-one say I didn't do *my* little best. But *how* greatly I loathed myself, and life, and everything all the time'; and (amidst Burmese rain, to Gye):

> There are few things more conducive to modesty and moral stock-takings of the gloomiest description than to lie kept awake for hours through the black dark by the adamantine roar of the rain on a thatched roof overhead. I conceived the liveliest conviction of my sins.[34]

Perhaps constant prayer while on his journeys through Burma, and seeing the Buddha's relic in the Arakan, restored some merit, through good karma. He had done ugly and injurious things, betraying his beliefs, promoting intolerant bellicosity, condemning pacifism and abusing conscientious objection. Farrer's self-culture suffers a serious setback in the face of pressure from his national culture; that is, an unprecedented warfare, a grave national emergency, and his commitment to repay for his life of privilege by participating in the defeat of the enemies: Germany, the Austro-Hungarian Empire, and the Ottoman Empire. So we see in the individual life some of the damage that war can do.

If Farrer's defence against irony with respect to sentimentality was straightforwardness, a redeeming feature of *Void* consists of such moments when he is on leave, as it were, from propaganda and description. On p. 185 of *Void*, in a 'letter' from the Hotel Ritz in the Place Vendôme, Paris, he writes:

> My brain and nerves have all gone wrong. I cannot sleep, and I cannot do anything slowly enough. Time has somehow swollen, and life rattles inside it. Can you understand what I mean? My brain is always some way ahead of myself. If I allow half an hour to do a thing, or go anywhere, I get the thing done in ten minutes, and then there is vacancy, with my brain drumming on ahead through it, and myself agonizing behind in the effort to catch up. It is a most odd dreadfulness, like racing onward in staggers through a nightmare, unable to stop.

This passage reads like a personal letter from the archives, thus showing the advantages of directness gained by Farrer's response to Buchan's advice, and his use of the epistolary form. There is a simplicity and straightforwardness in the immediacy with which these feelings are described. Feelings induced probably by the experience of being shelled, and by being caught up in hate, consequent guilt, and the other strong emotions released by his task just behind the lines. We must also not discount the psychological effect of encountering corpses in mile after mile of countryside torn up by shellfire. Farrer had taken a short ride in a tank (p. 11), which no doubt added to the horror of seeing burned-out tanks (pp. 98–99). He had visited dark damp cellars with suspicious cloth bundles of rottenness still in them; cellars and dugouts inhabited by crazed and blinded cats (pp. 94–95, 97–98, 113–15). Coming on top of eighteen months in a hysterical capital city and, before that, the immensities of remote Asia, the effect on him, as he plainly writes, was quite powerful. In his described feelings in the Hotel Ritz, Farrer testifies to modernity: the psychological effect of radical modernisation — specifically of unprecedented industrial warfare, into which he has been precipitated by the demands of another mode of modernity, the new phenomenon of government-sponsored propaganda. The modernist product of Farrer's experience is the book, *Void*, itself, pieced together like a conceptual jigsaw puzzle from 266 small sections, adopting a form invented 150 years before by an author whose work was being used and identified by the Russian Formalist critic Viktor Shklovsky, at almost the exact moment as Farrer's adoption of it, as modern and exemplary.[35] In analogous ways the painter Edouard Manet had modelled his modernist *Olympia* (1865) on Goya's *Nude Maja* (c. 1799) and Titian's *Venus of Urbino* (1538); and James Joyce was using the *Odyssey* as the model for *Ulysses* (1922).

Letter XII, Section 1, 'Hospital Barges' is the 133rd section in Farrer's book and therefore at the book's centre. In it, contemplating from a canal bridge in Saint-Omer the sight of hospital barges full of wounded floating quietly beneath him, Farrer manages references to Jane Austen's *Emma* and *Northanger Abbey*, and one to his other favourite literary character, Sarah Gamp of *Martin Chuzzlewit*. He tries to make the advance of medical care demanded by modern war a reason for optimism and a cause of social progress. He admires the 'beautiful orderliness and calm' he sees in the barges; wishes he were 'a doctor to these fellows'; and reflects that, for ordinary privates, 'It is a paradox, but however ill they might have been in England, they would never have had anything like this, hardly even in the best of hospitals.' (pp. 164–65) He even manages a reference to his own major theme: 'I suppose it is because these reflections are so obvious that they make one feel so sentimental.' This central section therefore delivers a hope that social progress will come out of the war. It does so by describing the peace and orderliness of the hospital barges as they take men away from combat; the consequence, but antithesis, of the 'whirl of the actual fighting [...] mess and muddle' (p. 164). However, such progress has not yet happened, so Farrer subjects his own 'sentimental' feelings to an ironic turn, through reference to Jane Austen's *Northanger Abbey* and in it General Tilney's complacent and patronising reflection to Catherine about: 'the accommodations and comforts by which the labours of her inferiors were softened'.[36] In *Void*, Farrer was caught between his task of producing propaganda, and the staggering sights he encountered and feelings he experienced on the battlefields. He sullied his Buddhism in doing his job; and tried to retain some dignity as a skilful creator of literature.

In the last paragraph of the book, after the collapse of the Italian Front, he writes:

> It is not that I want to preach, or overstate things: but I am really frightened by this Italian business. It seems to throw such a huge new responsibility on one's own personal firmness in courage and conviction and optimism. When you are halfway across a plank bridge over an abyss, it is no time to begin wobbling. (pp. 305–06)

This passage emerges from a general discussion of the meaning of the Front's collapse, but communication of the idea of defeat successfully marries the personal to the strategic. Farrer used a very similar motif in his letter to Osbert Sitwell reflecting on the damage that the war had done and his part in adding to that damaging 'slumgullion'; now giving it a Faustian tremor: 'It was like going straight forward, desperately, along a tight-rope, over Hell.'[37]

★ ★ ★ ★ ★

A late thought about his book made part of another letter from Burma, this one to Aubrey Herbert. Farrer describes the book now as a 'poor thing' that 'nobody read.' At the same time', he continues: 'I felt it *had* to be done, and the very best I could possibly do went into it; and it took a damned lot out of me, too, for nothing so appallingly difficult and — responsible, have I ever undertaken.'[38]

Notes to Chapter 9

1. A useful general history of British Great War propaganda is provided in M. L. Sanders and P. Taylor, *British Propaganda During the First World War, 1914–18* (London: Macmillan, 1982).
2. Sue Malvern, *Modern Art, Britain and the Great War: witnessing, testimony and remembrance* (New Haven: Yale University Press, 2004), p. 46.
3. Ibid.
4. Ibid., pp. 46–47.
5. Ibid., p. 47.
6. Ibid., p. 47.
7. 'The Organisation of the Services of Military Secrecy, Security and Publicity. Prepared by General Staff War Office' October 1917, Public Record Office, INF 4/9, quoted by Malvern, p. 47.
8. D. H. Lawrence, *Kangaroo*, p. 237.
9. Letter from John Buchan, Department of Information, to Farrer, 12/12/1917, RBGE GB235, RJF 2/1/4/2.
10. The 'absent person' is Émile Benveniste's formulation for the third person pronoun, according to Benveniste not really a linguistic 'person' at all. Émile Benveniste, *Problèmes de Linguistique Générale* (Paris: Gallimard, 1968), 'La nature des pronoms', pp. 251–57.
11. Farrer, *The Void of War: Letters from Three Fronts* (Boston: Houghton Mifflin Company, 1918), p. 53. Subsequent page numbers are given in the main text.
12. A. C. Swinburne, *Love's Cross-Currents. A Year's Letters* (London: Chatto & Windus, 1905), p. 136.
13. Bairnsfather published a comic drawing on this subject as one of his famous '"The Bystander's" Fragments from France': see 'Still More Bystander Fragments from France', vol. III (London: "The Bystander", n.d., but 1917).

14. Canto 4, stanza 79:

> The Niobe of nations! there she stands,
> Childless and crownless, in her voiceless woe;
> An empty urn within her withered hands,
> Whose holy dust was scatter'd long ago;
> The Scipios' tomb contains no ashes now;
> The very sepulchres lie tenantless
> Of their heroic dwellers: dost thou flow,
> Old Tiber! through a marble wilderness?
> Rise, with thy yellow waves, and mantle her distress!

15. Constance Babington-Smith, *Air Spy: the Story of Photo Intelligence in World War II* (New York: Harper, 1957), pp. 190–91.
16. Dion Fortune, *Psychic Self-Defence*, pp. 72–73.
17. Sara Mason, 'The Ingleborough Estate: home of Reginald Farrer', in Illingworth and Routh, *Reginald Farrer*, pp. 81–88 (p. 86).
18. On the significance of views from high places in literature by Ford and Tolkien related to the Great War, see Michael Charlesworth, 'Panorama, the Map, and the Divided Self: *No Enemy, No More Parades*, and Tolkien's *The Lord of the Rings*' in *Ford Madox Ford's Parade's End: The First World War, Culture, and Modernity*, International Ford Madox Ford Studies 13, ed. by A. Chantler and R. Hawkes (Amsterdam: Rodopi, 2014), pp. 95–106.
19. John Milton, *Paradise Regained*, Book 4, ll. 163, 182, 210.
20. Christopher Marlowe, *Dr. Faustus*, Act 3, Chorus, ll. 20–22, in *The Complete Plays*, ed. by M. T. Burnett (London: J. M. Dent and Charles E. Tuttle, 1999).
21. Rob Linrothe, 'Travel Albums and Revisioning Narratives: A Case Study in the Getty's Fleury "Cachemire" Album of 1908', in *Photography's Orientalism: New Essays on Colonial Representation*, ed. by Ali Behdad and Luke Gartlan (Los Angeles: Getty Research Institute, 2013), pp. 171–84 (p. 177).
22. See Liz Wilson, *Charming Cadavers: Horrific Figurations of the Feminine in Indian Buddhist Hagiographic Literature* (Chicago: Chicago University Press, 1996). Thanks to Jishnu Shankar for suggesting this reference. See also George Bond, 'Theravada Buddhism's Meditations on Death and the Symbolism of Initiatory Death', *History of Religions* 19, 3 (1980), 237–58, which focusses on the southern Buddhist tradition so strong in Sri Lanka.
23. Bond, 'Theravada Buddhism's Meditations on Death', p. 237.
24. I am very grateful to Professor Loos for showing me a photograph she found that shows the Prince-Priest on the islet in the company of skulls and a skeleton. For this episode, see her study of Prince Prisdang, the Prince-Priest, Tamara Loos, *Bones Around My Neck: The life and exile of a prince provocateur* (Ithaca, NY: Cornell University Press, 2016), p. 124.
25. Quoted in the *Ceylon National Review*, 7 (August 1908), p. 304, as part of the answer to Question 142. The revision of the *Catechism* was undertaken by the High Priest, Sri Sumangala, who had received Farrer into the community in February 1908. The quotation continues: 'But every being may equally reach Nirvana, by conquering ignorance and gaining wisdom.'
26. The word 'baresarkness' is Farrer's rendition of a berserk state: uncontrolled aggression of an all but insane person. Originally induced in Viking warriors by the ingestion of small amounts of fly agaric mushroom.
27. His Holiness the Dalai Lama of Tibet, *The Joy of Living and Dying in Peace* (New York: HarperCollins, 1997), p. 11.
28. Farrer's letter to Osbert Sitwell (1920).
29. Lawrence, *Kangaroo*, pp. 236–37.
30. '"Panting Eyes" ', *Times Literary Supplement*, December 12, 1918, p. 614. The passage quoted from *Void* is from the section 'Ira Sacra', pp. 155–56.
31. Richard H. Davis, *The Bhagavad Gita* (Princeton: Princeton University Press, 2014)
32. Lawrence, *Kangaroo*, p. 236.
33. *The Joy of Living and Dying*, pp. 11–12. The Dalai Lama explains that in this book he is not adding

anything new to traditional Buddhist teaching: 'I have nothing to say that has not been said before', p. ix.

34. RBGE, RJF 4/1/1, letter of 26/7/1919.

35. Shklovsky, famous for his admiration of Sterne's writings, a Revolutionary commissar in 1917–1918, published his own book entitled *A Sentimental Journey* in 1923. It deals with his life in the period 1917–1922.

36. On this theme, see the discussion of this section of Farrer's book in Claudia L. Johnson, *Jane Austen's Cults and Cultures* (Chicago: University of Chicago Press, 2012), pp. 105–10.

37. Farrer's letter to Sitwell (1920).

38. Letter to Aubrey Herbert from Hpimaw Fort, Upper Burma, 9/X/1919, Somerset County Archives, Taunton, DD\HER/38.

CHAPTER 10

Into the Halls of Heaven:
The Rainbow Bridge

On page 116 of *The Rainbow Bridge* Farrer wrote: 'In the powdered gold of early sunset I rode leisurely into the Halls of Heaven'. As this book was published after news of his death had reached Britain, and obituaries had appeared in the gardening journals, the *Geographical Journal* and *The Times*, the emotional effect of this sentence would have been very different for its first readers, who had known Farrer, than it is for us in the 21st century. *The Rainbow Bridge* was Farrer's last published book. There is little reason to doubt that this sentence provoked tears, at least in his friends and family. In it he seems uncannily to be describing his life after death, as a continuity with his descriptions of his life before. In fact 'the Halls of Heaven' is his translation of the Chinese name of a Tibetan Buddhist monastery, Tien Tang.

If in *On the Eaves of the World* Farrer presents, within a slice of his own auto-biography, his rejection of certain pervasive elements of Western civilisation, and his acceptance, even embrace, of Eastern civilisation; and if his paintings allow the viewer to observe the processes of making — itself a staple of French art since the 1860s at least, but for the amateur Farrer a self-revelation amounting to a close extension of his personality; what does he achieve in *The Rainbow Bridge*, more than just a continuation and completion of his autobiographical narrative of events from several years before? The short answer is that in the book he completely re-invents his narrative mode.

The Preface to *The Rainbow Bridge* is dated May 19, 1918, and a footnote on page 225 states that the material on that page was written in June 1918. By mid-September he had reached page 292[1] (of a total of 380). These signs indicate a date of composition from the spring to the autumn of 1918, between his employment earlier in the year as a guide to the battlefields, and the Armistice, followed by his third intestinal operation, in November that year. The domestic background is thus Farrer's lodging in the '*louche*' *ménage* of Jim Baird's household in Queen's Gate. The account of the second year of the China-Tibet expedition (1915) is therefore heavily retrospective, and thoroughly permeated by a sense of all the disaster and suffering (for the Western world, at least) experienced since.

In *The Rainbow Bridge* there is a smoother flow of narrative, a more integrated account, without the sudden jumps that mark *On the Eaves of the World*. Farrer controls his narrative more closely, and is more careful. Seeking to convey the beauty of things he saw, for the most part he relies on the effect of beauty being in the things seen and described, rather than in the poetry of his use of words. At times there is also a more careful botanical attention to the distinguishing structure of the plants encountered.

Farrer's change in narrative mode was related to the mixed reviews received by *On the Eaves of the World*. The *Saturday Review* (a journal associated with Laurence Binyon) loved the earlier book's descriptions of flowers in the wild, and found the work 'a most illuminating book about China.' But the *Spectator* wrote that: 'Mr. Farrer writes simply and admirably' about 'daily life' and 'civilization' in Northern China; 'but when he gets to flowers his language becomes bombastic and turgid [...] when he girds up his loins for "fine writing" he is lamentably bad.'[2] Along the same lines, the *Times Literary Supplement* thundered:

> We can share Mr. Farrer's delight when he comes upon a new plant and could share it more fully if he had learnt the first secret of writing — to use no more words than are needed [...] Where the Abbé [Huc] would use one word he uses three, and does not choose them well. It is enough for him if they are unusual.

And the reviewer chose to quote: 'a sentence certainly worse than most, but which we quote to show what he can do.'[3] (The sentence is a Meredithian one of five nested clauses about *Rodgersia pinnata* and the Giant Lily, in *On the Eaves of the World*, I, pp. 146–47). The review drops the insulting tone when congratulating Farrer on his knowledge and description of Chinese 'character' and culture. Quoting Farrer on Chinese postmen, it concludes: 'Passages like this show that Mr. Farrer can write well enough when he does not try to write finely.'

The Pall Mall Gazette, however, had liked the book: 'excellent in all its aspects.'[4] A similar pattern continued in journals published too late to affect the writing of *The Rainbow Bridge*: Cyrus C. Adams, writing in the American *Geographical Review*, cordially disliked *On the Eaves of the World* in a dismissive short review; but *The Alpine Journal* (a journal for mountaineers, not plant enthusiasts) was comfortably complimentary:

> Buddhism interests [Farrer] intensely. [Through reading the book] we have gained an unexpectedly comprehensive view of Chinese life and manners and of Chinese mentality [...] a very remarkable sketch of the strange mixture of forces whose interaction makes up the living politics of the Tibetan march of Kansu. [...] he is at his best — and his best is exceedingly good — when the conscious employment of literary artifice is least apparent [and it is most apparent in the sections about botanizing ...] the big facts of geography interest him, and he handles them with ease and skill [...] in his particular blend of mountaineering with botany, Mr. Farrer has succeeded in discovering, or at any rate 'introducing to cultivation' something very like a *species nova* in Alpine literature.[5]

Farrer referred to reviews of *On the Eaves of the World* early in *The Rainbow Bridge*, caricaturing them as divided between those that liked the botanical passages and disliked the description of people, and vice versa (p. 95). The hostile criticism evidently irked: when writing the word 'donkeys' he added the footnote: 'Hands off, critics; this is the spelling of the Divine Jane.' (p. 79). Apostrophes of the critics feature an ostentatious and impenitent return to alliteration: 'Oh, you dyspeptic people, who despise the pleasures of others, and with peevish pens depreciate rapture into rhapsody, it is already clear that you must not come with *me* to Tibet' (p. 115). It is noticeable that these passages are the only ones in *The Rainbow Bridge* where alliteration and assonance are so obvious; as if Farrer were deliberately flaunting an exaggerated version of himself as a challenge, and as a memory of terrain already fought over by himself and the critics.

Critics are still in view when, in a key passage, he reveals his values and purposes in writing at all:

> In no case [...] expect from me, in dealing with either plants or scenes of people, that jejune and dust-coloured dullness of expression that alone, I gather, passes current as sincerity among those who have no emotions to render, and no words to render them if they had. In sum: criticism here, criticism there, it is all helpful and guiding, but I must remind myself, as I here remind you, that I am writing this book for the relief and release of one person only in the world. I am strenuously re-living, in fact, the dead years, in order to win free for a while from the present; and, out of my own memories and stored emotions, spinning a rainbow bridge, far-flung over black depths, towards the golden irrecoverable past. As the need is greater now, and the gulfs deeper and darker, and the distance farther, this bridge must be higher and stronger, of firmer texture and closer construction than that which first took me back to the Eaves of the World: but the material must still be the same — *my* experiences, *my* pleasures, observations, ardours and achievements, with 'I,' 'I,' 'I,' for the inevitably recurring rivet of the whole. (p. 95)

The different character of the book ('firmer texture and closer construction') arises from the circumstances that have intervened between the events recounted and the time of writing: the horrors, dangers, and emotions of the War, as well as the gulf of temporal and geographical distance. To that extent the new literary quality owes nothing to the critics, Farrer states. But he also promises a greater subjective tone in *The Rainbow Bridge*. When the *Times* and the *Spectator* use the expression 'fine writing' (or a variant), the implication is that there exists a level of excellence that can be comprehended and judged by other people: a sort of objectively-perceptible standard. Farrer's reply in defence is that he writes to express his enthusiasm: the satisfaction is subjective. As part of his warning to the reader of the new 'contract', (as it were), he brings a familiar image back: 'On the perilous tightrope of creation, it is vital to concentrate entirely and undeviably on one's own footsteps.' And he goes on: 'No real book was written for anybody but its writer [...] and only afterwards [...] for the greater or lesser multitude of other people, who reflect his various facets and react to his personality' (p. 96).

It is interesting to consider that this last assertion is being made by a man who, as a boy, must have been bewildered by his inability to communicate, feeling himself a freak or an outsider. But it is also illuminating as an assertion of one way in which the subjective can become external. Subjective experience, communicated, awakens an echo in the (not unsympathetic) reader, whose reward is to visit Tibet with an entertaining companion. And there is a rather intellectually and psychologically deeper reward as well: we might say, in relation to this, that Farrer's approach is built upon the insights about personality, subjectivity, and impressionism achieved by Walter Pater. For Pater, according to a recent account:

> Historical ideas, philosophical systems, take their true form and are only comprehended through the individuals in whom they are manifested, which means that they are inextricable from certain biases of temperament, sometimes from afflictions of personality or psychosomatic maladies. But their force in the world is discovered through the drama they enact in and between persons. [...] 'Personality' is a word made to work notoriously hard in *Studies*, where it is conceived in terms of structural laws and inner moods, the awakening of which produces artworks. As such it is understood to be the basis of style, and an example of that vital aesthetic quality of *intimité*. Artworks have the capacity to move us as personalities do in life.[6]

The 'structural law' of personality in Farrer's understanding of the world is that individuals (whether people, animals or plants) respond to the determining conditions around them, but they do so in unpredictable ways that correspond to free-will. So Farrer's sympathetic readers ('my little band of the elect', he calls them, p. 115), by accompanying Farrer through the pages of his book, begin to understand another human being. They see the workings of psychology, and can compare Farrer in these respects to what they already know, and make a judgement based on that comparison. Readers find an example being set that can act as a touchstone; and they can get to understand what subjectivity is, and thus can contemplate related concepts such as objectivity, relationship, and persuasiveness. They also, of course, see a remote place, a set of circumstances, and third parties. Some of these points are made by a further review in the *Times Literary Supplement*, embracing both *The Rainbow Bridge* and *On the Eaves of the World* together as 'A Classic of Travel'. The book, 'vitalized by an extraordinary unflagging energy, [...] burns with the zest of life. [...] This is a conscious work of art'.[7]

The underlying Paterian idea surfaces overtly in various parts of *The Rainbow Bridge*, especially when Farrer contemplates the odd feeling of proprietorship that 'the vast loveliness of the world' seen from a high place gives:

> as if one somehow owned it, or were responsible for it, and had a right to be proud of it. And yet, I suppose, a glory so great that it floods and overwhelms one, and absorbs one wholly into its possession, does also, by that very fact pass into one's own possession, too, becomes an inseparable part of one for evermore. The mere fact of perceiving and assimilating such things means that one is storing their glory up to render again for others, even as the giant tree ferns who assimilated the glow of the Coal Age, now render it out again in flame. So that I, indeed, become the medium, the middleman, the mere conduit, to pour forth upon all you who read, a trickle or so, no matter how diluted and defiled and wasted, of the torrential beauty that held me breathless and stupid up on that Tibetan Ma-Chang that you will otherwise never see. (p. 221)

As Pater put it: 'Every moment some form grows perfect in hand or face; some tone on the hills or the sea is choicer than the rest; some mood of passion or insight or intellectual excitement is irresistably real and attractive to us.'[8] Farrer's 'glory' is an impression, or set of impressions, that seem huge, to engulf the subject. Yet the subject owns them as his impressions, and can attempt to communicate them to people who will never see the sights that caused them. Farrer is wrestling with the questions of how he feels and why he is writing, and provides an epitome here of the impulse which motivated him throughout his adult life. In a letter from Burma to Ernest Gye in February 1920, Farrer says that if he is forced home through being unable to find mules for his expedition, he will be 'infertile'.[9] So spreading discoveries, whether through writing or by sending seeds home, has become a deeply internalised, life-perpetuating, psychologically vital pursuit.

We should note in passing, in the lengthy passage just quoted from *The Rainbow Bridge*, Farrer's use of the pronoun 'who' to belong to tree ferns. 'Which' or even 'that' would have been more conventional. His unusual usage reminds us that plants are personalities. In the same way it is no affectation for him to call a 'pigmy hare [...] like a wee short-eared rabbit with a dark brown face' that he made 'friends' with: 'a pleasant person' (p. 135).

The new narrative tone, featuring control, contains a lot of possessiveness. Farrer refers to a capitalized 'My Primula' and 'My Own Primula' (pp. 186, 206) and the possessiveness is far from limited to these examples; in fact it runs as an undercurrent throughout the narrative, so we are left in no doubt that Farrer is proprietor of the expedition and discoverer of the plants. There is also in the narrative much less campy reference to male good looks than featured in *On the Eaves of the World*. He even goes out of his way to explain that he and Bill sleep in different tents, and the expedition servants in a third. However, the narrator cannot disguise his happiness when Gomer (who reminded him of Balliol's *jeunesse dorée* in the earlier book) returns (p. 37). He's also interested in transvestism in the Chinese theatre (p. 35–36), and points out 'phallic' mountains (p. 368 and, quoted here, p. 82): 'dark fantastic pillars of dolomite jetting up from the slopes in phallic towers with streaming flanks of wetness in the sunshine'. Separated from Bill for a few weeks on the return journey, in an impulse we have already noted, Farrer characterizes himself as a Dickensian woman: 'feeling like Mrs. Gummidge, lorn and lone, and widowed by my William' (p. 332). What seems, to his western eyes, the cross-dressing aspect of Chinese men's clothes is no longer played up, but when he meets a fashionable Chinese couple in a rustic inn, he finds the woman to be:

> My Lady, a very comely and capable-looking person, clearly of the most decided views and temper, resplendent in a short blue coat, crimson tabard, and tight black trousers. She was accompanied by a very fat little semi-demi-palace-dog, which she perilously hugged out of harm's way from the mules, holding it all anyhow as they do, or waving it about by one leg, till I could not help laughing at its expression of pompous resignation in untoward circumstances. (pp. 322–23)

In Britain in 1915–1921 no woman would wear trousers, especially tight black ones, so the paradoxes of Chinese dressing, and its gender implication for western readers, continue in the female sex.

Rejection of Western civilization continues, throughout the book. One lengthy passage celebrates Chinese labourers' approach to work, featuring a short break for rice, a smoke and a joke, every two or three hours, after which work is resumed with redoubled effort. To Farrer 'the Chinese system seems the sane, simple and psychological one', with its 'lightness and elasticity, and creed of mutually advantageous give and take.' In contrast, the 'cruder theory' in Britain, featuring 'stereotyped hours and meal-times', 'builds an adamantine unyielding programme of hours and intervals, trusting to nobody's honour and implicating nobody's interest.' (p. 362). The argument is against alienation in work. It is just one part of the cultural superiority of the China of 1915. Towards the end of his journey, Farrer writes: 'Never before had I so poignantly realized this dear kind land, so colossal in its calm and strength; and the direct wise people who have made it.' (p. 364). The extremity of the contrast between West and East has been given earlier, when Farrer's mind goes back to the Great War battlefields:

> Not so long since, I stood on the levelled land out beyond Ypres [...] the waste was pitted universally with shell-holes like bleared eyes, full of foul water [...] where, down in the filmy clear depths of a pool, the eye followed the strange line of a seeming tree-stump, pale and gnarled, until it startled to discern the tranquillity of an upturned mouldering chin at its end, or discovered a clenched mummified hand, brown as smoked old ivory.
> The pleasant garden of European civilization! (pp. 250–51)

When the misery became too much to bear, he writes, he remembered: 'obliterating and triumphant, the reverberating cliffs of Tien Tang, rugged and high and radiant in the rose and gold of sunshine [...] and their overpowering fragrance of pleasantness and warmth and peace' (p. 251). This is also an example of Farrer's theory of the value in personal memory. Memories of being happy (inevitably linked to place) can function as antidote to the poisons and anxieties of the present moment. He uses the phrase 'medicine-bottles' about them; effective because ugliness is evanescent and beauty eternal. Farrer was an optimist.

Part of the tighter control in the book has been to accept the passage of time between time of living the events and time of writing. No longer occluded, as in *The Void of War* and *On the Eaves of the World*, the gap of time becomes a structuring principle of the new book, giving the reader a better opportunity to understand how time and contrasting experiences affect the narrator's view of past life. Farrer reminds us that plants he has brought back (and that the reader sees being first discovered) are already growing in British gardens (p. 145), and tells us that he 'ransacked' the Petrograd Herbarium on his way home in 1916 (p. 214: the book ends before his return journey is described). Of 'his' gentian, he says that 'already special pilgrimages go to Edinburgh in August and September, to see those jungles of my Gentian, a yard through, with some three hundred gigantic trumpets opening at once.' (p. 282). Indeed, rather poignantly, perhaps given the idea by reading this very passage, Farrer's mother and father made such a pilgrimage in 1922.[10]

Among the many uses of this time-shift device, the main recurring theme is best exemplified in a passage from a section describing the journey from Tien Tang to Chebson Abbey:

> For, dull and long though they may sometimes seem in the going, how infinitely golden, really, and in retrospect, are those days of effortless uneventful abstraction, drifting across the enormous immemorial smile of China, in perfect openness of light and air, in perfect openness of freedom from all earthly cares, duties, ties and domesticities, with nothing to think about at all. (p. 154)

The Rousseauean overtones of reverie are clear, though distanced because this is also a memory, suffused with nostalgia. Nevertheless, the new openness about time also forms part of Farrer's impressionism; which is to say, that the book is written in a way that allows the reader to see its construction; it gives a sense of how it has been made; the reader can glimpse its inner workings. A range of other moments, not now about the strangeness of the passage of time, but about the question of how the narrator is going to write the book, contribute to this. We have already looked at the most important of these, the emphasis on the subjective, introduced as it is by Farrer's thoughts about the critical views of *On the Eaves of the World*. There are also apostrophes such as this: 'The delicious place it was, and the delicious day, and the ecstasy of my heart, almost irrecoverable now, even by the long arm of memory!' (p.112) At other times he specifies the writing process itself: 'There are no joys in life, I suppose, more restfully rapturous than the discovery of a new lovely flower. I have expatiated on this often, and will not do so here again.' (p.184) Later he addresses the reader directly about his feeling of sadness in having to leave high Asia and end the expedition: 'Yet do not be misled if I seem to grizzle and peeve as I return. [...] In fact, for the fun of the thing, I exaggerate my attitude, to make you the better share that fun.' (p. 241)

Farrer tells us explicitly that the book is made up of his memories and emotions. It is therefore about impressions and, in a Paterian sense, about moods: the moods of Farrer as he writes, and of Reg as he experiences the tedium, frustrations, and rewards of the quest, as well as the grand spectacle of Chinese and Buddhist civilizations. The moods of Bill, Mafu, Gomer, Buddhist monks and Chinese officials, and the way they are related to cultural ideas and traditions, or psychologies, also feature. There is also comedy, and Farrer shows an engaging ability to laugh at himself.

Impressionist painting was, in great part, concerned with breaking up the accomplished finish of normal French painting, by which only an immaculate surface is presented to the viewer, all decisions and revisions (in this normative or traditional mode) about how to make the work having been puzzled out in a series of preliminary sketches and studies. This earlier type of finish was normal (though not universal) in French painting in the first half of the nineteenth century, led by the work of David and Ingres. When Edouard Manet and the Impressionists appeared in the 1860s and 70s they began painting in short, plainly visible dabs and touches of paint: the dabs and touches being individual to the artist, so that Monet's or Cezanne's touches look unlike those of Renoir or Van Gogh. Monet's *Impression, Soleil Levant* (1872) provided such an extreme example of this that it looks like a visual manifesto of the new independent art. Such an approach allows the viewer to see how the touches of paint have been applied; which came first and which later; whether the brush was relatively dry or slickly wet; how the painter's hand and arm moved through space and time; in short, it opens up the spectacle of the painter's

FIG. 10.1. Ma Da-ren's garden: one of 4 photographs on a page of the album Farrer prepared for William Purdom. (Lakeland Horticultural Society. Photo: RBGE).

FIG. 10.2. Ma Da-ren's garden: from the same album page,
Purdom picking a sprig of *Viburnum farreri*.

decisions being made. Farrer's painting achieves something similar (figures 8.9 and 8.10 make good examples). So for his narrative of travels in China and Tibet to include moments that invite the reader to think about how the narrative has been written; what the time-shifts and time-lapses were; how the writer was deciding what kind of book it should be even as he was writing it; all this is consistent with Farrer's visual art, and amounts to a form of impressionism in words. It is about the writer's mental processes. Inevitably, the reader follows these processes (or doesn't follow them) in ways that engage his or her own mental processes too. Farrer opens up his own decision-making process to the reader very early on in the book, and continues doing so throughout.

Impressionism also features in a more obvious way, through Farrer's evocation of colours. Looking at plants in the Da-Tung alps, for example:

> Corydalis, in humped blobs of snow-flecked turquoise, squatting on its sumptuous blue foliage over the raw red face of the scree. Under a sky so imminent and black the air takes on a cold ghastly pallor in which flowers seem actually to flame; on the charnel-house gloom of that voor alp, the blues and purples and yellows of the blossoms were like multitudinous flecks of electric fire, luminous as ghost-lights. (p. 265)

Arguably impressionism also comes through a less obvious route, in Farrer's enlivening use of analogies: little dabs of language and sensibility combined. The expedition meets a grandmother: 'as old as the world, but infinitely more cheerful' (p.194). Moorland turf is 'dead as Queen Anne' (p. 202). Conglomerate rock: 'as hard as hate' (p.186). A mountain is as 'high as Heaven' and 'quite as monotonous' (p. 239). Accumulated letters and newspapers 'burst, in a quite unprofitable bomb-explosion' (p. 102). The analogies come from his experience as a Western man: from the society in which he is obliged to live and work.

Bill and Reg enjoyed their winter stay in Lanchow, the book tells us. They also took pleasure in a shorter stay in Sining. Here Reg took some beautiful photographs inside the garden of the military governor, Mâ Dâ-ren (figures 10.1, 10.2). In these photographs Farrer seems to have captured the peaceful winter, the feeling of tranquillity that he experienced in his happiest moments in China. The swaying forms of the winter trees testify to life and a certain elegance; a life and elegance that are both natural and, since we are in a garden, man-made. The winter trees admit plenty of the light of a radiant late-winter sky. Farrer has adjusted the focus to allow the print a slight blur of softness.[11] In the background of 10.2 Bill plucks some twigs from a flowering *Viburnum farreri* for a photograph of his own. 'It was the first time, too,' writes Farrer, 'that I had ever seen *Vibernum fragrans* blooming in its full magnificence out of doors — an epoch-marking instant in anyone's life.' (*RB*, p. 69) The garden had a tranquil feeling of neglect. Bill and Reg found it 'a noble sight' when 'spring in Sining floods the whole city in a sudden sea of pink peach-blossom.' The garden was 'all a haze of shell-pinkness', amounting to:

> a big open park in the heart of the town [...] there are complicated rockeries and pavilions [...] in the shade of huge spreading poplars, high over the tangles beneath, of peach and plum, and lilac and rose, and barberry and viburnum,

FIG. 10.3. The picnic with the travelling lamas. (RBGE).

FIG. 10.4. Landscape of the borderlands, showing the Da-Tung alps and the 'Tibetan' bridge. (Lakeland Horticultural Society. Photo: RBGE).

and aged masses of tree-peony. [...] Gasping with the loveliness of that sad abandoned ground, we roamed and sauntered, [...] and wandered among the desolate cloisters and corridors and grey old pleasure rooms crumbling to decay.

Unlike the first year's experience, the main places of civilization in this second summer of plant-hunting were not towns but the Tibetan abbeys.[12] There were two that made the expedition welcome: Tien Tang and another (smaller and richer) that Farrer names 'Chebson' and likens to a well-endowed Oxford college.[13] Despite his liking for the very self-assured 'prior' of this latter establishment, it is Tien Tang that suffuses Farrer's memory with a golden glow:

> It is there, amid its Iris fields and friendly crowds of monks and novices and pilgrims of devotion, that one's memory most fondly lingers, rather than in the leisurely and expensive emptinesses of Chebson Abbey, despite the charm of its fat old Prior, a typical ecclesiastic, full of unction and twinkles (with heavy artificial-looking eyebrows, and the great mobile face of a Coquelin), as placidly the equal of his guests as any College Dean assured and portly.[14]

Tien Tang is full of people, interesting conversation with monks and officials, pilgrims (often women), and the atmosphere of a 'poor and populous parish'.[15] There are also absorbing and perilous walks to be had, and fun with the boy acolyte-monks over photographs (eagerness to have a photograph taken, rather than shyness, being an issue). A crowd watches Reg paint a water-colour. Bill or Reg also had to photograph, and reproduce many times, a postcard of the Potala at Lhasa with the Dalai Lama's head uncannily appearing in the sky; and an esteemed *thangka* painting. An outing for plants in the neighbouring mountains brings a chance-meeting with travelling Lamas on their way to the abbey (figure 10.3). This meeting gives rise to an impromptu picnic, at which the Lamas' comestibles 'hard as marble' prove too much for Farrer's false teeth, and for a moment his 'general defectiveness of construction' has to be openly acknowledged and apologised for (p. 143). The way from Wolvesden to Tien Tang crossed 'the finest Tibetan bridge in Northern Asia' (p. 111), built by the monks of Tien Tang, who charged a toll (figures 10.4, 10.5). So Farrer basks in Buddhist civilization. When the expedition departed from Tien Tang the first time: 'with us tumultuously in a crowd poured the monks and acolytes, these last in brand new petticoats of deep violet, brief and bunchy as a ballerina's, which, under their equally new upper swathings of bright scarlet, made them look just like old-fashioned fuchsias.' (p. 144). Farrer in a small way contributes to the civilisation that he enjoys, deprecating Bill's wish to shoot a Big Horn sheep, because: 'I hold the Holy Law myself' (and rejoicing that the shooting is a failure, pp. 119, 125–26); objecting to the killing of moths (p. 195); and, when the youngest expedition servants wish to kill a small weasel-type animal, he: 'repressed their degrading ardours.' (p. 266). Here 'degrading' is used very precisely, since Reg ensured that the servants avoided accumulating bad karma needlessly.

Defending the 'superstitions and practices of Lamaism' in his article on the Tibetan abbeys, Farrer argues that they are no worse than either Roman Catholic or Orthodox Christianity (and his defence includes counter-attack against the missionaries). Obviously feeling provoked by considering calumnies against Lamas,

FIG. 10.5. 'The finest Tibetan bridge in northern Asia'.
(Lakeland Horticultural Society. Photo: RBGE).

WOLVESDEN HOUSE.

FIG. 10.6. Wolvesden House from *The Rainbow Bridge* (1921).

he lets fly some counter-provocation of his own: 'And who is to say, anyhow, in any creed, that an act of faith, if sincere, is necessarily powerless to react upon the material world?'[16]

Most of the summer was spent in more primitive buildings than those of the abbeys: a muleteers' shelter in a high pass of the Da-Tung alps, named 'Wolvesden' by Farrer, who also gives its Chinese name: Lang Shih Tang or Lang Shih Gô (p. 86; figure 10.6). From this base at c. 11,000 feet altitude, the expedition could make its forays to above 14,000 feet in search of plants. The altitude made the going slow, gave Farrer ear-ache, heart pangs, and difficulty breathing. Sun-stroke confused him. He also worried that the haul of plants would not satisfy his financial backers in Britain. But there were huge rewards in the visual, sensory and spatial delights of the mountains. On the western slopes of Wolvesden Pass: 'All the uppermost zigzags and open scree banks were dense with rounded low clouds of the Violet Delphinium, among which stalwartly stood up the azure spires of the Celestial Poppy. It was a stupefying sight, and one of these combinations that Nature alone can effect with complete success.' (p. 254) From a distance the delphinium gave the effect of a 'purple haze'.[17] And when he and Bill come upon several square miles of the blue 'Harebell Poppy,' *Meconopsis quintuplinervia*, filling a high shallow valley, both are reduced to silence:

I wondered to myself what he was feeling, or how at last he would try to put into words the pain of a pleasure so intense. Then, after the silence had grown too heavy, he turned to me and said in a half-whisper, "Doesn't it make your guts ache?" It was exactly right: no other words could have nailed the truth so absolutely.

This is, however, the account of the moment that Farrer read to the Royal Geographical Society on 11 March 1918, and published in the Society's journal.[18] In *The Rainbow Bridge* the incident is dressed up a little:

What was he thinking then? How was the sight striking home to him? But who can ever know what even these dearest and nearest are doing and enduring in the secret inmost rooms of the soul? We continued together, voiceless and smitten.

And then at last he turned to me, and in the awe-stricken whisper of one overwhelmed by a divine presence, he said: "Doesn't it make your very soul ache?" And it was right, the absolute and final word. It did. (p. 223)

The different build-up here is effective enough. But to deprive Bill of his true word vitiates the whole effect of the anecdote, which, substituting 'very soul' for 'guts' becomes a pious conventionality after all. It also erodes the effectiveness of the very next sentence, in which Farrer elaborates on Bill's original insight: 'It twisted one's very being, in the agony to absorb the sight wholly, to get outside it, possess it, delay its passing, tear it away from its native hills and keep it with one for ever — flesh of one's flesh, and brain of one's brain.' The metaphor from digestion and absorption is clear enough, and indicates that the substitution of 'soul' for 'guts' is the work of a more conventional and cowardly mind than his own. Farrer had already given the more earthy version of the incident in public, to an important audience, and that fact, taken together with the metaphor from absorption, militates against the possibility that he made the change himself. The later stages of preparation of the book for publication came after Farrer's death. At the moment we cannot say whether the change was made by a family member or the publisher.[19]

At any rate, such moments of discovery in the field are what drove Farrer onwards, taking his risks. No doubt he committed several what we could perhaps call orientalist blunders, admiring landscape when it reminded him of Britain (although there is plenty that he admired which didn't), making an abbey seem to be a transplanted Oxford College, seeing Tibetan Buddhism through the matrix of a vocabulary developed for a different and (considered from a Protestant point of view) problematic faith, referring to some locations under coined English names rather than bothering with their Chinese names. But this moment, and others like it on this and other travels, are what drove Farrer on, what he lived for; in the high stony places of the world to find an incomprehensible and inexpressible beauty made by flowers, if possible beyond human life and human interference. 'But beauty is so big and enduring, and we so small and evanescent,' he wrote, that 'trying to pack the incommensurable inside the infinitesimal' sometimes produces 'almost physical pain.' (p. 223) In the valley of *Meconopsis quintuplinervia* a sensation of beauty has resisted, for minutes, conversion into an impression, which happens when the mind can begin to reflect upon the sensation. In putting the matter in this way I mean to give a model that abides by nineteenth-century reasoning, in keeping with theories of impressionism. Walter Pater's terse but very clear comments on such feelings in his 'Conclusion' contribute to this view, and John Abercrombie is quite clear that sensation, as sense-datum, precedes impression.[20] When a sensation resists assimilation to impression, Farrer's experience is that the corresponding feeling verges on pain. By insisting on writing about his actions and feelings in a way that dwells very often on the small-scale, seemingly insignificant level of events, Farrer has found considerable depth in his meditation about what it feels like to be alive.

The plants he finds are also small-scale, each a small, almost minimal, unit contributing to the composition of the vast landscapes Farrer relishes; yet they give rise to thoughts about the relationship between them as individual parts of the complete landscape, and as parts of greater wholes: the relationship between an individual and a species, in fact:

> It is only on a vast number of living individuals that you can satisfactorily establish a general formula for a 'species', since only a vast number can yield you its one common factor, by giving full perception of the plant's range of variation, so that you can arrive at the one point (or more) in which it never varies at all. Thus, Meconopsis Prattii [...] may [...] have flowers of every shade from pure white through all tones of azure, mauve and lilac, to clean pink; it may have quite narrow foliage, or foliage so broad as to seem, in the second-year seedlings, almost round; the leaves may be quite entire or faintly waved along their edge; and the footstalks can be either quite short or strict and long; it may have the widest diversities in the shape of its pods and in the length of its styles. But it never varies in the smallest degree from the ashen-cream colour of its anthers. And thus, out of an incalculable multitude of diverse individuals on the mountains, I generalize a definite species. (pp. 233–34) [An anther is the pollen-discharging organ at the end of the stamen.]

Determination of species was not a straightforward pursuit, and in fact is constantly open to opinion and revision. Farrer's point here is that you need to see the plant 'wild and abundant' before you can distinguish the crucial common factor. Obviously Balfour, in Edinburgh, or the Russian experts in the Petrograd Herbarium, cannot do so. This is an argument for allowing primacy to a good field botanist. It is also, on a more general philosophical level, an argument for toleration of difference, and for not indulging in unnecessary minute distinctions. Also for recognizing kinship or similarity in a great number of seemingly unlike individuals. There is, it seems, an underlying determinism: members of a species share a common factor or a small set of common factors. Yet there is plenty of room for individuation on other levels: of colour, form, growth, and (though unstated here by Farrer) ability to adapt to seemingly unpropitious circumstances of habitat (growing conditions).

Such thoughts about psychological process and biological truths, that at the same time offer possibilities of extension to other forms of life, co-exist with enjoyment of the imagination and the brink of the metaphysical. Another impressionist metaphorical undercurrent of the text is furnished through its many references to magic. Tibet was, of course, regarded by people such as Blavatsky and Crowley as the land of 'practical' real magic. References to magic and transformation scenes — the magic of the theatrical stage-manager — abound in Farrer's landscape descriptions. *Lloydia alpina* is named by him the 'Fairy Bell'. The 'blares and explosions' of Tibetan music are 'muted to sweetness' by 'the tranquillity of the morning': 'like fairy horns in the distance' (p. 135). There are many instances of this class of use and language. Yet the expedition brings with it its own practical 'magics' (at least, that is how they were regarded by the local inhabitants): the ice-cream machine, the mincer, and the soda siphon (pp. 88–89; Farrer insisted on carrying with him thousands of soda bulbs, on the grounds that drinking flat water made him sick). There were also the clock and the camera (p. 93). Back in Britain after the end of the expedition, Farrer tells us proleptically, he has met people who invested him with metaphysical powers simply because he had been in Tibet. When he once preyed upon this gullibility, or wish to believe, he:

> told somebody at a party that I saw in her a mongoose being evoked, the poor lady immediately turned pale and faintly shrieked, and sank in a swoon upon the teacups, declaring that she felt herself becoming one indeed. (p. 257)

A contemporary student of the occult, for whom magic is an activation of the will, would say that Farrer, despite his scepticism and disavowals, had in fact worked magic upon her.[21] 'As for the powers,' he wrote, 'who is there that shall prescribe limits to will-force, and to will-feebleness? [...] Of what mysterious and supra-normal feats the Living Buddhas in Tibetan monasteries are capable, I cannot rightly speak; everything is possible, but nothing is proven. But the Mahatmas and the Maskelyne-Cookeries are mere inventions of a scheming folly' (pp. 258–59). The last references are to Madame Blavatsky's 'Mahatmas' (supposedly special orders of being living in Tibet with exceptional magical powers over space and time) and to a famous family of stage-magicians in Britain (Maskelyne and stage-partner Cook). Nevertheless, one way or another the many references to magic, and the faery-world, have built up a certain force of acceptance in the reader by the time late in the book when Farrer characterizes two soldiers seconded by a Chinese governor to accompany and safeguard the expedition as it returns to Peking. These hapless persons are described by Farrer as: 'a brace of unbelievable degraded atoms, like the fading ghosts of two malignant yet imbecile Elementals, chinless and spidery' (p. 347). In referring to Elementals, Farrer reveals himself fully versant with occult lore. Such strange beings, non-human and allied to the four elements, can sometimes be picked up accidentally from the Astral Plane at the moment of conception by a human couple; otherwise they can be called up by a magician who doesn't really know what he's doing. They can look like humans, but it can be disastrous for a human to marry one. Such is the short version defining them as recounted by Dion Fortune.[22]

Fortune would also have recognized Farrer's eerie feeling in high open Tibetan valleys: 'close up under the immediate lid of the sky [...] their pretence of being mere lowlands seems an evil sham, and with an evil magic their very dullness, hot and sterile, seems haunted, and the marmots themselves are a magic population, imprisoned by a spell in their present gollywog shape' (p. 145). Fortune writes

FIG. 10.7. Farrer's photograph of Shwa-y-Goo, China. (RBGE).

about: 'this peculiar terror with which the great hills can obsess mankind' as being felt even by mountaineers, and would no doubt have approved the way in which Reg: 'chanted snatches of song to charm away the weight of that watchful stillness'.[23] In addition, Fortune and Farrer would no doubt have agreed that it was largely through Blavatsky that Tibetan Buddhism came to be dragged into the world of European occultism.

A rainbow contains all the colours of all the Buddhas. A bridge is a way between two places. In various cultures a 'rainbow bridge' connects the earthly domain with a heaven, or an abode of the gods. The rainbow bridge of Farrer's title can thus be taken to stand for a path to enlightenment. It took Farrer to far northwestern China, and far northeastern Tibet, roaming a debatable region between the city of Lanchow and the lake of Koko Nor. In fact, to: 'the remote high heart of Asia, so old, so weary, and so wise.' In the lecture from which these phrases come, he generalized his experience in an exultant tribute:

> Once let Asia lay her hold on you, and you will never know peace again. Asia, ugly, desolate, tedious, difficult, and dangerous [...] once captured, never can your soul get free, amid the clamorous follies and futilities of Western life, from the deepening hunger that will always gnaw you for those wild and lonely lands, for that vast and vocal silence which everlastingly fills the remote high heart of Asia, so old, so weary, and so wise.[24]

Within this passionate loyalty, Tien Tang held a particular place in Farrer's heart. Returning to Peking by the end of the expedition, off his food, worn out by the nerve-strain of two years' travel (p. 328), in a 'general condition of urticaria' (hives), his feelings for the comfort and companionship of that idealized Tibetan Buddhist community became very strong. Travelling south-east, he looks at a distant view of mountains and clouds: 'Out into the sumptuous solemn chaos of the West I strained my eyes, in anguished longing for some lost glimpse of that sacred and mysterious Land, still not so very far away out there, but so soon to be lost for ever' (p. 326). Plants, views and villages still delighted him. Some places pre-figured home: 'Big fells [...] recalled Whernside' and 'a vast fell panorama [...] might have been Ribblehead on a huge scale' (pp. 318, 294). He sees:

> a very wide prospect over the country, now a panorama of low rolling lines, largely cultivated and largely green in grass [...] The air was autumnal, the banks all gay with Asters [...] Dark violet storms now pursued us on a violent gale, and broke in thunder and sharp squalling flaws of cold rain as we lumbered down the steep far descent on the other side, [...] arrived, under a cleared radiant sky, at Shwa-y-goo, neatest perhaps and cleanest and newest-looking of all these naked, neat and new-looking villages of Kansu. (p. 318; figure 10.7)

So there are moments; but in general, sadness over the necessity of return and regret for Tien Tang, as the finest part of an unrepeatable experience, predominate. By this time Reg is exhausted, and is carried along in a mule-litter. Even a description of this device becomes an opportunity for philosophico-moral insight: 'The movement is undulating and bland, the hours slide by in a stupor of incredible comfort, so acute as to be plausibly mistaken for happiness' (p. 316). To put it the other way: physical comfort is not happiness; a thought aimed at the legacy of Edwardian British thirst for material comforts. It is Tien Tang's hold over his emotions, though, that sets the tone of the last 90 pages of the book: 'through blurred eyes of memory I still see each step of the way as blurred as I did then — looking back and looking back, till that golden bay of sunshine was hidden finally from sight'. The way from Tien Tang has to be taken, yet is felt to be 'the wrong direction' (p. 292).

And yet, in another and surprising way, Farrer gives the last word to a different place. Possessiveness had made him feel that Wolvesden House, the primitive muleteers' shelter he had rented for the summer, ('our happy little house', p. 289) remains perpetually his property. 'Dear little house', he apostrophizes it, 'how dull you sometimes were; how desirable you always are! — sitting up there, far away, lost and lone in your deep groove of the great Tibetan Alps.' In another sentence that no doubt caused great emotional upset among his friends and relations reading it in 1921, he tells us that:

> Those who may wish (in days I hope still distant) to commune with my ghost must take a long journey; to where it will be found cheeping and chittering wanly round the mud-plastered walls of Wolvesden. (p. 289)

Notes to Chapter 10

1. That page refers to an event 'exactly three years ago today as I write'. The event came two days after September 13 (*The Rainbow Bridge*, p. 290). Page numbers in *The Rainbow Bridge* will hereafter be in the main text.
2. Both reviews, dated December 1917, reproduced in *Book Review Digest*, ed. by Mary Reely, Alice Sterling and Pauline Rich (New York: Wilson, 1919), p. 149. The *Spectator*'s review is unsigned, but a leading light on the paper was Lytton Strachey's cousin, John St. Loe Strachey.
3. *Times Literary Supplement*, November 15, 1917, p. 551 (hereafter *TLS*).
4. Quoted in *The Nation*, vol. 106.
5. Unsigned review, *The Alpine Journal*, vol. XXXII (London: Longmans, 1920), pp. 130–33; Cyrus Adams in *The Geographical Review*, vol 9 (New York, Jan-June 1920), pp. 218–19.
6. Stephen Cheeke, '"Fantastic Modernism": Walter Pater, Botticelli, and Simonetta', *Word & Image*, 32, 2 (April-June 2016), 195–206, p. 201. *Studies* refers to Pater's *Studies in the History of the Renaissance* (1873).
7. 'A Classic of Travel', *TLS*, November 10, 1921, p. 729.
8. Pater, the 'Conclusion' to *The Renaissance: Studies in Art and Poetry*, the 1893 text, ed. by Donald L. Hill (Berkeley: the University of California Press, 1980), p. 188. This is the 4th edition of the work by Pater in footnote 6 above.
9. RBGE RJF 4/1/1–13, letter of 26/2/1920.
10. J.A. Farrer's 'Annual Narrative', NYCRO. This is the Narrative's only mention of Reginald after his death.
11. This happens in other photographs, where it is probably not intentional; nevertheless, we could give Farrer the allowance of working towards the end of an era of Pictorialism in photography, with its enjoyment of soft focus prints.
12. Farrer's 'Some Tibetan Abbeys in China', *Quarterly Review*, vol. 227, no. 450 (Jan. 1917), 59–77, makes the point that Tibetan abbeys exist in China and adds further analysis of the vexed politics of the borderlands.
13. Reg overhears a monk calling Tien Tang 'Chorten Tang' (*RB*, p. 129). It is marked by this name on maps made by Karl E. Ryavec for his *A Historical Atlas of Tibet* (Chicago: University of Chicago Press, 2015). I can't identify the smaller establishment that Farrer calls 'Chebson'.
14. 'Some Tibetan Abbeys in China', p. 77.

15. Ibid.
16. Ibid., p. 76.
17. Farrer, 'My Second Year's Journey on the Tibetan Border of Kansu', *The Geographical Journal*, LI, 6, (June 1918) 341–59, p. 351.
18. Ibid.
19. Typists or editors struggling with Farrer's handwriting made occasional mistakes: Ardjeri is misrendered 'Ardgen' (p. 147) and the meaningless '(Fzoi)' of p. 236 was presumably F.201, the botanical number for a plant. But the present substitution of 'soul' for 'guts' can't be attributed to error of the same kind.
20. John Abercrombie, *Inquiries concerning the Intellectual Powers, and the Investigation of Truth* (1828: edition edited by Jacob Abbott, Boston and Philadelphia, 1835), p. 39.
21. Magic as a process of motivating the will is an idea argued by Éliphas Lévi (Alphonse-Louis Constant), *Dogme et Rituel de la Haute Magie*, Tome premier (4th edition, Paris: Alcan, 1903; facsimile published by Elibron Classics, 2006), p. 65. The idea is taken up by Anthony Powell in his *Daily Telegraph* review of Enid Starkie's *Arthur Rimbaud* (1962), reprinted in Powell, *Under Review: Further Writings on Writers, 1946–1990* (Chicago: University of Chicago Press, 1991), p. 434.
22. Dion Fortune (Violet Firth), *Psychic Self-Defence* (London: Rider & Co., 1930; facsimile reprint as *Psychic Self-Defense*, York Beach, Maine: Weiser, 1992), pp. 80–90. The character Theodora Clare, in Farrer's *Through the Ivory Gate*, may well be an Elemental.
23. *RB*, ibid.; Fortune, *Psychic Self-Defence*, p. 85.
24. Farrer, 'The Kansu Marches of Tibet', *Geographical Journal* XLIX (Jan to June, 1917), 106–24, p. 122. A paper read at a meeting of the Royal Geographical Society on 20 November 1916.

AFTERWORD

Transports of the Garden of Ingleborough Hall

A full history of the landscape garden at Ingleborough Hall is the work of a different project. Here, to fill out the picture of Farrer's work in landscape design, I will present a sketch only, and one particularly designed to emphasize Farrer's comprehension of the garden, and the changes he made to it. To distinguish him for generations of previous Farrers who made the garden, I shall refer to him throughout as Reginald.

Any landscape garden aspires to conceal the art by which it is made, and to look like a product of time and natural process. There are no clipped hedges, no geometrical layouts, no fountains spouting jets skywards. Nothing looks artificial: everything looks natural. This type of garden emerged in the eighteenth century, in England. The High Romantic landscape garden at Ingleborough Hall was made in the 1830s and 40s by Reginald's ancestors. The centrepiece of it was the lake, dammed and formed in Clapdale, the valley of the Clap Beck, in the 1830s.[1] At the north end of the village of Clapham is the dam, where spectacular waterfalls bring water from the lake into the village. A bridge over the sluice from the lake bears the inscribed date '1836' (figure A.1). To the east of the lake is a limestone cliff, half of it bare in Reginald's time but now completely overgrown with trees and bushes. To the west and north of the lake woodland was planted, and through it a track, originally a carriage drive, provides visitors with a path to follow. The track passes a seat made from cyclopean water-shaped limestone rocks. It passes over the Craven fault, the geological feature that allows at the surface the acidic Silurian rock strata buried over a thousand feet down everywhere else in the region. The track winds through woodland, and passes a splendid gothic covered seat, incorporating fantastically formed water-shaped stones. The seat gave a view (now almost completely occluded by invasive trees, mainly sycamore) up a grassy slope to a cliff: an outcrop of the scar limestone that stretches between Ingleborough and Pen-y-Ghent that is often mentioned by Reginald in his novels and travel books.

One characteristic of this landscape garden is that, once the visitor is within it, he or she can quickly forget about the outside world of farm tractors, economic activities, shops, and normal life. The garden seems to constitute a world of its own; sheltered by the trees not only from the sun's heat and the worst of the wind and rain, but from incursive reminders of the outside world. Views are within the garden; across the lake; to intriguing trees and other plants (figure A.2). Rock, and

FIG. A.1. The bridge at the lake, Ingleborough Hall, Clapham. Photo: author, 2016.

FIG. A.2. The lakeside. Photo: author, 2016.

Fig. A.3. Trow Ghyll. Photo: author, 2016.

stones, are prominent features. The view to the cliff of scar limestone is a view limited in lateral extent to a rare and interesting feature that itself betrays little or no evidence of the everyday world of human activities. The garden becomes a world of its own.

The track continues. The edge of the wood is reached, and beyond it about two hundred yards up the enclosed narrow valley lies the entrance to still another world: the strange world under the mountain: Ingleborough Cave, developed as a visitor attraction by Farrers from Victorian times on. The stream (beck) flows out of the cave and is crossed by a bridge taking the track another few hundred yards up the increasingly narrow valley to the gorge known as Trow Ghyll (figure A.3). Here a nineteenth-century visitor would have to descend from a carriage and walk. If he or she successfully climbed out of the top end of Trow Ghyll, the visitor would emerge on a plain into which drops the famous pothole, the 'prodigious abyss',[2] of Gaping Ghyll (first descended by a bold Frenchman in the 1890s). Reginald's own descent of this deep cleft is recorded in one of his articles.[3] The ghyll, in fictional guise, and a fictional descent of it, features at the plot climax of The Sundered Streams. Beyond and above the ghyll towers the summit of Ingleborough, from which the climber gains stupendous panoramic views absolutely removed from the mundane world suggested by suburbs, or the commuter train in and out of Leeds, or London.

So this is the garden (and the reader will see that I have appropriated to it a gorge, pothole, and mountain not strictly within the garden itself, if that be more literally defined) into which Reginald found himself emerging in his childhood (he had no doubt visited before his parents took up residence in 1889). How did it strike him?

Reginald's book, *In a Yorkshire Garden*, tells us very directly what he found valuable about the landscape garden. He delights in the lake, 'A noble work' (p. 267). Of the cliff over the lake, he describes humorously his parents' attempts to make a path along it or over it (267–68); and celebrates their surprising success:

> Now, envy my feelings when first I trod that path. In the first place, as one goes from the House [...] the prospect is really extremely beautiful and perfect. For a few yards you go under Beech-trees, on the shoulder of the hill, and then you come round that shoulder and out upon the very sheer bluff itself, with black vacancy beneath your feet, and the whole of the Lake exposed to view. Nor could you desire a view of finer composition; each pace almost gives you a fresh scheme, a fresh decorative effect. For, all along the cliff, here and there a huge arching wild-Rose far thrown over the water, or twisted Black-thorn by the path, or wryed Ash-sapling in the bank, gives you a new foil or foreground to the Lake, and the woods, and the hills behind. (268–69)

'Composition', 'scheme' (these are words implying planning), 'decorative effect'; 'arching wild-Rose', 'twisted Black-thorn', 'wryed Ash-sapling': all these phrases indicate a triumph for the picturesque, apprehended in its aesthetic sense (rather than its alleged social sense).[4] The forms of the plants frame views comprised of large landscape features: cliff, Lake, woods, hills, and it is the variety of such numerous views that purveys satisfaction in the aesthetic experience. The fore-fathers are involved, along with the parents, in that the Ash and the Blackthorn were planted, or at least not weeded out, longer ago than the time of the parents' work.

But if the parents have their triumphs, as they did with this path, they also make disasters. In his most important account of one of these, Reginald also shows a hugely, crucially, vitally, important characteristic of a great garden, in showing its value to him as an individual. Another of his parents' paths: 'doubles back into the darkness of the Yew-forest' that grows towards the top of the Cliff (288). These 'very ancient and autochthonous Yew-trees' (267) are low and spreading in habit. Reginald writes:

> But no one will ever see here what I have seen — once only and never again. For the Powers that rule created this path with noble energy and ingenuity, in and out and up through the impenetrable Yew-forest to the summit of the hill. And, when it was first opened to family inspection I walked along, and fairly gasped with the wonderfulness of it [...] For the path led on and up and round and up, through a uniform black silence of Yew-trees, dark and sombre and mysterious — a place haunted by immemorial mystery, where no sound or life had ever penetrated, and the very ground under the trees lay naked and bare. It was the actual forest in which Mélisande wandered with the Queen on her first arrival at Allemonde. And so I trusted it might continue. But the Powers that rule have a great passion for making everything plain and bare and open; so they chopped away every Yew-bough that they could possibly chop, and stripped the trunks to about six feet from the ground [...] so [...] whereas formerly, in that place of holy mystery, you wandered blindly on under the

soft darkness, having lost all trace of where you had come from, as well as any notion of where you were going to, or how you were to get to it, you can see now the whole zigzag climb from top to bottom, and it is all perfectly open and obvious and respectable, without any remnant of the glamorous mystery that once, to me, lent it so much of its commanding charm. (288–89).

Reginald describes here a state of mind that approaches an 'altered state', induced by the rarity and intensity of stimulus from the conditions; a state of forgetting where you come from, and where you are going; a feeling of being shifted into the world of the imagination (in this case into mediaeval legend); a state rare and extraordinarily valuable — one that was destroyed by his parents. 'Wonderfulness' and 'glamorous mystery' (making use of the old and original meaning of 'glamour' as magic) are set against 'plain', 'bare', 'open' and 'respectable' in a clash of values. The parents' values could perhaps be most suitable — in other walks of life; but in the aesthetics of the garden, and an attempt to harness the beautiful suggestions of the natural world, they become a disastrous inhibition.

Similar feelings of transportation to another world occur to Reginald in 'Alice's Valley' (Spring Valley), which branches off eastwards from Clapdale at the head of the Lake. The whole power of gardens to induce altered states, and take us away from the normal world to another time, or a remote place, or an alternative universe even, are not celebrated enough by garden historians. And it was such a feeling that a Chinese exile also experienced in the landscape garden of Ingleborough Hall one day in the 1930s. To understand this, we first have to comprehend how Reginald changed the garden that other Farrers had made.

He planted up the Cliff east of the Lake with alpines of various kinds. Around the bottom of the Cliff and to the north he planted, among many other plants: bulbs, anemones, trilliums, flowering cherry trees, three species of rodgersia, *Bambusa senanensis, Arundinaria nitida,* and other bamboos, some of which survive, including in 'Alice's Valley', where in *In a Yorkshire Garden* he celebrates the naturalness of the place. We saw him in Chapter 3 spending part of the winter of 1917–1918 planting the 'Black Ark', which is the rocky valley of the beck just upstream from the Lake, with his Chinese plants and with rhododendrons obtained from Edinburgh. He had previously planted bamboos next to the waterfalls there too. The Black Ark featured a series of waterfalls, and had been planted by the ancestors with oaks, firs and pines (figure A.4 shows it as illustrated in *In a Yorkshire Garden*; note the conifer at the very back of the photograph — probably a Noble Fir, at least one very tall specimen of which still survives in the valley). Rhododendrons and bamboos of Reginald's own planting still grow there. He wanted to turn the place into a 'Chinese Ghyll' (the new name in his letter to Balfour of 13/11/1917).

This brief sketch at least indicates that Reginald was interested in conjuring Asian landscape, and converting the Black Ark gorge from a perhaps Scottish or North American feeling, to an evocation of China.

Chiang Yee (1903–1977) found himself a not altogether voluntary exile in Britain from 1933 onwards.[5] In China he had been a modern man: a chemist, and after becoming the magistrate of a district, he had wanted to use aerial photography to discover property boundaries for taxation purposes. He became the enemy of one

THE BLACK ARK.

FIG. A.4. Farrer, 'The Black Ark', from *In a Yorkshire Garden*.

Fig. A.5. The three-part waterfall into the village of Clapham. Photo: author, 2016.

of China's notorious warlords. The chaotic political state of the nation eventually obliged him to seek exile. In Britain, in accordance with the conservative culture of his home upbringing, he became a traditional Chinaman, and the chemist became an artist, poet and prose writer. He started to teach Chinese language at the School of Oriental Studies (as it was; now SOAS) and he published a series of little books, prose accounts of visiting famous places in Britain, embellished by his poetry and reproductions of his paintings, all bearing titles beginning *The Silent Traveller in [...]*. In general, Chiang is very interested in the beauties of landscape and nature, proud to have been born on the slopes of Lu Mountain, a place in central China famous to the Chinese literati of previous centuries for its landscape beauties. His visits to celebrated British landscape, such as the Lake District and North Wales, tended, however, to be disappointing in one respect. He always hoped that the places would remind him strongly of China, and he writes that he was constantly disappointed. Chiang's book that is relevant to our purposes, *The Silent Traveller in the Yorkshire Dales,* appeared in 1941, but the visits to the region that occasioned the book had started in the late 1930s, after his visits to Wales and the Lakes, when this lonely homesick Chinaman had been befriended by Sir William Milner, of Parcevall Hall, Appletreewick. In the book Chiang Yee recounts a visit the two men paid to Clapham.

On this occasion the visit begins with an appointment for tea with Reginald's brother, Sydney (1882–1946), and his wife in their house at Newby Cote (finances of the Ingleborough estate had evidently necessitated a move out of Ingleborough Hall). Chiang is shown flower-paintings by Reginald. Sydney tells him that he himself is just learning water-colour drawing, and Chiang looks at his efforts. The party visits the garden at Ingleborough Hall. Chiang describes:

> I was led by my host to a hillside along the foot of which there ran a narrow path. We had to walk in single file as a large pool bordered the path. [...] I was most surprised to see all around me familiar garden forms. By the pool grew dwarf bamboos, willows, maples, cherry trees and peach trees. In the light of the spring afternoon the fresh red of the peach blossoms mingling with the new green leaves of the bamboos took me back in a flash to my homeland. Here was really something of China. My mind had suddenly filled with a picture of endless blossoming peach groves by a certain stream I used to know, and of azaleas smiling over hill slopes with their blood-red lips apart. Presently I realized that my host was speaking to me in a foreign language, and it came back to me that I was not in China but in Yorkshire. The stillness of the atmosphere — there was not a ripple on the surface of the pool — had allowed my mind to carry me unawares to the other side of the earth.[6]

This is it. This is the only place (until he reaches the park of Buttes-Chaumont in Paris, after the Second World War) that takes Chiang home. It is, as he clearly states, the plants that perform this power; and we can recognize in the phrase: 'azaleas smiling over hill slopes with their blood-red lips apart' a homage to Reginald Farrer. Chiang tells us that the garden also reminds him of Chinese gardens (for example, the three-part waterfall into the village, figure A.5) and he even mentions a famous Chinese garden in Souchow,[7] but there is a difference between being 'reminded' of a place and the stronger mental sensation of being 'taken' to his homeland, and its landscape (rather than its gardens). Chiang Yee, worried about war in general, the Japanese invasion of his homeland in particular, and depressed by the recent death of his brother, needed this respite; this refreshing brief visit to his beloved home. Reginald Farrer had aimed to make his garden 'the miracle of England'.[8] The Great War, and his early death, had foreclosed on that possibility. But he had at least worked a miracle for one lonely Chinese exile.

Notes to the Afterword

1. John Buglass and Michael Pearson give the date of 1828 for beginning of the works: 'Austwick Hall, Near Settle, Yorkshire: An Archaeological Survey of a Woodland Landscape', *Garden History*, 42:2 (2014), 266–73, p. 270. They cite Beck (see next note) p. 121, who, however, does not himself cite a source for the date.
2. 'Professor T. McKenny Hughes', quoted in Howard M. Beck, *Gaping Gill: 150 years of exploration* (London: Robert Hale, 1984), p. 24. On the entire landscape of Ingleborough, I strongly recommend the little book by Kevin Dixon, *Gaping Gill: a guide for visitors to Gaping Gill pothole and surface* (York: Geospatial3D, 2015).
3. 'Gaping Ghyll', *Blackwoods Magazine* (July, 1908), 93–103.
4. For a discussion of the picturesque, see Michael Charlesworth, 'Theories of the Picturesque', in *A Companion to British Art 1600 to the Present*, ed. by Dana Arnold and David Peters Corbett (Chichester: Wiley-Blackwell, 2013), pp. 351–72.

5. See the biography by Da Zheng, *Chiang Yee: the Silent Traveller from the East* (Piscataway, New Jersey: Rutgers University Press, 2010).

6. Chiang Yee, *The Silent Traveller in the Yorkshire Dales* (London: Methuen, 1941), p. 72.

7. Ibid., p. 73. Chiang likes the Black Ark, and wants to linger there, but is moved on by the Farrers and Milner before his admiration of it is complete. The Chinese garden he mentions is 'Chueh-Cheng-Yuan'.

8. Letter to his mother, 27/7/1910: see Chapter 1 n. 26.

APPENDIX

Vasanta the Beautiful

Farrer's verse drama, *Vasanta the Beautiful: a Homily in Four Acts* was published, apparently by Farrer himself, in 1913. Description of it is included here as an Appendix
because I don't regard it as critically problematic. Nor is it about landscape. But as
evidence of Farrer's understanding of Buddhism, and of his poetry, it merits a place
in this study.

The genre of the verse drama — poetry never intended for theatrical performance,
but presented in the form of a play — arguably reached its high moment nearly
a century before with such works by Shelley and Byron, or a little later with
Swinburne's *Atalanta in Calydon*. W. B. Yeats still used the form, at least until the
1920s, but the genre's life in the twentieth century was a rapid process of dwindling
to an obsolete status. Farrer was interested in real plays, as his time as drama critic
for *The Speaker*, and his writing of 'Hearts and Diamonds', that competent amateur
farce, show. He had also published a previous verse drama, *The Dowager of Jerusalem:
A Romance in Four Acts* (1908). The interest for us in *Vasanta the Beautiful* lies in its
Buddhist theme. In working out this theme, the poem also demonstrates Farrer's
conviction that the accidental and unpredictable have to be embraced in the process
of developing as a human being; the process of creating understanding, even
wisdom, in an individual, in perhaps what might even be termed a human spirit.

The poem is set in a non-specific ancient past of India. It gains its title ('vasanta'
meaning the season of Spring in Sanskrit) from its protagonist, Vasanta, the most
beautiful dancer and most beautiful woman any of the other characters has ever
seen. Unfortunately she is also a courtesan, whose rapacity is made clear in the first
act as she beggars a rich man, Varshakara, who lusts for possession of her. Outside
the house in which this transaction takes place, and quite by chance, Ananda, the
Buddha's disciple, passes by, accompanying the king as he returns from a meeting
with the Buddha. The company invite Ananda up into the house. Vasanta thus meets
him, and, jaded as she is by male appetites, nevertheless develops a genuine, and
amorous, interest in him. Ananda refuses to engage in private meetings with her.

Act Two takes place by night in the forest in which the Buddha lives (though at
a distance from him). Vasanta bumps into the King, who, despite having had an
audience with the Buddha the previous day, is experiencing back-sliding (following
the Buddha's way is not a miracle; it takes will-power). He develops a passion for
Vasanta. He tries to see her as 'only bones and blood' (p. 27), which would be a

Buddhist discipline, but fails. In fact, musing on the nature of love, he aligns with the theme and view of love taken in Farrer's novel *The Sundered Streams*. Vasanta says, 'Why do you love me?' The King replies:

> What sage or saint can tell us why we love?
> — Some flash of ancient memory seen by chance...
> Some cry of dead things robed anew in flesh
> And unforgotten. There's no clue but that,
> Why thousands pass unnoticed, and then *one,*
> Going swiftly by, with a glance or turn of the head,
> Consumes our life in hers for evermore
> As dust in licking flame... And so — you are I! (p. 26).

This view of love is entirely possessive. The King feels, in Vasanta, 'something intimate and known | And mine, through aeons — potent and magical, | And *mine.* — '

During their conversation it transpires that Vasanta would like the King to kill Varshakara, to whom she is now committed by a financial and legal agreement. The King promises. A distant bell is heard, as is a chorus singing: 'I take my refuge in the Brotherhood, the Truth, and in the Perfect One.' The King echoes each statement, and, recalled to his better self by hearing this version of the vows of commitment to Buddhism, abruptly leaves (p. 31). While Vasanta's bad servant makes a speech urging her to pursue the path of what all the world admires: 'Success made proudly manifest in gold' (which would mean breaking her undertaking to Varshakara and seducing the King), her good servant, Mandara, fetches Ananda. He tells Vasanta that she is not following the way of peace: 'You crave the calm | And the tempest too, with all its ecstasies.' Vasanta addresses him in a way that shows the phallic element imperfectly concealed:

> You are the one sole need I have!
> And the ivory glory of your manhood's strength,
> So white and bare beneath your single robe,
> Shines clearer than the wisdom of all Kings —
> O moonlight gleaming through the darkened grove,
> O pillar of marble lonely on the hills,
> The shape of your wonder tugs my secret self
> To thoughts that have not moved its depths before —
> O dawn of spring on the mountains, O young lion,
> O chill fresh wind of the snows, blow down on me,
> To cool my desert sands — (pp. 33–34).

Ananda promises to be there when she really needs peace, and leaves. Vasanta, thirsty, asks a passing poor woman for a drink of water. The Buddha has that night made the woman the same request, and drunk from her bowl. Rather than break the bowl or revere it by not allowing it to be used again, the woman reasons that: 'He set me free | So I must do for all as He for me.' (p. 38) Vasanta drinks from this highly auspicious bowl that has touched the Buddha's lips.

A woman appears, a stranger, a better dancer than Vasanta. Her name is Samsara, and she is 'Love', she tells Vasanta. 'Samsara' is the term for the never-ending cycle of rebirths to which we are doomed if we cannot become enlightened. Farrer called this 'the bitter sea of life and death' in *The Garden of Asia*. A better dancer, this stranger is also more beautiful than Vasanta; and Vasanta has consistently put her faith in her own beauty and dancing ability and the way she can manipulate men. The stranger goes to sleep with her head on Vasanta's lap. The bad servant urges Vasanta to strangle her, but she refrains; and in the depth of the night a voice 'like a vast bell' is heard:

> All things that were are as all things to be;
> And the same slumber waits for me and thee.
> We move on endless roads, and, in our change,
> Form passes into wonders new and strange.
> Yet all those shapes of cloud are born in pain,
> To part, and meet; and meet, to part again,
> Unfixed, unresting always; — set your store,
> Where life meets life indeed, and parts no more.
> So read that book which lies upon your knee,
> Whose word shall rend the veil and set you free. (pp. 41–42).

By now the stranger has become a skeleton. Vasanta leaps up in horror and disgust, scattering the bones, and addresses the skull: 'Are you my *self*? The thing I trust [...] Ah, who has shown me that this my world is smoke | And my faith a shadow?' The answer, of course, provided by Mandara, is 'Lord Buddha'. The transformation of Samsara has been an object-lesson in *Anicca*, impermanence.

Act III sees Vasanta divided against herself, and backsliding. As pledged to, she meets Varshakara in (what is now) her opulent house (once his). She is reluctant to bestow sexual favours on him. He grapples her to him. They struggle. Vasanta, wishing only to deter his lusts before they arrive at rape, stabs him with her knife, but unfortunately kills him. She and the servants pile cushions on the corpse, and Vasanta entertains the King on the soft heap. Before things can come to a climax, however, Varshakara's brother bursts in and the corpse is discovered. Then ensues a working-out of karma: disgusted with himself as a result of the previous conversation with Vasanta about the desirability of Varshakara's death, the King has turned over the administration of justice for a week to Varshakara's brother.

The scene of Act IV is the graveyard. Mutilated and blinded, Vasanta has been thrown there. She and her faithful servant Mandara are revealed in a *coup de théatre*: after some minor characters have described her fate and left, Mandara throws back a covering that had concealed the pair as part of the shadowy background. Vasanta curses her tormentors. She feels her soul to be a loom, frantically active, weaving nothing. She wishes Ananda were with her, still perceiving beauty in him — but not bodily beauty anymore; instead something dimly seen within or through him. She realizes that her previous approach to Ananda's beauty and love were framed in 'harlot's language' and 'words of shame' (p. 78). She hears someone approaching. Ananda appears. In bitterness, assuming he will mock her, she offers him her severed hands:

> take those pale cold hands
> That have lain like snowflakes fallen from strange heavens
> Upon the fevered breasts of many Kings;

> And these my feet, so dead and waxen-white,
> Went lightly once as moonbeams o'er a pool
> Among dark branches dancing: now they are still. (p. 79)

Vasanta still regrets that she can no longer offer him her physical charms, or, as she puts it:

> My whole abundance in the days gone by.
> I was fragrant as the lotus then, and sweet
> As breath of blossoms in a temple-shrine;
> And crowned with jasmine, and wreathed about with gems,
> And radiant with great suns of diamond,
> And bathed in love [...]

Ananda tells her that her beauty is in her heart. Vasanta begins to feel more calm. She understands that she has been 'evil' and that she 'struggles in hates and angers' (p. 80). Ananda urges the abandonment of desire. Vasanta, repudiating her former beauty that: 'served me as a trap | To snare the beautiful things that lived in me | And turn them dreadful', demonstrates by saying this that she understands that the crucially important factor is not whether she ensnared weak men (their karmic fate, after all, was up to them), but instead the dynamics at work inside *her*. She asks if her present love for Ananda is evil. He replies, 'You are I'; says, 'I am wholly you'; and calls her 'beautiful' (p. 82). This first phrase, used by the King earlier in the service of his possessiveness, but now collapsing the intersubjective exchange that is the foundation of separation and distinction, recurs here in a very different context, where Ananda and Vasanta are not grasping after each other physically, but turning towards a whole. In the last pages there is just an intimation that individual loves, pursued through ages of past lives (as in the plot of *The Sundered Streams*) are subsumed within the 'All'. Ananda says:

> The walls are down
> That hid your beauty always from my gaze
> Through lives of waiting search.
> *Vasanta:*   O, glad farewell
> To everything I was, since now I stand
> Unveiled and known at last by what I sought
> Unwitting in those many shadow-shapes.

This exchange intimates a time-span beyond that of the play, or, indeed, of single lives. Vasanta questions subjectivity: 'I love you... and I think I leave you now... | I-? I-? What *I* takes on this load of mine?' She has overcome desire and hate, and her last words are: 'Raise me... I take my refuge in the Truth... | I take my Refuge on the Royal Path... | — My final... Refuge... in the Perfect One!' The last words of the poem, however, belong to Ananda, assuring a bereft and grieving Mandara of what seems very like an 'All': 'For all roads meet in the great end of things | Where all roads cease...' (p.84).

   This reading therefore sees the play as a more optimistic working out of things than was allowed to the protagonist, Kingston Darnley, of Farrer's most Buddhist novel. By the end of *The Sundered Streams* Kingston's future is to be looking after his mad wife, mourning his dead son, and wondering how his mad love for a dead woman brought disaster upon them all. Precisely because it is set in mythic times, with mythic characters, and deals with death and Buddhist consolation, *Vasanta* achieves a solemnity of its own. A reader of Farrer's Buddhist fiction will not absorb a view of *nirvana* that aligns it with a chief nineteenth-century European objection, that of nihilism.[1] The ideas of progress (for Isabel in the novel) and consolation (for Vasanta in the poem) emerge very strongly.

In verse drama Farrer can indulge the poetry that sometimes interferes with his realist novels. For the most part it is not very memorable poetry; but it has its moments. The final act, at least the part of it that features Vasanta, is short. The poetry of it is subdued, shorn of flourishes, rather straightforward. Its presentation of a dying Vasanta, agonizing and enraged, humiliated and terrified, without her hands, feet and eyes, struggling for self-control, with Ananda able to give her comfort, is poignant, plaintive and affecting. This part of the play amounts to bleak but rather good poetry about dying: about overcoming resentment, desire and anger to achieve a good death, which features trust, faith and peace of mind.

★   ★   ★   ★   ★

I think it is obvious, from what I have said about Farrer's Buddhism throughout these pages, that, of the three 'refuges' which he had embraced that day (5th February 1908) in Ceylon, the one from which he was never able to withdraw his scepticism, was the *sangha* (the Buddhist community — which means the entire institution of Buddhism, in which the monastic community is predominant). He took refuge in the Buddha, often using the term 'the Perfect One'. He says himself, in *The Rainbow Bridge*, that he holds 'the Law' (that is, the *dharma*). But his view of monks and monastic communities was always tinged with scepticism (although, as we have seen, he also defended them). The community that most attracted him, at Tien Tang, held the attractions of humanity and enabled him to indulge his delight in fellow human beings, but his descriptions of it do not feature the spiritual idea particularly strongly (though that, of course, is implicit). The spiritual element comes over more resoundingly in his rapturous description of the 'Pink Temple' above Siku. In London he was part of a kind of Buddhist community (the Buddhist Society of Great Britain), as was his friend from Japan, Eric Collier, and the Yorkshire landowner the 5th Earl of Mexborough, among others. Yet the Society hardly counted as equivalent to the strength implied by the *sangha*. In *Vasanta* the *sangha* is represented, if at all, by Ananda; but since Ananda was the first and best of the Buddha's disciples, and is dramatized on his own in the play, he is exceptional rather than representative of a community of monks.

This leads to the thought that Buddhism was attractive to Farrer because of its belief that a person's fate lies in their own thoughts and actions. No redeemer stands in for us; no Calvinistic deity condemns us before we are even born. No god judges us. The idea of being responsible for his own destiny was no doubt liberating for Farrer. Although Buddhism is famous for requiring the abandonment of the ego, and for declaring the lack of fixed personality or inherent existence (*anatta*), nevertheless its teaching that the individual's fate is of their own making (*karma*) was freeing. It enabled a conjunction, or lack of contradiction, to occur between

Buddhist beliefs, on one hand, and Farrer's lifelong search for individuation, on the other. In response to Vasanta's offer of her body (an offer that indicates she is content to live within her physical or material appetites and the usual way she has of attaining them) Ananda says to her in Act II of Farrer's verse drama, 'You are... emptiness | [...] never yet have you found the You in you, | The thing abiding.' (p.36). Telling her she is emptiness, Ananda means that Vasanta (as everybody in this view) is without inherent existence, that Farrer termed 'fixed personality' — a difficult concept sometimes translated during Farrer's own lifetime as 'soul', in accordance with the Christian idea of a consciousness persisting beyond death.[2] Denying that she has found 'the You in you', Ananda says that Vasanta has not developed the potential Buddhahood in herself, (the Buddha-germ, *tathāgatagarbha*). Such a belief makes sense of Ananda's speech, and accords with some of the ideas discussed in Chapter 4. In this view the rejection of the idea of a self as inherently existing is an act of free will, while a continuation in living within the idea of an inherent existence allows a person to be preyed upon by all the determinisms of the world. And in the meantime a strong grasp on Buddhist teaching acts to guide followers past the difficulties and pitfalls presented by chance events, thus allowing such accidental happenings to become understood as part of the process of personal growth. Ananda resists all sorts of temptations, and refuses various charitable donations on the grounds that they are tainted by the way they have been acquired by the would-be giver. Unlike the other characters, he thinks of the consequences of his actions, rather than simply whether they would suit present desires or instant gratifications.

So individuation, the conscious process of creating the self, of learning how to live as an individual whose fate is of one's own making, all of which involves the choice of what self the individual wishes to be, can be pursued beyond the delusion of personality and its entrapping impulse of entitlement. When Vasanta questions the ego on the last page ('I -- ? I -- ? What *I* takes on this load of mine?) the action is part of her process of finding the 'You' that Ananda has spoken of previously, and sloughing off the mistaken idea of self that simply used her sexuality to pursue material things. Farrer's most profound lifelong impulses — to understand what it is to be an individual; and to learn the processes by which an individual responds to circumstances; were greatly helped and stimulated by Buddhist teaching and practice as he understood those.

Notes to the Appendix

1. This topic is analyzed in Guy Welbon, *The Buddhist Nirvāna and its Western Interpreters* (Chicago: The University of Chicago Press, 1968). See also Ananda Wickremeratne, *The Genesis of an Orientalist: Thomas William Rhys Davids and Buddhism in Sri Lanka* (Delhi: Motilal Banarsidass, 1984), pp. 195–97, 220–23.

2. Farrer employs the term 'without fixed personality' for the Pali word *anatta* in *In Old Ceylon*, p. 347. The Sanskrit word is *Anātman*. The equation of *ātman* with 'soul' is described in Judith Snodgrass, *Presenting Japanese Buddhism to the West: Orientalism, Occidentalism, and the Columbian Exposition* (Chapel Hill: University of North Carolina Press, 2003), pp. 6, 220, 237.

BIBLIOGRAPHY

Archive Collections

The major Reginald Farrer archive is held by the Royal Botanic Gardens Edinburgh: GB RJF.

The Royal Horticultural Society, Lindley Library, London: Farrer, Purdom and E.A. Bowles holdings.

North Yorkshire County Record Office, Northallerton: Farrer family at Ingleborough Hall, Clapham.

Somerset County Archives, Taunton: Aubrey Herbert papers.

Sri Lanka National Archives, Colombo: *The Times of Ceylon*; and the Branch library at Kandy: Government Agent's Diary.

West Yorkshire Archive Service, Leeds: Ingleborough estate papers.

Harry Ransom Humanities Research Center, University of Texas at Austin: Farrer's letter to Osbert Sitwell, Sitwell archive.

Select Bibliography of Farrer's Works

Published in London unless otherwise specified.

'The Geisha: a Faithful Study', *The Nineteenth Century*, LV (April 1904), pp. 630–36.

The Garden of Asia: Impressions from Japan (Methuen, 1904).

'Some British Alpines', *Flora and Sylva*, III, (1905), pp. 330–34.

The House of Shadows (Arnold, 1906).

My Rock Garden (Arnold, 1907).

The Sundered Streams: the history of a memory that had no full stops (Arnold, 1907).

'Gaping Ghyll', *Blackwoods Magazine* (July, 1908), pp. 93–103.

In Old Ceylon (Arnold, 1908).

Alpines and Bog Plants (Arnold, 1908).

Ways of Rebellion (Arnold, 1908).

The Dowager of Jerusalem: a Romance in Four Acts (Arnold, 1908).

In a Yorkshire Garden (Arnold, 1909).

The Anne-Queen's Chronicle (Rivers, 1909).

Among the Hills: a book of joy in high places (Headley Brothers, Bishopsgate, 1911).

Through the Ivory Gate (Palmer, 1912).

The Rock-Garden (T.C. & E.C. Jack, 1912).

The Dolomites: King Laurin's Garden (Black, 1913).

Vasanta the Beautiful: a homily in four acts (verse drama, probably self-published: 1913).

'In Central China', *The Spectator* (May 23, 1914: unpaginated copy at RBGE (RJF 2/1/3/6).

'The "White Wolf "in Kansu', *Quarterly Review* (April 1915), pp. 353–69.

'Some Tibetan Abbeys in China', *Quarterly Review*, vol. 227, no. 450, (Jan. 1917), 59–77.

'The Kansu Marches of Tibet', *The Geographical Journal* XLIX (Jan to June, 1917), 106–24.
'Catalogue of an Exhibition of Water-colours by Reginald Farrer of Scenes and Flowers in Western China and Tibet' (The Fine Art Society, 148 New Bond Street: April, 1917).
'Jane Austen, ob. July 18 1817', *Quarterly Review* (July 1917), 1–30.
On the Eaves of the World, 2 vols. (Arnold, 1917).
'My Second Year's Journey on the Tibetan Border of Kansu' *The Geographical Journal* LI, 6, (June 1918), 340–59.
The Void of War: Letters from Three Fronts (Constable, 1918).
The English Rock Garden, 2 vols. (T.C. & E.C. Jack Ltd., 1919).
The Rainbow Bridge (Arnold, 1921).
The most comprehensive bibliography of Farrer's works remains that compiled by W. T. Stearn for E.H.M. Cox's *The Plant Introductions of Reginald Farrer* (London: New Flora, 1930). Although Stearn painstakingly lists all Farrer many contributions to the *Royal Horticultural Society Journal* and to *The Gardener's Chronicle*, his list is not quite complete: it lacks the articles from 1905, 1908 and May 1914 listed above. Neither Stearn nor I list Farrer's theatre reviews in *The Speaker: the Liberal Review* (1904–1905).

Other Authors

ABERCROMBIE, JOHN, *Inquiries concerning the Intellectual Powers, and the Investigation of Truth* (1828: edition edited by Jacob Abbott, Boston and Philadelphia, 1835).
ALDINGTON, RICHARD, *Death of a Hero* (London: Chatto & Windus, 1929. London: The Hogarth Press, 1984).
ALDRICH, JOHN, *Cultural Encounters and Homoeroticism in Sri Lanka: Sex and Serendipity* (London: Routledge, 2004).
ANON ('A Native of Craven'), *Horae Momenta Cravenae, or, The Craven Dialect, Exemplified in Two Dialogues between Farmer Giles and his neighbour Bridget, to which is annexed a glossary* (London, n.p., 1824).
ANON, *Insight Guides: Sri Lanka* (Singapore: Apa Publications, 2009).
ARNOLD, DANA, and DAVID PETERS CORBETT, eds, *A Companion to British Art 1600 to the Present* (Chichester: Wiley-Blackwell, 2013).
AUSTEN, JANE, *Lady Susan, The Watsons, Sanditon* (Harmondsworth: Penguin, 1974).
BABINGTON-SMITH, CONSTANCE, *Air Spy: the Story of Photo Intelligence in World War II* (New York: Harper, 1957).
BAIRNSFATHER, BRUCE, 'Still More Bystander Fragments from France', VOL. III (London: "The Bystander", n.d., but 1917).
BANN, STEPHEN, *The Clothing of Clio: A study of the representation of history in nineteenth-century Britain and France* (Cambridge: Cambridge University Press, 1984).
—— *Ways Around Modernism* (London: Routledge, 2007).
BATEMAN, JOHN, *The Great Landowners of Great Britain* (London: 4th edition, 1883).
BECK, HOWARD M., *Gaping Gill: 150 years of exploration* (London: Hale, 1984).
BENNETT, ALAN, *Untold Stories* (London: Faber and Faber, 2005).
BENVENISTE, ÉMILE, *Problèmes de Linguistique Générale* (Paris: Gallimard, 1968).
BLACKBURN, ANNE, *Locations of Buddhism: Colonialism and Modernity in Sri Lanka* (Chicago: The University of Chicago Press, 2010).
BOND, GEORGE, 'Theravada Buddhism's Meditations on Death and the Symbolism of Initiatory Death', *History of Religions* 19, 3 (1980), 237–58.
BRADSHAW, D., and K. J. H. DETTMARR, eds, *A Companion to Modernist Literature and Culture* (Oxford: Blackwell, 2006).
BUCKLEY, THEODORE, *Aristotle's Treatise on Rhetoric, literally translated from the Greek* (3rd edn, 1846: London: Bohn, 1853).

BUGLASS, JOHN, and MICHAEL PEARSON, 'Austwick Hall, Near Settle, Yorkshire: An Archaeological Survey of a Woodland Landscape', *Garden History*, 42:2 (2014), 266–73.

BURNET, THOMAS, *The Sacred Theory of the Earth* (London, n. p., 1684).

CARACCIOLO, PETER, 'Buddhist Teaching Stories and their Influence on Conrad, Wells, and Kipling: the Reception of the Jataka and Allied Genres in Victorian Culture', *The Conradian*, 11, 1 (May 1986), 24–34.

—— 'Buddhist Typologies in "Heart of Darkness" and "Victory" and their Contribution to the Modernism of Jacob Epstein, Wyndham Lewis and T. S. Eliot', *The Conradian*, 14, 1/2 (December 1989), 67–91.

CARUS, P., and M. VERHOEVEN, *The Gospel of Buddha According to Old Records* (various editions before 1915; Peru, Illinois: Open Court, 2004).

CHANTLER, A., and R. HAWKES (eds.) *Ford Madox Ford's Parade's End: The First World War, Culture, and Modernity*, International Ford Madox Ford Studies 13 (Amsterdam: Rodopi, 2014).

CHARLESWORTH, MICHAEL, *Landscape and Vision in Nineteenth-Century Britain and France* (Aldershot: Ashgate, 2008).

CHEEKE, STEPHEN, '"Fantastic Modernism": Walter Pater, Botticelli, and Simonetta', *Word & Image*, 32, 2 (April-June 2016), 195–206.

CHIANG, YEE, *The Silent Traveller in the Yorkshire Dales* (London: Methuen, 1941).

COHN, DORRIT, *Transparent Minds: Narrative Modes for Presenting Consciousness in Fiction* (Princeton: Princeton University Press, 1978).

CONDER, JOSIAH, *Landscape Gardening in Japan* (1893: reprint New York: Dover, 1964).

COOMARASWAMY, ANANDA KENTISH, 'An Open Letter to the Kandyan Chiefs' (Kandy: 1905; New Edition, Colombo: Arts Council of Ceylon, 1957).

CORBETT, DAVID PETERS, 'Crossing the Boundary: British Art across Victorianism and Modernism', in *A Companion to British Art 1600 to the Present* ed. Dana Arnold and David Peters Corbett (Chichester: Wiley-Blackwell, 2013), pp. 131–55.

COX, E. H. M., *Farrer's Last Journey: Upper Burma 1919–20* (London: Dulau, 1926).

—— *Plant Hunting in China: A History of Botanical Exploration in China and the Tibetan Marches* (London: Collins, 1945).

DA ZHENG, *Chiang Yee: the Silent Traveller from the East* (Piscataway, New Jersey: Rutgers University Press, 2010).

DANGERFIELD, GEORGE, *The Strange Death of Liberal England* (London: Constable, 1936).

DAVIDS, T. W. RHYS, *Lectures on the Origin and Growth of Religion as Illustrated by Some Points in the History of Indian Buddhism* (London: Williams and Norgate, 1881).

DAVIS, RICHARD H., *The Bhagavad Gita* (Princeton: Princeton University Press, 2014).

DAVIS, WADE, *Into the Silence: The Great War, Mallory, and the Conquest of Everest* (New York: Knopf, 2012).

DIDUR, JILL, '"The Perverse Little People of the Hills": Unearthing Ecology and Transculturation in Reginald Farrer's Alpine Plant Hunting', in E. DeLoughry, J. Didur, A Carrigan, eds, *Global Ecologies and the Environmental Humanities: Postcolonial Approaches* (London: Routledge, 2015), pp. 51–72.

DISSANAIKE, A., 'The Land Settlement Policy under the Waste Lands Ordinance in Ceylon', *Ceylon National Review* 9 (March 1910), 130–32.

DIXON, KEVIN, *Gaping Gill: a guide for visitors to Gaping Gill pothole and surface* (York: Geospatial3D, 2015).

DOAN, LAURA and JANE GARRITY, 'Modernism Queered', in D. Bradshaw and K. J. H. Dettmarr, eds, *A Companion to Modernist Literature and Culture* (Oxford: Blackwell, 2006), pp. 545–48.

ELLIOTT, CLARENCE, 'The Late Reginald Farrer: an Appreciation', *The Gardeners' Chronicle*, (15 January 1921), 31.

EVANS, T. F., ed., *George Bernard Shaw: The Critical Heritage* (London: Routledge, 1997).

FARRER, CECIL, LORD FARRER, *Some Farrer Family Memorials: Being a Selection from the Papers of Thomas Henry, First Lord Farrer 1819–1899, on Various Matters Connected with his Life; together with Notes relating to some Branches of the Family of Greystoneley, Ingleborough, Abinger, between 1610 & 1923, made by his Son, Thomas Cecil, Second Lord Farrer* (London: Privately Printed, 1923).

FISHER, F. H., ed., *Reginald Farrer, Author, Traveller, Botanist and Flower Painter* (The Alpine Garden Society: A Bound Edition of the *Alpine Garden Society's Bulletin* vol. 1 no. 10, 1932).

FITZHERBERT, MARGARET, *The Man who was Greenmantle: a biography of Aubrey Herbert* (London: Murray, 1983).

FLETCHER, IAN, *Swinburne* (Harlow: The Longman Group for the British Council, 1973).

—— *W. B. Yeats and his Contemporaries* (New York: St. Martin's Press, 1987).

FONTANIER, PIERRE, *Les Figures du Discours* (1827. Paris: Flammarion, 1977).

FORD, FORD MADOX, *Joseph Conrad: A Personal Remembrance* (1924. New York, Ecco Press, 1989).

—— *Parade's End* (1924–1928. London: Campbell, 1992).

FORTUNE, DION (Violet Firth), *Psychic Self-Defence* (London: Rider, 1930).

FUSSELL, PAUL, *The Great War and Modern Memory* (Oxford: Oxford University Press, 1975).

GOUGH, PAUL, 'The Living, the Dead, and the Imagery of Emptiness and Re-appearance on the Battlefields of the Western Front', in *Deathscapes:New Spaces for Death, Dying, and Bereavement* (Farnham: Ashgate, 2010), pp. 263–81.

GYATSO, TENZIN, HIS HOLINESS THE 14TH DALAI LAMA OF TIBET, *The Joy of Living and Dying in Peace* (New York: Harper Collins, 1997).

—— *The Meaning of Life: Buddhist Perspectives on Cause and Effect*, 1992 (Boston: Wisdom, 2000).

HARISCHANDRA, W., *The Sacred City of Anuradhapura, with forty-six illustrations* (1908; New Delhi: Asian Educational Services, 1985).

HARMER, J. B., *Victory in Limbo: imagism, 1908–1917* (London: Secker & Warburg, 1975).

HARRIS, E., *Theravada Buddhism and the British Encounter: Religious, Missionary and Colonial Experience in Nineteenth-Century Sri Lanka* (London: Routledge, 2006).

HASLAM, SARA, *Fragmenting Modernism: Ford Madox Ford, the Novel and the Great War* (Manchester: Manchester University Press, 2002).

HAWKES, JACQUETTA, *A Land* (London: The Cresset Press, 1951).

HAZAMA, JIKŌ, 'The Characteristics of Japanese Tendai', *Japanese Journal of Religious Studies* 14, 2–3 (1987), 101–12.

HINTON, WILLIAM, *Shenfan: the Continuing Revolution in a Chinese Village* (New York: Vintage, 1984).

HOLMES, C. J., *Self and Partners (Mostly Self): Being the Reminiscences of C. J. Holmes* (New York: Macmillan, 1936).

HOLT, J. C., and P. B. MEEGASKUMBURA, eds, *Identity and Difference: Essays on Society and Culture in Sri Lanka* (Kandy: Intercollegiate Sri Lanka Educational Program, 2006).

ILLINGWORTH, JOHN, and JANE ROUTH, eds, *Reginald Farrer: Dalesman, Planthunter, Gardener* (Lancaster: Centre for North-West Regional Studies, University of Lancaster, Occasional Paper no. 19, 1991).

INGWERSEN, W. E. TH., 'Reginald Farrer and his Influence on Present-Day Rock Gardening', in *Reginald Farrer, Author, Traveller, Botanist and Flower Painter*, ed. by F. H. Fisher (The Alpine Garden Society: A Bound Edition of the *Alpine Garden Society's Bulletin* Vol. 1 No. 10, 1932), 34–38.

JAMES, HENRY, 'The Art of Fiction' (1884, rev. ed. 1888) in W. Veeder and S. M. Griffin, eds, *The Art of Criticism: Henry James on the Theory and Practice of Fiction* (Chicago: University of Chicago Press, 1986).

JOHNSON, CLAUDIA L., *Jane Austen's Cults and Cultures* (Chicago: University of Chicago Press, 2012).

KARUNARATNE, NIHAL, *Udavattekälē: the Forbidden Forest of the Kings of Kandy* (Colombo: Department of National Archives, 1986).

KERN, STEPHEN, *The Culture of Time and Space 1880–1918* (New Haven: Harvard University Press, 1983 & 2003).

KIPLING, RUDYARD, *Kim* (London: Macmillan, 1901).

KIRKPATRICK, B. J., 'Virginia Woolf — unrecorded TLS reviews', *Modern Fiction Studies*, 38, 1 (1992), 279–301.

LAWRENCE, D. H., *Kangaroo* (1923. Harmondsworth: Penguin, 1977).

LEOSHKO, JANICE, 'What is in *Kim*? Rudyard Kipling and Tibetan Buddhist Traditions', *South Asia Research*, 21, 1 (2001), 51–75.

LESDAIN, COUNT DE, *From Pekin to Sikkim Through the Ordos, the Gobi Desert, and Tibet* (London: Murray, 1908).

LÉVI, ÉLIPHAS, (Alphonse-Louis Constant), *Dogme et Rituel de la Haute Magie* Tome premier (4th edition, Paris, 1903; facsimile published by Elibron Classics, 2006).

LINROTHE, ROB, 'Travel Albums and Revisioning Narratives: A Case Study in the Getty's Fleury "Cachemire" Album of 1908', in Ali Behdad and Luke Gartlan, eds, *Photography's Orientalism: New Essays on Colonial Representation* (Los Angeles: Getty Research Institute, 2013), 171–84.

LLOYD, CHRISTOPHER, 'The Jarman Garden Experience' in *Derek Jarman: A Portrait*, ed. by R. Wollen (London: Thames and Hudson, 1996), pp. 147–52.

LOOS, TAMARA, *Bones Around My Neck: The life and exile of a prince provocateur*, (Ithaca, NY: Cornell University Press, 2016).

LOPEZ, DONALD S., JR., *Buddhism and Science: A Guide for the Perplexed* (Chicago: The University of Chicago Press, 2008).

—— '"Lamaism" and the Disappearance of Tibet', *Comparative Studies in Society and History*, 38, 1 (Jan 1996), 3–25.

LOTI, PIERRE, *Japan (Madame Chrysanthème)* trans. Laura Ensor (New York: Frederick A. Stokes Company, n.d.).

LYTE, CHARLES, *The Plant Hunters* (London: Orbis, 1983).

MACADAM, THOMAS, 'A Wonderful New Kind of Rock Garden', *Country Life in America*, v. 21, (April 15, 1912), 49.

MALVERN, SUE, *Modern Art, Britain and the Great War: witnessing, testimony and remembrance* (New Haven: Yale University Press, 2004).

MARLOWE, CHRISTOPHER, *The Complete Plays*, ed. M. T. Burnett (London: Everyman, 1999).

MARSH, DAVID '"An Amateurish Effort"? The Foundation of the National Botanic Gardens of Burma, 1914–22', *Garden History* 43, 2 (2015), 182–98.

MATHER, JEFF, 'Camping in China with the Divine Jane: The Travel Writing of Reginald Farrer', *Journeys* 10, 2 (2009), 45–64.

MEREDITH, GEORGE, *The Egoist: A Comedy in Narrative*, 1879 (London: Penguin, 1968, reprinted 1987).

—— *One of Our Conquerors*, 1897 (New York: Charles Scribner's Sons, 1899).

MITCHELL, W. R., *Reginald Farrer: At home in the Yorkshire Dales* (Giggleswick: Castleberg, 2002).

MOORE, G. E., *Principia Ethica* (1903; New York: Prometheus, 1988).

MUEGGLER, ERIK, 'The Eyes of Others: Race, "Gaping", and Companionship in the Scientific Exploration of Southwest China', in *Explorers and Scientists in China's Borderlands 1880–1950*, D. M. Glover et al., eds (Seattle: University of Washington Press, 2011), pp. 26–56.

PATER, WALTER, *The Renaissance: Studies in Art and Poetry, the 1893 text,* ed. Donald L. Hill (Berkeley: University of California Press, 1980).

——'STYLE' (1888), in *Appreciations, with an Essay on Style* (1889; London: Macmillan, 1927).

POWELL, ANTHONY, *Under Review: Further Writings on Writers, 1946–1990,* (Chicago: University of Chicago Press, 1991).

RAY, JOHN, *The Wisdom of God Manifested in the Works of the Creation* (London, 1691).

ROSENFIELD, JOHN M., and ELIZABETH TEN GROTENHUIS, *Journey of the Three Jewels: Japanese Buddhist Paintings from Western Collections* (New York: The Asia Society, 1979).

RUVIGNY and RAINEVAL, MARQUIS OF, *The Plantagenet Roll of the Blood Royal: The Mortimer-Percy Volume. Being a Complete Table of all the Descendants now living of Edward III, King of England. Containing the Descendants of Lady Elizabeth Percy, née Mortimer* (London, n. p., 1911).

SAITO, YURIKO, 'Japanese Aesthetics: Historical Overview', *The Encyclopedia of Aesthetics,* Michael Kelly and others, eds, 4 vols (New York: Oxford University Press, 1998) v. 2, 545–53.

SANDERS, M. L., and P. TAYLOR, *British Propaganda During the First World War, 1914–18* (London: Macmillan, 1982).

SAUNDERS, MAX, and S. HASLAM, eds, *Ford Madox Ford's The Good Soldier: Centenary Essays,* International Ford Madox Ford Studies 14 (Leiden: Brill, 2015).

SCHMITHAUSEN, LAMBERT, *Plants in Early Buddhism and the Far eastern Idea of the Buddha-Nature of Grasses and Trees* (Lumbini, Nepal: Lumbini International Research Institute, 2009).

SCHOPEN, GREGORY, 'Archaeology and Protestant Suppositions in the Study of Indian Buddhism', *History of Religions* 31:1 (1991), 1–23.

——'The Buddhist "Monastery" and the Indian Garden: Aesthetics, Assimilations, and the Siting of Monastic Establishments', *Journal of the American Oriental Society* vol. 126, 4 (Oct-Dec 2006), 487–505.

SHELLEY, PERCY BYSSHE, *Poetical Works,* ed. Thomas Hutchinson, 1904 (New edition, Oxford: Oxford University Press, 1970).

SHIFF, RICHARD, *Cezanne and the End of Impressionism: A Study of the Theory, Technique, and Critical Evaluation of Modern Art* (Chicago: University of Chicago Press, 1984).

SHULMAN, NICOLA, *A Rage for Rock Gardening: The Story of Reginald Farrer, gardener, writer & plant collector* (2002; Boston: Godine, 2004).

SITWELL, OSBERT, *Noble Essences* (London: Macmillan, 1950).

SNODGRASS, JUDITH, *Presenting Japanese Buddhism to the West: Orientalism, Occidentalism, and the Columbian Exposition* (Chapel Hill: University of North Carolina Press, 2003).

SOUTHAM, B. C., ed., *Jane Austen: The Critical Heritage Vol. 2 1870–1940* (London: Routledge, 1987).

SPENCER, JONATHAN, ed., *Sri Lanka: History and the Roots of Conflict,* (London: Routledge, 1990).

SWINBURNE, A. C., *Love's Cross-Currents. A Year's Letters* (London: Chatto & Windus, 1905).

TACHIBANA, SETSU, S. DANIELS, C. WATKINS, 'Japanese Gardens in Edwardian Britain: Landscape and Transculturation', *Journal of Historical Geography* 30, 2 (2004), 364–95.

TAMBIAH, STANLEY JEYARAJA, *Levelling Crowds: Ethnonationalist Conflicts and Collective Violence in South Asia* (Berkeley: University of California Press, 1996).

TATSUI TEIEN KENKYUJO, *Garden Views III: Water and Stream Gardens* (Tokyo: Kenchiku Shiryō Kenkyusha, 1991).

THOMAS, EDWARD J., *The Life of the Buddha as Legend and History,* (1927. London: Routledge, 1975).

WARD, FRANK KINGDON, 'REGINALD FARRER', *Geographical Journal* 57, 1 (January 1921), 69–70.

WELBON, GUY, *The Buddhist Nirvāna and its Western Interpreters* (Chicago: The University of Chicago Press, 1968).

WICKREMERATNE, ANANDA, *The Genesis of an Orientalist: Thomas William Rhys Davids and Buddhism in Sri Lanka* (Delhi: Motilal Banarsidass, 1984).

WIESENFARTH, JOSEPH, 'Death in the Wasteland: Ford, Wells and Waugh', in *Ford Madox Ford's Parade's End: The First World War, Culture, and Modernity: International Ford Madox Ford Studies 13* (Amsterdam: Rodopi, 2014), 197–206.

WILDE, OSCAR, *Intentions,* (1891; London: Unicorn, 1945).

WILSON, LIZ, *Charming Cadavers: Horrific Figurations of the Feminine in Indian Buddhist Hagiographic Literature* (Chicago: Chicago University Press, 1996).

WOOLF, LEONARD, *An Autobiography, I: 1880–1911* (1960, 1961; Oxford: Oxford University Press, 1980).

——*Diaries in Ceylon 1908–1911: Records of a Colonial Administrator* (*Ceylon Historical Journal,* Vol. IX — July 1959 and April 1960 Nos 1–4; published in book form by Tisara Press, Dehiwala, Sri Lanka: 1962; 2nd edition, 1963).

YATE, A. C., 'The Russian Débâcle and the East', *The Nineteenth Century and After,* 83 (May 1918), 1062–77.

YOUNGHUSBAND, LIEUTENANT-COLONEL SIR FRANCIS, 'Geographical Work in India for this Society', *The Geographical Journal,* XLIX, 6 (June 1917), 401–15.

YULE, HENRY, and A. C. BURNELL, *Hobson-Jobson: The Anglo-Indian Dictionary* (1886. Ware: Wordsworth, 1996).

INDEX

CPSIA information can be obtained
at www.ICGtesting.com
Printed in the USA
BVHW021547230719
554054BV00036B/115/P